national
**STATISTICS**

# Social Trends

**No 31**

**2001 edition**

| | |
|---|---|
| Editors: | Jil Matheson |
| | Carol Summerfield |
| | |
| Authors: | Jenny Church |
| | Jackie Jackson |
| | Victoria Jackson |
| | Ashley Kershaw |
| | Christine Lillistone |
| | Anne-Marie Manners |
| | Nina Mill |
| | Dave Sharp |
| | Conor Shipsey |
| | Mike Short |
| | |
| Production team: | Nicola Amaranayake |
| | Max Bonini |
| | John Chrzczonowicz |
| | Sunita Dedi |
| | Shaun Flanagan |
| | Nigel King |
| | Liza Murray |
| | Katie White |
| | Steve Whyman |
| | |
| Design & Artwork: | Michelle Franco |
| | Angela Cannell |
| | Dave Pike |
| | Kim Slatter |
| | |
| Maps: | Alistair Dent |
| | Pam Owen |

London: The Stationery Office

Applications for reproduction:
Copyright Manager, Office for National Statistics
Zone B1/09, 1 Drummond Gate,
London SW1V 2QQ
fax: 020 7533 5685
e-mail: copyright@ons.gov.uk

**Contact points**
For enquiries about this publication, contact
the Editor, Carol Summerfield:
Tel: 020 7533 5780
E-mail:  carol.summerfield@ons.gov.uk

To order this publication, call The Stationery Office
on **0870 600 5522**. See also back cover.

For general enquiries, contact the National Statistics
Public Enquiry Service on **0845 601 3034**
(minicom: 01633 812399)
E-mail: info@statistics.gov.uk
Fax: 01633 652747
Letters: room DG/18, 1 Drummond Gate,
LONDON SW1V 2QQ

You can also find National Statistics on the internet -
go to **www.statistics.gov.uk**.

**About the Office for National Statistics**
The Office for National Statistics (ONS) is the government agency responsible for compiling, analysing and disseminating many of the United Kingdom's economic, social and demographic statistics, including the retail prices index, trade figures and labour market data, as well as the periodic census of the population and health statistics. The Director of ONS is also the National Statistician and the Registrar General for England and Wales, and the agency that administers the statutory registration of births, marriages and deaths there.

**A National Statistics publication**
National Statistics are produced to high professional standards set out in the National Statistics Code of Practice. They undergo regular quality assurance reviews to ensure that they meet customer needs. They are produced free from any political interference.

# Contents

# Contents

## 3: Education and Training

Page

# Contents

Social Trends 31, © Crown copyright 2001

## 6: Expenditure

## 7: Health

# Contents

Page

## 9: Crime and Justice

# Contents

Page

## 12:Transport

# Contents

Social Trends 31, © Crown copyright 2001

# Introduction

This is the 31st edition of *Social Trends* – one of the flagship publications from the Office for National Statistics. It draws together statistics from a wide range of government departments and other organisations to paint a broad picture of British society today, and how it has been changing. Each of the 13 chapters focuses on a different social policy area, described in tables, charts and explanatory text. This year *Social Trends* also features an article on '200 Years of the Census of Population', to mark the bicentenary of the census; it has been written by Muriel Nissel, the first editor of *Social Trends*.

*Social Trends* is aimed at a very wide audience: policy makers in the public and private sectors; service providers; people in local government; journalists and other commentators; academics and students; schools; and the general public.

The editorial team always welcomes readers' views on how *Social Trends* could be improved. Please write to the Editors at the address shown below with any comments or suggestions you have.

### New material and sources
To preserve topicality, over half of the 321 tables and charts in the chapters of *Social Trends 31* are new compared with the previous edition, and draw on the most up-to-date available data.

In all chapters the source of the data is given below each table and chart, and where this is a major survey the name of the survey is also included. At the end of each chapter a list of contact telephone numbers is given, including the contact number for the chapter author and, for the first time in *Social Trends*, a list of useful website addresses. The list of further reading, directing readers to other relevant publications, can now be found towards the back of the book, beginning on page 238. Regional and other sub-national breakdowns of much of the information in *Social Trends* can be found in the ONS's publication *Regional Trends*, published by The Stationery Office.

### Appendix
The Appendix gives definitions and general background information, particularly on administrative and legal structures and frameworks. Anyone seeking to understand the tables and charts in detail will find it helpful to read the corresponding entries in the Appendix, as well as the footnotes on the tables and charts. A full index to this edition starts on page 263.

### Availability on electronic media
Social Trends 31 is now available electronically via the National Statistics website, www.statistics.gov.uk.

### Contributors
The Editors wish to thank all their colleagues in the National Statistics and contributors in other organisations, without whose help this publication would not be possible. Thanks also go to onsdesign.

Jil Matheson
Carol Summerfield
Social and Regional Division
Office for National Statistics
B5/10
1 Drummond Gate
London
SW1V 2QQ

# 200 Years of the Census of Population[1]

## Muriel Nissel

April 29th 2001 is a very important date, Census Day. It will be just over 200 years since the first census was taken on 10th March 1801 and it will reveal a very different country. In 1801 there were 10 million inhabitants in Great Britain and about 2 million households. Now there are 58 million people and 24 million households. Two hundred years ago the country was evolving from an agricultural into an industrial nation. Today it is a predominantly service economy with less than two per cent of people employed in agriculture.

Census taking has a long history. The Babylonians, the Egyptians and the Chinese all collected statistics about their people, mainly for military and taxation purposes, but also, as in Egypt, for other purposes such as planning the building of the Pyramids and sharing out the land after the annual flooding of the Nile. The Roman census required each man to return to his place of origin and, according to St Luke's gospel, it was the census ordered by Caesar Augustus which brought Mary and Joseph to Bethlehem when Jesus was born. The Hebrews had also carried out censuses, including one by King David. It was interrupted by plague and never completed, so leading to a belief at the time that census-taking was a dangerous practice likely to incur the wrath of God.

In Britain the 7th century document *Senchus fer n'Alba* was a Gaelic forerunner of the first census in England, the *Domesday Book,* taken in 1086. Regular census-taking came much later. Quebec had completed one as early as 1666, Iceland in 1703 and Sweden in 1749. In the middle of the 18th century censuses were also taken in Germany and other European states. In the United States, however, religious opposition, based on fears of what befell the Israelites in the time of King David, delayed census-taking until 1790.

The first census in Great Britain in 1801 was a simple count of the number of people and their houses with a very broad idea of occupations. The illustration below shows the form used by enumerators to record the data. Over the last 200 years, the number and types of questions have changed dramatically as more information has been needed to target the resources governments give to fund policies across the country. In April 2001, the census will ask for a wide variety of information including age, education, ethnic group, where people work, and whether people care for others. In all, there are ten questions relating to the household and some 30 questions for each individual: about half the individual questions do not apply to children and the elderly.

**An Overseer's schedule from the 1801 Census**

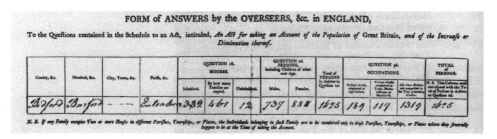

1 The censuses in England and Wales and in Scotland are carried out under the Census Act 1920. In Northern Ireland there is a similar but separate act, the Census Act (Northern Ireland) 1969. Under devolution, the census is a devolved responsibility in Scotland and Northern Ireland but not in Wales. This has led to increased diversity in the questions to be asked in 2001. This article deals with the main changes in the census over time and does not describe the more specific variations between countries. Full details of the questions asked, however, are included in the Appendix at the end of this article on page 26.

### The early censuses

An attempt by Parliament in the middle of the 18th century to hold a census ran up against political objections based on the fear that the results might reveal weaknesses of the country to foreign enemies, or that it would impair the liberty of the individual. As in the United States, there was also a suspicion that it might incur the wrath of God and some great public misfortune might result. However, during the second half of the century when it was becoming clear that the population was rising, fears about the consequences were fuelled by the publication in 1798 of Thomas Robert Malthus's *Essay on the Principle of Population.* This argued that, whereas food supplies tend to increase steadily year on year, population grows at an ever increasing rate. A series of bad harvests at the end of the century helped to make sure that, when a second Census Bill came before Parliament in 1800, it had an easy passage.

A population census in Great Britain is usually taken every ten years. The original returns for the first four censuses no longer survive but the published Abstracts include statistics and accompanying commentaries. These indicate some of the reasons for the topics selected and the definitions chosen, or for classifying the results in a particular way. They are of particular interest in that they throw light, not only on the economic state of the country and the political issues current at the time, but also on the living conditions and characteristics of the population. These commentaries might thus be regarded as precursors of *Social Trends,* first published in 1970.

There was little change in the information collected in the first four censuses. However, in 1821, a growing demand particularly from Friendly Societies for accurate life tables, led to a first attempt to analyse the population by age. Enumerators were given discretion:

# A.1

**Population present on Census night: by gender and age[1]**

**Great Britain**

Millions

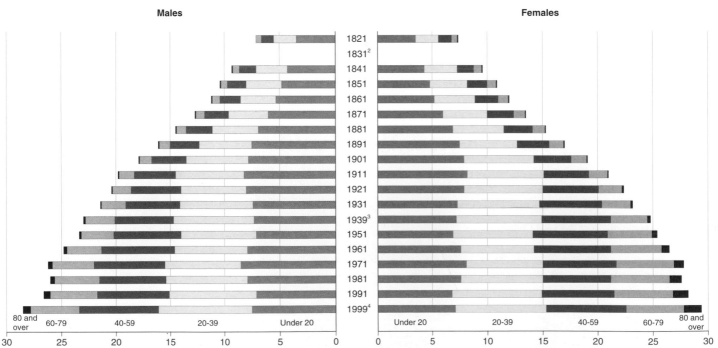

1 The data are not fully comparable over the full time span as different categories of people, including the armed forces, were treated differently at different times.
2 There was no age breakdown in the 1831 Census.
3 Data for 1939 refer to the United Kingdom, not Great Britain and are not census counts.
4 Data for 1999 are mid-year population estimates.

**Source: Census**

*If you are of the Opinion that - - - the Ages of the several individuals can be obtained in a Manner satisfactory to yourself, and not inconvenient to the Parties, be pleased to state - - - the Number of those who are under 5 Years of Age, of those between 5 and 10 Years of Age - - - distinguishing Males from Females.*

The question was not repeated in 1831, presumably because it was considered that once the age distribution had been determined there was no need to up-date it. From 1841 onwards the age of people was collected in single years instead of five-year age bands.

There were also modifications in these early censuses to the question on occupation. In 1801 a question asking for an individual's occupation was not understood. Traditionally, the family rather than the individual had been regarded as the economic unit. By 1801 agriculture was gradually giving way to industry. Even when a family ceased to be employed in agriculture and moved to the mill or the mine, the organisation of labour in the early stages still very often operated in family units. In the two subsequent censuses the question was rephrased to relate to families. The 1831 Census, however, began to move towards the concept of an individual occupation, and in 1841 family occupation was dropped.

The problem census takers had in defining work and classifying the unpaid labour of family workers demonstrates, perhaps more clearly than any other topic, the way in which changes in society and prevailing attitudes are reflected in the questions asked and the analyses adopted. For example, whereas we are now familiar with the concepts of childhood, retirement, unemployment and student status, the early census takers were not. At first everybody was included in the occupational classification. The retired were allocated to their previous occupations and students to their potential ones. Even 'lunatics' and prisoners were ascribed to an occupation. It was not until 1881 that most retired people were classed as unoccupied. In 1891 the concept of childhood was finally given a status of its own

when the cut-off point for occupations was given as ten years, the age at which children could be employed in factories. Unemployment was taken to be only a temporary break from active status. Although still included within the occupational classification, it had to wait for the severe economic depression of 1931 before it was separately classified. Perception of these different concepts came slowly and it may well be that present changes in the way we work will once again make terms, such as retirement, difficult to define.

The occupation question continued to give trouble throughout the rest of the 19th century. Thus the decision to exclude unpaid family workers from the working population in 1841 was reversed in 1851 and the number of occupied women in 'active' employment jumped from 1.8 to 2.8 million. Those who designed the census were aware that people can be both 'housewives' and carry on other occupations at the same time, and they were confused about how to deal with the problem of double-counting. The 1881 Census once again excluded household work from the definition of economic activity but in 1911 all family workers, male and female, were included and only those engaged in housework alone omitted. This kind of problem demonstrates the ever-present dilemma of making changes to census questions whilst retaining comparability with past censuses.

## The census from 1841 to 1901

One of the problems in organising the early censuses was that there was no local government or other established means of collecting the returns. The enumerators were either the Overseers of the Poor or, failing them, 'constables, tithingmen, headboroughs or other peace officers'. In Scotland responsibility was placed on schoolmasters. However, when in 1837 a Registrar General was appointed in England and Wales to record births, deaths and marriages, he was also given responsibility for the censuses of population. The 1841 census could therefore be carried out using the local organisation for the new registration service.

This made it practicable to introduce a radical change in the way the English and Welsh censuses were conducted. Self-completion forms were introduced which each householder was legally obliged to fill in for all those in the household. In a sense 1841 could thus be regarded as the first 'modern' census. Instead of a simple count of numbers, enumerators recorded the names and details of each individual on to special sheets. The full returns were then sent to the General Register Office (GRO) in London where hundreds of clerks carefully tabulated with pen and pencil on large sheets of paper details for every individual in the country. It is difficult to imagine today what a tremendous feat this must have been, particularly at a time when the majority of the population of England and Wales of 16 million was largely illiterate. The new system

remained more or less unaltered until 1911 when punched cards and mechanical sorting enabled machines to process the data. The next major development had to wait until 1961 when computers were first used to process the punched cards, thus halving the time taken.

The Appendix on page 26 at the end of this article shows the broad subject areas covered from 1801 until the present day. In 1851, for the first time, exact age, marital status and relationship to head of household were asked for. Once the concept of a personal occupation became generally accepted, it was perhaps hardly surprising at the time that it was the father or husband in a family who was referred to as 'head' and as the person who determined its social status.

A major innovation in 1851 was the way Dr William Farr, the 'compiler of abstracts' in the GRO, used the increasingly detailed data available to classify people by occupation and age. This was particularly important because, used in conjunction with the information on registration of deaths, it made possible detailed study of occupational mortality. In later years the expanded use of the census in this way by linking it to other sources was a major development in statistical analysis. The results of Farr's work were included in a supplement to the census, subsequently published under the title of the Decennial Supplement of Occupational Mortality in England and Wales. A similar publication continues to the present day.

In his Fourteenth Report, for the year 1851, the Registrar General of England and Wales, George Graham, drew on Farr's material in colourful language:

*While much has been written about the diseases of shoemakers, weavers, tailors, miners, and bakers, the extraordinary mortality of butchers appears to have escaped observation. Calculation alone has taught us that the red, injected face of the butcher is an indication of a frail habit of body. Here is an important problem for solution. On what does the great mortality of the butcher depend? On his diet, into which too much animal*

**FILLING UP THE CENSUS PAPER.**

*Wife of his Bosom.* "UPON MY WORD, MR. PEEWITT! IS THIS THE WAY YOU FILL UP YOUR CENSUS SO YOU CALL YOURSELF THE 'HEAD OF THE FAMILY'—DO YOU—AND ME A 'FEMALE!'"

*Reproduced from Punch vol xx, 1851*

*feed and too little fruit and vegetables enter? — on his drinking to excess? — on his exposure to heat and cold? — or, which is probably the most powerful cause, on the elements of decaying matter by which he is surrounded in his slaughter-house and its vicinity?*

As far back as 1839 Farr recognised the importance of cohort or longitudinal analysis to help solve these problems. Research on mortality, for example, can be greatly helped if the circumstances of a death can be given perspective by linking it to earlier events in a person's life and to the home and working conditions which provide the lifetime background. Farr himself wrote:

*To determine a question of this sort it would be necessary to take a large number of individuals, as 400,000 or 500,000, indiscriminately selected from all ranks and orders of the community, and to trace their lives from the moment of their birth, marking the exact period of the demise of each individual - - - But governments, which alone have the means of framing tables on an adequate scale, and with the necessary precautions, have been singularly inattentive to their duty in this respect.*

It was over a century before the type of study envisaged by Farr was set up using the census, the ONS Longitudinal Study.

Associated with the 1851 Census were two important enquiries into education and religion. Growing public interest in the state of elementary education was reflected in the Registrar General's Annual Report for 1839 when he reported that 33 men in a 100 and 49 women in a 100 during the previous three years had signed the marriage register with marks instead of signatures. Questions on both education and religion were intended to be included as part of the 1851 Census itself but, as completion of the form was compulsory, the House of Lords raised objections to the penalties that could be imposed on people withholding information. The legal advisers to the Crown upheld this view and the two enquiries were therefore carried out on a voluntary basis.

Nearly 150 years later a question on religion is being asked in the questionnaire for 2001. Again, following representation by the House of Lords, there will be no penalty for failing to respond to the question.

The problem of including sensitive questions is always a delicate one. On many occasions the possibility of asking for information on income has been considered but rejected. Not only is accurate information difficult to collect but the possible antagonism of the public might prejudice the reliability of the rest of the census. A similar difficulty has arisen in more recent years over ethnicity, and the topic was only included in 1991 after extensive testing of the best way of asking such a question. An earlier example was that of infirmity. In 1851, in response to the considerable interest of societies concerned with the welfare of the blind and the 'deaf and dumb', questions were included in the census on these topics. Later, in 1871, 'imbecile or idiot' and 'lunatics' were added to the list of questions. Not surprisingly the replies were thought to be unreliable, and in his report for 1881 Census the Registrar General admitted that:

*It cannot be expected, for instance, that a mother will return her child ... as an idiot, however much in her own heart she may believe or fear this to be the case; for to acknowledge it as such would be to abandon all hope.*

In 1891 the term 'idiot' was replaced by 'feeble-minded'. At the beginning of the 20th century a Royal Commission on the Care and Control of the Feeble-minded reported that the census was not a suitable or reliable medium for getting this kind of information. Accordingly after 1911 enquiries into infirmities were dropped until 1991 when a question was introduced on long-standing illness.

During the second half of the 19th century the tables in the reports and the commentaries by the Registrars General and their statistical superintendents became increasingly sophisticated. There was, however, little change in the content of the census itself. The main development, due to growing popular concern about housing conditions, was a question first asked in 1861 in Scotland about the number of rooms with one or more windows. A question was introduced in England and Wales in 1891 about the number of rooms in each house. This could then be related to household size to give a measure of overcrowding. Unfortunately, as overcrowding was illegal, it was highly likely that a householder with a large family living in a crowded dwelling would have given the widest possible interpretation to the word 'room'. Accordingly when the question was repeated precise definitions were issued.

## The early 20th century censuses

At the dawn of the new century there was a keen interest in fertility. The pronounced fall in birth rates at the end of the 19th century was as much a matter of concern to many as the rise had been to Malthus a century earlier, particularly as the number of children born to upper and middle class families was relatively low. A question about the number of children born to married women was included in the 1911 Census. The scope of the

questions were restricted to the fertility of current marriages. The question was dropped in 1921 and did not re-appear until 1951.

There was an interest of a rather different character, particularly by life insurance societies, in differential mortality rates in various strata of society. Some means of analysing data was needed. This led to the first systematic attempt led by Dr Thomas Stevenson to rank occupations and group them into social classes. These classes were designed to represent as far as possible different social grades intended to reflect wealth and culture. Social class mortality tables, using 1911 Census data and based on this new classification, were subsequently included in the Decennial Supplement from 1923.

In the period between the First and Second World Wars the main changes in the content of the census in England and Wales were questions on place of work and education. As people moved out of cities into suburban residential areas the number of daily journeys to and from work by train and bus increased. A question on place of work was therefore included in the 1921 Census. There was also for the first time a separate question on education. There had been no detailed information available since the voluntary enquiry in 1851, and local education authorities wanted up-to-date and comprehensive data about people of all ages living in their areas.

No census was held in 1941. The Second World War broke out on 3 September 1939 and less than a month later, on 29th September, the population of the United Kingdom was enumerated in order to compile a National Register. This was used for issuing National Identity Cards and for supporting a number of other wartime measures, such as food and clothes rationing, and the deployment of labour in military and other essential industries and services. Some of the statistics were published in 1944 but they are not comparable with those in the censuses.

# A.2

## Workforce: by selected industry

**Great Britain**

Percentages

1 There was no Census in 1941.

**Source: Census, Office for National Statistics**

## The post-war years: social change

The years in the second half of the 20th century following the end of the Second World War ushered in a period of exceptional social change. These inevitably had a substantial impact on the census. In real terms gross domestic product per head trebled. Population rose only slightly but there were relatively many more old people. There was also a far greater proportion born overseas or belonging to minority ethnic groups. Household size fell sharply and both the number and quality of the houses in which people lived changed dramatically. The Welfare State brought with it a big expansion in health and education facilities. The car, the spread of motorways and air travel enabled people to move around in way never before imagined. Telephones, radio, television and the Internet transformed communications.

By the end of the century Britain had become a predominantly service economy. Three-quarters of the workforce were employed in these industries. In contrast, manufacturing industry, which continued to grow until the end of the Second World War, contracted sharply. A fundamental change was the greatly increased proportion of women in employment, particularly in education and health and the distributive trades

Many of the jobs in the growing service economy could be organised on a part-time basis and were thus particularly congenial to married women with children. Numerous other factors combined to make it possible for them to seize the opportunity to take paid work outside the home. In particular the widespread use of contraception, and above all the advent of the contraceptive 'pill' in the 1960s, enabled those in all social classes to take control of the number and spacing of their children in unprecedented ways.

The increased numbers of women in employment and the shift in the industrial structure, combined with changes in the workplace, had far reaching implications for the existing occupationally based social classification that had originally been designed by Farr in 1851 and redefined by Stevenson in 1911. A major revision of the classification, based on the type of work performed rather than the skill required, was published In May 2000. The new National Statistics Socio-Economic Classification (NS-SEC) will be used for output from the 2001 Census.

Whereas the concept of social class, first introduced into census classifications in 1911, seemed relatively simple at the time, it has become progressively less meaningful. As originally designed there were five social classes plus separate categories for textile workers, miners and agricultural labourers. These classes were arranged around a grouping of occupations designed to bring out differences in morbidity and mortality. The analyses on mortality and social class, published after the 1971 Census, were used extensively by Sir Douglas Black in his 1980 report on the Working Group on Inequalities in Health.

Although occupation continues to be a reasonably good discriminator of life chances it has increasingly come under attack as a basis for social class analysis. In the run-up to the 1991 Census, the Secretary of State for Health, Kenneth Clarke, argued that it was not a satisfactory way of analysing what appeared to be increasing differences in health inequalities. After further discussion between Ministers and the Government Statistical Service, it was accepted that social class analysis should continue to be used, but that future Government publications would make it clear that the classification was a grouping of occupations and not hierarchical in nature.

NS-SEC is based around the concept of employment conditions and relations, rather than skill. The classification first makes a distinction between employers, the self-employed and employees. Employees are then further divided into classes reflecting conditions and relations, such as how their work is regulated by their employers. This new classification is of particular interest in the light of recent studies, such as the study of health and stress in the Civil Service (Whitehall II), which indicates that stress-related morbidity increases as control over one's work decreases, with people in top jobs suffering least and those at the bottom end suffering most.

Another even more far-reaching problem that has recently been emerging is the idea of using 'head of household' for analysis. It has become misleading, not only because of the growing participation of women in the labour force and the growth of two-earner families, but because of the increasing variety and fluidity of household structures. In 1981 provision was made in the census form for 'joint' heads of household with the first person mentioned on the schedule usually being regarded as the household reference person for analytical purposes. Follow-up studies suggested that around 97 per cent of married household heads were male. The definition thus inherently selected men rather than women.

The term 'head of household' is no longer being used. In the 2001 census a different approach is being adopted whereby a full matrix showing the relationship of each person in the household to every other person will be completed. The instructions ask the person filling in the form to start with the householder or joint householders. The 'household reference person' will be determined as one of the joint householders if they are aged 16 or over. If neither of the first two people on the form is 16 or over, then the first person on the form aged 16 or over will be the 'household reference person'.

## The census in the post-war years

As the Appendix on page 26 shows, there has been an enormous expansion in the range of questions asked in the census reflecting the rapid changes in society in the second half of the 20th century. Fuller and better information has been needed following greater government involvement in the economic and social life of the country, both at central and local levels. A service-orientated economy has called in particular for more statistics on educational and skill qualifications.

Housing has been another topic with high priority. The 1951 Census form included questions on the availability of basic amenities, ranging from a kitchen sink to a fixed bath. As slum clearance and higher standards were implemented, the basic list was shortened and other amenities added, such as sole use of an inside WC and central heating. In 2001 the only questions remaining are those relating to central heating, sole use of bath/shower and toilet, and floor level of accommodation.

The 1991 Census asked about long-standing illness and in 2001 a further question will be added about general health. Of particular interest are new questions on time spent in a voluntary capacity caring for people with long-term physical or mental illness or disability, or problems related to old age. These topics reflect concerns, not only about health generally, but about the growing number of old people in our society and anxiety as to who is to help look after them. Women, who have traditionally been the main carers, are increasingly working away from home and are no longer able to look after the young and old in a way they did a few generations ago.

There has been a demand for more information about the increasing ethnic diversity of the population. For a long time this was thought to be too sensitive a subject for inclusion in the census. Pre-tests in Haringey in 1979 met with organised opposition. The results showed that almost a third of form fillers from Asian and West Indian households thought it wrong to include such a question in the census. There were also doubts about whether the ethnic group of individuals was recorded accurately by the head of the household. In particular, less than half of those who were in households headed by someone who was 'Black' had their ethnic group recorded correctly during the 1979 test. There was particular objection to the questions on parents' country of birth as there were fears that they might be linked to proposals to change the nationality laws. Consequently, no question on ethnic group was included in 1981.

In 1983 a Sub-committee of the House of Commons Home Affairs Committee on Race Relations and Immigration recommended that:

*Questions on ethnic or racial origin should be asked in future Censuses, subject to*
*a. adequate reassurances on confidentiality, the misuse of data, and abuse of data in the future*
*b. the unequivocally-stated objective being to improve existing programmes against racial discrimination and disadvantage and to provide evidence for the development of new ones when policies are shown to be inadequate, ineffective or discriminatory.*

Meanwhile the wish to know more about minority groups generally, and a better understanding of the value of ethnic monitoring, enabled a carefully worded question to be included in 1991. It will again be included, but in an updated form, in 2001.

A major influence on the census in the post-war years has been the collection of statistics through sample surveys. These surveys can go into great depth on an individual topic and have helped to eliminate some of the detail in the census. They are particularly useful for giving a general overall picture of the country but, unlike the census, they cannot provide information for very small geographical areas on a nationwide basis.

A significant development in the use of the census has built on linkage with administrative sources. Farr pointed the way forward in the middle of the 19th century with the publication of his research on occupational mortality using the census and registration of deaths. He also looked forward to the time when longitudinal studies would trace individual histories. Such a major development, the Longitudinal Study (LS), had to wait until the 1971 Census, when a one per cent sample of the population was drawn by including all individuals born on four selected dates in any year. Data have been added to the sample from the 1981 and

1991 Censuses and it is proposed to extend the records further by including 2001 Census data for the same people. Data are also added from the registrations of births, deaths and cancers. The LS database will be held securely within the Office for National Statistics, with strictly controlled access.

Although the census collects information from each person and household in the country, it is not concerned with facts about individuals as such. Its purpose is to produce statistics and aid research about the community, and groups within the community as a whole. In extending the use of the census, for example, by linkage with administrative data and as a sample frame, great care is taken not to reveal any information about identifiable individuals or households. Special precautions apply to statistical outputs for small areas.

There is a well-established tradition of maintaining census confidentiality and at each census assurances are given to the public that the Census Offices will treat all information in strict confidence. Only people under the authority of the Registrars General or their agents have access to personal census information. Great care is taken to ensure the physical protection of documents.

## The census in 2001

The census in 2001 will mark another milestone in the history of census taking. While the traditional concept of collecting information on a particular day from each person and household in the country remains important, in many other respects it will be very different. In addition to information on household accommodation, the householder, or joint householders, will be required to supply full details of the relationships of the various people in the household, including 'partners' and step-relationships. Personal details will be filled in on a page-per-person form. The new approach reflects the marked changes in recent years in family relationships and attitudes towards divorce, separation, cohabitation and single parent families. It is thought to be more acceptable when answering sensitive questions, particularly in households of unrelated individuals. Those who wish to do so will be able to fill in their own census forms.

A further change is that the public will be asked to post their forms back in pre-paid envelopes. Different patterns of living have been making the task of collecting census forms more challenging. For example, people are away from home more frequently and there has been a significant increase in the number of one-person households and entry-phones into buildings. Enumerators will still deliver the forms and follow-up those households that have not returned a form, but the new procedure should allow more resources to target those areas which in the past have shown a lower response, such as inner cities, areas of high elderly population, young single males, substantial ethnic minorities or multi-occupied buildings.

Advances in technology, such as the use of automatic scanning and recognition of documents, should significantly reduce the clerical effort needed for processing. Harmonisation of concepts, definitions and classifications, designed to make it easier to make comparisons with other government sources of statistics, have played an important part in both the question design and the output of the census. The primary means of dissemination will be electronic. There will again be a standard set of tables but there will also be a service tailored to customers' needs.

Considerable attention will be given to validating the results. In an exercise as large and complex as the census it is inevitable that errors will occur. Responses that are missed or inconsistent will be resolved using other data so as to avoid a 'not stated' category. In 1991 it was estimated that over a million residents, or more than 2 per cent of the total, were missed. One of the reasons may have been the effect of the Community Charge, or 'Poll Tax'. Although the fear was unfounded, some people may not have been prepared to complete their forms lest the information should be transferred across on to the Community Charge Register. Another reason may have been alienation of some people from government and

authority in general. Final estimates for the total population in 1991 were arrived at by a variety of methods including using rolled-forward data from the 1981 Census, the Census Validation Survey and comparisons with administrative records.

In 2001 the Census Offices are planning extensive awareness campaigns through the media and via contacts with community groups, students and schools in order to strengthen response. They will also conduct a large Census Coverage Survey after the main fieldwork has finished. The results of this interviewer survey, in conjunction with the census data, will be used to yield a consistent set of counts that represents the best estimate of the total population, including the people and households who were missed during the census itself.

## The future

Traditionally the main purpose of a population census was to count heads. As time passed governments became increasingly concerned with basic information about the characteristics of this population, such as age, sex, marital status, place of birth, economic activity, health and housing. The data are used in a variety of ways and have become much more important. For example, central government pays out many billions of pounds per year by way of revenue support grants to local authorities and grants to health authorities. One of the main criteria for sharing it out is the kind of population in each local area. For example, local government uses the number of elderly when planning the level of services and education authorities need to know the numbers of children at different ages. Reliable information for small local areas has thus become essential to good government, both in its own right and for comparison with the wider picture. The results are also widely used by voluntary organisations, academics and local communities involved in planning and delivering services.

There is growing interest in harmonisation of information across countries. In 1997 the European Commission and the United Nations

Economic Commission for Europe jointly recommended that, around the year 2000, the Community should synchronise the collection of censuses or census-type data and compile a set of standardised tables. Those countries that do not conduct full censuses were recommended to carry out representative sample surveys or prepare tables based on registers or other administrative files. A number of European countries, notably Denmark, keep up-to-date population registers that record addresses and migration that can be used in conjunction with administrative and other data to provide census-type information.

The census is the most widely used of all government data sources and more information is steadily being asked for. Not only is it much in demand as a benchmark and to stratify samples for surveys but, alone amongst data sources, it can provide specific information on a comparable basis data for very fine geographical areas. The census has thus shifted away from its main original purpose - that of a simple count of numbers of people - to become a sophisticated tool for providing information for research and implementing policy at many levels.

## Bibliography

Dale A and Marsh C, eds. *The 1991 Census Users' Guide,* HMSO, London, 1993

Diamond I, *The Census* in Dorling D and Simpson S, (eds.) *Statistics in Society*, London, 1999

Farr W, *A Statistical Account of the British Empire Volume 1*, (Ed. J R Mc Culloch), London, 1839

General Register Office, *Second Annual Report of the Registrar-General of Births, Deaths and Marriages in England*, London, 1840

General Register Office, *Fourteenth Annual Report of the Registrar-General of Births, Deaths and Marriages in England*, London, 1855

General Register Office, *Census of England and Wales, 1881 volume IV General Report*, London, 1883

Hakim C, *Census Reports as Documentary Evidence: the Census Commentaries, 1801-1951*, in *The Sociological Review, Vol.28 no.3*, London, August 1980

Halsey A H with Webb J, (eds.) *Twentieth Century British Social Trends*, Macmillan, London, 2000

House of Commons, *Abstract of the Answers and Returns made pursuant to an Act, passed in the First Year of His Majesty King George IV*, London, 2 July 1822

House of Commons, *Abstract of the Answers and Returns made pursuant to an Act, passed in the Forty-First Year of His Majesty King George III*, London, 21 December 1801

House of Commons, *Second Report from the Home Affairs Committee Session 1982-83, Ethnic and racial questions in the Census, Volume I*, London, 1983

Mathias P, *The First Industrial Nation: an Economic History of Britain, 1700-1914*, Second Edition, Methuen & Co, London, 1983

Mills I, *Developments in Census-taking since 1841* in *Population Trends*, 48, London, 1987

Nissel M, *People Count: A History of the General Register Office*, HMSO, London, 1987

Office of Population Censuses and Surveys and General Register Office, Edinburgh, *Guide to Census Reports, Great Britain, 1801-1966*, HMSO, London, 1977

Registrar General, *The Story of the General Register Office and its Origins from 1536 to 1937*, HMSO, London, 1937

Teague A, *Innovation and Change in Population Census Taking*, ASC Conference, London, September 1999

Thompson E J, *The 1991 Census of Population in England and Wales*, in the *Royal Statistical Society Journal*, Series A Part 2, London, 1995

Townsend P, Margaret Whitehead, Nick Davidson, (eds.) *Inequalities in Health: The Black Report and The Health Divide Second edition*, Penguin, London, 1990

Vivian S P, Registrar General, *The History of the Census*. 1923, unpublished lecture given at the General Register Office

White P, *A question on ethnic group for the census: findings from the 1989 census test post-enumeration survey*, Population Trends 59, London, 1990

## Appendix

### Census topics

| Subject | 1801 | 1811 | 1821 | 1831 | 1841 | 1851 | 1861 | 1871 | 1881 | 1891 | 1901 | 1911 | 1921 | 1931 | 1951 | 1961[1] | 1971 | 1981 | 1991 | 2001 |
|---|---|---|---|---|---|---|---|---|---|---|---|---|---|---|---|---|---|---|---|---|
| **Names** | – | – | – | – | GB | GB | GB | GB | GB | GB | GB | GB | GB | GB | GB | GB | GB | GB | GB | GB |
| **Sex** | GB | GB | GB | GB | GB | GB | GB | GB | GB | GB | GB | GB | GB | GB | GB | GB | GB | GB | GB | GB |
| **Age**[2] | – | – | GB | – | GB | GB | GB | GB | GB | GB | GB | GB | GB | GB | GB | GB | GB | GB | GB | GB |
| **Marital status** | – | – | – | – | – | GB | GB | GB | GB | GB | GB | GB | GB | GB | GB | GB | GB | GB | GB | GB |
| relationship to head of household | – | – | – | – | – | GB | GB | GB | GB | GB | GB | GB | GB | GB | GB | GB | GB | GB | GB | GB[3] |
| **Migration** | | | | | | | | | | | | | | | | | | | | |
| Address one year ago | – | – | – | – | – | – | – | – | – | – | – | – | – | – | – | – | GB | GB | GB | GB |
| Address five years ago | – | – | – | – | – | – | – | – | – | – | – | – | – | – | – | – | GB | – | – | – |
| Years at present address | – | – | – | – | – | – | – | – | – | – | – | – | – | – | – | GB | – | – | – | – |
| **Country of birth/birthplace** | – | – | – | – | GB | GB | GB | GB | GB | GB | GB | GB | GB | GB | GB | GB | GB | GB | GB | GB |
| **Year of entry to UK** | – | – | – | – | – | – | – | – | – | – | – | – | – | – | – | – | GB | – | – | – |
| **Parents' countries of birth** | – | – | – | – | – | – | – | – | – | – | – | – | – | – | – | – | GB | – | – | – |
| **Nationality**[4] | – | – | – | – | GB | GB | GB | GB | GB | GB | GB | GB | GB | GB | GB | GB | – | – | – | – |
| **Ethnic group** | – | – | – | – | – | – | – | – | – | – | – | – | – | – | – | – | – | – | GB | GB |
| **Education** | | | | | | | | | | | | | | | | | | | | |
| whether scholar or student | – | – | – | – | – | GB | GB | GB | GB | S | S | GB[5] | GB[5] | – | GB[5] | GB | – | – | – | GB |
| age at which full-time education ceased | – | – | – | – | – | – | – | – | – | – | – | – | – | – | GB | GB | – | – | – | – |
| qualifications | – | – | – | – | – | – | – | – | – | – | – | – | – | – | – | GB | GB | GB | GB | GB |
| **Employment** | | | | | | | | | | | | | | | | | | | | |
| **Activity:** whether in job, unemployed, retired etc. | – | – | – | – | GB | GB | GB | GB | GB | GB | GB | GB | GB | GB | GB | GB | GB | GB | GB | GB |
| Students of working age | – | – | – | – | – | – | – | – | – | – | – | – | – | GB | GB | GB | GB | – | – | – |
| **Working full-time or part-time** | – | – | – | – | – | – | – | – | – | – | – | – | – | – | GB | GB | GB | – | – | – |
| **Weekly hours worked** | – | – | – | – | – | – | – | – | – | – | – | – | – | – | – | GB[6] | GB | – | GB | GB |
| **Employment status** | | | | | | | | | | | | | | | | | | | | |
| whether employee, self-employed, etc. | – | – | – | – | – | GB[7] | GB[7] | GB[7] | GB[7] | GB | GB | GB | GB | GB | GB | GB | GB | GB | GB | GB |
| Apprentice or trainee | – | – | – | – | – | – | – | – | – | – | – | – | – | – | GB | GB | GB | GB | – | – |
| **Name and nature of business** | | | | | | | | | | | | | | | | | | | | |
| **of employer** ('industry') | – | – | – | – | – | – | – | – | – | – | – | GB | GB | GB | GB | GB | GB | GB | GB | GB |
| **Address of business** | – | – | – | – | – | – | – | – | – | – | – | – | GB | – | – | – | – | – | GB | GB |
| **Occupation** | GB[8] | – | – | GB[8] | – | GB | GB | GB | GB | GB | GB | GB | GB | GB | GB | GB | GB | GB | GB | GB |
| **Family occupation**[9] | – | GB | GB | GB | – | – | – | – | – | – | – | – | – | – | – | – | – | – | – | – |
| **Occupation one year ago** | – | – | – | – | – | – | – | – | – | – | – | – | – | – | – | – | GB | – | – | – |
| **Workplace** | – | – | – | – | – | – | – | – | – | – | GB[10] | GB[10] | E, W | – | GB | GB | GB | GB | GB | GB |
| **Transport to work** | – | – | – | – | – | – | – | – | – | – | – | – | – | – | – | – | GB | GB | GB | GB |
| **Time since last worked** | – | – | – | – | – | – | – | – | – | – | – | – | – | – | – | – | – | – | GB[11] | GB |
| **Workplace size** | – | – | – | – | – | – | – | – | – | – | – | – | – | – | – | – | – | – | – | GB |
| **Supervisor status** | – | – | – | – | – | – | – | – | – | – | – | – | – | – | – | – | – | GB | – | GB |
| **Marriage and fertility** | | | | | | | | | | | | | | | | | | | | |
| year and month of birth of children born alive in marriage | – | – | – | – | – | – | – | – | – | – | – | – | – | – | – | – | GB | – | – | – |
| number of children born alive in marriage | – | – | – | – | – | – | – | – | – | – | – | GB[12] | – | – | GB | GB | – | – | – | – |
| whether live child born in last 12 months | – | – | – | – | – | – | – | – | – | – | – | – | – | – | GB | GB | – | – | – | – |
| year and month of first marriage and of end, if ended | – | – | – | – | – | – | – | – | – | – | – | – | – | – | – | GB[13] | GB | GB | – | – |
| duration of marriage | – | – | – | – | – | – | – | – | – | – | – | GB | – | – | GB | GB | – | – | – | – |
| **Social conditions** | | | | | | | | | | | | | | | | | | | | |
| religion | – | – | – | – | – | GB[14] | – | – | – | – | – | – | – | – | – | – | – | – | – | GB[15] |
| dependency: number and ages of children under 16 | – | – | – | – | – | – | – | – | – | – | – | – | GB | – | – | – | – | – | – | – |
| orphanhood: father, mother or both parents dead | – | – | – | – | – | – | – | – | – | – | – | – | GB | – | – | – | – | – | – | – |

| Subject | 1801 | 1811 | 1821 | 1831 | 1841 | 1851 | 1861 | 1871 | 1881 | 1891 | 1901 | 1911 | 1921 | 1931 | 1951 | 1961[1] | 1971 | 1981 | 1991 | 2001 |
|---|---|---|---|---|---|---|---|---|---|---|---|---|---|---|---|---|---|---|---|---|
| infirmity: deaf, dumb, blind, etc. | – | – | – | – | – | GB | GB | GB | GB | GB | GB | GB | – | – | – | – | – | – | – | – |
| eligibility to medical benefit | – | – | – | – | – | – | – | – | – | – | – | – | S | S | – | – | – | – | – | – |
| limiting long-term illness | – | – | – | – | – | – | – | – | – | – | – | – | – | – | – | – | – | – | GB | GB |
| provision of unpaid care | – | – | – | – | – | – | – | – | – | – | – | – | – | – | – | – | – | – | – | GB |
| general health | – | – | – | – | – | – | – | – | – | – | – | – | – | – | – | – | – | – | – | GB |

**Language spoken**

| Subject | 1801 | 1811 | 1821 | 1831 | 1841 | 1851 | 1861 | 1871 | 1881 | 1891 | 1901 | 1911 | 1921 | 1931 | 1951 | 1961[1] | 1971 | 1981 | 1991 | 2001 |
|---|---|---|---|---|---|---|---|---|---|---|---|---|---|---|---|---|---|---|---|---|
| Welsh | – | – | – | – | – | – | – | – | – | – | W | W | W | W | W | W | W | W | W | W |
| Gaelic | – | – | – | – | – | – | – | – | S | S | S | S | S | S | S | S | S | S | S | S |

**Absent persons** whole or

| Subject | 1801 | 1811 | 1821 | 1831 | 1841 | 1851 | 1861 | 1871 | 1881 | 1891 | 1901 | 1911 | 1921 | 1931 | 1951 | 1961[1] | 1971 | 1981 | 1991 | 2001 |
|---|---|---|---|---|---|---|---|---|---|---|---|---|---|---|---|---|---|---|---|---|
| part returns | – | – | – | – | – | – | – | – | – | – | – | – | – | – | – | GB | GB | GB | GB | – |

**Housing**

| Subject | 1801 | 1811 | 1821 | 1831 | 1841 | 1851 | 1861 | 1871 | 1881 | 1891 | 1901 | 1911 | 1921 | 1931 | 1951 | 1961[1] | 1971 | 1981 | 1991 | 2001 |
|---|---|---|---|---|---|---|---|---|---|---|---|---|---|---|---|---|---|---|---|---|
| number of rooms[16] | – | – | – | – | – | – | – | – | – | E,W | E,W | E,W | E,W | E,W | GB | GB | GB | GB | GB | GB |
| number of rooms with one or more windows | – | – | – | – | – | – | S | S | S | S | S | S | S | S | – | – | – | – | – | – |
| sharing accommodation | – | – | – | – | – | – | – | – | – | – | – | – | – | – | – | GB | GB | GB | GB | GB |
| tenure | – | – | – | – | – | – | – | – | – | – | – | – | – | – | – | GB | GB | GB | GB | GB |
| housing type | – | – | – | – | – | – | – | – | – | – | – | – | – | – | – | – | – | – | GB | GB |
| lowest floor level | – | – | – | – | – | – | – | – | – | – | – | – | – | – | – | – | – | – | S | GB |
| furnished/unfurnished | – | – | – | – | – | – | – | – | – | – | – | – | – | – | – | – | – | – | GB | S |

**Amenities** whether exclusive use, shared use, or lacking

| Subject | 1801 | 1811 | 1821 | 1831 | 1841 | 1851 | 1861 | 1871 | 1881 | 1891 | 1901 | 1911 | 1921 | 1931 | 1951 | 1961[1] | 1971 | 1981 | 1991 | 2001 |
|---|---|---|---|---|---|---|---|---|---|---|---|---|---|---|---|---|---|---|---|---|
| cooking stove | – | – | – | – | – | – | – | – | – | – | – | – | – | – | GB | GB | GB | – | – | – |
| kitchen sink | – | – | – | – | – | – | – | – | – | – | – | – | – | – | GB | GB | GB | – | – | – |
| piped water supply | – | – | – | – | – | – | – | – | – | – | – | – | – | – | GB | GB | – | – | – | – |
| hot water supply | – | – | – | – | – | – | – | – | – | – | – | – | – | – | – | – | – | – | – | – |
| fixed bath or shower | – | – | – | – | – | – | – | – | – | – | – | – | – | – | GB | GB | GB | GB | GB | GB[17] |
| inside WC | – | – | – | – | – | – | – | – | – | – | – | – | – | – | GB | GB | GB | GB | GB | GB[17] |
| outside WC | – | – | – | – | – | – | – | – | – | – | – | – | – | – | – | GB | GB | GB | GB | |
| central heating | – | – | – | – | – | – | – | – | – | – | – | – | – | – | – | – | – | – | GB | GB |

**Cars or vans**

| Subject | 1801 | 1811 | 1821 | 1831 | 1841 | 1851 | 1861 | 1871 | 1881 | 1891 | 1901 | 1911 | 1921 | 1931 | 1951 | 1961[1] | 1971 | 1981 | 1991 | 2001 |
|---|---|---|---|---|---|---|---|---|---|---|---|---|---|---|---|---|---|---|---|---|
| Cars or vans | – | – | – | – | – | – | – | – | – | – | – | – | – | – | – | – | GB | GB | GB | GB |

**Principal returns made by enumerators**

| Subject | 1801 | 1811 | 1821 | 1831 | 1841 | 1851 | 1861 | 1871 | 1881 | 1891 | 1901 | 1911 | 1921 | 1931 | 1951 | 1961[1] | 1971 | 1981 | 1991 | 2001 |
|---|---|---|---|---|---|---|---|---|---|---|---|---|---|---|---|---|---|---|---|---|
| **Number of houses** | GB | GB | GB | GB | GB | GB | GB | GB | GB | GB | GB | GB | GB | GB | GB | GB | – | – | – | – |
| **Families per house** | GB | GB | GB | GB | – | – | – | – | – | – | – | GB | GB | GB | GB | GB | – | – | – | – |

**Vacant houses** or

| Subject | 1801 | 1811 | 1821 | 1831 | 1841 | 1851 | 1861 | 1871 | 1881 | 1891 | 1901 | 1911 | 1921 | 1931 | 1951 | 1961[1] | 1971 | 1981 | 1991 | 2001 |
|---|---|---|---|---|---|---|---|---|---|---|---|---|---|---|---|---|---|---|---|---|
| household spaces | | GB | GB | GB | GB | GB | GB | GB | GB | GB | GB | GB | GB | GB | GB | GB | GB | GB | GB | GB |
| House or household spaces otherwise unoccupied | GB | GB | GB | GB | GB | GB | GB | GB | GB | GB | GB | GB | GB | – | – | – | GB | GB | GB | GB |
| **Shared access** to accommodation | – | – | – | – | – | – | – | – | – | – | – | – | – | – | – | – | GB | GB | GB | – |
| **Non-permanent** structures | – | – | – | – | – | – | – | – | – | – | – | – | – | – | – | GB | GB | GB | GB | – |

*Note:* GB = Great Britain = England, Wales and Scotland; E = England; W = Wales; S = Scotland

1 Education, employment, migration and household composition were collected from a 10 per cent sample in 1961.
2 1821-1841: in 5 year age groups;
  1851-1911: age in years;
  1921-1961: age in years and months;
  1971 onwards: exact date of birth.
3 More extensive relationship matrix.
4 1841: only for persons born in Scotland or Ireland: 1851-91 whether British subject or not.
5 Also whether full-time or part-time.
6 Asked of part-time workers only.
7 Asked of farmers and tradesmen only.
8 Only distinguishing (a) agriculture, (b) trade, manufacture or handicraft, (c) others.

9 1811-31: only distinguishing (a) agriculture, (b) trade, manufacture or handicraft, (c) others.
10 1901-11: restricted to whether those carrying on trade or industry worked at home.
11 Whether worked in the last 10 years.
12 Also number living and number dead.
13 Date first marriage ended not asked.
14 Separate voluntary enquiry.
15 Voluntary question.
16 1891-1901: only required if under 5 rooms; 1921-61; returned by the enumerator.
17 Whether exclusive use of bath/shower and toilet.

# Chapter 1 Population

### Population profile

- In 1999 the population of the United Kingdom was estimated to be 59.5 million, the 20th largest in the world. In 1851, it was 22.3 million. (Table 1.1)

- Just over a quarter of the population of Great Britain were aged under 20 in 1999, compared with just under half in 1821. (Chart 1.2)

- In 1999, 16 per cent of the population in the United Kingdom was aged 65 and over. The country in the EU with the highest proportion was Italy with 18 per cent and that with the lowest was the Irish Republic with 12 per cent. (Table 1.4)

- About one person in 15 in Great Britain is from an ethnic minority group. (Table 1.5)

### Population change

- The number of births in the United Kingdom peaked in 1920 at more than 1.1 million, the highest number in any year of the 20th century. (Chart 1.8)

- The annual number of deaths remained relatively constant during the 20th century, even though the population rose – there were 629 thousand deaths in the United Kingdom in 1999 compared with 632 thousand in 1901. (Table 1.9)

### International perspective

- The world's population in 2000 was nearly 6.1 billion - more than six times larger than it was in 1800. (Table 1.16)

- In 1999 Western Sahara and Mongolia had the lowest population densities at 1 person per square kilometre, while Hong Kong and Singapore had 6 thousand people per square kilometre. (Chart 1.17)

# 1.1

## Population[1] of the United Kingdom

Thousands

| | 1801 | 1851 | 1901 | 1951 | 1991 | 1999 | 2021 | 2026 |
|---|---|---|---|---|---|---|---|---|
| England | 8,305 | 16,764 | 30,515 | 41,159 | 48,208 | 49,753 | 53,715 | 54,443 |
| Wales | 587 | 1,163 | 2,013 | 2,599 | 2,891 | 2,937 | 3,047 | 3,062 |
| Scotland | 1,608 | 2,889 | 4,472 | 5,096 | 5,107 | 5,119 | 5,058 | 5,016 |
| Northern Ireland[2] | .. | 1,443 | 1,237 | 1,371 | 1,607 | 1,692 | 1,821 | 1,835 |
| United Kingdom | .. | 22,259 | 38,237 | 50,225 | 57,814 | 59,501 | 63,642 | 64,355 |

1 Data are census enumerated for 1801 to 1951; mid-year estimates for 1991 and 1999; 1998-based projections for 2021 and 2026.
See Appendix, Part 1: Population estimates and projections.
2 No census was taken in Ireland in 1801.

*Source: Office for National Statistics; Government Actuary's Department; General Register Office for Scotland; Northern Ireland Statistics and Research Agency*

# 1.2

## Population: by gender and age, 1821 and 1999

**Great Britain**

Millions

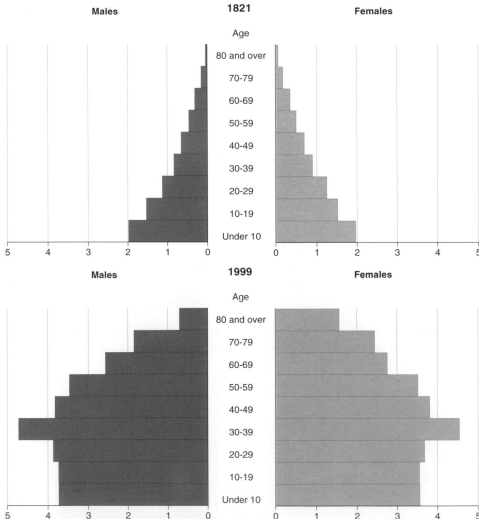

*Source: Census; Office for National Statistics; General Register Office for Scotland*

## Population profile

Information on the size and structure of the population is important for understanding many aspects of society such as the labour market and household composition. Changes in demographic patterns also have implications for public policy decisions, including those on housing and the provision of health, education and social services.

There are now more people living in the United Kingdom than at any time in the past. In 1999 the population was estimated to be 59.5 million (Table 1.1), the 20th largest in the world. The population of the United Kingdom increased by 37 million between 1851 and 1999, although there have been variations in the rate of increase between the constituent countries. The population of England almost trebled over the period, while Northern Ireland's increased by around a sixth.

Projections, using assumptions based on past trends, suggest that growth in the population of the United Kingdom will continue until it peaks at nearly 65 million people in 2036. It is then anticipated that the population will gradually decline. Different rates of growth are expected in the four constituent countries. A small decline in the population of Scotland is projected, while the populations of Wales and Northern Ireland are projected to peak in around 30 years' time and then start to fall. The population of England is still projected to be rising in around 30 years' time, but at a decreasing rate of growth.

The number of people in any age group within the population is dependent on how many are born in a particular period, and how long they survive. It is also dependent on the ages of migrants moving into and out of the country. Further information on factors affecting population change can be found in the Population change section of this chapter, which begins on page 33.

## 1.3

The 1821 Census was the first to record people's ages. Then, as now, there were more females in total than males living in Great Britain, and the ratio of females to males increased with age. In 1821 women began to outnumber men by their 20s, whereas they are now in the minority until their 50s. This is due to a rapid improvement in male mortality at younger ages.

In 1821 just under half of the population of Great Britain was aged under 20 and around a quarter were aged between 20 and 39 (Chart 1.2). The number of people in each ten-year age band decreased sharply with age, reflecting the poor survival rates at the time. In contrast, the 1999 age distribution was more even. A far higher proportion of the population was in the older age bands than in 1821, with over two-fifths aged 40 or over and just over a quarter aged under 20. Higher survival rates during the 20th century have resulted in the current age distribution, which follows patterns in the numbers of births more closely than it did in the 1800s.

The United Kingdom has an ageing population (Table 1.3). Historically, ageing was largely a result of the fall in fertility that began towards the end of the 19th century. Early in the 20th century lower mortality helped to increase the number of people surviving into old age, but the effects of improved survival were greater among younger people which operated as a counterbalance to the trend towards population ageing. More recently, there have been improvements in mortality rates for older people, and lower fertility rates, both of which have contributed to the ageing of the population. Projections suggest these trends will continue so that by 2016 it is expected the number of people aged 65 and over will exceed those aged under 16.

**Population: by gender and age**

| United Kingdom | | | | | | | | Percentages |
|---|---|---|---|---|---|---|---|---|
| | Under 16 | 16-24 | 25-34 | 35-44 | 45-54 | 55-64 | 65-74 | 75 and over | All ages (=100%) (millions) |

| | Under 16 | 16-24 | 25-34 | 35-44 | 45-54 | 55-64 | 65-74 | 75 and over | All ages (=100%) (millions) |
|---|---|---|---|---|---|---|---|---|---|
| **Males** | | | | | | | | | |
| 1901[1] | 34 | 20 | 16 | 12 | 9 | 6 | 3 | 1 | 18.5 |
| 1931[1] | 26 | 18 | 16 | 13 | 12 | 9 | 5 | 2 | 22.1 |
| 1961[1] | 25 | 14 | 13 | 14 | 14 | 11 | 6 | 3 | 25.5 |
| 1991 | 21 | 14 | 16 | 14 | 12 | 10 | 8 | 5 | 28.2 |
| 1999 | 21 | 11 | 16 | 15 | 13 | 10 | 8 | 5 | 29.3 |
| 2011[2] | 19 | 12 | 13 | 14 | 15 | 12 | 9 | 6 | 30.7 |
| 2026[2] | 18 | 10 | 13 | 13 | 12 | 14 | 10 | 9 | 32.1 |
| **Females** | | | | | | | | | |
| 1901[1] | 31 | 20 | 16 | 12 | 9 | 6 | 4 | 2 | 19.7 |
| 1931[1] | 23 | 17 | 16 | 14 | 12 | 9 | 6 | 2 | 24.0 |
| 1961[1] | 22 | 13 | 12 | 13 | 14 | 12 | 9 | 5 | 27.3 |
| 1991 | 19 | 12 | 15 | 13 | 11 | 10 | 9 | 9 | 29.6 |
| 1999 | 20 | 10 | 15 | 14 | 13 | 10 | 9 | 9 | 30.2 |
| 2011[2] | 18 | 11 | 12 | 14 | 14 | 12 | 9 | 9 | 31.1 |
| 2026[2] | 17 | 10 | 12 | 13 | 12 | 14 | 11 | 11 | 32.3 |

1 Data for 1901, 1931 and 1961 for under 16 and 16 to 24 relate to age bands under 15 and 15 to 24 respectively. Data for 1901 and 1931 are census enumerated; data for later years are mid-year estimates. 1931 figures for Northern Ireland relate to the 1937 Census.
2 1998-based projections.
**Source: Office for National Statistics; General Register Office for Scotland; Northern Ireland Statistics and Research Agency**

## 1.4

**Percentage of the population aged 65 and over: EU comparison**

| | | | | | Percentages |
|---|---|---|---|---|---|
| | 1960 | 1970 | 1981 | 1991 | 1999[1] |
| Italy | 9.3 | 10.8 | 13.2 | 15.1 | 17.6 |
| Sweden | 11.7 | 13.6 | 16.4 | 17.8 | 17.2 |
| Greece | 9.4 | 11.1 | 13.1 | 13.9 | 16.8 |
| Belgium | 12.0 | 13.3 | 14.2 | 15.0 | 16.5 |
| Spain | 8.2 | 9.5 | 11.2 | 13.8 | 16.4 |
| France | 11.6 | 12.8 | 13.8 | 14.1 | 15.8 |
| United Kingdom | 11.7 | 13.0 | 15.0 | 15.7 | 15.7 |
| Germany | 11.5 | 13.5 | 15.5 | 14.9 | 15.7 |
| Austria | 12.1 | 14.0 | 15.3 | 15.0 | 15.3 |
| Portugal | 8.0 | 9.7 | 11.4 | 13.6 | 15.2 |
| Denmark | 10.5 | 12.2 | 14.5 | 15.6 | 14.8 |
| Finland | 7.2 | 9.0 | 12.1 | 13.5 | 14.6 |
| Luxembourg | 10.8 | 12.5 | 13.6 | 13.4 | 14.3 |
| Netherlands | 8.9 | 10.1 | 11.6 | 12.9 | 13.6 |
| Irish Republic | 11.1 | 11.1 | 10.7 | 11.4 | 11.6 |
| EU average | 10.6 | 12.1 | 13.9 | 14.7 | 16.0 |

1 Population at January 1st 1999.
**Source: Eurostat**

# 1.5

## Population: by ethnic group and age, 1999-00[1]

| Great Britain | | | | | Percentages |
|---|---|---|---|---|---|
| | Under 16 | 16-34 | 35-64 | 65 and over | All ages (=100%) (millions) |
| **White** | 20 | 26 | 39 | 16 | 53.1 |
| **Black** | | | | | |
| Black Caribbean | 22 | 28 | 40 | 10 | 0.5 |
| Black African | 33 | 35 | 30 | .. | 0.4 |
| Other Black groups | 56 | 31 | 13 | .. | 0.3 |
| All Black groups | 34 | 31 | 30 | 5 | 1.2 |
| **Indian** | 24 | 31 | 38 | 7 | 0.9 |
| **Pakistani/Bangladeshi** | | | | | |
| Pakistani | 36 | 35 | 25 | 4 | 0.7 |
| Bangladeshi | 40 | 34 | 23 | .. | 0.3 |
| All Pakistani/Bangladeshi | 37 | 35 | 24 | 4 | 0.9 |
| **Other groups** | | | | | |
| Chinese | 16 | 40 | 39 | .. | 0.1 |
| None of the above | 36 | 30 | 31 | 3 | 0.6 |
| All other groups[2] | 33 | 32 | 32 | 3 | 0.8 |
| **All ethnic groups[3]** | 20 | 26 | 38 | 15 | 56.9 |

1 Population living in private households. Combined quarters: Spring 1999 to Winter 1999-00.
2 Includes those of mixed origin.
3 Includes those who did not state their ethnic group.

**Source: Labour Force Survey, Office for National Statistics**

# 1.6

## Population of working age[1]: by gender and social class, Spring 2000

**United Kingdom**

Percentages

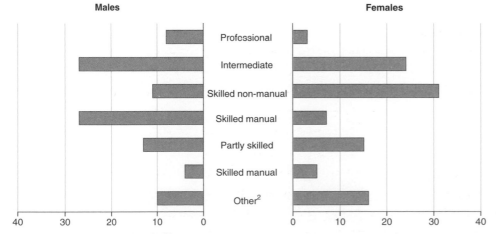

1 Males aged 16 to 64, females aged 16 to 59.
2 Includes members of the armed forces, those who did not state their current or last occupation and those who had not worked in the last eight years.

**Source: Labour Force Survey, Office for National Statistics**

An ageing population is a characteristic the United Kingdom shares with the other countries in the European Union (EU) (see Table 1.4 on previous page). In 1999 the proportion of the population aged 65 and over in the United Kingdom was 16 per cent, almost the same as the EU average. The percentage of the EU population aged 65 and over has increased by half since 1960. The largest increases were in Spain and Finland, where the proportions doubled. Conversely, the proportion in the Irish Republic, the country with the lowest proportion of people aged 65 and over in 1999, has remained steady since 1960.

The age profile of the population varies between ethnic groups. Members of ethnic minority groups were present in the United Kingdom in small numbers throughout the period of the British Empire. However, their numbers increased dramatically after the Second World War. This growth was initiated by large scale immigration from the countries of the New Commonwealth following the passing of the *1948 British Nationality Act*. This trend was subsequently curtailed by legislation passed in the 1960s and 1970s.

In Spring 2000, about one person in 15 in Great Britain was from an ethnic minority group (Table 1.5). In general, ethnic minority groups have a younger age structure than the White population, reflecting past immigration and fertility patterns. The 'Other Black' group has the youngest age structure with 56 per cent aged under 16. The Bangladeshi group also has a young age structure, with 40 per cent aged under 16 in 1999-00. This was double the proportion of the White group. In contrast, the White group had the highest proportion of people aged 65 and over at 16 per cent, compared with 4 per cent of the Pakistani/Bangladeshi group. Progressive ageing of the ethnic minority population is anticipated in the future, but changes will be dependent upon fertility levels, mortality rates and patterns of migration.

**1.7**

The occupational composition of the population has also changed during the 20th century. Among men, there has been a strong upward trend in the share of professional, managerial and supervisory grades. There have also been increases in the numbers of women in higher socio-economic occupations, albeit more slowly than for men, along with rises in clerical and unskilled manual groups. In Spring 2000 men of working age were three times more likely than women of working age to be in professional occupations (Chart 1.6). Conversely, women were three times more likely than men to be in the skilled non-manual group. This reflects the predominance of women in certain occupations such as clerical and secretarial jobs. These trends are accompanied by other factors such as the increasing participation of women in the workforce. Further information on economic activity rates is presented in Chart 4.4 on page 76 of the Labour Market chapter.

## Population change

The speed of population change depends upon the net natural change – the difference between the numbers of births and deaths – and the net effect of people migrating to and from the country. Most of the population growth of the United Kingdom during the 20th century can be attributed to net natural change (Table 1.7). However, in recent years net inward migration has become an increasingly important determinant of population growth. Between 1991 and 1999 net natural change in the United Kingdom as a whole was almost matched by net migration and other change.

The fastest population growth of the 20th century occurred in the first decade, when the population increased by an average of 385 thousand each year. This rapid growth at the start of the century, and again during the 1960s, was due to the high

**Population change[1]**

| United Kingdom | | | | | | Thousands |
|---|---|---|---|---|---|---|
| | | | | Annual averages | | |
| | Population at start of period | Live births | Deaths | Net natural change | Net migration and other | Overall change |
| **Census enumerated** | | | | | | |
| 1901-1911 | 38,237 | 1,091 | 624 | 467 | -82 | 385 |
| 1911-1921 | 42,082 | 975 | 689 | 286 | -92 | 194 |
| 1921-1931 | 44,027 | 824 | 555 | 268 | -67 | 201 |
| 1931-1951 | 46,038 | 785 | 598 | 188 | 25 | 213 |
| **Mid-year estimates** | | | | | | |
| 1951-1961 | 50,287 | 839 | 593 | 246 | 12 | 258 |
| 1961-1971 | 52,807 | 962 | 638 | 324 | -14 | 310 |
| 1971-1981 | 55,928 | 736 | 666 | 69 | -27 | 42 |
| 1981-1991 | 56,357 | 757 | 655 | 103 | 43 | 146 |
| 1991-1999 | 57,814 | 744 | 637 | 107 | 104 | 211 |
| **Mid-year projections[2]** | | | | | | |
| 1999-2001 | 59,501 | 716 | 627 | 88 | 140 | 228 |
| 2001-2011 | 59,954 | 701 | 614 | 87 | 95 | 182 |
| 2011-2021 | 61,773 | 712 | 620 | 92 | 95 | 187 |

1 See Appendix, Part 1: Population estimates and projections.
2 1998-based projections.

**Source: Office for National Statistics; Government Actuary's Department; General Register Office for Scotland; Northern Ireland Statistics and Research Agency**

**1.8**

**Births and deaths[1]**

**United Kingdom**

Millions

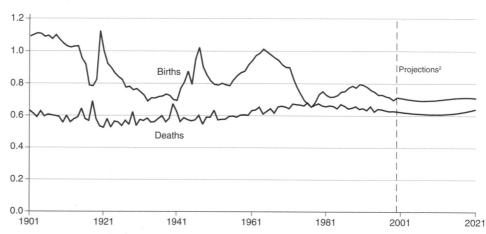

1 Data for 1901 to 1921 exclude the Irish Republic, which was constitutionally a part of the United Kingdom during this period.
2 1998-based.

**Source: Office for National Statistics; Government Actuary's Department; General Register Office for Scotland; Northern Ireland Statistics and Research Agency**

# 1.9

## Deaths: by gender and age

**United Kingdom**                                         Death rates per 1,000 in each age group

| | Under 1[1] | 1-15 | 16-34 | 35-54 | 55-64 | 65-74 | 75 and over | All ages | All deaths (thousands) |
|---|---|---|---|---|---|---|---|---|---|
| **Males** | | | | | | | | | |
| 1961 | 26.3 | 0.6 | 1.1 | 5.0 | 22.4 | 54.8 | 142.5 | 12.6 | 322 |
| 1971 | 20.2 | 0.5 | 1.0 | 4.8 | 20.4 | 51.1 | 131.4 | 12.1 | 329 |
| 1981 | 12.7 | 0.4 | 0.0 | 4.0 | 18.1 | 46.4 | 122.2 | 12.0 | 329 |
| 1991 | 8.3 | 0.3 | 0.9 | 3.1 | 14.2 | 38.7 | 110.6 | 11.1 | 314 |
| 1999 | 6.3 | 0.2 | 0.9 | 2.8 | 11.5 | 32.1 | 103.8 | 10.3 | 299 |
| 2011[2] | 3.7 | 0.2 | 0.9 | 2.4 | 9.5 | 24.6 | 88.1 | 9.7 | 298 |
| 2021[2] | 3.1 | 0.2 | 0.9 | 2.3 | 8.1 | 23.0 | 80.7 | 10.3 | 327 |
| **Females** | | | | | | | | | |
| 1961 | 18.2 | 0.4 | 0.6 | 3.2 | 11.0 | 31.6 | 110.4 | 11.4 | 310 |
| 1971 | 15.5 | 0.4 | 0.5 | 3.1 | 10.3 | 26.6 | 96.6 | 11.0 | 317 |
| 1981 | 9.5 | 0.3 | 0.4 | 2.5 | 9.8 | 24.7 | 90.2 | 11.4 | 329 |
| 1991 | 6.3 | 0.2 | 0.4 | 1.9 | 8.4 | 22.3 | 83.9 | 11.2 | 332 |
| 1999 | 5.0 | 0.2 | 0.4 | 1.8 | 7.0 | 19.5 | 84.8 | 11.0 | 330 |
| 2011[2] | 3.1 | 0.1 | 0.3 | 1.8 | 6.2 | 15.7 | 78.7 | 10.0 | 311 |
| 2021[2] | 2.4 | 0.1 | 0.3 | 1.7 | 5.5 | 14.9 | 69.0 | 9.8 | 314 |

1 Rate per 1,000 live births.
2 1998-based projections.

**Source: Office for National Statistics; Government Actuary's Department; General Register Office for Scotland; Northern Ireland Statistics and Research Agency**

# 1.10

## Population density: by area[1], 1801 and 1999

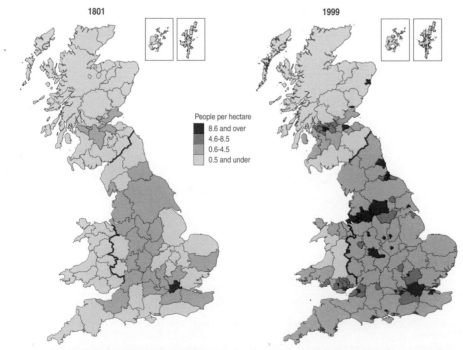

**1801**   **1999**

People per hectare
- 8.6 and over
- 4.6-8.5
- 0.6-4.5
- 0.5 and under

1 Unitary authorities and counties for 1999. Ancient counties for 1801. Densities for Scotland based on measurements from 1861.
**Source: Census, Office for National Statistics; National Assembly for Wales; General Registry Office for Scotland**

number of births during these decades. The considerable fall in the number of births following the 1960s' 'baby boom' helps to explain the slower population growth of the 1970s.

The two World Wars had a major impact on the number of births and, to a lesser extent, deaths in the United Kingdom (see Chart 1.8 on previous page). There was a noticeable fall in births during the First World War, followed by a post-war 'baby boom' when the number of births peaked at more than 1.1 million in 1920 – the highest number in any year of the 20th century. The number of births then decreased and remained low during the 1930s' depression and the Second World War. This was followed by a 'baby boom' shortly after the Second World War and another in the 1960s.

One factor influencing trends in the number of births is the number of women of reproductive age. For example, the number of births rose during the 1980s as the women born during the 1960s 'baby boom' entered their peak reproductive years. As these women have got older the number of births each year has fallen. More information about fertility is contained in the Family formation section of Chapter 2: Households and Families (page 48).

Despite the considerable population growth since 1901, the annual number of deaths remained relatively constant during the 20th century. There were 629 thousand deaths in the United Kingdom in 1999 compared with 632 thousand in 1901. However, this masks large declines in mortality rates. Early in the 20th century, infant and childhood mortality declined considerably, while in more recent years the death rates among older people have also fallen. Rising standards of living and new developments in medical technology and practice help to explain these declines in mortality rates.

Death rates are higher for males than for females in all age groups (Table 1.9), resulting in the life expectancy of females being higher than that for males (see Table 7.1 on page 128 in the Health chapter). The fact that the overall crude death rate has been higher for women than for men since 1991 can be explained by the older age structure of the female population compared with that for males. Death rates among both men and women in Scotland were higher at most ages in 1999 than among those in the other constituent countries of the United Kingdom.

## Geographical distribution

In 1999 the majority of the population of the United Kingdom (about 84 per cent) lived in England, with Northern Ireland having the smallest population of the four constituent countries at 1.7 million (3 per cent) (see Table 1.1 on page 30). The population density of the four countries varies considerably: in 1999 England had about 381 inhabitants per square kilometre compared with only 66 people per square kilometre in Scotland.

There are difficulties in tracing population distribution and density over time, not least due to boundary and classification changes. Although the maps shown in Chart 1.10 use different boundaries, it is still possible to see that London had by far the greatest concentration of people in both 1801 (when it fell within the county of Middlesex) and 1999, while the Highlands of Scotland had the lowest population density in both years. The maps also reveal the relatively high population densities of the counties of the South of England compared with those of Northern England, Scotland and Wales.

By 1831, today's large cities were already established. London was the largest urban area, even discounting those areas such as Brixton and Southwark, which were at the time officially towns in their own right. Glasgow and Edinburgh had larger populations than many English towns in 1831 which have since overtaken them in size of population (Table 1.11). Despite this, large scale movement into urban areas was not yet under way. This was in part because travel over large distances was still difficult and expensive, and industry providing employment was not yet centred on large towns but based around the existing rural craft centres. It was not until the last quarter of the 19th century that there was a large increase in urbanisation. Improvements in transport, better education and agricultural depression were factors in this change. In 1831 one in six people lived in areas designated at the 1831 Census as towns or cities, compared with just under two in three living in areas designated as urban in the 1901 Census.

The population of Great Britain has been highly urbanised for much of the 20th century. By 1991 almost 90 per cent of the population were living in urban areas. The largest of these urban areas is Greater London which, with a resident population of 6.4 million, had more than two and a half times the population of the next largest metropolitan counties, the West Midlands and Greater Manchester.

**Urban areas with largest populations[1]**

**Great Britain**

| 1831 | 1901 | 1991[3] |
|---|---|---|
| London[2] | London | London |
| Glasgow | Glasgow | West Midlands |
| Manchester | Liverpool | Manchester |
| Edinburgh | Manchester | West Yorkshire |
| Liverpool | Birmingham | Tyneside |

1 Resident population.
2 Includes London within and without the walls and the City of Westminster.
3 Metropolitan counties.
**Source: Census**

## Migration

Migration flows influence the size, growth and profile of the population. Regional populations are affected by people relocating within the country, supplemented by international migration flows. During much of the 20th century there has been a movement of population from the old coal, shipbuilding and steel industries in the north of England, Scotland and Wales to the light industries and services of the south of England and the Midlands. Population gains and losses due to internal migration have important implications for local land use and housing planning, as well as for the provision of welfare services.

During 1999 Wales gained 5 thousand people due to internal migration, while Scotland and Northern Ireland experienced net losses of population of 4 thousand and 1 thousand respectively. In England the numbers of people moving in and out was more or less balanced. At a regional level within England, the greatest fall in population occurred in London where 65 thousand more people moved to other regions of the United Kingdom than moved into the region (Table 1.12). However, this was more than offset by the net inflow of international migrants settling in the capital. Two-fifths of people leaving London for elsewhere in the United Kingdom moved into the neighbouring South East region. The South West experienced the highest net gain of all the regions due to internal migration, of 33 thousand people.

# 1.12

**Inter-regional movements[1] within the United Kingdom, 1999**

**United Kingdom**  Thousands

| | | | | | | | Origin | | | | | | | |
| --- | --- | --- | --- | --- | --- | --- | --- | --- | --- | --- | --- | --- | --- | --- |
| | North East | North West | York-shire and the Humber | East Mid-lands | West Mid-lands | East | London | South East | South West | Eng-land | Wales | Scot-land | Nor-thern Ireland | United King-dom |
| **Destination** | | | | | | | | | | | | | | |
| North East | . | 6 | 8 | 3 | 2 | 3 | 4 | 4 | 2 | 33 | 1 | 4 | 1 | 39 |
| North West | 7 | . | 18 | 10 | 13 | 7 | 11 | 12 | 8 | 86 | 9 | 8 | 2 | 105 |
| Yorkshire and the Humber | 10 | 19 | . | 16 | 8 | 8 | 8 | 11 | 6 | 86 | 3 | 5 | 1 | 95 |
| East Midlands | 4 | 11 | 18 | . | 16 | 17 | 11 | 18 | 8 | 103 | 3 | 4 | 1 | 111 |
| West Midlands | 3 | 13 | 8 | 14 | . | 8 | 10 | 14 | 13 | 82 | 8 | 3 | 1 | 94 |
| East | 3 | 8 | 8 | 14 | 8 | . | 59 | 29 | 10 | 139 | 3 | 5 | 1 | 148 |
| London | 5 | 13 | 10 | 10 | 11 | 29 | . | 54 | 16 | 148 | 5 | 8 | 2 | 163 |
| South East | 5 | 14 | 11 | 14 | 14 | 30 | 88 | . | 34 | 211 | 8 | 8 | 1 | 228 |
| South West | 2 | 10 | 7 | 9 | 17 | 14 | 22 | 47 | . | 128 | 10 | 5 | 1 | 143 |
| England | 38 | 94 | 88 | 89 | 88 | 117 | 214 | 190 | 96 | . | 51 | 51 | 10 | 112 |
| Wales | 1 | 12 | 3 | 3 | 10 | 4 | 6 | 9 | 9 | 56 | . | 2 | - | 58 |
| Scotland | 4 | 8 | 5 | 3 | 3 | 5 | 7 | 8 | 4 | 47 | 2 | . | 2 | 51 |
| Northern Ireland | - | 2 | 1 | 1 | 1 | 1 | 2 | 1 | 1 | 9 | - | 2 | . | 12 |
| United Kingdom | 44 | 115 | 97 | 96 | 102 | 126 | 228 | 209 | 110 | 112 | 53 | 55 | 12 | . |

1 Based on patients re-registering with NHS doctors in other parts of the United Kingdom. Moves where the origin and destination lie within the same region do not appear in the table.

**Source: Office for National Statistics; General Register Office for Scotland; Northern Ireland Statistics and Research Agency**

# 1.13

Young adults are the most mobile age group, reflecting in part the move most young people make from their parental home either to study, seek employment or set up their own home. In 1999 London experienced the largest net increase of people aged 15 to 24 due to migration within the United Kingdom, of 18 thousand, while the West Midlands experienced the biggest net loss of people in this age group, of 4 thousand. However, London also experienced the largest net losses among all other age groups, particularly those aged 35 to 44 and those aged under 15. The regions with the highest net gains in these age groups were the South West, East of England and South East. Further information about some of the reasons why people move home can be found in Table 10.17 on page 185 in the Housing chapter.

The pattern of people entering and leaving the United Kingdom changed over the 20th century. There was a net loss due to international migration during the first three decades of the 20th century and again during the 1960s and 1970s. However, since 1983 there has been net migration into the United Kingdom.

Over the period 1994 to 1998, net international migration to the United Kingdom averaged 73 thousand a year (Table 1.13). This was nearly four times the annual average of the preceding five years. Between 1994 and 1998, 17.5 thousand more people per year migrated to the United Kingdom from the EU than between 1989 and 1993, compared with 17.6 thousand more from all other regions. Of those migrating from the United Kingdom to other countries between 1994 and 1998, most were leaving for the EU or Old Commonwealth countries, such as Canada, Australia and New Zealand.

Between 1990 and 1998 the numbers of UK nationals living outside the United Kingdom but within the European Union (EU) increased overall. This increase was greatest in Portugal, where the number of resident UK nationals has risen by

**Average international migration[1]: by region of next or last residence, 1989-1993 and 1994-1998**

| United Kingdom | | | | | | Thousands |
| --- | --- | --- | --- | --- | --- | --- |
| | 1989-1993 | | | 1994-1998 | | |
| | Inflow | Outflow | Balance | Inflow | Outflow | Balance |
| New Commonwealth | 49.9 | 25.9 | 24.0 | 49.3 | 23.5 | 25.8 |
| European Union | 66.4 | 61.3 | 5.1 | 83.9 | 62.3 | 21.7 |
| Old Commonwealth | 52.7 | 57.6 | -4.9 | 57.0 | 50.9 | 6.1 |
| United States of America | 25.3 | 34.8 | -9.5 | 30.5 | 24.9 | 5.6 |
| Middle East | 9.0 | 11.3 | -2.3 | 11.4 | 8.9 | 2.5 |
| Rest of Europe | 12.5 | 9.7 | 2.8 | 13.4 | 12.3 | 1.0 |
| Rest of America | 2.3 | 3.6 | -1.3 | 2.8 | 2.9 | -0.1 |
| Other | 24.4 | 19.4 | 4.9 | 29.3 | 18.6 | 10.6 |
| All countries | 242.5 | 223.6 | 18.9 | 277.6 | 204.4 | 73.2 |

1 Derived from International Passenger Survey migration estimates only. Excludes migration between the United Kingdom and the Irish Republic. Excludes asylum seekers. See also Appendix, Part 1: International migration estimates.

**Source: International Passenger Survey, Office for National Statistics**

# 1.14

**Acceptances for settlement: by selected region of origin**

**United Kingdom**

Thousands

1 Includes all European Economic Area (EEA) countries throughout the period covered. EEA nationals are not obliged to seek settlement and the figures relate only to those who chose to do so.

**Source: Home Office**

# 1.15

**Asylum applications[1] and decisions[2]: by region of origin, 1999**

United Kingdom                                                                                       Thousands

| | Europe and Americas | Africa | Middle East | Rest of Asia | Not known | All areas |
|---|---|---|---|---|---|---|
| **Applications received** | 30.3 | 18.4 | 4.2 | 17.5 | 0.8 | 71.2 |
| **Decisions taken** | | | | | | |
| Recognised as a refugee and granted asylum | 6.5 | 0.8 | 0.4 | 0.1 | 0.1 | 7.8 |
| Not recognised as a refugee but granted exceptional leave | 0.1 | 0.7 | 0.4 | 1.2 | - | 2.5 |
| Refused asylum and exceptional leave | 3.4 | 2.9 | 0.3 | 4.4 | - | 11.0 |
| Granted asylum or exceptional leave to remain under backlog criteria | 3.5 | 5.6 | 0.3 | 1.6 | 0.1 | 11.1 |
| Refused leave under backlog criteria | 0.4 | 0.7 | - | 0.1 | - | 1.3 |
| Total decisions | 13.9 | 10.7 | 1.4 | 7.4 | 0.3 | 33.7 |
| **Applications withdrawn** | 0.3 | 0.3 | - | 0.1 | - | 0.7 |
| **Applications outstanding at end of year** | 41.8 | 28.6 | 8.0 | 22.1 | 0.9 | 101.5 |

1 Excluding dependants.
2 Excludes South East Asia refugees. Information is for initial determination decisions, excluding the outcome of appeals or other subsequent decisions. Decisions figures do not necessarily relate to applications made in 1999. See Appendix, Part 1: Asylum.
**Source: Home Office**

# 1.16

**World population**

                                                                                                     Millions

| | 1800 | 1850 | 1900 | 1950 | 2000 |
|---|---|---|---|---|---|
| Asia | 635 | 809 | 947 | 1,402 | 3,683 |
| Africa | 107 | 111 | 133 | 224 | 784 |
| Europe | 203 | 276 | 408 | 547 | 729 |
| Latin America and Caribbean | 24 | 38 | 74 | 166 | 519 |
| North America | 7 | 26 | 82 | 172 | 310 |
| Oceania | 2 | 2 | 6 | 13 | 30 |
| World | 978 | 1,262 | 1,650 | 2,524 | 6,055 |

**Source: United Nations**

almost 60 per cent. Only three countries had fewer resident UK nationals in 1998 than in 1990: Italy, Spain and Greece.

Nationals of the European Economic Area (EU plus Norway, Iceland and Liechtenstein) have the right to reside in the United Kingdom provided they are working or able to support themselves financially. Nearly all other overseas nationals wishing to live permanently in the United Kingdom require Home Office acceptance for settlement. The number of people accepted for settlement in the United Kingdom increased by 27 thousand to 97 thousand between 1998 and 1999, the highest annual number since July 1962 when Commonwealth citizens became subject to immigration control, and equivalent to 0.2 per cent of the UK population (see Chart 1.14 on previous page). The number of people accepted from other European countries doubled between 1998 and 1999, mainly due to asylum-related settlement from the Federal Republic of Yugoslavia and to a lesser extent Turkey.

There have also been high percentages of acceptances from Asia and Africa in recent years, again mainly asylum-related, but also reflecting the increase in spouses of those already accepted for settlement from South Asia, after the abolition of the primary purpose rule, in June 1997. This rule required applicants to satisfy the Home Office that they had not married primarily in order to gain entrance to the UK. The number of acceptances from the Americas declined between 1998 and 1999, returning to a level similar to that seen before the evacuation of Monserrat due to volcanic activity in 1997.

The United Kingdom has a tradition of granting protection to those in need, and has certain obligations under the 1951 United Nations Convention, and the 1967 Protocol, relating to the Status of Refugees. These provide that refugees (those who have been granted asylum) should enjoy treatment at least as favourable as that accorded to the indigenous population.

The number of people seeking asylum varies considerably from year to year, although there has been an overall increase from about 4 thousand a year from 1985 to 1988 to around 71 thousand in 1999 (Table 1.15). The countries from which people arrive to claim asylum varies with world events. In 1999, most asylum seekers came from the Federal Republic of Yugoslavia, Somalia, Sri Lanka and Afghanistan, areas which have seen escalations of internal conflict.

## International perspective

Population growth in Europe has been considerably slower than the average growth rate for the world in recent years. The world's population is now more than six times larger than it was in 1800 (Table 1.16). Much of this increase has occurred in the 20th century: in 2000 the population was more than three and a half times the size it was in 1900. In October 1999 the world's population exceeded 6 billion people, and reached nearly 6.1 billion in 2000, an increase of three and a half billion in the previous 50 years. China, with 1.3 billion is currently the country with the largest population, although India is expected to have overtaken it by 2050.

Population density varies considerably throughout the world. In 1999 Western Sahara and Mongolia had the lowest densities at 1 person per square kilometre, while both Hong Kong and Singapore had 6 thousand people per square kilometre (Chart 1.17). The countries which have the highest population densities are not always those which have the highest populations. The population of China in 1999 was around 410 times that of Albania but, as it covers 33 times the area, the densities of these regions are the same - 130 people per square kilometre.

**World population densities, 1999**

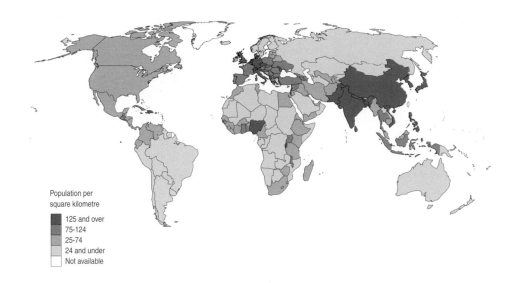

Population per square kilometre

- 125 and over
- 75-124
- 25-74
- 24 and under
- Not available

*Source: United Nations*

## Websites

| | |
|---|---|
| National Statistics | www.statistics.gov.uk |
| General Register Office for Scotland | www.gro-scotland.gov.uk |
| Government Actuary's Department | www.gad.gov.uk |
| Home Office Immigration and Asylum Statistics | www.homeoffice.gov.uk/rds/index.htm |
| National Assembly for Wales | www.wales.gov.uk/statisticswales/statistics_e.htm |
| Northern Ireland Statistics and Research Agency | www.nisra.gov.uk |
| Scottish Executive | www.scotland.gov.uk |
| Eurostat | http://europa.eu.int./comm/eurostat |
| United Nations Population Information Network | www.undp.org/popin/popin.htm |

## Contacts

| | |
|---|---|
| **Office for National Statistics** | |
| Chapter author | 020 7533 5786 |
| Internal migration | 01329 813 889 |
| International migration | 01329 813 255 |
| Labour market enquiries helpline | 020 7533 6094 |
| Population estimates general enquiries | 01329 813 318 |
| **General Register Office for Scotland** | 0131 314 4254 |
| **Government Actuary's Department** | 020 7211 2622 |
| **Home Office** | 020 8760 8280 |
| **National Assembly for Wales** | 029 2082 5085 |
| **Northern Ireland Statistics and Research Agency** | |
| Population enquiries | 028 9034 8132 |
| **Eurostat** | 00 352 4231 13727 |
| **United Nations** | 020 7630 2709 |

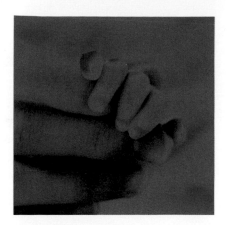

# Chapter 2 Households and Families

### Households and families

● The population of Great Britain increased by more than half during the 20th century, and the number of households tripled over the same period to almost 24 million in Spring 2000. (Page 42)

● Almost three in ten households in Great Britain comprised one person living alone in Spring 2000, more than two and a half times the proportion in 1961. (Table 2.2)

● Among families with dependent children in Great Britain in Spring 2000, nearly half of those headed by a Black person were lone parent families compared with one in 13 Indian families. (Table 2.4)

### Partnerships

● Among non-married women aged under 60 in Great Britain, the proportion cohabiting almost doubled between 1986 and 1998-99 from 13 per cent to 25 per cent. For men it more than doubled from 11 per cent to 26 per cent over the same period. (Page 45)

● In 1999, 179 thousand first marriages took place in the United Kingdom – less than half the number in 1970. (Chart 2.8)

### Family formation

● The mean age of women at childbirth in England and Wales rose from 26.2 years in 1971 to 29.0 in 1999. (Page 50)

### Family relationships

● In 1998-99, step-families (married and cohabiting), where the head of the family was aged under 60, accounted for about 6 per cent of all families with dependent children in Great Britain. (Page 53)

● Most people acknowledge the importance of grandparents – about three-quarters of adults agreed that 'families with working mothers need grandparents help more and more' and only one in ten agreed that grandparents have 'little to teach the grandchildren of today'. (Table 2.24)

# 2.1

## Households[1]: by size

| Great Britain | | | | | Percentages |
|---|---|---|---|---|---|
| | 1961 | 1971 | 1981 | 1991 | 2000[2] |
| One person | 14 | 18 | 22 | 27 | 29 |
| Two people | 30 | 32 | 32 | 34 | 35 |
| Three people | 23 | 19 | 17 | 16 | 16 |
| Four people | 18 | 17 | 18 | 16 | 14 |
| Five people | 9 | 8 | 7 | 5 | 5 |
| Six or more people | 7 | 6 | 4 | 2 | 2 |
| All households (=100%)(millions) | 16.3 | 18.6 | 20.2 | 22.4 | 23.9 |
| Average household size (number of people) | 3.1 | 2.9 | 2.7 | 2.5 | 2.4 |

1 See Appendix, Part 2: Households.
2 At Spring 2000.

**Source: Census; Labour Force Survey, Office for National Statistics**

# 2.2

## Households[1]: by type of household and family

| Great Britain | | | | | Percentages |
|---|---|---|---|---|---|
| | 1961 | 1971 | 1981 | 1991 | 2000[2] |
| **One person** | | | | | |
| Under state pension age | 4 | 6 | 8 | 11 | 14 |
| Over state pension age | 7 | 12 | 14 | 16 | 15 |
| **Two or more unrelated adults** | 5 | 4 | 5 | 3 | 3 |
| **One family households** | | | | | |
| Couple[3] | | | | | |
| No children | 26 | 27 | 26 | 28 | 29 |
| 1-2 dependent children[4] | 30 | 26 | 25 | 20 | 19 |
| 3 or more dependent children[4] | 8 | 9 | 6 | 5 | 4 |
| Non-dependent children only | 10 | 8 | 8 | 8 | 6 |
| Lone parent[3] | | | | | |
| Dependent children[4] | 2 | 3 | 5 | 6 | 6 |
| Non-dependent children only | 4 | 4 | 4 | 4 | 3 |
| **Multi-family households** | 3 | 1 | 1 | 1 | 1 |
| **All households[5]** (=100%)(millions) | 16.3 | 18.6 | 20.2 | 22.4 | 23.9 |

1 See Appendix, Part 2: Households and Families.
2 At Spring 2000.
3 Other individuals who were not family members may also be included.
4 May also include non-dependent children.
5 Includes couples of the same gender in 2000, but percentages are based on totals excluding this group.

**Source: Census; Labour Force Survey, Office for National Statistics**

Changes in the population structure, in society's values and also in social legislation have resulted in something of a transformation of the characteristics and dynamics of the so-called 'traditional' household and family.

## Households and families

While the population of Great Britain increased by more than half during the 20th century (see Table 1.1 in Chapter 1 on page 30), the number of households tripled during the same period, from just under 8 million at the beginning of the century to almost 24 million in Spring 2000. This stronger growth in the number of households is a result of family sizes decreasing, an increase in longevity, a trend towards living alone – particularly among the elderly – and the demand for separate, smaller accommodation units. During the 19th and early part of the 20th century many households contained members of the extended family and some households also contained domestic servants. The average size of households almost halved during the 20th century – from 4.6 to 2.4 persons per household (Table 2.1). The Continuous Household Survey estimated that, in 1998-99, the average household size in Northern Ireland was 2.7, slightly higher than in Great Britain.

If recent trends continue, official projections in England suggest that between 1996 and 2021, there will be steady growth of 3.4 million in the private household population and 3.8 million in the number of households. In Wales the private household population figure is projected to rise by 0.1 million over the same period to almost 3 million, while the number of households is projected to increase by 0.2 million to 1.3 million. At the same time the average household size in England has been projected to decline from 2.4 people in 1996 to 2.2 in 2021. The comparable figures in Wales are for a decline from 2.5 people to 2.2.

## 2.3

The so-called 'nuclear' or 'traditional' family household consisting of a couple with dependent children living in their own home has been predominant since at least the late 16th century, and probably since the late 14th century. Household composition, however, has transformed in recent decades. The trend towards people living alone has become increasingly notable. In Spring 2000 almost three in ten households in Great Britain comprised one person living alone, which was more than two and a half times the proportion in 1961 (Table 2.2). The proportion of couple family households with dependent children fell from almost two-fifths in 1961 to less than a quarter in Spring 2000, while the proportion of lone parent households with dependent children tripled. Multi-family households formed 3 per cent of all households in 1961, but have since declined to around 1 per cent. During the 1970s and 1980s there was emphasis towards the provision of first public, and then private, housing which encouraged the acquisition of separate accommodation. There is also evidence that lone parents, who historically were more likely than other families to live in multi-family households, increasingly became one-family households throughout the period.

Whereas Table 2.2 shows that almost three-fifths of the households in Great Britain were headed by a couple in Spring 2000, Table 2.3 is based on people. It shows that almost three-quarters of people living in private households were in a couple family household. The 'traditional' family household was the most common type of family in which people lived in Spring 2000. However, during the last four decades of the 20th century, the proportion living in such households fell by a quarter and the proportion of people living in couple family households with no children increased from less than a fifth to a quarter. One in ten people in Great Britain in Spring 2000 and one in seven people in Northern Ireland in 1998-99 lived in a lone parent household.

### People in households[1]: by type of household and family in which they live

| Great Britain | | | | | Percentages |
| --- | --- | --- | --- | --- | --- |
| | 1961 | 1971 | 1981 | 1991 | 2000[2] |
| **One family households** | | | | | |
| Living alone | 4 | 6 | 8 | 11 | 12 |
| Couple | | | | | |
| No children | 18 | 19 | 20 | 23 | 25 |
| Dependent children[3] | 52 | 52 | 47 | 41 | 39 |
| Non-dependent children only | 12 | 10 | 10 | 11 | 9 |
| Lone parent | 3 | 4 | 6 | 10 | 10 |
| **Other households** | 12 | 9 | 9 | 4 | 6 |
| **All people in private households** | | | | | |
| (=100%)(millions) | .. | 53.4 | 53.9 | 55.4 | 57.0 |
| **People not in private** | | | | | |
| **households** (millions) | .. | 0.9 | 0.8 | 0.8 | .. |
| **Total population** (millions) | 51.4 | 54.4 | 54.8 | 56.2 | .. |

1 See Appendix, Part 2: Households and Families.
2 At Spring 2000.
3 May also include non-dependent children.
**Source: Census; Labour Force Survey, Office for National Statistics**

Different demographic structures, cultural traditions and economic characteristics of the various ethnic groups in Great Britain underlie distinctive patterns of family and household size and composition. In Spring 2000, of families with dependent children in Great Britain, nearly half of those headed by a Black person were lone parent families compared with one in 13 Indian families (see Table 2.4 overleaf). Indian and Pakistani/Bangladeshi households tended to be larger than those from other ethnic groups, at 3.5 and 4.6 persons per household respectively. Such households may contain three generations with grandparents living with a married couple and their children. Even once age structure has been taken into account, the South Asian groups still have the largest households.

Earlier in this section, the increase in the proportion of one person households was highlighted as being one of the most notable differences seen in household composition during the past 40 years in Great Britain. Indeed, the

# 2.4

**Families with dependent children[1]: by ethnic group, Spring 2000**

**Great Britain**                                                                                                   Percentages

|  | White | Black | Indian | Pakistani/ Bangladeshi | Other groups[2] | All ethnic groups[3] |
|---|---|---|---|---|---|---|
| Couples | 79 | 51 | 92 | 85 | 71 | 78 |
| Lone parents | 21 | 49 | 8 | 15 | 29 | 22 |
| | | | | | | |
| All[4] (=100%)(millions) | 6.6 | 0.2 | 0.2 | 0.2 | 0.3 | 7.2 |

1 May also include non-dependent children.
2 Includes those of mixed origin.
3 Includes those who did not state their ethnic group.
4 Excludes cases where the dependent child is the family unit, for example, foster child.
**Source: Labour Force Survey, Office for National Statistics**

# 2.5

**One person households[1]: by gender and whether aged under 65 or aged 65 and over**

**England & Wales**

Percentages

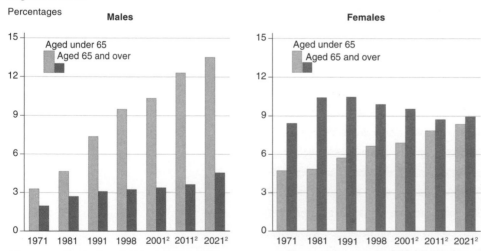

1 Percentage of heads of household that were living alone as a percentage of all households.
2 1996-based household projections.
**Source: Department of the Environment, Transport and the Regions; National Assembly for Wales**

number of such households increased from almost 2 million in 1961 to around 7 million in Spring 2000. However, the percentage increase has not been uniform across all categories of those living alone. In 1998 women aged 65 and over formed the largest proportion of households living alone in England and Wales (Chart 2.5), and this proportion has remained fairly stable since the beginning of the 1970s. In recent years, the largest increase in one person households has been among men under the age of 65: 10 per cent in 1998 which was almost three times the proportion in 1971. At the same time the proportion of women aged under 65 and living alone has almost doubled. These increases in part reflect the decline in marriage and the rise in separation and divorce, as well as people first marrying at an older age these days. The Department of the Environment, Transport and the Regions' 1996-based household projections suggest that the size of the group of men aged under 65 and living alone will continue to increase and will overtake women aged 65 and over to form the largest category of one-person households by 2001.

## Partnerships

The pattern of partnership formation has changed since the mid-1970s, and although the majority of men and women still get married, that majority is not quite so large as it once was. While the proportion of men and women who are marrying has been declining, the proportion cohabiting has been increasing, and the proportion living outside a partnership has also increased. In a combined estimation and projections exercise, undertaken

# 2.6

by the Government Actuary's Department and the Office for National Statistics, it was estimated that there were just over one and a half million cohabiting couples in England and Wales in 1996 – representing about one in six of the adult non-married population – and that the number of cohabiting couples would almost double by 2021.

The proportions of both men and women cohabiting has increased since 1986 which is the earliest year for which data are available on a consistent basis. For non-married women aged under 60, the proportion cohabiting in Great Britain almost doubled from 13 per cent to 25 per cent between 1986 and 1998-99. For men, it more than doubled from 11 per cent to 26 per cent over the same time period. The longest time series on cohabitation exists for women aged 18 to 49. Between 1979 and 1998 the proportion of non-married women in Great Britain who were cohabiting almost tripled, from 11 per cent to 29 per cent. In Northern Ireland, although the proportion of non-married people aged under 60 who were cohabiting has also increased since the mid-1980s, this proportion has remained below that of Great Britain. Data from the 1986 Continuous Household Survey show that 2 per cent of non-married men aged between 16 and 59 and 2 per cent of non-married women of the same age in Northern Ireland were cohabiting. Combined data for 1996-97 and 1998-99 suggest that this increased to around one in ten non-married people aged 16 to 59.

Combined data from the 1996-97 and 1998-99 General Household Surveys show that three in ten men and over a quarter of women in Great Britain who had ever been married had cohabited before their first marriage. The proportion who had cohabited with their future partner before their wedding increased with age at marriage. Around three-fifths of people who were aged 35 to 39 when they married for the first time had cohabited with their future partner (Table 2.6). An analysis undertaken using data from the British Household Panel Survey (BHPS) demonstrated that for women whose first partnership was a cohabitation which dissolved, almost all of those who repartnered cohabited in their second partnership. It was estimated that after a cohabiting first partnership had dissolved, the median duration to the next partnership was around five years.

Results from the 1998 BHPS indicate that nearly three-quarters of never married childless people aged under 35 who were cohabiting expected to marry each other. Seven out of eight of those cohabiting expected to marry at some time. Thus, for most people, cohabitation is part of the process of getting married and is not a substitute for marriage. About two-fifths of the cohabiting adults perceived advantages to just living together rather than marrying. Among those who did, about half mentioned the idea of 'trial marriage' and another three in ten mentioned 'no legal ties' as the first advantage to this type of union.

Cohabitation does not always result in marriage. In 1998-99, 15 per cent of men and 13 per cent of women reported at least one cohabitation not leading to marriage. Cohabitation is not restricted to periods before first marriage. Combined data from the 1996-97 and 1998-99 General Household Surveys illustrate that 12 per cent of separated women and 36 per cent of divorced women aged 25 to 34 were cohabiting.

**Cohabitation prior to first marriage[1]: by age at first marriage and gender, 1996-1999[2]**

| Great Britain | | Percentages |
|---|---|---|
| | Males | Females |
| **Age at first marriage** | | |
| 16-19 | 14 | 12 |
| 20-24 | 19 | 23 |
| 25-29 | 39 | 50 |
| 30-34 | 56 | 60 |
| 35-39 | 63 | 59 |
| 40-59 | 57 | 49 |
| | | |
| All aged 16 to 59 | 30 | 27 |

1 Those who cohabited with their future partner prior to their first marriage as a proportion of all ever married men and women.
2 Combined years: 1996-97 and 1998-99.

*Source: General Household Survey, Office for National Statistics*

# 2.7

## Women remaining 'never married' by certain ages: by year of birth

**England & Wales**
Percentages

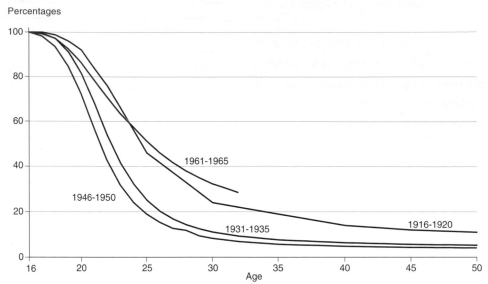

Source: Office for National Statistics; London School of Hygiene and Tropical Medicine

# 2.8

## Marriages and divorces

**United Kingdom**
Thousands

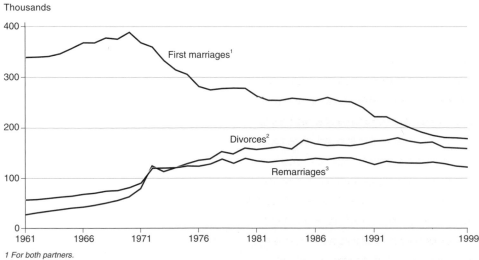

1 For both partners.
2 Includes annulments.
3 For one or both partners.

Source: Office for National Statistics; General Register Office for Scotland; Northern Ireland Statistics and Research Agency

Some people never marry. The proportion of women remaining never married in England and Wales is compared in Chart 2.7 for four cohorts of women born between 1916 to 1920, 1931 to 1935, 1946 to 1950 and 1961 to 1965. A higher proportion of women from the cohort born in the 1960s remain never married in their early 30s than in previous groups at the same age. By the age of 32, only 7 per cent of the 1946 to 1950 cohort, 9 per cent of the 1931 to 1935 and 22 per cent of the 1916 to 1920 cohort remained unmarried compared with 28 per cent of those born between 1961 and 1965. The relatively large proportion of women born in the 1916 to 1920 cohort remaining never married by the age of 32 is likely to be as a consequence of the Second World War.

There are similar trends for men in the proportion remaining never married by cohort. For both men and women, this is partly reflecting a shift towards later marriage. If current trends continue, official projections suggest that over 10 per cent of women and 16 per cent of men born in the 1960s cohort will neither have married nor be in a permanent cohabiting union by the time they reach the age of 50. This compares with 4 per cent of women and 8 per cent of men born in the 1940s cohort.

The Marriage Act 1836 and the Registration Act 1836 came into force in 1837 in England and Wales, and provided the statutory basis for regulating and recording marriages. At the time the minimum legal age at marriage was 14 for boys and 12 for girls and this was increased to 16 for both males and females under the Age of Marriage Act 1929. The annual number of marriages during the first year of civil registration to mid-1838 was over 110 thousand in England and Wales. Annual numbers of marriages rose steadily from the 1840s to the 1940s, apart from peaks and troughs in and around the years of the two World Wars. At the beginning of the 1960s there were around 340 thousand first marriages a year in the United Kingdom (Chart 2.8). Marriage was fashionable in the 1960s, despite it being the so-called 'permissive age'. The growth in the number of marriages in the mid- to late 1960s was largely as a result of three factors: babies born in the post-war boom were passing through the marriageable ages; people were marrying younger; and a higher proportion of people were getting married. The number of first marriages peaked in 1970 at almost 390 thousand, and since then has decreased to less than half this number – 179 thousand in 1999. Remarriages increased by about a third between 1971 and 1972 following the introduction of the *Divorce Reform Act 1969*. In 1999 there were 122 thousand remarriages for one or both partners, accounting for two-fifths of all marriages.

There has been a tendency for first marriages to take place later in life. In 1971 the average age at first marriage for both partners in England and Wales was 24 for men and 22 for women; by 1999 these had risen to 29 and 27 respectively. Rises in pre-marital cohabitation help to explain the recent trend towards later marriage, but other factors such as the increased and longer participation in further and higher education, particularly among women, have also contributed.

Three out of four marriages in England and Wales were solemnised with a religious ceremony during the years following the First World War, and the proportion remained at this level until the early 1960s. By the mid-1970s the proportion had fallen to about one in two and the ratio remained at about this level until the early 1990s. In 1999 around two in five marriages in Great Britain were solemnised with a religious ceremony (Table 2.9). Differences exist between the types of ceremonies for first and subsequent marriages. Just over a fifth of second and subsequent marriages were solemnised with a religious ceremony in 1999 compared with over half of first marriages.

In England and Wales, the enactment of the *Marriage Act 1994* permitted marriages to be solemnised in approved premises such as castles,

**Marriages: by type of ceremony**

| Great Britain | | | Percentages |
| --- | --- | --- | --- |
| | Religious ceremonies | Civil ceremonies | All marriages (=100%)(thousands) |
| **First marriages**[1] | | | |
| 1981 | 69 | 31 | 255 |
| 1991 | 67 | 33 | 215 |
| 1999 | 54 | 46 | 173 |
| **Remarriages**[2] | | | |
| 1981 | 19 | 81 | 134 |
| 1991 | 25 | 75 | 126 |
| 1999 | 21 | 79 | 121 |
| **All marriages** | | | |
| 1981 | 52 | 48 | 388 |
| 1991 | 51 | 49 | 341 |
| 1999 | 40 | 60 | 293 |

1 For both partners.
2 For one or both partners.
**Source: Office for National Statistics; General Register Office for Scotland**

parks, halls, manors and hotels. The introduction of approved premises from April 1995 has led to a small acceleration in civil marriages in England and Wales from 52 per cent of all marriages in 1994 to 62 per cent in 1999. By 1999 almost a quarter of civil marriages occurred in approved premises.

Prior to 1857 a private Act of Parliament was the only means of obtaining a divorce in England and Wales, and thus was only available to a very wealthy few. The *1857 Matrimonial Causes Act* enabled divorce to be petitioned and granted in a civil court. The Act allowed civil divorce on the sole ground of adultery, although a wife could only petition for divorce if her husband had committed one or more other matrimonial offences besides adultery. As it was more difficult for wives to petition for divorce than husbands, a larger proportion of decrees were granted to husbands than wives – approximately 60 per cent of decrees were awarded to husbands from 1858 to 1900. The additional conditions for petitioning wives were abolished in 1924 and the grounds for divorce were widened in 1938. By 1999, about 70 per cent of divorces were granted to wives.

# 2.10

## Divorce: by gender and age

| England & Wales | | | | | Rates per 1,000 married population |
|---|---|---|---|---|---|
| | 1961 | 1971 | 1981 | 1991 | 1999 |
| **Males** | | | | | |
| 16-24 | 1.4 | 5.0 | 17.7 | 25.4 | 29.0 |
| 25-29 | 3.9 | 12.5 | 27.6 | 31.0 | 31.5 |
| 30-34 | 4.1 | 11.8 | 22.8 | 27.8 | 28.4 |
| 35-44 | 3.1 | 7.9 | 17.0 | 20.0 | 21.7 |
| 45 and over | 1.1 | 3.1 | 4.8 | 5.6 | 6.3 |
| | | | | | |
| All aged 16 and over | 2.1 | 5.9 | 11.9 | 13.5 | 13.0 |
| **Females** | | | | | |
| 16-24 | 2.4 | 7.5 | 22.3 | 28.7 | 30.3 |
| 25-29 | 4.5 | 13.0 | 26.7 | 30.7 | 32.3 |
| 30-34 | 3.8 | 10.5 | 20.2 | 25.0 | 27.3 |
| 35-44 | 2.7 | 6.7 | 14.9 | 17.3 | 19.4 |
| 45 and over | 0.9 | 2.8 | 3.9 | 4.5 | 5.1 |
| | | | | | |
| All aged 16 and over | 2.1 | 5.9 | 11.9 | 13.4 | 12.9 |

*Source: Office for National Statistics*

# 2.11

## Percentage of first marriages[1] ending in separation within five years: by year of marriage and gender, 1998-99

| Great Britain | | Percentages |
|---|---|---|
| | Males | Females |
| **Year of marriage** | | |
| 1965-1969 | 7 | 7 |
| 1970-1974 | 10 | 10 |
| 1975-1979 | 14 | 13 |
| 1980-1984 | 10 | 14 |
| 1985-1989 | 13 | 16 |

1 For people born between 1940 and 1978 and first married aged under 30.

*Source: General Household Survey, Office for National Statistics*

The number of divorces doubled between 1961 and 1969 in the United Kingdom, and had doubled again by 1972 (see Chart 2.8). This latter increase was partly a 'one-off' effect of the *Divorce Reform Act 1969* in England and Wales, which came into effect in 1971. The Act introduced a single ground for divorce – irretrievable breakdown – which could be established by proving one or more of certain facts: adultery, desertion, separation either with or without consent, or unreasonable behaviour.

Although there was a drop in the number of divorces in 1973 in the United Kingdom, the number increased again in 1974 and peaked in 1993 at 180 thousand. The annual number of divorces was 12 per cent lower at 159 thousand in 1999.

The rate of divorce per 1,000 married people in England and Wales rose between 1961 and 1991, then fell slightly. Since the 1970s this rate has been highest for those aged between 25 and 29. However, in 1999 the divorce rate for both males and females aged between 16 and 24 was almost as high as that for those aged 25 to 29 (Table 2.10).

Table 2.11 shows the percentage of marriages that ended in separation within five years based on those who were born between 1940 and 1978 and first married under the age of 30. Among those who were married in the latter half of the 1980s, around one in eight men and one in six women had separated within the first five years. This was double the proportion for those who first married 20 years earlier. Teenage marriages were also more likely to break down than those which occurred later in life. Among those married in the late 1980s, 24 per cent of women who were under 20 when they first married had separated within five years compared with 8 per cent of women married between the ages of 25 and 29. The earlier a partnership is formed, the more likely it is to breakdown. Other demographic factors that have been implicated in marital breakdown include having a pre-marital birth, cohabiting prior to marriage and having a spouse who has previously been married.

The *Matrimonial and Family Proceedings Act 1984* reduced the minimum period after marriage before a petition for divorce could be filed. The new law allowed couples to file for divorce after their first wedding anniversary whereas under former legislation they could not usually do so until their marriage had lasted at least three years.

In 1999 the most common reason for women to be granted divorce in England and Wales was the unreasonable behaviour of the husbands, while for men it was separation for two years with consent. Results from the BHPS showed that in 1998 around four in ten adults in Great Britain either strongly agreed or agreed that 'divorce is better than an unhappy marriage'.

## Family formation

Changes to fertility patterns influence the size of households and families, and also affect the age structure of the population. Most British middle-class families practised contraception by the

# 2.12

1900s, although it was still condemned by some professional bodies for its supposed spiritual and physical adverse effects. Contraception was not taught in medical schools until 1928. One of the major changes in access to birth control seen during the late 1960s was the introduction of the oral contraceptive pill. It first went on sale in 1961, and was later made freely available through the National Heath Service for unmarried as well as married women. Use of the oral contraceptive pill was highest in the 1970s and early 1980s. Usage then fell and has never reached the same level. In 1998, 24 per cent of women aged 16 to 49 used oral contraceptives in Great Britain.

The total number of conceptions was 797 thousand in England and Wales in 1998, when 78 per cent of conceptions led to a maternity (Table 2.12). During the last ten years or so the percentage of conceptions that were inside marriage and led to a maternity fell by 12 percentage points to 44 per cent. The percentage of conceptions that occurred outside marriage and led to a maternity inside marriage also fell slightly. Over the same time period the percentage of conceptions that led to a birth outside marriage increased by around 10 percentage points to 30 per cent. In 1998 the conception rate was highest among women aged 25 to 29, at 123 per thousand women (Table 2.13).

Better contraception does not necessarily mean lower fertility, although it should mean less unwanted fertility. The *1967 Abortion Act*, which applied across Great Britain, was amended by the *1990 Human Fertilisation and Embryology Act*. The amendment included the introduction of a new upper time-limit of 24 weeks for most abortions, but removed the upper time-limit in the following circumstances: risk to the life of the mother, risk of grave permanent injury, and risk of serious foetal handicap. In 1998, 22 per cent of conceptions in England and Wales led to abortion. Within marriage, abortions were uncommon: 9 per cent of conceptions inside marriage lead to an

abortion compared with 35 per cent of those to unmarried women. The percentage of conceptions that lead to abortion is generally higher among teenagers and women over 40 than among those in their twenties and thirties.

Trends in abortion rates vary by the age of the women (see Chart 2.14 overleaf). Abortions amongst those aged between 16 and 24 rose particularly rapidly following the introduction of the *1967 Abortion Act*, and reached 18.0 abortions per thousand women aged 16 to 19 and 15.7 per thousand women aged 20 to 24 in 1974. Apart from fluctuations apparent during the mid-1970s and 1990s, abortion rates among women of these ages have increased and by 1999 the abortion rate for women aged 20 to 24 was 29.9 abortions per thousand women, higher than for any other age group. The rate for those aged 16 to 19 was 26.0 abortions per thousand women.

Changes in family size have a long-term impact on the population structure. It has been estimated that an average family size of 2.1 children per woman is needed to maintain the population at its current size, if mortality rates are constant and there is no net migration.

## Conceptions[1]: by marital status and outcome

| England & Wales | | | | Percentages |
| --- | --- | --- | --- | --- |
| | 1987 | 1991 | 1995 | 1998 |
| **Conceptions inside marriage leading to** | | | | |
| Maternities | 56 | 52 | 49 | 44 |
| Legal abortions[2] | 5 | 4 | 4 | 4 |
| **Conceptions outside marriage leading to** | | | | |
| Maternities inside marriage | 5 | 4 | 3 | 3 |
| Maternities outside marriage[3] | 20 | 25 | 28 | 30 |
| Legal abortions[2] | 14 | 15 | 16 | 18 |
| **All conceptions** (=100%)(thousands) | 850 | 854 | 790 | 797 |

1 See Appendix, Part 2: Conceptions.
2 Legal terminations under the 1967 Abortion Act.
3 Births outside marriage can be registered by one parent only, usually the mother (sole registrations), or by both parents (joint registrations).
**Source: Office for National Statistics**

# 2.13

## Conception[1] rates: by age of woman at conception

| England & Wales | Rates per 1,000 women | |
| --- | --- | --- |
| | 1991 | 1998 |
| Under 18[2] | 45 | 47 |
| 18-19 | 89 | 92 |
| 20-24 | 120 | 109 |
| 25-29 | 135 | 123 |
| 30-34 | 90 | 96 |
| 35-39 | 34 | 42 |
| 40 and over[2] | 7 | 9 |
| All ages[2] | 78 | 74 |

1 See Appendix, Part 2: Conceptions.
2 Rates for women aged under 18, those aged 40 and over and all ages are based on the population of women aged 15 to 17, 40 to 44 and 15 to 44 respectively.
**Source: Office for National Statistics**

# 2.14

## Abortion rates[1]: by age

**England & Wales**

Rates per 1,000 women

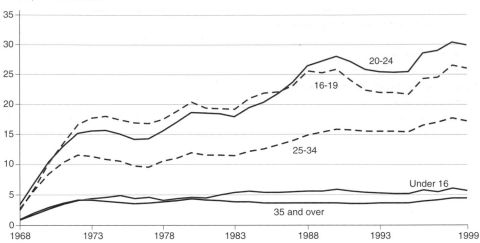

*1 The rates for women aged under 16 are based on the population of women aged 14 and 15. The rates for women aged 35 and over are based on the population of women aged 35 to 49.*

**Source: Office for National Statistics**

# 2.15

## Fertility rates: by age of mother at childbirth

**United Kingdom**                                                                 Live births per 1,000 women

|  | 1961 | 1971 | 1981 | 1991 | 1999 |
|---|---|---|---|---|---|
| Under 20[1] | 37 | 50 | 28 | 33 | 30 |
| 20-24 | 173 | 154 | 107 | 89 | 72 |
| 25-29 | 178 | 155 | 130 | 120 | 99 |
| 30-34 | 106 | 79 | 70 | 87 | 89 |
| 35-39 | 51 | 34 | 22 | 32 | 40 |
| 40 and over[2] | 16 | 9 | 5 | 5 | 8 |
| All ages[3] | 91 | 84 | 62 | 64 | 57 |

*1 Live births to women aged under 20 per 1,000 women aged 15 to 19 at last birthday.*
*2 Live births to women aged 40 and over per 1,000 women aged 40 to 44.*
*3 Total live births per 1,000 women aged 15 to 44.*

**Source: Office for National Statistics; General Register Office for Scotland; Northern Ireland Statistics and Research Agency**

The overall level of fertility in the United Kingdom fluctuated during the 20th century, although it was lower (57 live births per 1,000 women aged 15 to 44) at the end of the century than at the start (115 live births per 1,000 women aged 15 to 44). Fertility patterns have also varied by age and there has been a shift towards later childbearing. The mean age at childbirth in England and Wales rose from 26.2 years in 1971 to 29.0 in 1999. Women aged 25 to 29 are still the most likely to give birth, but since 1992 those in the 30 to 34 age group have been more likely to give birth than those aged 20 to 24 (Table 2.15).

Not all couples have children and the proportion of women remaining childless has risen during recent years. Increasing childlessness may be related to the later age at which couples are married. About 16 per cent of women born in 1924 were childless by the age of 45. It is projected that 23 per cent of women born in 1974 will be childless when they reach the age of 45.

Most children are born to married couples but an increasing proportion of births occur outside marriage. With the exception of the periods immediately after the two World Wars, few births occurred outside marriage during the first 60 years of the 20th century in the United Kingdom (Chart 2.16). During the 1960s and 1970s, this proportion rose and growth became more rapid from the late 1970s onwards. The proportion of live births that occurred outside marriage in the United Kingdom was almost five times greater in 1999 than in 1971. In 1999 nearly two-fifths of births were outside marriage. Much of this growth can be accounted for by the increase in births to cohabiting couples, that is parents living at the same address.

In 1999, 80 per cent of all births outside marriage in Great Britain were jointly registered by both parents. For about three-quarters of these births (that is around 60 per cent of all births outside marriage), the parents were living at the same address. The proportion of births registered solely by the mother remained steady at around 8 per cent of all live births between 1996 and 1999. The proportion of births outside marriage has always been highest for teenagers; in 1999, 90 per cent of births to women under 20 occurred outside marriage. In 1999, 27 per cent of births to teenagers were sole registrations compared with only 4 per cent of births to women in their late thirties or early forties. The average age of mothers at childbirth is lower for births that occur outside marriage than those occurring inside marriage – 26.4 and 30.6 years respectively in England and Wales in 1999.

Throughout most of Western Europe, teenage birth rates fell during the 1970s, 1980s and 1990s, but the UK rates have stuck at the early 1980s level or above. The United Kingdom, with an average live birth rate of around 30 per 1,000 women aged under 20, had the highest rate of live births to teenage women in the European Union in 1996 (Chart 2.17).

Data from the Health Education Monitoring Survey undertaken in 1998 show that, in England, only 29 per cent of 16 to 19 year old women had not had a sexual partner. Among 20 to 24 year olds, a quarter had had their first sexual partner when they were aged under 16. Between 1975 and 1999-00 the proportion of girls aged under 16 visiting family planning clinics increased from 1 per cent to 7 per cent. The proportion of girls aged 16 to 19 visiting family planning clinics increased from 12 per cent in 1988-89 to 23 per cent in 1999-00. In contrast, the proportion of women aged 20 to 34 using these services fell from 21 per cent to 12 per cent between 1975 and 1999-00. The number of women attending family planning clinics was roughly 1.5 million in each year from 1975 to 1985; by the early 1990s the number had fallen to below 1.1 million, and it rose gradually to just under 1.2 million in 1999-00.

**2.16**

**Births outside marriage as a percentage of all live births**

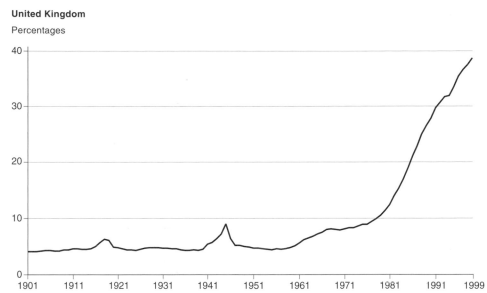

United Kingdom

Percentages

*Source: Office for National Statistics; General Register Office for Scotland; Northern Ireland Statistics and Research Agency*

**2.17**

**Live births to teenage women[1]: EU comparison, 1996**

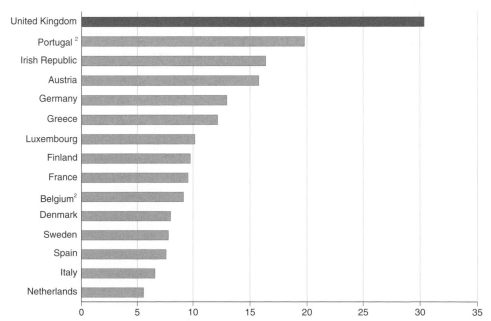

Live births per 1,000 women

1 See Appendix, Part 2: Average teenage fertility rate.
2 Data are for 1995.

*Source: Council of Europe*

# 2.18

**Percentage of dependent children[1] living in different family types**

**Family relationships**

| Great Britain | | | | Percentages |
|---|---|---|---|---|
| | 1972 | 1981 | 1991-92 | 2000[2] |
| **Couple families** | | | | |
| 1 child | 16 | 18 | 17 | 17 |
| 2 children | 35 | 41 | 37 | 38 |
| 3 or more children | 41 | 29 | 28 | 26 |
| **Lone mother families** | | | | |
| 1 child | 2 | 3 | 5 | 6 |
| 2 children | 2 | 4 | 7 | 7 |
| 3 or more children | 2 | 3 | 6 | 6 |
| **Lone father families** | | | | |
| 1 child | - | 1 | - | 1 |
| 2 or more children | 1 | 1 | 1 | 1 |
| **All dependent children**[3] | 100 | 100 | 100 | 100 |

1 See Appendix, Part 2: Families.
2 At Spring 2000.
3 In Spring 2000, includes cases where the dependent child is a family unit, for example, a foster child.
**Source: General Household Survey and Labour Force Survey, Office for National Statistics**

Families and especially those with children are the focus for many policy issues. Government measures, including Sure Start and the Policy Forum on Parenting, are aimed at tackling the early years between birth and school and providing support for parents of older children. The type of family in which a child grows up has changed over the past 30 or so years, with a decrease in the percentages of dependent children living in couple families and an increase in those living in lone-parent families (Table 2.18). Nevertheless, the traditional couple family remains the most common type of family in which dependent children live in Great Britain – 80 per cent lived in such a family in Spring 2000. The percentage of dependent children living in lone mother families more than tripled between 1972 and Spring 2000 to almost one in five. Although divorced lone mothers were the most numerous of all the lone mother marital statuses throughout most of the 1970s and 1980s, single lone mothers overtook divorced lone mothers in relative numbers from the beginning of the 1990s. The proportion of all lone mothers who were single started to increase quite sharply around 1986, when the incidence of births outside marriage began to rise at a faster rate. Lone father families accounted for 2 per cent of all families with dependent children in Spring 2000. As a whole, one parent families tend to be more vulnerable than couple families, whether from the point of view of economic deprivation, greater health problems or general social disadvantage.

As was seen earlier in the chapter, there was an increase in the number of divorces following the implementation of the *Divorce Reform Act 1969* in 1971. The percentage of children experiencing divorce consequently increased (Chart 2.19). The number of children aged under 16 in England and Wales who experienced the divorce of their parents peaked at almost 176 thousand in 1993. Since then the number has fallen to 148 thousand

# 2.19

**Children of couples divorced: by age of child**

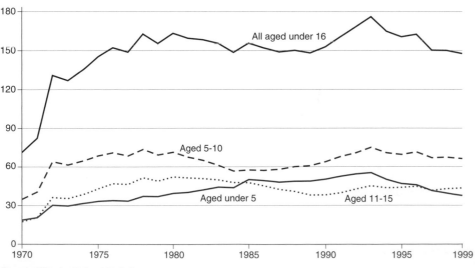

**England & Wales**
Thousands

*Source: Office for National Statistics*

# 2.20

in 1999 when around one in four children affected by divorce were under five years old and seven in ten were aged ten or under.

There is some evidence that experiencing divorce has an impact upon children's relationship formation later in life. Analyses of the National Child Development Study suggest that people who experience parental divorce during childhood are more likely to form partnerships at a younger age than those whose parents did not divorce. For example, 48 per cent of women born in 1958 who had experienced parental divorce during childhood had entered their first co-residential partnership as a teenager, compared with 29 per cent of women brought up with both parents. Furthermore, by the age of 33, men and women born in 1958 who had experienced parental divorce were also more likely to have experienced partnership and marriage dissolution themselves.

Stepfamilies are one reflection of the diversity of family life that young people experience. Such family types may be formed when lone parents, whether single, separated or widowed, form new partnerships. According to the General Household Survey, in 1998-99, stepfamilies (married and cohabiting) where the head of the family was aged under 60 accounted for about 6 per cent of all families with dependent children in Great Britain. There is a tendency for children to remain with their mother after a partnership breaks up. Almost nine in ten stepfamilies consisted of a couple with at least one child from a previous relationship of the female partner (Chart 2.20).

Families may be formed or extended by the adoption of children. The annual number of adoptions increased after the introduction of the *Adoption Act* in 1926 in England and Wales. Further increases were seen following the Second World War and the numbers peaked in 1968 at just under 25 thousand. This rise was in part related to the gradual increase in the 1960s in the number of births outside marriage. Since the late 1960s the number of adoptions have fallen so that

the total of just over 4 thousand in 1999 was less than a fifth of the number at the peak just over 30 years earlier. In particular, the number of children available for adoption has fallen since the introduction of legal abortion. Other factors include the use of contraception and changes in attitudes towards lone parents. There were also large falls in adoption in 1976 and 1977, just after the implementation of the *1975 Children Act* (Chart 2.21).

As children get older and become adults they are more likely to have left the parental home. Results from the 1998-99 Survey of English Housing suggest that young women in England tend to start living independently, that is outside the parental home, earlier than young men. By the age of 20 or 21 years, 50 per cent of young women were living independently. In contrast, the proportion of young men living independently did not exceed 50 per cent until about the age of 24. This was only partly accounted for by the tendency of women to marry or start cohabiting at younger ages than men – women under the age of 20 were also more likely than men to head lone parent households, live alone or share with others.

## Stepfamilies[1] with dependent children[2]: by family type, 1998-99

**Great Britain**

Percentages

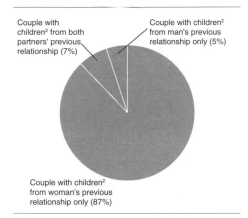

Couple with children[2] from both partners' previous relationship (7%)

Couple with children[2] from man's previous relationship only (5%)

Couple with children[2] from woman's previous relationship only (87%)

*1 Head of family aged 16 to 59.*
*2 One or more children.*

**Source: General Household Survey, Office for National Statistics**

# 2.21

## Children adopted

**England & Wales**

Thousands

**Source: Office for National Statistics**

# 2.22

**Relatives[1] living within half an hour's journey time: by age of respondent[2], 1999[3]**

Great Britain                                                                    Percentages

| | Number of relatives | | | |
| | 0 | 1 | 2 or more | All |
|---|---|---|---|---|
| **Age of respondent** | | | | |
| 20-29 | 45 | 15 | 40 | 100 |
| 30-39 | 46 | 17 | 37 | 100 |
| 40-49 | 43 | 31 | 26 | 100 |
| 50-59 | 55 | 26 | 19 | 100 |
| 60-69 | 59 | 20 | 21 | 100 |
| 70 and over | 60 | 24 | 15 | 100 |
| | | | | |
| All aged 20 and over | 55 | 23 | 20 | 100 |

1 Includes mother, father, eldest child or eldest grandchild.
2 Respondents living alone.
3 January and February 1999.
**Source: Omnibus Survey, Office for National Statistics; London School of Hygiene and Tropical Medicine; London School of Economics**

# 2.23

**Exchanges of help within families[1], 1999[2]**

Great Britain                                                                    Percentages

| | Receiving help | | Providing help | |
| | Mothers | Fathers | Mothers | Fathers |
|---|---|---|---|---|
| Money | 6 | 5 | 24 | 32 |
| Lifts in car | 33 | 20 | 16 | 24 |
| Paperwork/maintenance[3] | 21 | 15 | 23 | 23 |
| Domestic tasks[4] | 21 | 15 | 34 | 22 |
| Childcare | 1 | 2 | 27 | 19 |
| Shopping | 26 | 16 | 19 | 15 |
| | | | | |
| Any of the above | 50 | 38 | 55 | 58 |

1 Help exchanged between parents aged 50 years or over, with at least one surviving child, and their eldest child.
2 January and February 1999.
3 Includes helping to sort out paperwork, decorating, gardening or house repairs.
4 Includes preparing or cooking meals, washing, ironing or cleaning.
**Source: Omnibus Survey, Office for National Statistics; London School of Hygiene and Tropical Medicine; London School of Economics**

In situations where adult relatives do not live in the same household, more than half of people aged 20 and over and living alone in Great Britain had neither a parent, eldest child or eldest grandchild living within half an hour's journey time in 1999 (Table 2.22). The results from the January and February 1999 Omnibus Survey module, analysed by Grundy, Murphy and Shelton show that 40 per cent of people living on their own and aged between 20 to 29 had two or more of these relatives living within half an hour's journey time, compared with 15 per cent of people aged 70 and over.

Although relatively few adult children live with their parents, and the proportion of older people who live with their children is low, exchanges of help between generations are usual. Intergenerational exchanges of resources within the family are widely recognised as of central importance to both individual and social well being. Adult children and their older parents exchange a great deal of help with everyday tasks (Table 2.23). Overall, half of mothers and almost two-fifths of fathers aged 50 and over had had some kind of regular help from their eldest child in the previous 12 months. The types of help most often received were being given lifts in a car, especially important for mothers, help with shopping, domestic chores, paperwork or household maintenance tasks, such as decorating. Only small proportions had received financial help from their eldest child.

Older parents gave a great deal of help to their children. Over a quarter of mothers aged 50 or over regularly helped their eldest child with care of their children and a third helped with domestic tasks. Fathers were more likely to help with money or by giving lifts. As the questions only related to help given to or received from the eldest child the total extent of help given to, or received from, all children will be higher.

The wider family remains an important resource, particularly for groups such as mothers of young children. Most mothers can call on help from their

## 2.24

own mother (their children's maternal grandmother). Overall, three-quarters of women aged 20 to 49 with a dependent child at home were helped regularly by their own mothers and this proportion was higher (79 per cent) among those with a child under 5.

Most people acknowledge the importance of grandparents, according to data from the 1998 British Social Attitudes Survey. Only one in ten people aged 18 and over in Great Britain agreed that grandparents have 'little to teach the grandchildren of today' and about three-quarters agreed that 'families with working mothers needed grandparents help more and more' (Table 2.24). Half felt that the role of grandparents was not properly valued, and a slightly smaller proportion felt that parents, in particular, did not appreciate grandparents' help. Although most believed that grandparents could give a lot of help to parents, only one in five stated that they should be closely involved in decisions about how grandchildren were brought up.

This chapter has illustrated that families are constantly evolving structures as a result of life events such as childbirth or marital breakdown. Results from the BHPS indicate that families with children were more likely to have experienced family change than those families without children between 1997 and 1998 (Table 2.25). For both couples and lone parents with non-dependent children only, by far the most common change was the departure of children. The most likely change for couples with dependent children was the birth of a child. Around one in ten lone parents with dependent children experienced change as a result of joining a new partner.

The structures of both the household and family are becoming increasingly diverse, but remain important to society and retain an integral role in people's lives.

**Attitudes towards grandparenting[1], 1998**

Great Britain — Percentages

| | Respondent is | | | |
| --- | --- | --- | --- | --- |
| | Grand-parent | Grand-child | Linking parent | All[2] |
| With so many working mothers, families need grandparents to help more and more | 79 | 72 | 74 | 74 |
| People today don't place enough value on the part grandparents play in family life | 50 | 50 | 51 | 51 |
| Many parents today do not appreciate the help that grandparents give | 40 | 31 | 41 | 41 |
| In most families, grandparents should be closely involved in deciding how their grandchildren are brought up | 24 | 19 | 16 | 20 |
| Grandparents tend to interfere too much with the way their grandchildren are brought up | 9 | 10 | 8 | 11 |
| Grandparents have little to teach the grandchildren of today | 13 | 8 | 6 | 9 |

1 Percentage aged 18 and over who agreed with each statement.
2 Includes respondents who do not fall into the first three categories.
*Source: British Social Attitudes Survey, National Centre for Social Research*

## 2.25

**Adults'[1] experience of family change: by type of family, 1997 to 1998**

Great Britain — Percentages

| | Couple | | | | Lone parent | |
| --- | --- | --- | --- | --- | --- | --- |
| | Lone adult | Dependent children | Non-dependent children only | No children | Dependent children | Non-dependent children only |
| **No change** | 85 | 85 | 73 | 91 | 76 | 74 |
| | | | | | | |
| **Change** | | | | | | |
| Birth of child | 0 | 6 | 0 | 3 | 2 | 0 |
| Departure of child | 0 | 4 | 25 | 0 | 7 | 19 |
| Separation from partner | 0 | 4 | 1 | 2 | 0 | 0 |
| Death of partner | 0 | - | - | 1 | 0 | 0 |
| Join new partner | 5 | 0 | 0 | 0 | 10 | 1 |
| Other changes | 10 | 2 | 2 | 3 | 5 | 6 |
| | | | | | | |
| **All changes** | 15 | 15 | 27 | 9 | 24 | 26 |
| **All adults** | 100 | 100 | 100 | 100 | 100 | 100 |

1 Aged 16 and over.
*Source: British Household Panel Survey, Institute for Social and Economic Research*

## Websites

| | |
|---|---|
| National Statistics | www.statistics.gov.uk |
| Department of the Environment, Transport and the Regions | www.detr.gov.uk |
| General Register Office for Scotland | www.gro-scotland.gov.uk |
| National Assembly for Wales | www.wales.gov.uk |
| Northern Ireland Statistics and Research Agency | www.nisra.gov.uk |
| Scottish Executive | www.scotland.gov.uk |
| Teenage Pregnancy Unit | www.teenagepregnancyunit.gov.uk |
| ESRC Research Centre for Analysis of Social Exclusion, London School of Economics | www.lse.ac.uk |
| Institute for Social and Economic Research | www.iser.essex.ac.uk |
| National Centre for Social Research | www.natcen.ac.uk |

## Contacts

| | |
|---|---|
| **Office for National Statistics** | |
| Chapter author | 020 7533 6117 |
| Fertility | 020 7533 5113 |
| General Household Survey | 020 7533 5444 |
| Labour Market Enquiry Helpline | 020 7533 6094 |
| Marriages and divorces | 01329 813772 |
| **Department of the Environment, Transport and the Regions** | 020 7944 3303 |
| **Home Office Family Policy Unit** | 020 7217 8545 |
| **National Assembly for Wales** | 029 2082 5055 |
| **Northern Ireland Statistics and Research Agency** | 028 9034 8243 |
| **Institute for Social and Economic Research** | 01206 872957 |
| **ESRC Research Centre for Analysis of Social Exclusion, London School of Economics** | 020 7955 6679 |
| **London School of Hygiene and Tropical Medicine** | 020 7299 4614 |
| **National Centre for Social Research** | 020 7250 1866 |

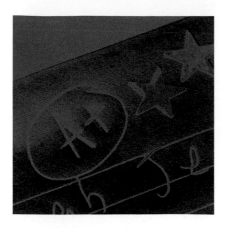

# Chapter 3  Education

### Schools, pupils and staffing

● The proportion of three and four year olds enrolled in schools in the United Kingdom tripled from 21 per cent in 1970/71 to 64 per cent in 1999/00. (Chart 3.2)

● Over 10 thousand children in England were permanently excluded from schools in 1998/99, with the number of boys excluded outnumbering girls by almost five to one. (Table 3.4)

● In 2000, 86 per cent of primary and 98 per cent of secondary schools in England were connected to the Internet, compared with 17 per cent and 83 per cent respectively in 1998. (Chart 3.6)

● Women comprised 53 per cent of all secondary school teachers in England and Wales in 1999 but only 28 per cent of head teachers. (Table 3.10)

### Post-compulsory education

● Around 75 per cent of both young men and young women aged 16 to 18 years in England were in education or training in 1999, compared with 64 per cent and 58 per cent respectively in 1986. (Table 3.12)

● In 2000, 96 per cent of Indian 16 year olds in England and Wales were in education and training compared with 85 per cent of White young people of the same age. (Chart 3.14)

● In Spring 2000, 5.7 million people of working age were studying towards a qualification in the United Kingdom, just over half of whom were aged between 16 and 24. (Table 3.16)

### Educational attainment

● The proportion of young women in the United Kingdom achieving two or more A levels or equivalent has doubled since the mid-1970s, to 24 per cent in 1998/99. For young men there has been an increase of just under a half to 20 per cent. (Chart 3.20)

A well-educated and trained population is important for the social and economic success of the labour market and for individuals themselves. Education plays a role in providing people with the knowledge and skills necessary to participate more effectively in society today.

## Schools, pupils and staffing

Education has been transformed over the last 200 years. In the early 1800s, schooling was entirely voluntary with no state funding. Fewer than ten private boarding schools were in existence although there were some grammar schools, private tuition and small 'dame' schools where pupils were taught by women in private houses. Some rudimentary teaching for the young was provided in Sunday schools and in elementary schools which were run by church-sponsored voluntary societies. There were four universities in Scotland and just two in England.

In 1870 the *Elementary Education Act* introduced the first state schooling and in 1880 schooling was made compulsory for all five to ten year olds. The *1918 Education Act* raised the school-leaving age to 14 and abolished fees in elementary schools, so that they catered largely for working class children up to the age of 14. A few brighter children, selected by examination at the age of 11, went on to local authority secondary schools. The vast majority of children however left school at 14 with no formal qualifications.

The school-leaving age was raised to 15 in 1947 and this, together with changes in the birth rate, has contributed to fluctuations in the number of children of school age. The declining births during the late 1970s (see Chart 1.8 on page 33 of the Population chapter) led to a fall in pupil numbers in the 1980s and early 1990s. Since then, pupil numbers have continued to increase but they are still below the peak level of the 1970s.

As well as the fluctuation in pupil numbers there have also been changes in the structure of secondary education. Prior to the introduction of comprehensive schools in England and Wales, children were required to take the '11 plus' examination which determined whether they would attend a grammar or secondary modern school. The '11 plus' had largely been abolished by the late 1960s and comprehensive schools replaced grammar and secondary modern schools. Comprehensive schools were introduced with the aim of providing equality of opportunity for all children. In 1999/00, 85 per cent of pupils attending secondary schools in the United Kingdom attended comprehensives while only 5 per cent went to grammar schools and 2 per cent attended secondary modern schools; this compares with 37 per cent, 19 per cent and 33 per cent respectively in 1970/71 (Table 3.1).

# 3.1

### School pupils[1]: by type of school[2]

| United Kingdom | | | | | Thousands |
|---|---|---|---|---|---|
| | 1970/71 | 1980/81 | 1990/91 | 1994/95 | 1999/00 |
| **Public sector schools[3]** | | | | | |
| Nursery[4] | 50 | 89 | 105 | 111 | 144 |
| Primary[4] | 5,902 | 5,171 | 4,955 | 5,230 | 5,338 |
| Secondary | | | | | |
| Comprehensive[5] | 1,313 | 3,730 | 2,843 | 3,093 | 3,277 |
| Grammar | 673 | 149 | 156 | 184 | 204 |
| Modern | 1,164 | 233 | 94 | 90 | 94 |
| Other | 403 | 434 | 300 | 289 | 283 |
| All public sector schools | 9,507 | 9,806 | 8,453 | 8,996 | 9,339 |
| **Non-maintained schools[3]** | 621 | 619 | 613 | 600 | 618 |
| **Special schools[6]** | 103 | 148 | 114 | 117 | 114 |
| **Pupil referral units** | . | . | . | . | 9 |
| **All schools** | 10,230 | 10,572 | 9,180 | 9,714 | 10,081 |

1 Headcounts.
2 See Appendix, Part 3: Main categories of educational establishments and stages of education.
3 Excludes special schools.
4 Nursery classes within primary schools are included in primary schools except for Scotland from 1990/91 when they are included in nursery schools.
5 Excludes sixth form colleges from 1980/81.
6 Includes maintained and non-maintained sectors.

**Source: Department for Education and Employment; National Assembly for Wales; Scottish Executive; Northern Ireland Department of Education**

# 3.2

There has been a major expansion of pre-school education in recent years with the Government stating their aim that all children should begin school with a basic foundation in literacy and numeracy. In 1970/71, 21 per cent of three and four year olds in the United Kingdom attended schools; by 1999/00 this had risen to 64 per cent (Chart 3.2). In addition, there are other forms of pre-school education which children attend. In January 2000, 16 per cent of all four year olds in England were enrolled in non-school education settings in the private and voluntary sector, such as local playgroups (see also Table 8.23 on page 156 in the Social Protection chapter).

Since 1998 all four year olds in England and Wales have been entitled to a free, part-time early education place if their parents wanted one. In January 2000, 97 per cent of children aged four in England had such a place. In September 2000 the Government announced its commitment to provide all three year olds with a free, part-time place from 2004. The interim aim is to increase the proportion of three year olds with free education places in England to 66 per cent by 2002. In January 2000, 76 per cent of children aged three in the 65 English LEAs where funding was available for 3 year olds in the voluntary and private sector had a funded education place. In total, 100 per cent of all four year olds and 86 per cent of all 3 year olds were in an early education place.

**Children under five[1] in schools as a percentage of all children aged three and four**

**United Kingdom**
Percentages

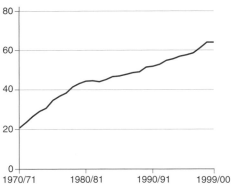

1 Pupils aged 3 and 4 at 31 December each year. Data for 1999/00 for Wales and Scotland relate to 1998/99.

*Source: Department for Education and Employment; National Assembly for Wales; Scottish Executive; Northern Ireland Department of Education*

# 3.3

## Class sizes in primary schools[1]: by region, 1999/00[2]

| | Key stage 1[3] | | Key stage 2[3] | | All primary schools | |
|---|---|---|---|---|---|---|
| | Average number in class | Percentage of classes of more than 30 pupils | Average number in class | Percentage of classes of more than 30 pupils | Average number in class | Percentage of classes of more than 30 pupils |
| Great Britain | 25.7 | 10.0 | 27.9 | 30.8 | 26.9 | 21.5 |
| North East | 25.2 | 7.5 | 27.4 | 27.0 | 26.3 | 18.3 |
| North West | 25.6 | 10.3 | 28.7 | 39.2 | 27.3 | 26.0 |
| Yorkshire and the Humber | 25.8 | 9.5 | 28.5 | 35.6 | 27.4 | 24.5 |
| East Midlands | 25.5 | 9.1 | 28.8 | 38.7 | 27.5 | 25.9 |
| West Midlands | 25.8 | 10.0 | 28.1 | 31.1 | 27.1 | 21.9 |
| East | 25.8 | 10.1 | 28.2 | 32.5 | 26.9 | 21.4 |
| London | 27.0 | 9.4 | 27.9 | 19.5 | 27.5 | 15.2 |
| South East | 26.3 | 11.4 | 28.5 | 34.8 | 27.4 | 24.0 |
| South West | 25.9 | 10.2 | 28.9 | 40.6 | 27.4 | 25.9 |
| England | 26.0 | 9.9 | 28.4 | 33.2 | 27.3 | 22.6 |
| Wales | 24.0 | 6.0 | 26.7 | 25.0 | 25.4 | 16.7 |
| Scotland[3] | 24.8 | 13.1 | 25.0 | 15.1 | 24.9 | 14.3 |
| Northern Ireland[4] | 23.3 | 4.3 | 24.8 | 11.7 | 23.8 | 7.2 |

1 Data for Scotland include composite classes covering more than one year group. Data for England, Wales and Scotland include classes where more than one teacher may be present. In Northern Ireland a class is defined as a group of pupils normally under the control of one teacher.
2 Data for Scotland relate to 1998/99. Data for Wales refer to September 1999 class size count.
3 In Scotland primary P1-P3 is interpreted to be key stage 1 and P4-P7, key stage 2.
4 Pupils in composite classes which overlap key stage 1 and key stage 2 are included in the total, but are excluded from all other categories.

*Source: Department for Education and Employment; National Assembly for Wales; Scottish Executive; Northern Ireland Department of Education*

# 3.4

## Permanent exclusions from schools: by gender

| England | | | Thousands |
|---|---|---|---|
| | Males | Females | All as a percentage of school population[1] |
| 1995/96 | 10.4 | 2.1 | *0.17* |
| 1996/97 | 10.5 | 2.1 | *0.17* |
| 1997/98 | 10.3 | 2.0 | *0.16* |
| 1998/99 | 8.6 | 1.8 | *0.14* |

*1 The number of permanent exclusions expressed as a percentage of the number (headcount) of full and part-time pupils of all ages (excluding dually registered pupils in secondary schools) in January each year.*

**Source: Department for Education and Employment**

# 3.5

## GCSE or equivalent[1] entries for pupils in their last year of compulsory education[2]: by selected subject

| Great Britain | | | | | Thousands |
|---|---|---|---|---|---|
| | 1991/92 | 1993/94 | 1995/96 | 1997/98 | 1998/99 |
| Mathematics[3] | 548 | 574 | 641 | 628 | 640 |
| English | 572 | 570 | 634 | 610 | 621 |
| English literature[4] | 420 | 416 | 478 | 473 | 489 |
| Science double award[4] | 308 | 401 | 458 | 455 | 465 |
| Design and technology[5] | 223 | 220 | 327 | 419 | 439 |
| French | 350 | 370 | 392 | 376 | 378 |
| Geography | 270 | 271 | 312 | 274 | 268 |
| History | 216 | 239 | 245 | 221 | 222 |
| German | 109 | 136 | 155 | 155 | 158 |
| Physical education | 51 | 68 | 98 | 107 | 118 |
| Computer studies[6] | 83 | 67 | 78 | 94 | 104 |
| Drama | 53 | 66 | 83 | 84 | 88 |
| Science single award[7] | 119 | 80 | 84 | 73 | 70 |
| Spanish | 22 | 31 | 38 | 44 | 44 |
| Vocational studies | 48 | 46 | 38 | 25 | 19 |
| Economics | 15 | 12 | 11 | 8 | 6 |
| Creative arts[4] | 9 | 7 | 13 | 1 | - |
| All entries[8] | 4,710 | 4,927 | 5,535 | 5,366 | 5,461 |

*1 In Scotland SCE Standard grades and, additionally up to 1993/94, SCE Ordinary grades.*
*2 Those in all schools who were 15 at the start of the academic year, ie 31 August. Pupils in Year S4 in Scotland.*
*3 Includes related subjects such as statistics.*
*4 England and Wales only.*
*5 Craft and design, graphic communications and technological studies in Scotland.*
*6 Includes information systems.*
*7 Standard grade in general science in Scotland.*
*8 Includes other subjects not listed; science double award is counted twice in this row.*

**Source: Department for Education and Employment; National Assembly for Wales; Scottish Executive**

Infant class-sizes in maintained schools have also been seen as an issue in the drive to improve standards, and the Government has set a target that, by September 2001, infant class sizes in England and Wales should be limited to 30 pupils. In 1999/00, 90 per cent of classes for 5 to 7 year olds in Great Britain and 69 per cent of those for 8 to 11 year olds contained 30 or fewer pupils (see Table 3.3 on the previous page). The latest available statistics for September 2000 show that 98 per cent of 5 to 7 year olds in England were in classes of 30 or below, compared with 89 per cent 12 months previously. The latest figures for average class sizes in 1999/00 for Scotland and Wales were 24.6 and 25.2 respectively. Regional differences exist: around 60 per cent of key stage 2 classes in the South West, North West and the East Midlands had 30 or fewer pupils in 1999/00 compared with 88 per cent in Northern Ireland and 85 per cent in Scotland.

When key stage 1 teachers were asked in a 1998 survey by the National Foundation for Educational Research about the impact of reducing class sizes, most felt it created a better environment for both teaching and learning. Teachers associated smaller classes with self-worth: they felt more in command; their motivation was keener; and teaching seemed more fulfilling.

There has been growing awareness of, and concern over, the number of children outside the education system. Some have been excluded from schools, while others play truant. In 1998/99, over 10 thousand children in England were permanently excluded from schools, around four-fifths of them were from secondary schools (Table 3.4). The number of boys excluded outnumbered girls by almost five to one. Between 1997/98 and 1998/99 the number of pupils permanently excluded from schools in England declined by nearly 2 thousand. Analyses by the Department for Education and Employment found that, in general, schools in England with the highest level of absence had the highest rates of permanent exclusions.

The Youth Cohort Study (YCS) found that the percentage of 16 year olds reporting that they had played truant in year 11 in England and Wales has continued to fall. Between the 1989 and 1998 surveys, the percentage reporting that they had ever played truant in year 11 fell from 50 per cent to 36 per cent. There remained a small but significant minority (4 per cent in 1998) who reported that they had played truant for 'weeks at a time' or for 'several days at a time'.

Between 1989 and 1996 the National Curriculum was introduced in England and Wales with the aim of ensuring that children receive a comparable and balanced programme of study throughout their compulsory schooling. The subjects taught to children between the ages of five and 16 in state schools are to a large extent determined by the National Curriculum, which has four key stages. The core subjects of the National Curriculum, compulsory at each of the four stages, are English (and Welsh in Wales), mathematics, science and physical education. The second level of the curriculum comprises the so-called 'foundation' subjects, such as history, geography, art, music and technology. A modern foreign language is added to the curriculum at key stage 3. At key stage 4, the study of many of the 'foundation' subjects becomes optional.

A major aspect of the curriculum is improving the numeracy and literacy levels of children in schools. In September 1998 there was a relaxation in the requirements of the non-core primary school curriculum to allow primary schools in England to devote an hour to literacy during each teaching day, and a daily numeracy lesson was added in September 1999. In addition, literacy and numeracy summer schools are now available to help those 11 year olds about to enter secondary education who have failed to meet the standards for English and mathematics. In 2000, approximately 32 thousand attended literacy schools and 20 thousand attended numeracy schools in England. Information on the proportions of pupils attaining expected standards at the key stages is given in Table 3.17 on page 67.

Alongside changes in the national curriculum there have been changes in the types of subjects students study at GCSE. Table 3.5 looks at GCSE subject entries in selected subjects for pupils in their last year of compulsory education in Great Britain. Data are not directly comparable over time for all subjects as a result of syllabus changes and the introduction of national curriculum subjects in England and Wales. As expected, compulsory

subjects such as mathematics, English, and English literature have the largest number of entries. Between 1991/92 and 1998/99 subjects such as economics decreased by well over half, while the number of entries for both physical education (PE) and Spanish doubled. Entries in geography and history remained relatively constant over the seven year period.

Society is becoming increasingly more dependent on technological knowledge and skills, as is the labour market (see Chart 3.24 on page 70). Students with little or no exposure to Information Communications Technology (ICT) in schools may face difficulties in making the transition to the modern labour market. Computers have been widespread as resources for learning in schools since the 1980s, and ICT has been part of the National Curriculum since 1990. Chart 3.6 shows results from the 1998, 1999 and 2000 ICT surveys of schools in England. Over this period there has been a considerable increase in the percentage of schools connected to the Internet. In 2000, 86 per cent of primary and 98 per cent of secondary schools in England were connected compared with 17 and 83 per cent respectively in 1998.

**Access to the Internet: by type of school[1]**

**England**
Percentages

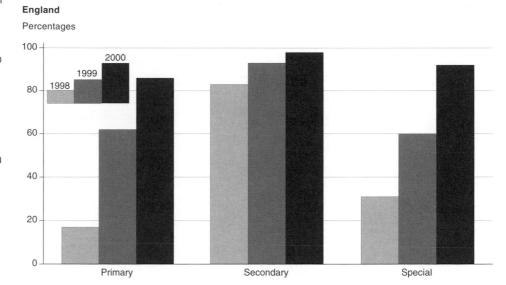

1 See Appendix, Part 3: Main categories of educational establishments and stages of education.
*Source: Department for Education and Employment*

| Key Stages of the National Curriculum | | |
|---|---|---|
| | Pupil ages | Year groups |
| Key stage 1 | 5–7 | 1–2 |
| Key stage 2 | 7–11 | 3–6 |
| Key stage 3 | 11–14 | 7–9 |
| Key stage 4 | 14–16 | 10–11 |

# 3.7

**Most popular sports played in school lessons[1]: by gender, 1994 and 1999**

**England**
Percentages

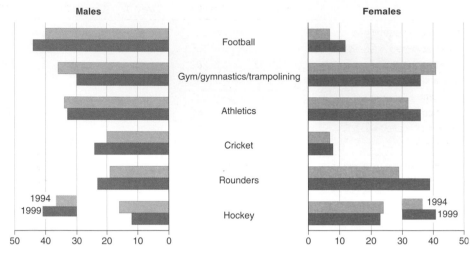

1 Percentage of pupils aged 6 to 16 who participated ten or more times in the last year.

**Source: National Survey for Young People and Sport, MORI for Sport England**

# 3.8

**Places available on holiday schemes and out of school clubs for five to seven year olds**

**England**
Thousands

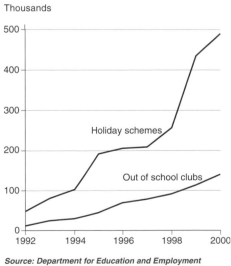

**Source: Department for Education and Employment**

The amount of time allocated to PE in the curriculum is important as PE provides young people with the opportunity of a rounded education that addresses their physical, as well as their intellectual, development. For some, school provides pupils with perhaps their only opportunity for sport. In 1994 the first national survey of sports participation among young people aged 6 to 16 in England was carried out and it was repeated in 1999. Overall, the proportion of young people spending an average of between 30 and 59 minutes a week in PE lessons increased from 5 per cent in 1994 to 18 per cent in 1999. However, the proportion of young people spending two hours or more on PE and sport decreased from 46 per cent to 33 per cent over the same period.

For many sports the change in participation between 1994 and 1999 was small (Chart 3.7). The biggest falls that took place were in participation in gymnastics, in particular, but also in swimming in primary schools and hockey in secondary schools. However there have been increases in participation in rounders, football and, to a lesser extent, athletics. There were also differences in both years in the participation rates of girls and boys. As might be expected, boys

were far more likely than girls to have participated frequently (ten or more times in the previous year) in football and cricket. In contrast, girls were more likely than boys to have participated frequently in rounders and hockey. Athletics was one sport in which there was little gender difference in participation levels.

For a child to succeed and progress through the education system support and care is also helpful outside of the school day. There is a growing demand for good quality childcare, with the increasing participation of women in the workplace (see Chart 4.1 on page 74) and a corresponding increase in households where both parents are in employment. There is a range of childcare arrangements currently used by parents. These include both 'informal' options (such as grandparents, partners, relatives, friends or neighbours) and 'formal' options (such as childminders, nannies, nurseries and 'out of school hours' clubs). (See also Table 8.23 on page 156).

Out of school clubs provide sessional care for four or five days a week before and/or after school. In 2000 there were around 4 thousand such clubs in England, providing 141 thousand places for children aged five to seven (Chart 3.8). The number of places available was almost 12 times higher than in 1992. Holiday play schemes or clubs provide care all day during school holidays and sometimes at half term. In 2000 there were 11.5 thousand holiday schemes providing 490 thousand places – ten times more than in 1992, with half of the increase taking place since 1998.

A recent report by the Cabinet Office on women's attitudes to combining paid work and family life found that most mothers preferred 'informal' childcare arrangements. Key factors in influencing a mother to choose 'formal' care arrangements were whether carers could be trusted to provide high quality care in a safe environment, affordability and accessibility in accommodating irregular working hours and school holidays.

# 3.9

Parental involvement in children's education is also important. Programmes to improve children's basic skills often try to encourage reading practice at home with the involvement of parents. Research from the 1970 Birth Cohort Study suggests that where parents had poor skills their children were also likely to have poor skills.

In 1996 Great Britain participated in the International Adult Literacy Survey which examined the levels of literacy of people aged 16 to 65. Respondents who had children aged 6 to 15 living with them were asked about literacy in the home environment. Respondents with low literacy levels themselves were less likely than those at higher literacy levels to report that their children would often see them or their partner reading (Table 3.9). There was no consistent pattern between parents' literacy levels and whether or not parents said their children had time set aside for reading or were limited in the amount of time they were allowed to watch television.

In the last decade there have been changes in the gender composition of primary and secondary school teachers. Women represented 83 per cent of all teachers in nursery and primary schools in England and Wales in 1999 but only 58 per cent of all nursery/primary head teachers; nevertheless this was an increase since 1990 (Table 3.10). In secondary schools, women represented 53 per cent of all teachers in 1999 but only 28 per cent of all head teachers were women.

There have also been changes in the age structure of teachers. For example, the proportion of women secondary school teachers aged under 40 declined from three-fifths in 1986 to around two-fifths in 1999. These changes in the age structure reflect a large cohort of teachers recruited in the 1970s, with smaller numbers of teachers recruited since then.

**Respondents[1] who reported various family literacy practices: by prose literacy level, 1996**

Great Britain · Percentages

| | Level 1 | Level 2 | Level 3 | Level 4/5 | All |
|---|---|---|---|---|---|
| **Children of respondent** | | | | | |
| Often see respondent or spouse reading | 68 | 89 | 96 | 99 | 89 |
| Are limited in amount of time allowed to watch TV | 48 | 55 | 54 | 46 | 51 |
| Have time set aside for reading | 46 | 55 | 47 | 52 | 50 |

1 Respondents with children aged 6 to 15 living with them. See Appendix, Part 3: Literacy levels.
**Source: Adult Literacy Survey, Office for National Statistics**

# 3.10

**Teachers in maintained schools who are women: by grade**

England & Wales · Percentages

| | Nursery/primary | | | Secondary | | |
|---|---|---|---|---|---|---|
| | 1990 | 1995 | 1999 | 1990 | 1995 | 1999 |
| Head | 49 | 52 | 58 | 20 | 23 | 28 |
| Deputy head | 65 | 69 | 73 | 34 | 34 | 36 |
| Classroom teacher | 88 | 88 | 88 | 49 | 52 | 55 |
| All teachers | 81 | 82 | 83 | 48 | 51 | 53 |

**Source: Department for Education and Employment**

# 3.11

## Enrolments[1] on teacher training courses[2]: by type of subject

England & Wales                                                                     Numbers

|  | 1990/91 | 1994/95 | 1999/00 |
|---|---|---|---|
| **Primary** | 14,331 | 15,087 | 13,378 |
| **Secondary** | | | |
| Science | 1,651 | 3,074 | 2,512 |
| English | 1,103 | 1,933 | 2,171 |
| Technology[3] | 1,379 | 2,247 | 1,825 |
| Languages | 1,101 | 1,936 | 1,611 |
| Mathematics | 1,091 | 2,050 | 1,395 |
| Physical education | 933 | 1,378 | 1,287 |
| Geography | 342 | 686 | 915 |
| History | 491 | 981 | 884 |
| Art | 475 | 805 | 853 |
| Religious education | 252 | 465 | 566 |
| Music | 341 | 526 | 552 |
| Other | 307 | 327 | 271 |
| All secondary subjects | 9,464 | 16,407 | 14,842 |
| **All enrolments** | 23,795 | 31,494 | 28,220 |

1 Data for 1990/91 represent full-time equivalents. For 1994/95 and 1999/00, data represent head-counts (the total of full-time and part-time recruitment).
2 Includes universities and other higher education institutes, SCITT and Open University.
3 Includes design and technology, engineering, computer studies, business studies, commerce, home economics, needlecraft and other technology.

*Source: Department for Education and Employment; National Assembly for Wales*

# 3.12

## Young people in education or training[1]: by gender and age

England                                                                              Percentages

|  | 1986 | 1988 | 1991 | 1993 | 1994 | 1995 | 1996 | 1997 | 1998 | 1999 |
|---|---|---|---|---|---|---|---|---|---|---|
| **Males** | | | | | | | | | | |
| 16 | 83 | 84 | 87 | 89 | 89 | 87 | 86 | 85 | 84 | 85 |
| 17 | 61 | 74 | 80 | 81 | 80 | 79 | 79 | 78 | 78 | 79 |
| 18 | 46 | 51 | 58 | 61 | 61 | 61 | 61 | 60 | 60 | 61 |
| All aged 16-18 | 64 | 70 | 75 | 77 | 77 | 76 | 76 | 74 | 74 | 75 |
| **Females** | | | | | | | | | | |
| 16 | 83 | 83 | 89 | 91 | 91 | 89 | 88 | 87 | 88 | 88 |
| 17 | 57 | 67 | 76 | 81 | 81 | 80 | 80 | 79 | 80 | 81 |
| 18 | 37 | 39 | 48 | 56 | 58 | 59 | 61 | 60 | 59 | 60 |
| All aged 16-18 | 58 | 63 | 71 | 76 | 76 | 77 | 77 | 76 | 75 | 76 |

1 Data are at end of each year. All in full-time education and government-supported training plus employer-funded training and other education and training. There is a slight discontinuity in the data series in 1994 due to changes in the data sources. See Appendix, Part 3: Discontinuity in further and higher education statistics.

*Source: Department for Education and Employment*

In 1999/00, around 28 thousand students were enrolled on teacher training courses in England and Wales, 19 thousand of whom were taking Post Graduate Certificate in Education (PGCE) courses (Table 3.11). The numbers enrolled on a mathematics teacher training course increased by 88 per cent between 1990/91 and 1994/95 and then decreased by 32 per cent to around 1.4 thousand enrolments in 1999/00. Substantial increases in teacher training enrolments over the last decade were also seen in geography, which tripled between 1990/91 and 1999/00, and in religious education, which doubled over the same period.

In 1999/00, the greatest percentage shortfall in the recruitment of teachers against the Government's targets was for technology, followed by languages, and then mathematics. A number of initiatives, including the introduction of financial incentives for initial teacher training, aim to attract more graduates to the teaching profession.

## Post-compulsory education

At age 16 young people are faced with the choice of whether to remain in education, go into training or seek employment. Over the last decade young people have become more likely to continue with their education.

At the end of 1999, around 75 per cent of both young men and women aged 16 to 18 in England were in education or training compared with 64 per cent and 58 per cent respectively in 1986 (Table 3.12). The proportion of 17 year olds in education or training increased markedly between 1986 and the early 1990s, after which it remained fairly stable. The increase in participation of 18 year olds has been most noticeable for women. In 1999, 60 per cent of 18 year old women were in education or training compared with 37 per cent in 1986.

# 3.13

Compulsory schooling ends at different ages in different European countries, varying between the ages of 14 and 18. The vast majority of young people in Europe choose to stay on in education beyond this age (Table 3.13). In 1998 Sweden had the highest proportion in education one year after school-leaving age – 98 per cent at age 16 – compared with 88 per cent in Spain and 81 per cent in the United Kingdom. Conversely, by the age of 20, Sweden had one of the lowest participation rates in education and training.

Analyses undertaken by the Youth Cohort Study (YCS) show that young people from most minority ethnic groups in England and Wales are more likely to be in education and training beyond school-leaving age than their White counterparts. In 2000, 96 per cent of Indian 16 year olds were in education and training compared with 85 per cent of White young people of the same age (Chart 3.14). The occupation of parents also had some effect on their children's participation in education and training. In 1999, 17 year olds in England with parents in professional and managerial occupations were more likely than those with parents in unskilled manual occupations to be in education or training post-16, at 89 and 60 per cent respectively.

There were 4 million students in further education in the United Kingdom during 1998/99, of which 56 per cent were female. The number of male further education students fell by 2 per cent between 1970/71 and 1990/91, whereas the number of female students increased by almost three-quarters (see Table 3.15 overleaf). Data for 1998/99 are not comparable with earlier years due to a change in definition. However, on a comparable 'snapshot' basis, enrolments in further education increased steadily, from around 2.2 million in 1990/91 to 2.5 million in 1997/98.

## Participation rates in education[1]: EU comparison, by age[2], 1998

Percentages

| | 16 | 17 | 18 | 19 | 20 | Age[3] at which compulsory education ends |
|---|---|---|---|---|---|---|
| Greece | 90 | 67 | 71 | 70 | 59 | 14.5 |
| France | 95 | 90 | 81 | 69 | 57 | 16 |
| Netherlands | 97 | 89 | 78 | 65 | 57 | 18 |
| Belgium | 94 | 94 | 80 | 67 | 55 | 18 |
| Spain | 88 | 79 | 66 | 58 | 54 | 16 |
| | | | | | | |
| Germany | 96 | 92 | 86 | 66 | 48 | 18 |
| Finland | 89 | 93 | 85 | 43 | 45 | 16 |
| United Kingdom | 81 | 68 | 49 | 47 | 43 | 16 |
| Irish Republic | 92 | 82 | 71 | 52 | 41 | 15 |
| Sweden | 98 | 97 | 95 | 41 | 41 | 16 |
| | | | | | | |
| Denmark | 93 | 82 | 74 | 57 | 40 | 16 |
| Portugal | 84 | 84 | 66 | 53 | 40 | 14 |
| Italy | 78 | 73 | 68 | 48 | 37 | 14 |
| Austria | 88 | 86 | 68 | 41 | 29 | 15 |

1 Full-time and part-time education. In Belgium, Germany and the Netherlands, the part-time compulsory schooling age is 18, 17 and 19 years respectively.
2 Age as at start of the academic year.
3 Age as at end of the academic year.

**Source: Organisation for Economic Co-operation and Development**

# 3.14

## Sixteen year olds in education or training[1]: by ethnic group, 2000

**England & Wales**

Percentages

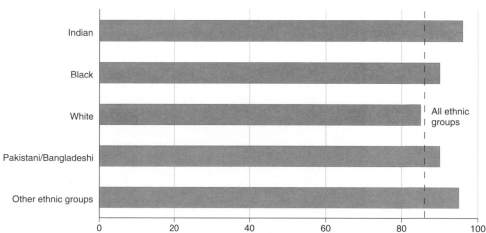

1 Includes those not in full-time education, government-supported training or employer funded training, but in other education or training.

**Source: Youth Cohort Study, Department for Education and Employment**

# 3.15

**Students[1] in further and higher education: by type of course and gender**

United Kingdom                                                             Thousands

| | Males | | | | Females | | | |
|---|---|---|---|---|---|---|---|---|
| | 1970/71 | 1980/81 | 1990/91 | 1998/99[2] | 1970/71 | 1980/81 | 1990/91 | 1998/99[2] |
| **Further education[3]** | | | | | | | | |
| Full time | 116 | 154 | 219 | 532 | 95 | 196 | 261 | 533 |
| Part time | 891 | 697 | 768 | 1,257 | 630 | 624 | 986 | 1,721 |
| All further education | 1,007 | 851 | 987 | 1,789 | 725 | 820 | 1,247 | 2,254 |
| **Higher education[4]** | | | | | | | | |
| Undergraduate | | | | | | | | |
| Full time | 241 | 277 | 345 | 528 | 173 | 196 | 319 | 599 |
| Part time | 127 | 176 | 193 | 229 | 19 | 71 | 148 | 305 |
| Postgraduate | | | | | | | | |
| Full time | 33 | 41 | 50 | 87 | 10 | 21 | 34 | 80 |
| Part time | 15 | 32 | 50 | 130 | 3 | 13 | 36 | 124 |
| All higher education | 416 | 526 | 638 | 974 | 205 | 301 | 537 | 1,107 |

1 Home and overseas students.
2 Data for 1998/99 are not directly comparable with earlier years which referred solely to snapshot pupils counted at a particular point in the year rather than whole year counts used in 1998/99.
3 Dates differ by country, but are snapshots taken at around November each year. Excludes adult education centres.
4 At December each year (except 1998/99 which is a whole year count). Includes Open University.

**Source: Department for Education and Employment; National Assembly for Wales; Scottish Executive; Department of Education Northern Ireland**

# 3.16

**People working towards a qualification[1]: by type of qualification and age, Spring 2000**

United Kingdom                                             Percentages

| | 16-24 | 25-34 | 35-44 | 45-54 | 55-59/64[2] | All aged 16-59/64[2] (=100%) (thousands) |
|---|---|---|---|---|---|---|
| Degree or equivalent | 56 | 22 | 14 | 6 | 1 | 1,491 |
| Higher education[3] | 34 | 28 | 24 | 12 | 2 | 539 |
| GCE A Level or equivalent | 80 | 8 | 8 | 3 | 1 | 1,273 |
| GCSE grades A* to C or equivalent | 72 | 11 | 10 | 6 | 1 | 771 |
| Other qualification[4] | 22 | 32 | 25 | 17 | 5 | 582 |
| Any qualification | 52 | 21 | 16 | 9 | 2 | 5,656 |

1 For those working towards more than one qualification the highest is recorded.
2 Males aged up to 64, females aged up to 59.
3 Below degree level.
4 Includes those who did not state which qualification.

**Source: Department for Education and Employment from the Labour Force Survey**

Alongside the increases in the proportions of young people staying on in education after the age of 16 there have also been substantial increases in the number of students going onto higher education in the United Kingdom. The number of enrolments by men on undergraduate courses more than doubled between 1970/71 and 1998/99. For women the increase was even more dramatic, with nearly five times as many enrolments in 1998/99 as in the early 1970s. In 1998/99 there were 2.1 million students in higher education, 53 per cent of whom were women. There were slightly more male postgraduate students than female, but at undergraduate level there were almost 150 thousand more females than males.

Not everyone working towards a qualification beyond the age of 16 will have worked their way continuously through the various levels of education. Table 3.16 shows that 5.7 million people of working age were studying towards a qualification in the United Kingdom in Spring 2000, and just over half were aged between 16 and 24 while just over a quarter were aged 35 and over. However, the age composition differed widely from qualification to qualification. For example, among those taking higher education qualifications below degree level, such as HNDs, only a third were aged 16 to 24 and two-fifths were aged 35 and over.

Many adults continue their education, either for enjoyment or to develop new skills. Among the many general courses that are available are subjects as diverse as languages, physical education/sport/fitness, and practical crafts such as embroidery and woodwork. Nearly seven out of ten of those enrolled on adult education courses in England in November 1999 were on courses that did not lead to a formal qualification. In total, there were 1.1 million adults in England and Wales enrolled on adult education courses, and enrolment rates were higher for women than for men.

3: Education and Training

# 3.17

## Educational attainment

School pupils in England and Wales are formally assessed at three key stages before GCSE level – at the ages of 7, 11 and 14. The assessment at all three key stages cover the core subjects of English (and Welsh in Wales), mathematics and science. The purpose of these tests is to help inform teachers and parents about the progress of individual pupils and to give a measure of the performance of schools. There are two forms of assessment: tests and teacher assessment. Pupils' attainment is shown as a level on the national curriculum scale. A typical 7 year old is expected to achieve level two, a typical 11 year old level four, and a typical 14 year old between levels five and six.

In 2000, the proportion of boys in England reaching the required standard for English, was lower than for girls at all key stages, particularly at key stages 2 and 3 (Table 3.17). However, similar proportions of boys and girls reached the expected level in tests for mathematics and science at all key stages. The proportion of pupils achieving the expected level generally reduced with age for both genders.

From the age of 14 onwards young people study for public examinations which, for some, mark the end of their compulsory education. In England, Wales and Northern Ireland young people aged 15 and 16 sit GCSEs, and Standard Grades are taken in Scotland. Table 3.18 shows the proportion of pupils in their final year of compulsory education in Great Britain who gained grades A* to C (or equivalent) in selected subjects. In 1998/99 girls performed far better than boys in English and were also more likely than boys to have obtained grades A* to C in modern languages and science.

Attainment at GCSE varies according to the family background of young people. The YCS study of 16 year olds found that the proportion of 16 year olds

**Pupils reaching or exceeding expected standards[1]: by key stage and gender, 2000**

England — Percentages

| | Teacher assessment | | Tests | |
|---|---|---|---|---|
| | Males | Females | Males | Females |
| **Key stage 1[2]** | | | | |
| English | 80 | 88 | . | . |
| Reading | . | . | 79 | 88 |
| Writing | . | . | 80 | 89 |
| Spelling | . | . | 67 | 77 |
| Mathematics | 87 | 89 | 89 | 91 |
| Science | 87 | 89 | . | . |
| **Key stage 2[3]** | | | | |
| English | 65 | 76 | 70 | 79 |
| Reading | . | . | 80 | 86 |
| Writing | . | . | 48 | 63 |
| Mathematics | 72 | 73 | 72 | 71 |
| Science | 78 | 80 | 84 | 85 |
| **Key stage 3[4]** | | | | |
| English | 56 | 73 | 55 | 72 |
| Mathematics | 65 | 68 | 64 | 65 |
| Science | 60 | 63 | 61 | 58 |

1 See Appendix, Part 3: The National Curriculum: assessments and tests.
2 Percentage of pupils achieving level 2 or above at key stage 1.
3 Percentage of pupils achieving level 4 or above at key stage 2.
4 Percentage of pupils achieving level 5 or above at key stage 3.

**Source: Department for Education and Employment**

# 3.18

**Pupils[1] achieving GCSE grades A* to C[2] or equivalent: by selected subject and gender**

Great Britain — Percentages

| | Males | | | Females | | |
|---|---|---|---|---|---|---|
| | 1988/89 | 1992/93 | 1998/99 | 1988/89 | 1992/93 | 1998/99 |
| English | 39 | 44 | 46 | 52 | 61 | 63 |
| Any science[3] | .. | 41 | 46 | .. | 41 | 49 |
| Any modern language | .. | .. | 32 | .. | .. | 48 |
| French | 14 | 20 | 22 | 23 | 31 | 34 |
| Mathematics | 38 | 40 | 44 | 34 | 40 | 47 |
| History | 15 | 17 | 18 | 17 | 22 | 22 |
| Geography | 20 | 22 | 24 | 16 | 20 | 21 |

1 Pupils in final year of compulsory schooling.
2 Or equivalent. See Appendix, Part 3: Qualifications.
3 Includes double award, single award and individual science subjects.

**Source: Department for Education and Employment; National Assembly for Wales; Scottish Executive**

Social Trends 31, © Crown copyright 2001

67

# 3.19

**Pupils achieving five or more GCSE grades A\* to C or equivalent[1]: by parents' socio-economic group, 1989 and 2000**

**England & Wales**
Percentages

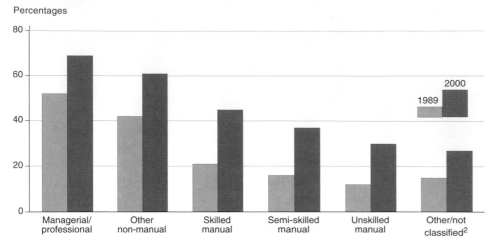

1 Includes equivalent GNVQ qualifications achieved in Year 11.
2 Includes a high percentage of respondents who had neither parent in a full-time job.
**Source: Youth Cohort Study, Department for Education and Employment**

# 3.20

**Achievement at GCE A level or equivalent[1]: by gender**

**United Kingdom**
Percentages

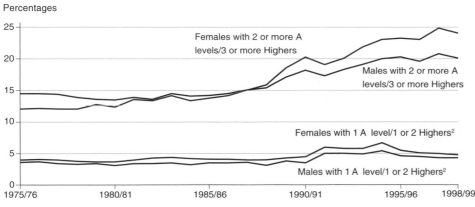

1 Based on population aged 17 at the start of the academic year. Data to 1990/91 (1991/92 in Northern Ireland) relate to school leavers. From 1991/92 data relate to pupils of any age for Great Britain while school performance data are used for Northern Ireland from 1992/93. Figures exclude sixth form colleges in England and Wales which were reclassified as FE colleges from 1 April 1993. Excludes GNVQ Advanced Qualifications throughout.
2 From 1996/97, figures only include two SCE Highers.

**Source: Department for Education and Employment; National Assembly for Wales; Scottish Executive; Northern Ireland Department of Education**

with parents in manual occupations who attained five or more GCSEs at grades A\* to C increased markedly between 1989 and 2000 (Chart 3.19). The proportion with parents from semi-skilled manual and unskilled manual occupations who achieved this more than doubled over the same period, to around a third in 2000. Large differences, however, remained between the socio-economic groups. For example, around two-thirds of young people with parents in non-manual occupations attained five or more GCSEs at grades A\* to C in year 11 in 2000, compared with a third of those with parents in skilled and semi-skilled manual occupations. However, the proportion of young people with parents in skilled manual occupations with the same level of qualifications increased from a fifth in 1989 to over two-fifths in 2000.

The YCS also found that ethnic origin was associated with achievement at GCSE. The rise in the proportion of 16 year olds gaining five or more GCSEs at grades A\* to C has been apparent among young people from all ethnic groups, but differences remain. Although there has been continued improvement in GCSE attainment among Black young people – just under 30 per cent of Black young people in England and Wales gained five or more GCSEs in 1998 – this was well below the proportions for Asian and White young people. The proportions of Indian and 'other' Asian young people who gained five or more GCSEs at grades A\* to C were higher than other groups, at 54 per cent and 61 per cent respectively.

There has been an increase in the proportion of young men and women in the United Kingdom achieving two or more A levels (or equivalent) over the last 25 years. (Chart 3.20). The proportion of young women who achieved this has doubled since the mid-1970s, to 24 per cent in 1998/99. The increase in the proportion of young men achieving this has been more modest, with a rise from around 14 per cent to 20 per cent. Up to 1987/88, a higher proportion of young men than

Highest qualification held[1]: by gender and ethnic group, 1999-00[2]

Great Britain                                                                                                                          Percentages

| | Degree or equivalent | Higher education[3] | GCE A level or equivalent | GCSE grades A* to C or equivalent | Other qualification | No qualifications | All |
|---|---|---|---|---|---|---|---|
| **Males** | | | | | | | |
| White | 16 | 8 | 31 | 18 | 13 | 14 | 100 |
| Black | 19 | 7 | 22 | 16 | 21 | 16 | 100 |
| Indian/Pakistani/Bangladeshi | 18 | 5 | 17 | 15 | 26 | 20 | 100 |
| Other groups[4] | 22 | 6 | 20 | 13 | 27 | 11 | 100 |
| All | 16 | 8 | 31 | 18 | 14 | 15 | 100 |
| **Females** | | | | | | | |
| White | 13 | 9 | 17 | 28 | 14 | 19 | 100 |
| Black | 13 | 12 | 16 | 24 | 20 | 15 | 100 |
| Indian/Pakistani/Bangladeshi | 10 | 5 | 14 | 16 | 25 | 31 | 100 |
| Other groups[4] | 16 | 7 | 15 | 16 | 31 | 14 | 100 |
| All | 13 | 9 | 17 | 27 | 15 | 19 | 100 |

1 Males aged 16 to 64, females aged 16 to 59.
2 Combined quarters: Spring 1999 to Winter 1999-00.
3 Below degree level.
4 Includes those who did not state their ethnic group.
*Source: Department for Education and Employment from the Labour Force Survey*

young women achieved two or more A levels. In 1987/88, an equal proportion of young men and women achieved two or more A levels (15 per cent) but since 1988/89 women have outperformed men at this level. It should be noted that these figures exclude young men and women achieving A level qualification in sixth form colleges, and Advanced General National Vocational Qualifications (GNVQ).

The highest qualification held by individuals is related to a number of factors, such as age, gender and socio-economic group. There is also variation across ethnic groups. In 1999-00, 14 per cent of men from the White group in Great Britain held no qualification compared with 20 per cent from the Indian/Pakistani/Bangladeshi group (Table 3.21). The gap between corresponding figures for women was bigger, at 19 per cent and 31 per cent respectively. White men were more likely to be qualified to A level standard or above than other groups, but there was little difference between the ethnic groups in the percentage of men with a degree.

3.22

National Learning Targets[1]: by gender

England                                                                                     Percentages

| | Males | | | Females | | | All | | |
|---|---|---|---|---|---|---|---|---|---|
| | 1998 | 1999 | 2000 | 1998 | 1999 | 2000 | 1998 | 1999 | 2000 |
| **Young people** | | | | | | | | | |
| 85 per cent of 19 year olds with an NVQ level 2 qualification | 70 | 74 | 72 | 74 | 75 | 77 | 72 | 75 | 75 |
| 60 per cent of 21 year olds with an NVQ level 3 qualification | 51 | 55 | 56 | 49 | 52 | 52 | 50 | 54 | 54 |
| **Adults**[2] | | | | | | | | | |
| 50 per cent of adults with an NVQ level 3 qualification | 48 | 49 | 51 | 38 | 40 | 41 | 44 | 45 | 47 |
| 28 per cent of adults with an NVQ level 4 qualification | 25 | 26 | 27 | 25 | 26 | 27 | 25 | 26 | 27 |

1 At Spring each year. Targets relate to objectives for the year 2002. See Appendix, Part 3: National Learning Targets.
2 Males aged 18 to 64 and females aged 18 to 59, who are in employment or actively seeking employment.
*Source: Department for Education and Employment from the Labour Force Survey*

# 3.23

## Destination of leavers from Work-based Training[1], 1998-99

| England & Wales | | Percentages |
|---|---|---|
| | Work-based Learning for Adults | Work-based Training for Young People[2] |
| In employment | 40 | 69 |
| Unemployed | 47 | 13 |
| In further education or training | 5 | 12 |
| Other | 8 | 7 |
| All leavers (=100%) (thousands) | 111 | 224 |
| Percentage who gained full qualification | 41 | 49 |

1 Status six months after leaving.
2 Excludes Foundation Modern Apprenticeships.
**Source: Department for Education and Employment**

In recent years there has been a focus on the concept of 'lifelong learning'. National Learning Targets for England have been set which state that by 2002, 85 per cent of 19 year olds should be qualified to NVQ level 2 or its equivalent and that 60 per cent of 21 year olds should be qualified to NVQ level 3 or its equivalent. Some progress has been made towards the targets. In 2000, 75 per cent of 19 year olds and 54 per cent of 21 year olds met these standards (see Table 3.22 on previous page).

In addition to these targets for young people, a set of targets also exists for adults of working age. The first states that by the year 2002, 50 per cent of the workforce should be qualified to NVQ level 3 or its equivalent, while the second states that 28 per cent of the workforce should have a professional, vocational, management or academic qualification at NVQ level 4 or above by the same year. In Spring 2000, 47 per cent and 27 per cent of economically active adults held level 3 and level 4 qualifications respectively.

## Training

There are a number of government-supported training initiatives in England and Wales. Work-based Training for Young People (WBTYP) was introduced with the aim of ensuring that all young people have access to post-compulsory education. Included within this initiative are Advanced Modern Apprenticeships and Foundation Modern Apprenticeships (formerly known as Modern Apprenticeships and National Traineeships respectively). Advanced Modern Apprenticeships were introduced in September 1998. They are aimed at developing technical, supervisory and craft-level skills among 16 to 24 year olds; they accounted for 48 per cent of all young people on government-supported training in England in June 2000. Participants usually have full-employed status and are provided with training to NVQ level 3 (equivalent to 2 A levels).

In 1999, 81 per cent of young people in England and Wales were either in employment or further education six months after leaving Work Based Training for Young People (Table 3.23). Another government-supported scheme is Work-based Learning for Adults. This is designed to help unemployed and disadvantaged adults find jobs through training and work experience, and is open to those aged over 25 who have been unemployed for six months or longer. The proportion of adult leavers who were in a job six months after leaving the scheme in 1998-99 was 40 per cent compared with 33 per cent in 1990-91.

Training is not just for school leavers or the unemployed; it is also an increasingly important aspect of working life for employees. The modern working environment now demands a broad range of skills such as computer literacy, communication skills, problem solving skills and customer handling skills. The Employers Skills Survey, conducted in 1999 on behalf of the Department for Education and Employment, looked at the extent, causes and implications of skill deficiencies as

# 3.24

## Skills sought by employers in connection with skill-shortage vacancies, 1999

**England**

Percentages

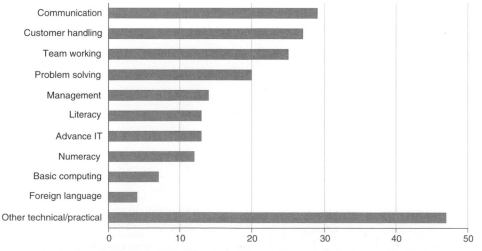

**Source: Skills Task Force Employers' Survey, Institute for Employment Research for Department for Education and Employment**

reported by employers. It estimated that almost 2 million employees in England in 1999 were considered by their employers to be less than fully proficient in their job.

Results from the survey also suggest that the main types of skill which employers with skill-shortage vacancies found hard to obtain were technical and practical skills other than IT (Chart 3.24). This was reported by almost half of establishments with such vacancies. Specific skills such as communication (29 per cent of all skill-shortage vacancies) and customer handling (27 per cent) were also important, particularly for vacancies in sales, personal service and clerical occupations. The principal effects of skill-shortage vacancies were reported to be: difficulties in meeting customer service objectives; delays in developing new products or services; increased operating costs; and loss of business or orders to competitors.

Almost half of establishments with skill gaps acknowledged that these were partly due to their own failure to train and develop staff. The other main factors felt to be causing skill gaps were the introduction of new working practices, the development of new products, recruitment problems and the introduction of new technology.

Some people undertake vocational training in order to help them find work; others receive training from employers. In Spring 2000, around 15 per cent of male and 18 per cent of female employees of working age had received some job-related training in the previous four weeks (Chart 3.25). Young people aged between 16 and 24 were the most likely to have received training while males aged 50 to 64 were the least likely.

Most employers now invest in their workforce by providing training opportunities and many have training plans and budgets. Regional differences exist (Table 3.26). In 1999, two in five employers in both the East Midlands and the South West

regions had provided off the job training in the last 12 months, – the highest proportion among the English regions. Employers in the South East were found to be more likely to have reported an increase in skill needs in the previous 12 months while employers in the North East were least likely. Employee training is vital in improving skill acquisition and, as the Employer Skills Survey showed, skill shortages can both have effects on the productivity of establishments and can have long term effects on economic performance.

# 3.25

**Employees[1] receiving job-related training: by gender and age, Spring 2000**

**United Kingdom**
Percentages

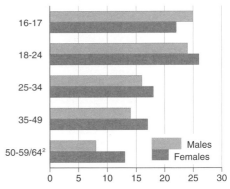

1 Percentage who received job-related training in the four weeks before interview.
2 Males aged 50 to 64 and females aged 50 to 59.
**Source: Department for Education and Employment from the Labour Force Survey**

# 3.26

**Changes in skill needs and employers' commitment to training[1]: by region, 1999**

Percentages

| | Reporting an increase in skills needed in an average employee | With a training plan | With a training budget | Providing off-the-job training in the last 12 months |
|---|---|---|---|---|
| England | 62 | 32 | 25 | 34 |
| North East | 52 | 31 | 24 | 34 |
| North West | 60 | 35 | 27 | 34 |
| Yorkshire and the Humber | 57 | 36 | 23 | 37 |
| East Midlands | 65 | 34 | 30 | 42 |
| West Midlands | 58 | 29 | 25 | 31 |
| East | 60 | 33 | 28 | 34 |
| London | 63 | 29 | 19 | 28 |
| South East | 70 | 31 | 24 | 32 |
| South West | 64 | 39 | 32 | 41 |

1 Fieldwork was carried out in November and December 1999 and asked if any training provision had been made 12 months prior to the interview. See Appendix, Part 3: Learning and Training at Work.
**Source: Learning and Training at Work, IFF Research Limited for Department for Education and Employment**

## Websites

| | |
|---|---|
| Department for Education and Employment | www.dfee.gov.uk |
| Cabinet Office | www.cabinet-office.gov.uk |
| Sport England | www.english.sports.gov.uk |
| Institute for Employment Research, University of Warwick | www.warwick.ac.uk/ier |
| National Foundation for Education Research | www.nfer.ac.uk |
| Organisation for Economic Co-operation and Development | www.oecd.org |

## Contacts

| | |
|---|---|
| **Office for National Statistics** | |
| Chapter author | 020 7533 6174 |
| Labour market statistics helpline | 020 7533 6094 |
| **Department for Education and Employment** | 01325 392658 |
| **National Assembly for Wales** | 029 2082 3507 |
| **Northern Ireland Department for Education** | 028 9127 9279 |
| **Scottish Executive** | 0131 244 0442 |
| **Sport England** | 020 7273 1941 |
| **Centre for Longitudinal Studies, Institute of Education** | 020 7612 6900 |
| **Institute for Employment Research University of Warwick** | 024 7652 4420 |

Social Trends 31, © Crown copyright 2001

# Chapter 4 Labour Market

### Overview

● Since the mid-1960s, employment rates for men have gradually fallen to reach 79 per cent of the working age population in 1999, whereas among women they have risen to 69 per cent in 1999. (Chart 4.1)

● In Spring 2000 there were 27 million people of working age in employment in the United Kingdom, the highest number since 1959 when current records began. (Table 4.2 and page 75)

### Economic activity

● Two in five economically inactive men were not looking for a job in Spring 2000 because of long-term sickness or disability. (Table 4.9)

● In Spring 2000, in around 16 per cent of households with at least one person of working age, no-one was in employment. (Chart 4.10)

### Patterns of employment

● Jobs in the service industries rose by 36 per cent between 1978 and 2000, compared with a fall of 39 per cent in manufacturing over the same period. (Chart 4.11)

● In Spring 2000 there were 855 thousand people working in information technology related occupations, an increase of 45 per cent in five years. (Page 82)

### Labour market dynamics

● In Spring 2000, one in ten employees of working age had been in their current job for less than six months, and a similar proportion had been in the same job for 20 years or more. (Table 4.26)

### Working lives

● In Spring 2000, about 6 per cent of full-time employees were looking for a new job; for 35 per cent of these men and 27 per cent of these women unsatisfactory pay in their current job was a trigger for looking for another one. (Table 4.32)

# 4.1

**Employment rates[1]: by gender**

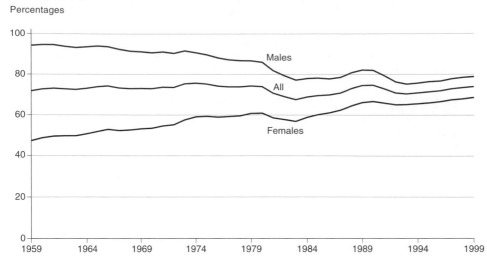

**United Kingdom**

Percentages

1 At Summer each year. In 1959 to 1971, males aged 15 to 64 and females aged 15 to 59; from 1972 onwards males aged 16 to 64 and females aged 16 to 59.

**Source: Department for Education and Employment**

Most people spend a large part of their lives in the labour force, though this proportion has been falling with the rise in participation in higher education and the increase in longevity and thus in the years spent in retirement. More women entering paid employment, the increase in employment in service industries and the fall in manufacturing have all been features of the changes which have taken place in the labour market during the post-war period.

## Overview

The proportion of the working age population in employment has varied between 70 and 75 per cent for most of the period from 1959 (when current records began) to 2000, peaking at almost 76 per cent in 1974 (Chart 4.1). There are business cycle effects in evidence – for example,

## Glossary of terms

**Employees (Labour Force Survey measure)** - a measure, obtained from household surveys, of people aged 16 and over who regard themselves as paid employees. People with two or more jobs are counted only once.

**Self-employed** - a measure, obtained from household surveys, of people aged 16 and over who regard themselves as self-employed, ie who in their main employment work on their own account, whether or not they have employees.

**In employment** - a measure, obtained from household surveys and censuses, of employees, self-employed people, participants in government employment and training programmes, and people doing unpaid family work.

**Government employment and training programmes** - a measure, obtained from household surveys, of those who said they were participants on Youth Training, Employment Training, Employment Action or Community Industry or a programme organised by a TEC/LEC.

**ILO unemployed** - an International Labour Organisation (ILO) recommended measure, used in household surveys such as the Labour Force Survey, which counts as unemployed those aged 16 and over who are without a job, are available to start work in the next two weeks, who have been seeking a job in the last four weeks or are waiting to start a job already obtained.

**Economically active** (labour force) - those **in employment** plus those **ILO unemployed.**

**ILO unemployment rate** - the percentage of the **economically active** who are **ILO unemployed.**

**The economically Inactive** - people who are neither in employment nor ILO unemployed. For example, all people under 16, those looking after a home or retired, or those permanently unable to work.

**Economic activity rate** - the percentage of the population in a given age group which is economically active.

the dip in employment rates between 1980 and 1983, and recovery from 1984 to 1989 – but over the period as a whole there is no sign of a long-run trend in either direction.

However, trends in the overall employment rate mask large differences for men and women. Since the mid-1960s, the trend in employment rates for men has been gradually downwards. Each time a dip in the economic cycle has resulted in a faster fall, the following recovery has not been sufficient to restore rates to their pre-recession levels, and these cyclical effects have been more marked since 1979. Taken over the 40 year period, the effect has been to reduce the male employment rate from 94 per cent to 79 per cent, a fall of 15 percentage points. There is some evidence that the downward trend has now stabilised with a gradual rise between 1993 and 1999.

The picture for women is very different. Employment rates among women rose from 47 per cent to 69 per cent between 1959 and 1999. As with men, the proportion of women in employment has followed the economic cycle, but for them such effects have generally been less marked. For example, between 1980 and 1983 the female employment rate fell less sharply than the male rate and recovered more quickly thereafter. However, since 1993 it has risen at virtually the same rate as the male employment rate.

The data in Chart 4.1 are provisional. The estimates for 1959 to 1983 have been designed by the Department for Education and Employment to be consistent with Labour Force Survey (LFS) estimates available from 1984, but the whole series is currently being refined (see Appendix, Part 4: Estimates of employment rates). The Office for National Statistics (ONS) estimates of employment rates for all aged 16 and over are expected to be published in Spring 2001; estimates for all of working age are expected to be published later in 2001.

**Population of working age[1]: by employment status and gender, 1986 and 2000**

United Kingdom
Millions

| | 1986 | | | 2000 | | |
|---|---|---|---|---|---|---|
| | Males | Females | All | Males | Females | All |
| **Economically active** | | | | | | |
| In employment | | | | | | |
| Full-time employees | 11.3 | 5.3 | 16.6 | 11.8 | 6.3 | 18.1 |
| Part-time employees | 0.3 | 3.9 | 4.2 | 1.0 | 4.7 | 5.7 |
| Self-employed | 2.0 | 0.6 | 2.7 | 2.2 | 0.8 | 2.9 |
| Others in employment[2] | 0.3 | 0.1 | 0.4 | 0.1 | 0.1 | 0.2 |
| All in employment | 13.9 | 10.0 | 23.9 | 15.0 | 11.9 | 27.0 |
| Unemployed[3] | 1.8 | 1.2 | 3.1 | 1.0 | 0.6 | 1.6 |
| All economically active | 15.8 | 11.2 | 26.9 | 16.0 | 12.5 | 28.6 |
| **Economically inactive** | 2.2 | 5.3 | 7.5 | 3.0 | 4.8 | 7.7 |
| **Population of working age** | 18.0 | 16.4 | 34.4 | 19.0 | 17.3 | 36.3 |

1 At Spring each year. Males aged 16 to 64, females aged 16 to 59.
2 Those on government employment and training schemes and unpaid family workers.
3 Based on the ILO definition. See Appendix, Part 4: ILO unemployment.
**Source: Labour Force Survey, Office for National Statistics**

In Spring 2000 there were 36.3 million people of working age in the United Kingdom, of whom 27.0 million were in employment (Table 4.2). This is the highest number of people in employment since the series began in 1959 – although the highest employment rate was recorded in 1974, it only represented 24.4 million people. Comparing the structure of the labour market in Spring 2000 with that in Spring 1986, we can see that the number of people working part time has increased as well as the number working full time, among both men and women. The number of people unemployed (on the ILO measure – see Glossary on page 74) has nearly halved. However, the number of men who are economically inactive has risen and the number of economically inactive women has fallen. The changes in economic inactivity result from increased early retirement among men because of long-term sickness and disability and the decreased likelihood of women staying at home for long periods looking after children.

# 4.3

**Employment rates[1]: by area[2], Spring 2000**

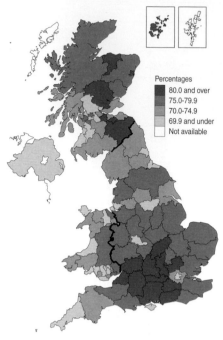

Percentages
- 80.0 and over
- 75.0-79.9
- 70.0-74.9
- 69.9 and under
- Not available

1 Total employed as a percentage of all people of working age.
2 Counties and former counties, except for Northern Ireland.
**Source: Labour Force Survey, Office for National Statistics**

Employment rates are not uniform across the country. Many inner city areas and former industrial areas had the lowest rates in Spring 2000 – for example, 53 per cent in Merthyr Tydfil and 59 per cent in Glasgow City (Chart 4.3). Conversely, the highest employment rates were in the South – for example, 85 per cent in Wiltshire and 84 per cent in Surrey – and the Scottish Borders and the Orkney Islands also had very high rates, at 84 and 96 per cent respectively. However, there can be much greater differences between employment rates within regions than between regions, and most regions have areas with high rates and areas with low rates. Nevertheless, all UK regions have employment rates above the EU average.

## Economic activity

This section concentrates on people who are economically active – those who are aged 16 and over and are considered to be in the labour force because they are either in work or actively looking for work.

The likelihood of being economically active varies with age (Chart 4.4). Around 66 per cent of women aged 16 to 24 were in the labour force in Spring 2000, virtually the same as in 1971. However, whereas in 1971 there was a sharp dip in the labour market participation to 54 per cent of women aged 25 to 44, the main child-bearing and child-rearing years, in 2000 participation rose in this age group to 76 per cent. The rate of decrease with age in economic activity rates for women aged 45 and over was virtually the same in 2000 as in 1971.

For men, labour market participation for all age groups was lower in 2000 than in 1971. For young men aged 16 to 24 increased participation in full-time further and higher education has had an impact. Although education participation rates have also increased among young women, it appears that this has been offset by a reduced likelihood of not being in the labour market because of bringing up a family. From the 45 to 54 age group onwards, male economic activity rates were much lower in 2000 compared with 1971 when the rates stayed above 95 per cent until the 60 to 64 age group. The dramatic effect of earlier retirement among men is illustrated by the fall in rates for the 60 to 64 age group from 85 per cent in 1971 to 50 per cent in 2000.

It would appear that a large proportion of older men who find themselves out of work are leaving the labour force completely rather than being

# 4.4

**Economic activity rates[1]: by gender and age, 1971 and 2000**

**United Kingdom**

Percentages

_[Line chart showing economic activity rates by age group (16-24, 25-44, 45-54, 55-59, 60-64, 65 and over), with four lines: Males 1971, Males 2000, Females 2000, Females 1971. Y-axis from 0 to 100.]_

1 The percentage of the population that is in the labour force. The definition of the labour force changed in 1984 when the former Great Britain civilian labour force definition was replaced by the ILO definition which excludes members of the armed forces.

**Source: Census and Labour Force Survey, Office for National Statistics**

unemployed and seeking work. An analysis from the British Household Panel Survey shows that many men aged 45 to 64 move from being unemployed to long-term sick, and from both unemployment and long-term sickness into retirement.

Economic activity rates are translated into numbers of men and women in the labour force in Table 4.5. This shows the rise in the number of women in the labour force over the last 30 years from 10 million in 1971 to 13 million in 1999, and projections indicate that the number will rise by another 1.1 million between 1999 and 2011. The rise over the last 30 years has been greatest among those in the 25 to 44 age bracket, the same group for whom female economic activity rates have also risen the most. Among men, the number in the labour force has risen much more slowly from 16.0 million to 16.2 million in 1999, and is set to increase by a further 0.3 million by 2011.

For a variety of cultural reasons, as well as because of differing age structures, economic activity rates vary between people of different ethnic groups in Great Britain (Table 4.6). Overall, the lowest activity rates for women are among the Pakistani and Bangladeshi communities at only 30 and 22 per cent respectively in 1999-00. Their activity rates are very low at all ages compared with other ethnic groups. Although economic activity among Pakistani and Bangladeshi men aged 25 to 44 is comparable with most other non-White groups, rates for older and younger men are also low. Conversely, the highest labour market participation is to be found among Indian and White men aged 25 to 44. However, this is the age range in which the differences in economic activity rates between ethnic groups are smallest.

## 4.5

**Labour force[1]: by gender and age**

**United Kingdom** — Millions

| | 16-24 | 25-44 | 45-54 | 55-59 | 60-64 | 65 and over | All aged 16 and over |
|---|---|---|---|---|---|---|---|
| **Males** | | | | | | | |
| 1971 | 3.0 | 6.5 | 3.2 | 1.5 | 1.3 | 0.6 | 16.0 |
| 1981 | 3.2 | 7.1 | 3.0 | 1.4 | 1.0 | 0.3 | 16.0 |
| 1991 | 3.1 | 8.1 | 3.0 | 1.1 | 0.8 | 0.3 | 16.4 |
| 1999[2] | 2.4 | 8.3 | 3.4 | 1.2 | 0.7 | 0.3 | 16.2 |
| 2001[3] | 2.4 | 8.2 | 3.4 | 1.3 | 0.7 | 0.3 | 16.3 |
| 2011[3] | 2.8 | 7.3 | 3.9 | 1.3 | 0.9 | 0.3 | 16.5 |
| **Females** | | | | | | | |
| 1971 | 2.3 | 3.5 | 2.1 | 0.9 | 0.5 | 0.3 | 10.0 |
| 1981 | 2.7 | 4.6 | 2.1 | 0.9 | 0.4 | 0.2 | 10.9 |
| 1991 | 2.6 | 6.1 | 2.4 | 0.8 | 0.3 | 0.2 | 12.4 |
| 1999[2] | 2.0 | 6.6 | 2.9 | 0.9 | 0.4 | 0.2 | 13.0 |
| 2001[3] | 2.1 | 6.4 | 3.0 | 0.9 | 0.4 | 0.2 | 13.1 |
| 2011[3] | 2.3 | 6.2 | 3.6 | 1.0 | 0.7 | 0.2 | 14.1 |

1 The former civilian labour force definition of unemployment has been used to produce the estimates for 1971 and 1981; in later years the ILO definition has been used and members of the armed forces excluded. See also Appendix, Part 4: Labour force.
2 At Spring.
3 Data for 2001 and 2011 are based on Spring 1997 Labour Force Survey and mid-1997 based population projections.
**Source: Census; Labour Force Survey, Office for National Statistics**

## 4.6

**Economic activity rates[1]: by ethnic group, gender and age, 1999-00[2]**

**Great Britain** — Percentages

| | Males | | | | Females | | | |
|---|---|---|---|---|---|---|---|---|
| | 16-24 | 25-44 | 45-64 | All aged 16-64 | 16-24 | 25-44 | 45-59 | All aged 16-59 |
| White | 78 | 94 | 78 | 85 | 70 | 78 | 71 | 74 |
| Black Caribbean | 77 | 89 | 65 | 80 | 63 | 78 | 72 | 75 |
| Black African | 50 | 84 | 77 | 76 | 40 | 65 | 71 | 61 |
| Other Black groups | 78 | 83 | .. | 81 | 59 | 72 | .. | 67 |
| Indian | 62 | 95 | 74 | 82 | 56 | 69 | 56 | 63 |
| Pakistani | 56 | 89 | 62 | 74 | 35 | 31 | 21 | 30 |
| Bangladeshi | 55 | 81 | 40 | 65 | 36 | .. | .. | 22 |
| Chinese | .. | 83 | 73 | 63 | .. | 63 | 64 | 57 |
| None of the above[3] | 55 | 86 | 79 | 76 | 50 | 56 | 65 | 57 |
| All ethnic groups[4] | 76 | 93 | 77 | 85 | 68 | 76 | 70 | 73 |

1 The percentage of the population that is in the labour force.
2 Combined quarters: Spring 1999 to Winter 1999-00.
3 Includes those of mixed origin.
4 Includes those who did not state their ethnic group.
**Source: Labour Force Survey, Office for National Statistics**

# 4.7

## Economic activity rates[1]: by gender, EU comparison, 1991 and 1999

Percentages

| | 1992 | | | 1999 | | |
|---|---|---|---|---|---|---|
| | Males | Females | All | Males | Females | All |
| Denmark | .. | .. | .. | 85.0 | 76.1 | 80.6 |
| Finland | .. | .. | .. | 78.9 | 73.9 | 76.4 |
| Sweden | .. | .. | .. | 78.8 | 74.0 | 76.4 |
| United Kingdom | 86.3 | 66.8 | 76.6 | 84.1 | 68.4 | 76.3 |
| Netherlands | 79.4 | 55.3 | 67.4 | 82.6 | 64.4 | 73.6 |
| Austria | .. | .. | .. | 80.5 | 62.7 | 71.6 |
| Germany | 80.9 | 61.1 | 71.1 | 79.3 | 62.9 | 71.2 |
| Portugal | 80.0 | 58.6 | 68.7 | 79.1 | 63.0 | 70.9 |
| France | 75.5 | 58.9 | 67.0 | 75.5 | 62.2 | 68.8 |
| Irish Republic | 76.4 | 43.4 | 60.0 | 78.3 | 54.4 | 66.4 |
| Belgium | 71.8 | 49.3 | 60.6 | 73.0 | 56.0 | 64.6 |
| Luxembourg | 77.6 | 47.5 | 62.8 | 75.7 | 50.2 | 63.1 |
| Greece | 76.2 | 41.7 | 58.3 | 76.9 | 49.7 | 62.9 |
| Spain | 76.0 | 41.8 | 58.7 | 76.2 | 48.5 | 62.1 |
| Italy | 74.0 | 42.0 | 57.8 | 73.7 | 45.6 | 59.6 |
| EU average | .. | .. | .. | 78.1 | 59.2 | 68.6 |

1 People aged 15 to 64, except for United Kingdom where data refer to those aged 16 to 64.
**Source: Labour Force Surveys, Eurostat**

# 4.8

## Economic activity status of women[1]: by marital status and age of youngest dependent child, Spring 2000

**United Kingdom**

Percentages

| | Age of youngest dependent child | | | | No dependent children | All[1] |
|---|---|---|---|---|---|---|
| | Under 5 | 5-10 | 11-15 | 16-18[2] | | |
| **Not married/cohabiting[3]** | | | | | | |
| Working full time | 11 | 18 | 32 | 51 | 46 | 39 |
| Working part time | 21 | 33 | 33 | 26 | 20 | 22 |
| Unemployed[4] | 8 | 8 | 7 | .. | 5 | 6 |
| Economically inactive | 60 | 41 | 28 | 20 | 28 | 32 |
| All (=100%)(millions) | 0.6 | 0.6 | 0.4 | 0.1 | 4.5 | 6.3 |
| **Married/cohabiting** | | | | | | |
| Working full time | 21 | 27 | 39 | 40 | 51 | 39 |
| Working part time | 39 | 49 | 40 | 38 | 25 | 34 |
| Unemployed[4] | 3 | 3 | 2 | .. | 2 | 2 |
| Economically inactive | 37 | 21 | 20 | 20 | 22 | 25 |
| All (=100%)(millions) | 2.4 | 1.7 | 1.2 | 0.4 | 5.3 | 11.0 |

1 Aged 16 to 59.
2 Those in full-time education.
3 Includes single, widowed, separated or divorced.
4 Based on the ILO definition. See Appendix, Part 4: ILO unemployment.
**Source: Labour Force Survey, Office for National Statistics**

The average economic activity rate among people aged 15 to 64 in the European Union in 1999 was 78 per cent for men and 59 per cent for women (Table 4.7). However, these averages mask a wide range of rates between countries, especially for women. In most of the southern European countries fewer than 50 per cent of women were active in the labour market – for example, 46 per cent in Italy and 48 per cent in Spain. In contrast, the Scandanavian countries showed the highest rates of economic activity among women – 76 per cent in Denmark and 74 per cent in both Finland and Sweden. Among men the rates varied within a rather narrower band, ranging from 73 per cent in Belgium to 85 per cent in Denmark.

Note that there is a wide range of factors underlying these comparisons: as well as economic cycle effects which will vary across countries for a given year, they will also be affected by population structures and differing retirement ages and participation in post-compulsory full-time education across countries. (See Table 1.4 on page 31 and Table 3.13 on page 65.)

One of the main themes already to emerge in this chapter is the increased labour market participation of women over the last decades. The labour market participation patterns of women without dependent children are now fairly similar whether they are married or cohabiting, or neither (Table 4.8).

However, the likelihood of women being economically active still varies considerably according to whether or not they have dependent children. Table 4.8 shows that for both lone mothers and for those with a partner, economic activity rates are lowest when they have a child under five. However, lone mothers with a pre-school child are half as likely to be working as mothers with a partner. This differential decreases with the age of the child, so that about three-quarters of women whose youngest child is aged 16 to 18 work, irrespective of marital status.

Not surprisingly, it is not only the age but also the number of dependent children which influences mothers' decisions about working. The larger their family, the less likely they are to work either full time or part time. The difference between lone mothers and those with a partner also persists, so that 75 per cent of lone mothers with four children or more were economically inactive in Spring 2000 compared with 54 per cent of mothers with a partner. For mothers with only one child, only 37 per cent of those without a partner, and 23 per cent of those with a partner, were economically inactive.

Overall, about 7.7 million people in the United Kingdom were classified as economically inactive in Spring 2000, about the same number as in 1995 (Table 4.9). These people are of working age, but for a variety of reasons are either not looking for paid work or not available to start work. The majority (70 per cent) do not want a job. We have already seen that looking after a family is a major factor in women's labour market participation and in fact this was the reason given by about half the women who said that they did not want a job. For men, long-term sickness or disability was the major reason given, and almost as many were students.

Table 4.9 shows that a further quarter of economically inactive people actually wanted a job, but had not actively sought one during the four weeks before interview. Over half of the men falling into this category were long-term sick or disabled, while around half of the women were looking after a family or home.

There is a small number of adults who have never had a paid job – nearly 2 million in the United Kingdom in Spring 2000 (1.2 million women and 0.7 million men). Around 43 per cent were in full-time education. Among those not in full-time education, 16 to 17 year olds were the least likely ever to have had a paid job with the proportions then increasing rapidly with age. However, the proportion of women who have never had a paid

**Reasons for economic inactivity[1]: by gender, 1995 and 2000**

United Kingdom                                                                                   Percentages

|  | 1995 | | | 2000 | | |
| --- | --- | --- | --- | --- | --- | --- |
|  | Males | Females | All | Males | Females | All |
| **Does not want a job** | | | | | | |
| Looking after family or home | 3 | 37 | 25 | 3 | 33 | 22 |
| Long-term sick or disabled | 28 | 13 | 18 | 25 | 14 | 18 |
| Student | 23 | 12 | 16 | 21 | 13 | 16 |
| Other | 16 | 9 | 12 | 19 | 10 | 14 |
| All | 70 | 71 | 71 | 68 | 71 | 70 |
| **Wants a job but not seeking in last four weeks** | | | | | | |
| Long-term sick or disabled | 11 | 4 | 7 | 16 | 6 | 10 |
| Looking after family or home | 2 | 14 | 10 | 2 | 12 | 8 |
| Student | 5 | 2 | 3 | 4 | 3 | 3 |
| Discouraged worker[2] | 2 | 1 | 1 | 1 | 1 | 1 |
| Other | 6 | 4 | 5 | 6 | 4 | 5 |
| All | 26 | 26 | 26 | 29 | 26 | 27 |
| **Wants a job and seeking work but not available to start[3]** | 5 | 3 | 4 | 3 | 3 | 3 |
| **All reasons** (=100%)(millions) | 2.8 | 5.0 | 7.8 | 3.0 | 4.8 | 7.7 |

1 At Spring each year. Males aged 16 to 64, females aged 16 to 59.
2 People who believed no jobs were available.
3 Not available for work in the next two weeks. Includes those who did not state whether or not they were available.
**Source: Labour Force Survey, Office for National Statistics**

job rises after the age of 60, reflecting the historical change in attitudes towards women working.

Disability has a considerable impact on an individual's labour market participation. Disabled people are nearly seven times as likely as non-disabled people to be out of work and claiming benefits. In Spring 2000 there were over 2.6 million disabled people out of work and on benefits: over a million of them wanted to work though many would not be able to start work straightaway due to health reasons. They are about twice as likely as non-disabled people to have no qualifications, a difference that is consistent across all age groups. Employment rates vary greatly between types of disability and are lowest for those with mental illness and learning disabilities.

# 4.10

**Proportion of working age households[1] where no-one is in employment**

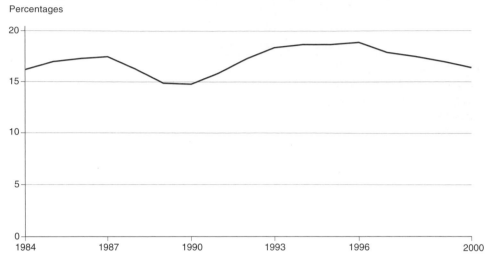

**United Kingdom**
Percentages

1984 1987 1990 1993 1996 2000

1 Households with at least one person of working age: males aged 16 to 64, females aged 16 to 59. Data for 1984 to 1991 are from individual datasets; data for 1992 to 2000 are from household datasets.
**Source: Labour Force Survey, Office for National Statistics**

Although there are now more people in the United Kingdom in employment than at any other time in the post-war period, there are still substantial numbers of workless households – that is, households where at least one person is of working age but no-one is in employment. Around 16 per cent of working age households were workless in Spring 2000, and although this proportion was virtually the same in 1984, during the early 1990s it rose to reach nearly 19 per cent in 1996 (Chart 4.10). These estimates are derived from the Labour Force Survey. Other research into longer run trends, based on the Family Expenditure Survey and thus not strictly comparable, appears to suggest that the fastest rise in workless households took place in the mid-1970s and early 1980s, and that rates were well below 10 per cent in the mid-1970s. Workless households as a proportion of all households rose over the period, as did the proportion of households with every adult member in work. Although a trend towards smaller households, and in particular one person households, will explain some of this change, there have been increases in workless households in all family types.

# 4.11

**Employee jobs[1]: by gender and industry**

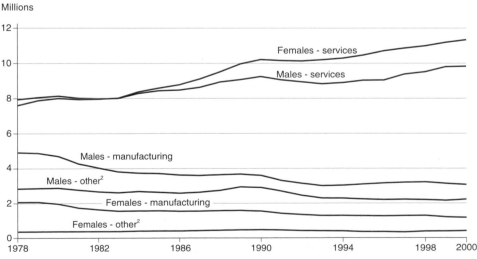

**United Kingdom**
Millions

Females - services
Males - services
Males - manufacturing
Males - other[2]
Females - manufacturing
Females - other[2]

1978 1982 1986 1990 1994 1998 2000

1 At June each year.
2 Includes agriculture, construction, energy and water.
**Source: Office for National Statistics**

## Patterns of employment

It is well-known that the UK economy has experienced structural change in the post-war period, with a decline in the manufacturing sector and an increase in service industries. Chart 4.11 illustrates the impact which this change has had on the labour market. Jobs in the service industries have increased by 36 per cent, from 15.6 million in 1978 to 21.2 million in 2000, while those in manufacturing have fallen by 39 per cent from 7.0 million to 4.2 million over the same period. Virtually all the increase in women's labour market participation has been through taking up jobs in the service sector. The total number of jobs done by men is now 15.1 million, compared with

# 4.12

13.0 million by women. Note that this chart is based on jobs rather than people – one person may have more than one job, and jobs may vary in the number of hours' work they involve.

The most common occupations among women employees continue to be in the clerical and secretarial sphere, followed by personal and protective services (Table 4.12). For men there was a fall of 4 percentage points between 1991 and 2000 in those working in craft and related occupations, again reflecting the decline in manufacturing industry. The proportion of male managers and administrators is nearly twice that of women, and these occupations have increased slightly in popularity since 1991: among both men and women the proportions rose by 3 percentage points between 1991 and 2000.

It is not only those employees whose occupation is as a manager or an administrator who have managerial responsibilities. The Labour Force Survey asks employees to allocate themselves to one of three groups: 'manager' – those who manage employees directly or through supervisors and have a general responsibility for policy or long-term planning; 'foremen and supervisors' – those who have day-to-day control over a group of workers whom they supervise; and those who fall into neither category. It is important to remember that those without managerial responsibility are not necessarily in low status jobs: for example, many professional people such as doctors and lawyers will be in this category.

Around 35 per cent of male employees and 25 per cent of females have some managerial or supervisory responsibility (Table 4.13). White men are more likely than those from the main ethnic minority groups to be managers, with Pakistani/Bangladeshi and Black men least likely (12 per cent and 13 per cent respectively).

**Employees[1]: by gender and occupation, 1991 and 2000**

United Kingdom        Percentages

| | Males | | Females | |
|---|---|---|---|---|
| | 1991 | 2000 | 1991 | 2000 |
| Managers and administrators | 16 | 19 | 8 | 11 |
| Professional | 10 | 12 | 8 | 10 |
| Associate professional and technical | 8 | 9 | 10 | 11 |
| Clerical and secretarial | 8 | 8 | 29 | 25 |
| Craft and related | 21 | 17 | 4 | 2 |
| Personal and protective services | 7 | 8 | 14 | 17 |
| Selling | 6 | 6 | 12 | 12 |
| Plant and machine operatives | 15 | 14 | 5 | 4 |
| Other occupations | 8 | 8 | 10 | 8 |
| All employees[2] (=100%)(millions) | 11.8 | 12.8 | 10.1 | 11.0 |

1 At Spring each year. Males aged 16 to 64, females aged 16 to 59.
2 Includes a few people who did not state their occupation. Percentages are based on totals which exclude this group.
**Source: Labour Force Survey, Office for National Statistics**

# 4.13

**Managerial responsibility of employees: by gender and ethnic group, Spring 2000**

Great Britain        Percentages

| | White | Black | Indian | Pakistani/ Bangla- deshi | Other | All employees |
|---|---|---|---|---|---|---|
| **Males** | | | | | | |
| Managers | 23 | 13 | 17 | 12 | 21 | 23 |
| Foremen and supervisors | 12 | 11 | 8 | .. | 11 | 12 |
| Not managers, foremen or supervisors | 65 | 76 | 75 | 81 | 68 | 65 |
| All employees (=100%)(millions) | 12.0 | 0.2 | 0.2 | 0.1 | 0.1 | 12.6 |
| **Females** | | | | | | |
| Managers | 14 | 12 | 10 | .. | 12 | 14 |
| Foremen and supervisors | 11 | 14 | 13 | .. | 13 | 11 |
| Not managers, foremen or supervisors | 74 | 75 | 77 | 82 | 76 | 74 |
| All employees (=100%)(millions) | 10.7 | 0.2 | 0.2 | 0.1 | 0.1 | 11.2 |

**Source: Labour Force Survey, Office for National Statistics**

# 4.14

### Self-employment: by gender and industry, 1991 and 2000[1]

| United Kingdom | | | | | | Percentages |
| --- | --- | --- | --- | --- | --- | --- |
| | 1991 | | | 2000 | | |
| | Males | Females | All | Males | Females | All |
| Construction | 29 | 2 | 22 | 27 | 1 | 20 |
| Distribution, hotels and restaurants | 21 | 29 | 23 | 18 | 21 | 19 |
| Banking, finance and insurance | 14 | 13 | 14 | 19 | 18 | 19 |
| Public administration, education and health | 4 | 14 | 6 | 5 | 22 | 10 |
| Manufacturing | 11 | 10 | 11 | 7 | 7 | 7 |
| Transport and communication | 6 | 2 | 5 | 8 | 3 | 7 |
| Agriculture and fishing | 10 | 7 | 9 | 7 | 4 | 6 |
| Other services | 5 | 22 | 9 | 9 | 23 | 13 |
| All industries[2] (=100%)(millions) | 2.6 | 0.8 | 3.4 | 2.3 | 0.8 | 3.1 |

1 At Spring each year.
2 Includes those in energy and water supply industries for which figures are not shown separately because of the small sample sizes. Also includes those who did not state industry and those whose workplace was outside the United Kingdom, but percentages are based on totals which exclude these groups.

**Source: Labour Force Survey, Office for National Statistics**

# 4.15

### Employees and self-employed in information technology occupations: by region of workplace, Spring 2000

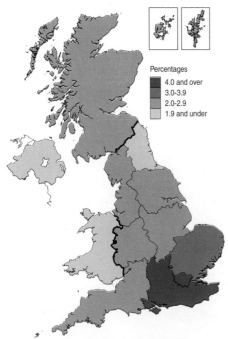

Percentages
- 4.0 and over
- 3.0-3.9
- 2.0-2.9
- 1.9 and under

*Source: Labour Force Survey, Office for National Statistics*

Although the last two items looked at the pattern of employment among employees only, the self-employed of course also form an important part of the labour force. Around 3.1 million people were self-employed in the United Kingdom in Spring 2000 (Table 4.14), representing 11 per cent of all in employment. This proportion has fluctuated between 11 and 13 per cent since 1984, though because of the increase in employment overall there were only 2.7 million self-employed people in 1984. Self-employment is much more common among men than among women – 15 per cent of men in employment were self-employed in Spring 2000 compared with 7 per cent of women in employment.

Men and women also vary considerably in the type of self-employed work they undertake. More than a quarter of self-employed men work in the construction industry but very few women do so. On the other hand, 23 per cent of self-employed women work in 'other services' – for example community, social and personal services – and a further 22 per cent are in public administration, education and health, areas where self-employed

men are comparatively under-represented. The biggest changes over the last 10 years in the type of self-employed work undertaken were the increase in the proportion of women in the public administration, education and health sector, which accounted for only 14 per cent of self-employed women in 1991, and a corresponding fall in the proportion working in distribution, hotels and restaurants.

There is a small group of people who work in an unpaid capacity for a business that either they or a relative own, known as unpaid family workers. On average, 109 thousand people were in this category in Spring 2000. A third of them worked in the distribution, hotels and restaurants sector. However, it is agriculture and fishing which has by far the highest rate of unpaid family workers at 42 per 1,000 people employed, with distribution, hotels and restaurants some way behind at only 76 per 1,000.

Although it is not possible to identify from the Labour Force Survey the number of people using computers in their work, it is possible to measure the numbers employed in the occupations most closely linked to Information Technology (IT) (see Appendix, Part 4: IT occupations). In Spring 2000, there were 855 thousand people employed in IT-related occupations in the United Kingdom, an increase of 45 per cent in only five years. The region with the highest proportion of employed people working in IT was London, at 4.8 per cent, followed by the South East with 4.4 per cent (Chart 4.15). Together, these regions accounted for 41 per cent of all those working in IT in the United Kingdom. Northern Ireland, Wales and the North East all had low proportions working in IT, at 1.3 per cent, 1.6 per cent and 1.9 per cent respectively.

In Spring 2000 around 0.7 million people in the United Kingdom were homeworkers – that is, they worked mainly in their own home – a number which was unchanged compared with 1996. Most

# 4.16

(0.5 million) were women. Homeworking was most common among women in personal and protective services, professional and craft and related occupations (Table 4.16). Most of those in personal and protective services were working in childcare and related occupations.

Many homeworkers could not do so unless they used both a telephone and a computer. These people are often known as teleworkers and there were almost a third of a million of them in Spring 2000. Just under half worked part time, and slightly more than half were women. A further 0.8 million teleworkers worked in various locations using home as a base, and 0.5 million people were occasional teleworkers. Nearly nine out of ten of the latter group were working in the management, professional and technical occupations.

Table 4.2 above showed that there were 5.7 million employees of working age working part time in the United Kingdom in Spring 2000, of whom 4.7 million were women. However, to distinguish only between 'part time' and 'full time' masks a wide variety of patterns of working hours which people experience. Chart 4.17 therefore shows the distribution of usual weekly hours of work, including regular paid and unpaid overtime, for both men and women in Spring 2000.

The most common length of working week for men was 40 hours followed by 60 hours and over; for women the most common length was only slightly shorter at 38 hours, and the second most common was 40 hours. Men were more likely than women to work in excess of 60 hours per week – nearly 1.5 million did so. However, note that there is a tendency for LFS respondents' reported hours to be bunched around five hour marks and so the distribution of hours worked has to be treated with some caution.

### Homeworking[1]: by occupation and gender, 1996 and 2000[2]

**United Kingdom**          Percentages

|  | 1996 | | | 2000 | | |
|---|---|---|---|---|---|---|
|  | Males | Females | All | Males | Females | All |
| Managers and administrators | 1 | 4 | 3 | 2 | 4 | 2 |
| Professional | 2 | 7 | 4 | 2 | 5 | 3 |
| Associate professional and technical | 2 | 2 | 2 | 3 | 2 | 3 |
| Clerical and secretarial | 4 | 5 | 5 | 5 | 4 | 4 |
| Craft and related | 1 | 5 | 4 | .. | 5 | 4 |
| Personal and protective | .. | 8 | 1 | 0 | 8 | 1 |
| Sales | .. | 5 | 3 | .. | 4 | 3 |
| Plant and machine operatives | 2 | .. | 1 | .. | 1 | 1 |
| All occupations[3] | 1 | 4 | 3 | 2 | 4 | 2 |

1 Percentage of those in employment in each occupation who were homeworkers excluding those on government training and employment schemes. Homeworkers covers those who work mainly in their own home but excludes those who work in the same grounds or buildings as their home, those who work in different places using their home as a base and those who sometimes do work at home.
2 At Spring each year.
3 Includes those with other occupations and those who did not state their occupation.
**Source: Labour Force Survey, Office for National Statistics**

# 4.17

### Distribution of usual weekly hours of work: by gender, Spring 2000

**United Kingdom**

Thousands

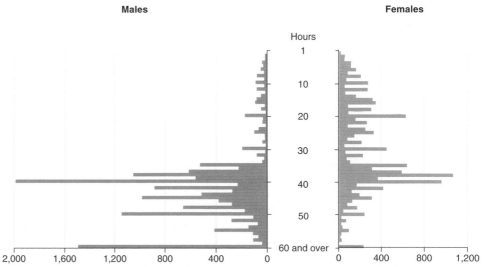

**Source: Labour Force Survey, Office for National Statistics**

# 4.18

**Average hours usually worked[1] per week by full-time employees: by gender, EU comparison, 1999**

| | | Hours |
|---|---|---|
| | Males | Females |
| United Kingdom | 45.2 | 40.7 |
| Greece[2] | 41.7 | 39.3 |
| Portugal | 41.5 | 39.4 |
| Irish Republic | 41.3 | 38.0 |
| Spain | 41.1 | 39.6 |
| Germany | 40.5 | 39.4 |
| Luxembourg | 40.5 | 38.0 |
| Austria | 40.3 | 39.9 |
| Sweden | 40.2 | 39.9 |
| France | 40.2 | 38.6 |
| Finland | 40.1 | 38.3 |
| Italy | 39.7 | 36.3 |
| Denmark | 39.6 | 37.9 |
| Netherlands | 39.2 | 38.3 |
| Belgium | 39.1 | 36.9 |
| EU average | 41.2 | 39.0 |

1 In main job; excludes meal breaks but includes regularly worked paid and unpaid overtime.
2 Data are for 1998.

**Source: Labour Force Surveys, Eurostat**

# 4.19

**Usual time taken to travel to work[1]: by gender, Autumn 1999**

**United Kingdom**

| | Males | | Females | | |
|---|---|---|---|---|---|
| | Full time | Part time | Full time | Part time | |
| 10 minutes or less | 22 | 32 | 27 | 41 | |
| Between 11 and 20 minutes | 23 | 22 | 26 | 26 | |
| Between 21 and 30 minutes | 16 | 10 | 17 | 11 | |
| Between 31 and 40 minutes | 5 | 2 | 5 | 2 | |
| Between 41 and 50 minutes | 6 | 3 | 6 | 3 | |
| Between 51 minutes and one hour | 5 | 3 | 5 | 2 | |
| More than one hour | 5 | 2 | 3 | 1 | |
| All in employment (=100%)(millions) | 13.9 | 1.3 | 6.9 | 5.4 | |

*Percentages*

1 Employees and self-employed working at a place separate from their home.

**Source: Labour Force Survey, Office for National Statistics**

The chart clearly illustrates that women are more likely to work part time than men, but it also shows the wide range of working hours which they undertake. Nearly 2 million women worked 15 hours or fewer, and a further 1.4 million worked between 16 and 20 hours.

Compared with the rest of the EU, full-time employees in the United Kingdom work on average the longest hours per week in their main job and this holds for both men and women (Table 4.18). Men's hours range from 39 per week in Belgium and the Netherlands to 42 in Greece and 45 in the United Kingdom. Women's hours all fall in the range 36 hours (Italy) to 41 hours (United Kingdom).

For some people, the time taken to travel to and from their work can add significantly to the length of their working day. On average, the time taken to travel to work in Autumn 1999 was 25 minutes, but underlying this is a wide range of journey times (Table 4.19). People working part time tended to have shorter journey times than those working full time, and women tended to have shorter journey times than men irrespective of their hours of work. The most significant regional difference in time taken to travel to work was between those who work in London compared with those in other regions. Employees and self-employed whose jobs were in central London took, on average, 56 minutes to get to work.

## Unemployment

The number of people unemployed is linked to the economic cycle, albeit with a time lag. Broadly speaking, as the country experiences economic growth so the number of jobs grows and unemployment falls, though any mismatches between the skill needs of the new jobs and the skills of those available for work may slow this process. Conversely as the economy slows and goes into recession, so unemployment tends to rise. The latest peak in unemployment occurred in 1993, when it reached just under 3 million (Chart 4.20). This recession had a much greater effect on unemployment among men than among women. Since then, the number of people unemployed has fallen to 1.6 million in Spring 2000, a rate of 5.5 per cent.

The ILO measure of unemployment shown in Chart 4.20 is based on Labour Force Survey estimates of the number of people without a job who are seeking work (see Glossary on page 74). It is based on internationally agreed definitions and is the ONS measure of unemployment. An alternative indicator of unemployment is available, known as the claimant count. This is a count of the number of people claiming unemployment-

# 4.20

related benefits and national insurance credits. It differs from the ILO measure in that not all those without a job are eligible to receive benefits, and some of those receiving benefits may not be immediately available for work. A key strength of the claimant count is that it can provide small area estimates at a lower level of geographic disaggregation than is possible from the LFS.

The ILO and claimant measures both tend to move in the same direction. In times of economic downturn, the claimant count tends to rise faster than the ILO measure so that at the trough of the last recession in 1993 the two measures were very close together. However, in times of economic upturn the claimant count tends to fall faster than the ILO measure. This is because economically inactive people become more optimistic about their employment prospects, start looking for work and hence become ILO unemployed.

Unemployment is not equally distributed across the UK labour force. Age, qualifications, gender, ethnicity and location all have an impact on the likelihood of becoming unemployed and on the time people spend out of work.

Young people are much more likely than older people to be unemployed, and men are more likely to be unemployed than women. In Spring 2000, 20 per cent of economically active 16 to 17 year old men were unemployed, as were 17 per cent of economically active women in the same age group, compared with only 6 per cent of men and 3 per cent of women within five years of state pension age (Table 4.21). Over the last ten years, the gap between the unemployment rates for 16 and 17 year olds and the rates for other age groups has widened for both men and women.

## Unemployment[1]: by gender

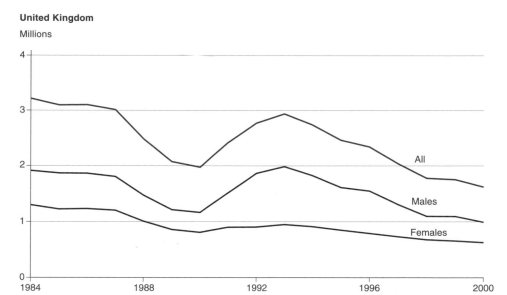

**United Kingdom**
Millions

1 At Spring each year. Unemployment based on the ILO definition. See Appendix, Part 4: ILO unemployment.
*Source: Labour Force Survey, Office for National Statistics*

# 4.21

## Unemployment rates[1]: by gender and age

**United Kingdom**                                                                                          Percentages

|  | 1991 | 1992 | 1993 | 1994 | 1995 | 1996 | 1997 | 1998 | 1999 | 2000 |
|---|---|---|---|---|---|---|---|---|---|---|
| **Males** | | | | | | | | | | |
| 16-17 | 15.4 | 17.7 | 18.5 | 18.8 | 19.2 | 21.3 | 19.4 | 18.1 | 21.5 | 20.1 |
| 18-24 | 15.7 | 19.0 | 21.1 | 19.3 | 17.7 | 17.2 | 14.8 | 13.1 | 12.6 | 11.8 |
| 25-44 | 8.0 | 10.5 | 10.9 | 10.2 | 8.9 | 8.7 | 6.9 | 5.7 | 5.6 | 4.8 |
| 45-54 | 6.3 | 8.4 | 9.4 | 8.6 | 7.5 | 6.4 | 6.1 | 4.7 | 4.9 | 4.8 |
| 55-59 | 8.4 | 11.2 | 12.3 | 11.6 | 10.3 | 9.8 | 8.0 | 6.7 | 6.4 | 5.4 |
| 60-64 | 9.9 | 10.2 | 14.2 | 11.6 | 9.9 | 8.9 | 7.6 | 6.9 | 6.4 | 5.8 |
| 65 and over | 5.9 | 4.9 | 4.6 | 3.7 | .. | 4.0 | 4.1 | .. | .. | .. |
| All aged 16 and over | 9.2 | 11.5 | 12.4 | 11.4 | 10.1 | 9.6 | 8.1 | 6.8 | 6.7 | 6.1 |
| **Females** | | | | | | | | | | |
| 16-17 | 14.3 | 14.0 | 15.1 | 16.9 | 15.5 | 15.3 | 16.0 | 15.3 | 14.0 | 16.9 |
| 18-24 | 10.5 | 11.0 | 12.9 | 11.8 | 11.6 | 10.2 | 9.8 | 9.4 | 9.3 | 8.5 |
| 25-44 | 7.1 | 7.3 | 7.3 | 7.0 | 6.7 | 6.3 | 5.4 | 5.1 | 4.8 | 4.5 |
| 45-54 | 4.6 | 5.0 | 5.0 | 5.0 | 4.5 | 4.1 | 3.7 | 3.1 | 3.2 | 2.9 |
| 55-59 | 5.5 | 4.5 | 6.0 | 6.5 | 4.7 | 4.3 | 4.8 | 3.5 | 3.5 | 3.1 |
| 60 and over | 4.4 | 3.1 | 3.9 | 2.9 | .. | .. | 2.1 | 2.0 | 1.9 | .. |
| All aged 16 and over | 7.2 | 7.3 | 7.6 | 7.3 | 6.8 | 6.3 | 5.7 | 5.3 | 5.1 | 4.8 |

1 At Spring each year. Unemployment based on the ILO definition as a percentage of all economically active. See Appendix, Part 4: ILO unemployment.
*Source: Labour Force Survey, Office for National Statistics*

# 4.22

### Unemployment rates[1]: by age, EU comparison, 1999

Percentages

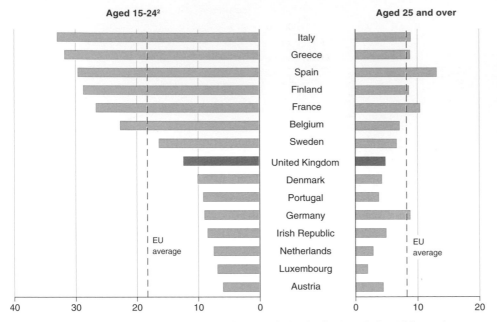

Aged 15-24[2]      Aged 25 and over

1 Unemployment based on the ILO definition as a percentage of all economically active. See Appendix, Part 4: ILO unemployment.
2 Data for United Kingdom refer to those aged 16 to 24.

**Source: Labour Force Surveys, Eurostat**

In April 1998 the Government introduced the New Deal for Young Unemployed people as part of its Welfare to Work strategy. The aim of the scheme is to help young people who have been unemployed and claiming jobseeker's allowance for six months or more to find work and to improve their longer-term employability. The impact of this scheme is discussed in the next section on Labour market dynamics.

Youth unemployment is a feature of the economies of all the countries of the European Union. The EU average unemployment rate for young people aged 15/16 to 24 was 18.3 per cent in 1999 compared with 8.2 per cent for those aged 25 and over. Chart 4.22 shows that Italy had the highest youth unemployment rate (32.9 per cent) and Austria the lowest (5.9 per cent). Among those aged 25 and over Luxembourg had the lowest unemployment rate (2.0 per cent) and

# 4.23

### Duration of unemployment[1]: by gender and age, Spring 2000

**United Kingdom**      Percentages

| | Less than three months | Three months but less than six months | Six months but less than one year | One year but less than two years | Two years but less than three years | Three years or more | All durations |
|---|---|---|---|---|---|---|---|
| **Males** | | | | | | | |
| 16-19 | 48 | 21 | 18 | 9 | .. | .. | 100 |
| 20-29 | 37 | 21 | 14 | 14 | 6 | 8 | 100 |
| 30-39 | 26 | 19 | 13 | 15 | 5 | 21 | 100 |
| 40-49 | 29 | 16 | 14 | 15 | .. | 20 | 100 |
| 50-64 | 24 | 15 | 15 | 16 | 6 | 24 | 100 |
| | | | | | | | |
| All aged 16 and over[2] | 33 | 19 | 15 | 14 | 5 | 15 | 100 |
| **Females** | | | | | | | |
| 16-19 | 52 | 23 | 17 | .. | .. | .. | 100 |
| 20-29 | 53 | 19 | 15 | 7 | .. | .. | 100 |
| 30-39 | 41 | 17 | 18 | 12 | .. | .. | 100 |
| 40-49 | 36 | 23 | 16 | 12 | .. | .. | 100 |
| 50-59 | 34 | 17 | 18 | .. | .. | .. | 100 |
| | | | | | | | |
| All aged 16 and over[2] | 44 | 20 | 17 | 10 | 4 | 5 | 100 |

1 Excludes those who did not state their duration of unemployment. Unemployment is based on the ILO definition. See Appendix, Part 4: ILO unemployment.
2 Includes males aged 65 and over and females aged 60 and over.

**Source: Labour Force Survey, Office for National Statistics**

Spain the highest (13.2 per cent). However, comparisons between countries at a point in time are affected by the fact that they are not all at the same point in the economic cycle, and so do not necessarily reflect the underlying nature of their labour markets.

Age and gender also influence the length of time that people spend unemployed. Young unemployed people are less likely to have been so for a long period compared with older people, and women are less likely than men to have been unemployed for a long period (Table 4.23). In Spring 2000, over half of unemployed women aged between 16 and 29 had been out of work for less than three months, and less than one in ten had been unemployed for a year or more. However, around a fifth of unemployed men in their thirties and forties had been unemployed for three years or more and this rose to nearly a quarter among those aged 50 to 64.

Qualifications also have an important influence on the likelihood of unemployment. Table 4.24 shows that those with no qualifications are the most likely to be unemployed, particularly among men, and those with the highest qualifications are the least likely. Over one in ten of people of working age who reported having no qualifications were unemployed on the ILO measure in Spring 2000.

A further factor underlying patterns of unemployment is location. In Spring 2000, rates within England were lowest in the South East (3.3 per cent) and in the East (3.6 per cent) and highest in the North East and London, 9.1 per cent and 7.0 per cent respectively (Chart 4.25). Rates were also high in Scotland (7.6 per cent) and Northern Ireland (7.0 per cent).

## 4.24

**Unemployment rates[1]: by highest qualification and gender, Spring 2000**

| United Kingdom | | | | | | Percentages |
|---|---|---|---|---|---|---|
| | Above A level | GCE A level or equivalent | GCSE grades A* to C or equivalent | Other | None | All[2] |
| Males | 2.5 | 4.5 | 7.5 | 8.6 | 13.7 | 6.1 |
| Females | 2.2 | 4.5 | 5.4 | 6.6 | 8.2 | 4.9 |
| All | 2.4 | 4.5 | 6.3 | 7.7 | 11.1 | 5.6 |

1 People of working age: males aged 16 to 64, females aged 16 to 59. Unemployment based on the ILO definition. See Appendix, Part 4: ILO unemployment.
2 Includes those who did not state their highest qualification.
**Source: Labour Force Survey, Office for National Statistics**

## 4.25

**Unemployment rates[1]: by region, Spring 2000**

Percentages

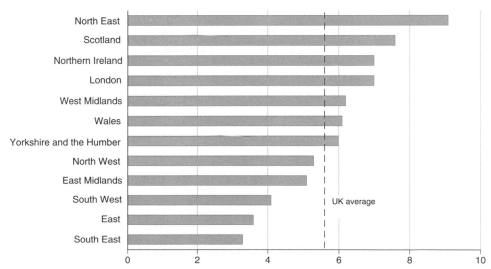

1 Unemployment based on the ILO definition as a percentage of all economically active. See Appendix, Part 4: ILO unemployment.
**Source: Labour Force Survey, Office for National Statistics**

# 4.26

## Length of service of employees[1]

United Kingdom | | | | Percentages

| | 1986 | 1991 | 1996 | 2000 |
|---|---|---|---|---|
| Less than three months | 5 | 5 | 5 | 5 |
| Three months but less than six months | 4 | 4 | 5 | 5 |
| Six months but less than one year | 9 | 10 | 9 | 10 |
| One year but less than two years | 11 | 13 | 12 | 13 |
| Two years but less than five years | 20 | 24 | 19 | 21 |
| Five years but less than ten years | 21 | 16 | 21 | 15 |
| Ten years but less than twenty years | 20 | 19 | 19 | 20 |
| Twenty years or more | 9 | 9 | 11 | 11 |
| All employees[2] (=100%)(millions) | 20.8 | 21.9 | 22.1 | 23.8 |

1 At Spring each year; males aged 16 to 64, females aged 16 to 59.
2 Includes those who did not state length of time in current employment, but percentages are based on totals that exclude this group.

**Source: Labour Force Survey, Office for National Statistics**

# 4.27

## Routes to unemployment[1]: by gender, Spring 2000

United Kingdom | | | Percentages

| | Males | Females | All |
|---|---|---|---|
| **Working** | | | |
| Made redundant | 21 | 9 | 16 |
| Temporary job came to an end | 13 | 6 | 10 |
| Resigned | 7 | 6 | 7 |
| Dismissed | 4 | 2 | 3 |
| Family or personal reasons | 2 | 3 | 2 |
| Health reasons | 2 | .. | 2 |
| Retired | .. | .. | .. |
| Other reason | 8 | 4 | 6 |
| All previously in work[2] | 62 | 33 | 51 |
| **In full-time education or training** | | | |
| **or on a scheme** | 19 | 18 | 19 |
| **Looking after family or home** | 5 | 39 | 18 |
| **Doing something else** | 14 | 9 | 12 |
| **All routes[3] (=100%)(millions)** | 1.0 | 0.6 | 1.6 |

1 Males aged 16 to 64, females aged 16 to 59. Unemployment based on the ILO definition. See Appendix, Part 4: ILO unemployment.
2 Immediately before job search began. Includes people who left their last job more than eight years ago who were not asked why they left, and those who did not give a reason.
3 Includes a small number of people who did not state what they were doing before they became unemployed. Percentages are based on totals which exclude this group.

**Source: Labour Force Survey, Office for National Statistics**

## Labour market dynamics

Information about the labour market experiences of individuals over the course of their working lives complements the sort of 'snap-shots' which other sections in this chapter provide. It enables us to build up a dynamic, as opposed to static, picture.

Table 4.26 gives some indication of how long people stay in a job. In Spring 2000, one in ten employees of working age had been in their current job for less than six months, but a similar proportion had been in the same job for 20 years or more. Most people – four out of five – had been in the same job for a year or more, and this proportion changed little between the years shown in the table. Although in 1986 unemployment was almost twice as high as in 2000 (see Chart 4.20 above), the proportion of people who had been in their job for more than a year was virtually the same.

Research using the Labour Force Survey by Paul Gregg and Jonathan Wadsworth (published in *The State of Working Britain*) indicates that in the late 1990s, typically when someone started a new job, it lasted about 15 months, but that the average job in progress lasted around 5.5 years. This is because most employees eventually find a long-term job match. Average job tenure has remained relatively stable since 1975. However, this masks sharp contrasts across gender. Job tenure has risen among women with children, partly as a result of the increased provision and use of maternity leave. However, it has fallen for men and for women without dependent children. The largest fall in job tenure has been among men aged 50 and over.

People may become unemployed via a number of routes. They may lose a job and not be able to find another one immediately, or they may move from being economically inactive – for example from looking after a family or from being a student – and spend a period of time looking for a job. In

# 4.28

### Redundancy rates[1]: by broad industry group

| United Kingdom | | | Rates per 1,000 employees |  |
|---|---|---|---|---|
|  | Manuf- acturing | Serv- ices | Other | All |
| 1992 | 15 | 8 | 26 | 11 |
| 1993 | 14 | 7 | 15 | 9 |
| 1994 | 11 | 6 | 16 | 7 |
| 1995 | 10 | 7 | 13 | 8 |
| 1996 | 11 | 6 | 19 | 8 |
| 1997 | 10 | 6 | 18 | 7 |
| 1998 | 12 | 6 | 10 | 7 |
| 1999 | 16 | 5 | 17 | 8 |
| 2000 | 16 | 5 | 11 | 7 |

*1 At Spring each year. Redundancy rates prior to Spring 1995 calculated using number of employees in current quarter. Rates from Spring 1995 onwards calculated using number of employees in previous quarter.*

**Source: Labour Force Survey, Office for National Statistics**

Spring 2000, half of those unemployed had been in work immediately before becoming unemployed and half had been economically inactive (Table 4.27). However, women were less likely than men to have been working immediately before becoming unemployed: two out of five unemployed women had been looking after their family or home before their job search began.

About one in six unemployed people had lost their job through being made redundant. Redundancies are of considerable interest as part of labour market dynamics: a change in the level or rate of redundancies is interpreted differently according to the situation of the labour market as a whole. For example, a rise in redundancy may reflect a general economic slow-down if it is associated with a net fall in total employment. Otherwise it may indicate a change in the structure of the economy, such as a switch in employment between a declining industrial sector to a growing one.

In Spring 2000 the rate of redundancies per thousand employees was highest in the manufacturing sector (16 per 1,000 employees) and lowest in the services sector (5 per 1,000 employees) (Table 4.28). Overall, the redundancy rate fell in the early 1990s but has remained fairly stable since 1994. However, the trends are somewhat different for the main industrial groups. By far the highest redundancy rates in 1992 were in the 'other' sector which includes the construction industry where the rate was 30 per 1,000 employees. Redundancy rates in the services sector have gradually fallen over the period. People in the craft and related occupations and plant and machine operatives experienced the highest redundancy rates throughout the period averaging 15 and 13 per 1,000 employees respectively.

Most people move from being unemployed into work. Table 4.29 shows the destination of those ceasing to claim unemployment-related benefits whose destination is known: in 1999-00 more than half of each age and gender group shown found work, either full time or part time. For young men and young women under 25, the next most likely destination was some type of training. In contrast, people over the age of 54 were more likely to begin claiming incapacity benefit or another benefit instead, though a significant minority ceased claiming because they moved abroad.

Participation in the Government's New Deal scheme is mandatory for 18 to 24 year olds who have claimed jobseeker's allowance continuously for six months. First there is a Gateway period which includes intensive careers advice and guidance and help with job search skills. The aim is to find unsubsidised jobs for as many as possible. Those who do not find a job then move onto one of four options: subsidised employment;

# 4.29

### Destination of leavers from the claimant count: by gender and age, 1999-00[1]

| United Kingdom | | | | | | Percentages |
|---|---|---|---|---|---|---|
|  | Males | | | Females | | |
|  | 16-24 | 25-54 | 55-64 | 16-24 | 25-54 | 55-59 |
| Found work | 68.9 | 72.6 | 55.5 | 64.5 | 69.2 | 51.9 |
| Full-time education | 2.3 | 0.6 | 0.1 | 3.3 | 0.8 | 0.1 |
| Transferred to government supported training/other training[2] | 14.4 | 7.8 | 4.5 | 10.4 | 6.0 | 4.2 |
| Claimed incapacity benefit | 3.7 | 6.9 | 10.3 | 4.1 | 6.8 | 12.3 |
| Claimed other benefit | 1.7 | 3.4 | 10.1 | 8.0 | 5.5 | 6.2 |
| Gone abroad | 3.3 | 4.7 | 8.0 | 4.7 | 7.0 | 11.2 |
| Automatic credits | . | . | 4.2 | . | . | 0.1 |
| Claim withdrawal | 3.6 | 3.1 | 5.1 | 4.2 | 4.4 | 6.8 |
| Other[3] | 2.2 | 0.9 | 2.2 | 0.8 | 0.2 | 7.1 |
| All leavers with known destination[4] (=100%)(thousands) | 508 | 1,024 | 133 | 264 | 381 | 43 |
| All leavers[5] (thousands) | 766 | 1,333 | 158 | 374 | 484 | 52 |

*1 People who left the claimant count between 8 July 1999 and 12 July 2000 inclusive.*
*2 Includes New Deal.*
*3 Includes those deceased, reached state pension age, were attending court, or gone to prison.*
*4 Excludes claimants who failed to sign and leavers whose destination is not known.*
*5 Includes claimants who failed to sign and leavers whose destination is not known.*

**Source: Office for National Statistics**

# 4.30

### People entering employment through the New Deal: by age and type of employment, January 1998 to July 2000

| Great Britain | | | Percentages |
|---|---|---|---|
| | 18-24 | 25 and over | All aged 18 and over |
| **Sustained employment** | | | |
| Unsubsidised | 66 | 66 | 66 |
| Subsidised | 11 | 19 | 12 |
| All | 76 | 85 | 78 |
| **Other employment** | | | |
| Unsubsidised | 22 | 14 | 21 |
| Subsidised | 2 | 1 | 2 |
| All | 24 | 15 | 22 |
| All entering employment (=100%)(thousands) | 237 | 51 | 288 |
| Those entering sustained employment as a percentage of all leavers | 40 | 16 | 32 |

*Source: Employment Service*

work experience with a voluntary organisation or on an environmental task force, both with training; or full-time education. For those reaching the end of their option without keeping or finding work, there is a follow-through period of support and further training if needed.

Of those young people aged 18 to 24 in Great Britain leaving the New Deal during the period January 1998 to July 2000, 40 per cent entered employment (Table 4.30). The National Institute for Economic and Social Research has estimated that the programme has reduced youth unemployment by approximately 30 thousand relative to what it otherwise would have been. This is equivalent to a reduction in youth long-term unemployment of nearly 40 per cent.

Among those aged 25 and over leaving the New Deal programme, a much lower proportion moved into employment – only 16 per cent – though the employment they find is more likely to be sustained.

## Working lives

Most people spend a large proportion of their lives at work. The quality of their working lives therefore has a major influence on their well-being more generally.

Any job is made up of a wide range of different characteristics. However, they can be divided into two main groups: those which are agreed parts of the contract between employer and employee such as financial rewards, working time, job security and opportunities for advancement; and those aspects which tend not to be written down but are nevertheless essential in making the employer/employee relationship work, for example the interest the worker finds in their job, relationships with others in the workplace, the pace of work and so on. All these aspects will play a part in how an employee views their job, but because each person will value each aspect differently, it is virtually impossible to devise an objective measure of 'job quality'.

# 4.31

### Employee job satisfaction[1]: by gender, 1998

| Great Britain | | | | | Percentages |
|---|---|---|---|---|---|
| | Males | | Females | | |
| | Full time | Part time | Full time | Part time | All employees |
| Very satisfied | 7 | 10 | 7 | 9 | 7 |
| Satisfied | 42 | 50 | 49 | 54 | 47 |
| Neither satisfied nor dissatisfied | 28 | 26 | 28 | 25 | 27 |
| Dissatisfied | 20 | 12 | 14 | 10 | 16 |
| Very dissatisfied | 4 | 1 | 2 | 2 | 3 |
| All | 100 | 100 | 100 | 100 | 100 |

*1 Employees in workplaces with 10 or more employees.*
*Source: Workplace Employee Relations Survey, Department of Trade and Industry*

It is possible however to measure job satisfaction. In 1998 the Workplace Employee Relations Survey asked employees in Great Britain how satisfied they were with their jobs. The answers can be interpreted as a summary assessment by the individual of all the different characteristics of their job. Overall, 54 per cent of employees were satisfied or very satisfied with their job (Table 4.31). Women had higher levels of job satisfaction than men, and part-time employees had higher levels of satisfaction than those working full time. Also, temporary and fixed term contract employees recorded higher levels of job satisfaction than those in permanent jobs.

# 4.32

Dissatisfaction with their current job is the main reason that prompts people to start looking for another one. In Spring 2000, about 6 per cent of both male and female full-time employees in the United Kingdom were looking for a new job (Table 4.32). For 35 per cent of these men and 27 per cent of the women, unsatisfactory pay in their current job was a trigger for looking for another one. A significant minority of women with dependent children were looking for a job with shorter hours than in their present job.

In 1998 the Cabinet Office carried out a survey of women's attitudes towards combining paid work and family life. Mothers who were not doing paid work at the time of interview or who had not had paid work for periods in the past were given a series of statements about not doing paid work. About two-thirds felt that it was 'very important' not to work because they enjoyed spending time with their children (Chart 4.33). However, there is evidence that for some the choice not to work is often at least partly an involuntary one. Nearly half thought that suitable childcare was too costly, and a third were unable to find the sort of childcare they would like. Significant minorities of mothers not doing paid work cited other obstacles such as finding work with suitable hours, finding work locally, and the pressure of juggling work and family life.

Of those mothers currently not in paid work, the majority intended to return to work when their children were older – only one in ten did not intend to go out to work even when their children left school.

**Reasons[1] full-time employees were for looking for a new job: by gender and presence of dependent children, Spring 2000**

United Kingdom | | | | Percentages

| | | Females | | |
| | Males | With dependent children | Without dependent children | All |
|---|---|---|---|---|
| Pay unsatisfactory in present job | 35 | 26 | 27 | 27 |
| Wants longer hours than in present job/ other reasons | 23 | 25 | 22 | 26 |
| Present job may come to an end | 16 | 13 | 14 | 14 |
| In present job to fill time before finding another | 9 | .. | 9 | 8 |
| Wants shorter hours than in present job | 8 | 13 | 5 | 7 |
| Journey unsatisfactory in present job | 7 | .. | 7 | 7 |
| Other aspects of present job unsatisfactory | 38 | 46 | 44 | 44 |
| | | | | |
| All looking for a new job (millions) | 0.7 | 0.1 | 0.3 | 0.4 |
| | | | | |
| All full-time employees (millions) | 11.8 | 1.8 | 4.6 | 6.4 |
| | | | | |
| Percentage of full-time employees looking for a new job | 6.1 | 6.3 | 6.6 | 6.5 |

1 More than one reason could be given.

*Source: Labour Force Survey, Office for National Statistics*

# 4.33

**Mothers' reasons for not doing paid work[1], Spring 1998**

**Great Britain**

Percentages

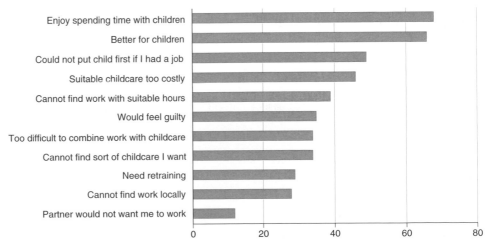

1 Percentage of mothers who were not doing paid work at the time of interview or had not had paid work for periods in the past who thought each reason was 'very important'.

*Source: Cabinet Office*

## Websites

| | |
|---|---|
| National Statistics | www.statistics.gov.uk |
| Department for Education and Employment | www.dfee.gov.uk |
| Cabinet Office Women's Unit | www.womens-unit.gov.uk |
| Department of Trade and Industry | www.dti.gov.uk |
| Employment Service | www.employment.gov.uk |
| Eurostat | www.europa.eu.int/comm/eurostat/ |
| National Centre for Social Research | www.natcen.ac.uk |

## Contacts

**Office for National Statistics**

| | |
|---|---|
| Chapter author | 020 7533 5783 |
| Labour market enquiry helpline | 020 7533 6094 |
| **Cabinet Office Women's Unit** | 020 7273 8880 |
| **Department of Trade and Industry** | 020 7215 6160 |
| **Employment Service** | 0114 273 6425 |
| **Eurostat** | 00 352 4301 33209 |
| **National Centre for Social Research** | 020 7549 9571 |

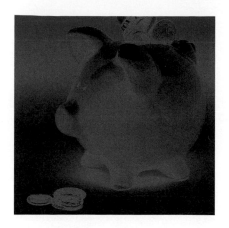

# Chapter 5  Income and Wealth

### Household income
- The advent of student loans has had a considerable impact on the composition of student incomes: they formed nearly a quarter of student incomes in 1998/99 while income from grants fell in importance, to make up 14 per cent of their incomes in 1998/99. (Table 5.4)

### Earnings
- In 2000 the lowest earnings were to be found in parts of Wales, such as Conwy, in Torbay and Cornwall, and in parts of Scotland. (Chart 5.8)

- The average usual gross earnings of an employee with a degree or equivalent were £520 per week in Spring 2000, compared with £200 per week for an employee with no qualifications. (Table 5.9)

### Income distribution
- During the 1980s, the distribution of household income became more unequal: in the first half of the 1990s inequalities appeared to stabilise but since then have started to widen. (Chart 5.16)

- Couples under pension age with no dependent children are nearly twice as likely as average to be in the top 20 per cent of the income distribution. (Table 5.17)

### Low incomes
- Children are disproportionately present in low income households: in 1998-99, 24 per cent of all children lived in households with below 60 per cent median equivalised income (before housing costs). (Chart 5.22)

- In 1999, around one in ten people reported that they could not afford 'to replace or repair electrical goods' or 'replace worn-out furniture', and 'money to keep their home in a decent state of decoration'. (Chart 5.24)

### Wealth
- Nearly one in ten households in Great Britain have no current account or investments: this proportion rises to one in six of those with total weekly income of less than £100. (Page 110)

People's incomes have a major influence on their well-being: they determine how much they are able to spend and save. Income levels depend on the level of activity within the economy as a whole – the national income – and on the way in which national income is distributed. Wealth, on the other hand, represents the ownership of assets valued at a point in time.

## Household income

The amount of income available for distribution to households depends on the overall level of economic activity. The most commonly used measure of economic activity is gross domestic product (GDP), sometimes also referred to as the amount of 'value added' generated within the economy of a country. The total income generated is divided between individuals, companies and other organisations (for example in the form of profits retained for investment), and government (in the form of taxes on production). Analysis of the trends in GDP may be found in the final section of this chapter.

Household income is derived not only directly from economic activity in the form of wages and salaries and self-employment income but also through transfers such as social security benefits. It is then subject to a number of deductions such as income tax, local taxes, and contributions towards pensions and national insurance. The amount of income remaining is referred to as household disposable income – the amount people have available to spend or save – and it is this measure which is commonly used to describe people's 'economic well-being'.

Household disposable income per head, adjusted for inflation, doubled between 1971 and 1999 (Chart 5.1). During the 1970s and early 1980s growth was somewhat erratic, and in some years there were small year-on-year falls, such as in 1974, 1977 and 1981. However, since then there has been growth each year, with the exception of 1998 when there was a very slight fall when adjusted for inflation. Over the period since 1971, a comparison of the patterns of growth of household disposable income and GDP per head shows that there has been a small shift between the shares of households and organisations in GDP in favour of households. Between 1998 and 1999, real household disposable income per head grew by 3.1 per cent compared with GDP per head growth of 1.7 per cent.

Table 5.2 illustrates how the shares of the various components of household income have changed since 1987. This shows a fall in the proportion derived from wages and salaries (including employers' social contributions for pensions and national insurance) from 59 per cent to 56 per cent in 1999, and small rises in most other components. More information about social benefits and the characteristics of their recipients may be found in Table 8.4 on page 146 of the Social Protection chapter.

# 5.1

**Real household disposable income per head[1] and gross domestic product per head**

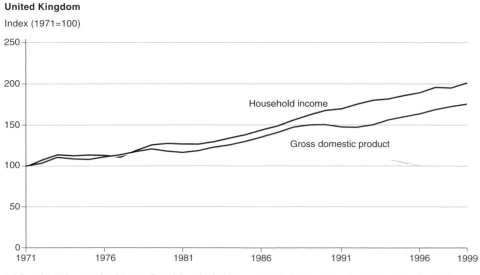

**United Kingdom**

Index (1971=100)

1 Adjusted to real terms using the expenditure deflator for the household sector. See also Appendix, Part 5: Household sector.

**Source: Office for National Statistics**

# 5.2

The data in Chart 5.1 and Table 5.2 are derived from the UK national accounts (see Appendix, Part 5: Household sector). In the national accounts the household sector is defined as including a variety of non-profit making institutions such as universities, charities and clubs, and people living in institutions such as nursing homes, as well as people living in private households. In most of the remainder of this chapter, the tables and charts are derived directly from surveys of households (such as the Family Resources Survey, the Family Expenditure Survey, the Labour Force Survey, the British Household Panel Survey, and the European Household Panel Survey) and surveys of businesses (such as the New Earnings Survey). Data from these surveys cover the population living in households and some cover certain parts of the population living in institutions, but all exclude non-profit making institutions. They can be used to analyse the distribution of household income between different sub-groups of the population, such as pensioners.

Survey sources differ from the national accounts not only in their population coverage but also in the way that household income is defined. One of the main differences is that the national accounts include the value of national insurance contributions made on behalf of employees by their employer as part of total household income, whereas survey sources do not.

The main sources of household income identified in Table 5.2 differ considerably in their importance between different types of households, particularly according to their family and employment circumstances. The following three tables show analyses of the composition of income for three groups of people: pensioners, students, and the disabled.

## Composition of household income[1]

| United Kingdom | | | | | | Percentages |
| --- | --- | --- | --- | --- | --- | --- |
| | 1987 | 1991 | 1996 | 1997 | 1998 | 1999 |
| **Source of income** | | | | | | |
| Wages and salaries[2] | 59 | 58 | 54 | 55 | 56 | 56 |
| Operating income[3] | 11 | 11 | 11 | 11 | 11 | 11 |
| Net property income | 7 | 8 | 9 | 9 | 9 | 9 |
| Social benefits[4] | 19 | 19 | 21 | 21 | 21 | 20 |
| Other current transfers[5] | 3 | 4 | 5 | 4 | 4 | 4 |
| | | | | | | |
| Total household income | | | | | | |
| (=100%)(£ billion at 1999 prices[6]) | 631 | 723 | 802 | 825 | 846 | 874 |
| **Taxes etc as a percentage of** | | | | | | |
| **total household income** | | | | | | |
| Taxes on income | 11 | 12 | 10 | 9 | 11 | 11 |
| Social contributions | 16 | 15 | 15 | 16 | 16 | 16 |
| Other current taxes | 2 | 2 | 2 | 2 | 2 | 2 |
| Other current transfers | 2 | 3 | 3 | 2 | 2 | 2 |
| | | | | | | |
| Total household disposable income | | | | | | |
| (£ billion at 1999 prices[6]) | 426 | 493 | 559 | 580 | 581 | 601 |

1 See Appendix, Part 5: Household sector.
2 Includes employers' social contributions.
3 Includes self-employment income for sole-traders and rental income.
4 Comprises pensions and benefits.
5 Mostly other government grants, but including transfers from abroad and non-profit making bodies.
6 Adjusted to 1999 prices using the expenditure deflator for the household sector.
**Source: Office for National Statistics**

The largest source of income for pensioner households in Great Britain, not surprisingly, is social security benefits, which include the state retirement pension (see Table 5.3 overleaf). In money terms in 1999, these were around £140 per week for all couples and around £100 per week for single pensioners, irrespective of age. Among couple pensioners under the age of 75, earnings continue to be a significant source of income, and couple pensioners are also more likely than single pensioners to have occupational pensions. In money terms, occupational pensions are higher for younger pensioners.

# 5.3

## Pensioners'[1] gross income: by age and source

**Great Britain**                                    Percentages

| | Couples[2] | | | Single | | |
| --- | --- | --- | --- | --- | --- | --- |
| | 1994-95 | 1996-97 | 1998-99 | 1994-95 | 1996-97 | 1998-99 |
| **Aged under 75** | | | | | | |
| Benefits | 42 | 40 | 40 | 58 | 57 | 56 |
| Occupational pensions | 28 | 30 | 29 | 23 | 25 | 23 |
| Investments | 16 | 16 | 17 | 11 | 10 | 12 |
| Earnings | 13 | 14 | 14 | 7 | 6 | 7 |
| Other | - | - | 1 | 1 | 1 | 1 |
| | | | | | | |
| All gross income (=100%) | | | | | | |
| (£ per week at July 1998 prices[3]) | 313 | 334 | 345 | 157 | 164 | 174 |
| **Aged 75 and over** | | | | | | |
| Benefits | 54 | 55 | 51 | 69 | 70 | 69 |
| Occupational pensions | 29 | 27 | 29 | 17 | 19 | 20 |
| Investments | 14 | 14 | 15 | 11 | 10 | 10 |
| Earnings | 3 | 4 | 4 | 2 | 1 | 1 |
| Other | - | - | - | 1 | - | - |
| | | | | | | |
| All gross income (=100%) | | | | | | |
| (£ per week at July 1998 prices[3]) | 251 | 256 | 275 | 136 | 142 | 149 |

1 Pensioner units - single people over state pension age (65 for males, 60 for females) and couples where the man is over state pension age.
2 Classified by age of man.
3 Adjusted to July 1998 prices using the retail prices index less local taxes.

**Source: Pensioners' Income Series, Department of Social Security**

# 5.4

## Composition of student[1] income

**United Kingdom**                              Percentages

| | 1988/89 | 1992/93 | 1995/96 | 1998/99 |
| --- | --- | --- | --- | --- |
| Student loan | - | 8 | 14 | 24 |
| Parental contribution | 32 | 26 | 22 | 16 |
| Grant | 38 | 38 | 23 | 14 |
| Earnings | 6 | 7 | 14 | 12 |
| Gifts | 9 | 7 | 11 | 11 |
| Loans[2] | 4 | 4 | 6 | 9 |
| Withdrawn savings | 4 | 2 | 6 | 8 |
| Other[3] | 8 | 8 | 4 | 5 |
| | | | | |
| All income (=100%) (£ per student per year at July 1999 prices[4]) | 4,395 | 4,048 | 4,951 | 5,575 |

1 Aged under 26 in higher education.
2 Includes overdrafts, credit cards and hire purchase.
3 Includes social security benefits, other student support and miscellaneous income.
4 Adjusted to July 1999 prices using the retail prices index (excluding mortgage interest payments).

**Source: Student Income and Expenditure Survey, Department for Education and Employment**

Incomes tend to be higher for younger pensioners than for older pensioners, for both single people and couples. Differences in income by age can be caused in different ways. First, older pensioners are less willing or able to work, due to their age. But second, there is influence from historical factors: for example, the rapid rise in occupational pension coverage in the 1950s and 1960s will have been more beneficial to someone born in 1930 than in 1910. A third reason is that whereas before retirement the value of occupational and other earnings-related pensions is broadly linked to earnings growth, the value of these pensions when they are paid is usually linked to prices. Thus all other things being equal, the value of such a pension to someone who has been retired for longer will be less than for the equivalent younger pensioner.

Although the series shown in Table 5.3, derived from the Family Resources Survey, is too short to provide an accurate picture of trends over time, evidence from the Family Expenditure Survey indicates that between 1979 and 1996-97 pensioners' disposable income (ie net of taxes) rose by over 60 per cent in real terms. This compares with growth of 36 per cent in average earnings deflated by the retail price index (all items) over the same period (see Chart 5.7 on page 98).

In 1988/89, the main source of income for students was their grant, followed by the contribution from their parents (Table 5.4). Student support arrangements changed substantially during the 1990s with gradual replacement from 1990/91 of the maintenance grant by student loans. By 1998/99, the portion of students' income accounted for by the grant had fallen by 24 percentage points and been replaced by student loans, which then formed 24 per cent of total income. The share of parental contributions had halved, while both earnings and gifts increased in importance. Overall, student incomes in 1998/99 were nearly 27 per cent higher in real terms than they were in 1988/89.

# 5.5

Incomes of households with at least one disabled person are lower than the incomes of all households. In 1996-97 disabled households received a larger share of their income from state pensions and other benefits than non-disabled households, and a smaller share from employment. Total income did not vary a great deal by severity of disablement, but the composition of income did (Table 5.5). While earnings decrease in importance with severity of disability, disability and other benefits increase to take their place. Overall, pensions as a proportion of income vary little with severity of disability.

The information presented in this section so far has been in terms of household income, since the household is generally considered to be the unit across which resources are shared (see Appendix, Part 2: Households for definition of a household). Thus total household income can be taken as representing the (potential) standard of living of each of its members. The assumption of equal sharing of resources between each member of the household is very difficult to test. Using certain assumptions it is possible to use household survey data to derive estimates of the income accruing to individuals, but it is not possible to infer their living standards from these.

The results of such an exercise are shown in Table 5.6 which compares the net and disposable personal incomes of men and women by family type. (See Appendix, Part 5: Individual income for details of how these estimates were derived.) Net income is after deduction of income tax and national insurance contributions, and disposable income is derived by making further deductions and additions such as shared housing costs, childcare and travel to work costs and payments/ receipts of maintenance and child support.

## Disabled households – gross income: by severity of disability[1] and source, 1996-97

**Great Britain**                                                                 Percentages

|  | Severity of disability[1] | | | | |
| --- | --- | --- | --- | --- | --- |
|  | 1-2 | 3-4 | 5-6 | 7-8 | 9-10 |
| Earnings | 41 | 35 | 34 | 26 | 22 |
| Self-employment income | 5 | 4 | 3 | 4 | 1 |
| Investments | 5 | 5 | 3 | 2 | 2 |
| State pension | 16 | 18 | 19 | 17 | 21 |
| Other pension | 15 | 14 | 11 | 10 | 9 |
| Disability benefits | 7 | 10 | 14 | 22 | 26 |
| Other benefits | 9 | 11 | 15 | 17 | 18 |
| Other income | 2 | 2 | 2 | 2 | 1 |
| All gross income (=100%)(£ per week) | 297 | 267 | 247 | 260 | 276 |

1 See Appendix, Part 5: Disability.
**Source: Disability follow-up to the Family Resources Survey, Department of Social Security**

# 5.6

## Mean individual income: by family type and gender, 1998-99

**Great Britain**                                                                 £ per week

|  | Net income[1] | | Disposable income[2] | |
| --- | --- | --- | --- | --- |
|  | Males | Females | Males | Females |
| Single people without children | 190 | 165 | 150 | 126 |
| Single pensioners | 155 | 132 | 140 | 122 |
| Lone parents | .. | 166 | .. | 142 |
| Couples without children | 307 | 155 | 263 | 120 |
| Pensioner couples | 203 | 86 | 193 | 76 |
| Couples with children | 352 | 147 | 296 | 97 |
| All adults | 264 | 144 | 224 | 112 |

1 After deduction of income tax and national insurance contributions. See Appendix, Part 5: Individual income.
2 After deduction of income tax, national insurance contributions and further deductions/additions such as childcare and travel to work costs and payments/receipts of maintenance and child support. See Appendix, Part 5: Individual income.
**Source: Women's Individual Income series, Department of Social Security**

# 5.7

**Average earnings index¹ and retail prices index²**

Percentage change over 12 months

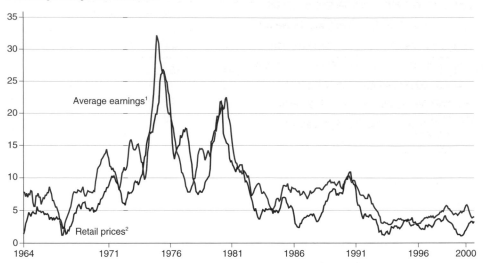

1 Data are for Great Britain.
2 Data are for United Kingdom.
**Source: Office for National Statistics**

# 5.8

**Average gross weekly earnings¹: by area²,
April 2000**

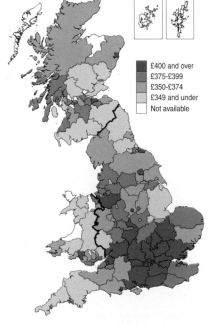

£400 and over
£375-£399
£350-£374
£349 and under
Not available

1 Earnings, including overtime, for full-time employees on adult rates whose
pay for the survey period was not affected by absence.
2 Areas refer to normal place of work, rather than normal place of residence.
**Source: New Earnings Survey, Office for National Statistics**

Men's incomes outstripped those of women in all types of family in 1998-99: the average net income of women was 55 per cent of that of men. However, this varied according to family type. The average net income of single women was 87 per cent of that of single men, whereas that of women living in pensioner couple households or couple households with children was 42 per cent of that of men in such households. For men, individual net incomes were highest for those in couple households with children, whereas for women they were highest for non-pensioners not living with a partner, whether or not they had children.

In terms of disposable income, the differentials between men's and women's incomes were virtually the same for single people without children as for single pensioners. However, for women living in couple families with children the difference in disposable incomes was larger than that based on net income – they had only 32 per cent of the income of men in such households. Among men, individual incomes remained the highest for those living with a partner and children, whereas among women lone mothers had the highest individual disposable incomes.

## Earnings

Income from employment is the most important component of household income. The average earnings index (AEI), a monthly measure of the pay of a representative sample of all employees across all sectors of the economy, is one of the indicators used to judge the state of the UK economy. If the index rises rapidly, this may indicate that the labour market is under-supplied with employees in the right numbers and with the right skills to meet the level of demand within the economy. In addition, a rapid rise may indicate that wage settlements are higher than the rate of economic growth, and this can sustain and thus create inflationary pressures. A fall in the index may be a reflection of reduced demand within the economy and may presage a fall in GDP and an increase in unemployment. The relationship between the AEI and the retail prices index (RPI) is also of importance. If the AEI rises faster than the RPI, this means that employees' pay is increasing faster than the prices they have to pay for goods and services and that therefore, all things being equal, their purchasing power will rise and they will feel 'better off'.

During the two decades from 1964, the AEI and RPI showed similar patterns of change, but with the RPI generally showing slower growth (Chart 5.7). For example, the peak in earnings growth over this period occurred in February 1975 when it reached an annual rate of 32 per cent. The peak in the RPI occurred in August that year at 27 per cent. During most of the 1990s, the AEI outpaced the RPI. This was made possible mainly through increases in productivity, enabling employers to pay higher wages while not increasing their prices to the same extent to finance their wage bill. The periods during which prices have risen faster than earnings – for example in the latter half of 1995 – have been times of economic downturn when a fall in demand for labour depressed earnings growth.

A wide variety of factors influence the level of earnings which an employee receives, such as their skills and experience, their occupation, the economic sector in which they work, the hours they work, and so on. The area of the country in which they work and their gender may also have an impact. The remainder of this section explores some of these factors. However, it should be borne in mind that these are all very much interlinked, and it is not possible here to disentangle the effect that any single factor may have.

Average gross weekly earnings for full-time employees in Great Britain in 2000 were highest in a central band of England running roughly from Warwickshire in the south midlands to Hampshire and West Sussex (Chart 5.8). Within this geographic band, gross earnings in the City of London were the highest at £765 per week, followed by Bracknell Forest Unitary Authority at £559 per week. A number of isolated pockets of high earnings also exist elsewhere: for example, in Aberdeen City where the North Sea industries have a substantial influence, earnings averaged £445 per week. The lowest earnings were to be found in parts of Wales such as Conwy, in Torbay and Cornwall, and in parts of Scotland.

The level of educational attainment can have a substantial impact on a person's earning power. In Spring 2000, average usual gross earnings for employees with a degree were £520 per week (Table 5.9). They then fell as educational attainment fell, so that employees with no qualifications had earnings of only £200 per week. There was a large increase in earnings for those aged 25 to 34 compared with those aged 16 to 24, across all attainment levels. However, there were further increases among those with GCE A levels or higher up to the age of 44, but little change for those with lower qualifications or none.

Wage rates can vary considerably between industrial sectors. Agriculture has traditionally been a relatively low-paid sector and this is still

the case, with 65 per cent of employees on wage rates of less than £6 per hour in Spring 2000 (see Table 5.10 overleaf). The hotel and restaurant sector is also relatively low paid, with 75 per cent earning less than £6 per hour and 34 per cent earning less than £4 per hour. At the other end of the scale, 39 per cent of those in financial intermediation earned more than £12 per hour. Averaged over all industries, 6 per cent of employees earned less than £4 per hour.

The national minimum wage (NMW) came into force in April 1999. The minimum wage rates were set at £3.00 per hour for 18 to 21 year olds and £3.60 for those aged 22 or over, with some exceptions for workers receiving training during the first six months of employment. The NMW has

# 5.9

**Usual gross weekly earnings of all employees: by highest qualification level attained and age, Spring 2000**

| United Kingdom | | | | | | £ per week |
|---|---|---|---|---|---|---|
| | 16-24 | 25-34 | 35-44 | 45-54 | 55-59/64 | All of working age[1] |
| Degree or equivalent | 280 | 470 | 600 | 610 | 560 | 520 |
| Higher education below degree level | 230 | 370 | 410 | 400 | 460 | 390 |
| GCE A level or equivalent | 180 | 340 | 390 | 360 | 330 | 320 |
| GCSE grades A*-C or equivalent | 140 | 270 | 270 | 300 | 270 | 240 |
| Other (including GCSE below grade C) | 180 | 260 | 280 | 260 | 290 | 260 |
| No qualifications | 100 | 220 | 200 | 210 | 210 | 200 |
| All[2] | 170 | 340 | 370 | 360 | 320 | 320 |

1 Males aged 16 to 64 and females aged 16 to 59.
2 Includes people who did not state their highest qualification.
**Source: Labour Force Survey, Office for National Statistics**

# 5.10

**Distribution of hourly[1] earnings: by industry, Spring 2000**

United Kingdom · Percentages

| | Less than £4 | £4 but less than £6 | £6 but less than £8 | £8 but less than £10 | £10 but less than £12 | £12 and over |
|---|---|---|---|---|---|---|
| Hotels and restaurants | 34 | 41 | 13 | 5 | 2 | 4 |
| Wholesale and retail trade | 11 | 44 | 19 | 10 | 5 | 12 |
| Agriculture, hunting, forestry and fishing | 8 | 57 | 21 | 6 | 4 | 4 |
| Health and social work | 6 | 28 | 21 | 15 | 12 | 18 |
| Real estate, renting and business activities | 5 | 27 | 19 | 12 | 9 | 28 |
| Construction | 4 | 19 | 31 | 19 | 10 | 17 |
| Education | 3 | 24 | 19 | 11 | 9 | 34 |
| | | | | | | |
| Manufacturing | 3 | 22 | 25 | 18 | 12 | 20 |
| Transport, storage and communication | 2 | 20 | 32 | 18 | 10 | 19 |
| Public administration and defence | 1 | 15 | 25 | 16 | 15 | 28 |
| Financial intermediation | 1 | 11 | 21 | 18 | 11 | 39 |
| Mining, quarrying, electricity, gas and water supplies | 1 | 7 | 17 | 23 | 18 | 34 |
| Other services | 12 | 30 | 21 | 13 | 7 | 17 |
| | | | | | | |
| All industries[2] | 6 | 26 | 22 | 14 | 10 | 22 |

1 Both full and part-time employees, including overtime payments, whose gross hourly earnings were less than £100.
2 Includes those whose workplace is abroad and those who did not state their industry.

**Source: New Earnings Survey, Office for National Statistics**

had an impact on the earnings distribution. The number of jobs paid at less than these rates fell from 1.5 million in Spring 1998 to 0.3 million in Spring 2000. These estimates cannot be used as a measure of non-compliance because it is not possible to discern from the data sources whether an individual is eligible for minimum wage rates. The rate for 18-21 year olds was increased to £3.20 per hour in June 2000 and the rate for those aged 22 and over was raised to £3.70 per hour in October 2000.

For some workers, the value of income 'in kind' forms an important part of their overall remuneration package. Such benefits may include a company car, free fuel, or private medical insurance. Information is available from the Inland Revenue on those benefits whose value to the recipient is liable to taxation. In 1998-99, 4 million people received such benefits (including 600 thousand company directors) and the amount received increased with their income (Table 5.11). The average value of taxable benefits was £2,320 per recipient.

The differential between the earnings of men and women has narrowed over the last 20 years, though women still earn less than men. In 2000 women's weekly earnings were only 74 per cent of men's, but because even those women working full time tend not to work as many hours as men, the gap for hourly earnings is narrower, with women's earnings at 82 per cent of men's.

Research carried out by the Cabinet Office's Women's Unit has simulated women's lifetime earnings. This indicates that skill level has the biggest impact on women's total earnings over their lifetimes rather than family-building (Chart 5.12). Women with high skill levels – at graduate level – have the highest earnings, with their marital status and whether or not they have children having little impact. However, for women with no qualifications child-bearing does have a substantial influence on lifetime earnings: a married mother with two children has half the total lifetime earnings of her childless counterpart, and a mother of four has less than a fifth of the total earnings of a childless woman.

# 5.11

**Selected taxable fringe benefits received by employees[1] and company directors: by gross annual earnings, 1998-99[2]**

United Kingdom

| | Company car | | Free fuel | | Private medical insurance | | Any benefit or expenses payment | |
|---|---|---|---|---|---|---|---|---|
| | Number of recipients (thousands) | Average value[3] (£) | Number of recipients (thousands) | Average value[4] (£) | Number of recipients (thousands) | Average value[5] (£) | Number of recipients[6] (thousands) | Average value[6] (£) |
| **Employees[1]** | | | | | | | | |
| Below £25,000 | 530 | 1,770 | 260 | 940 | 800 | 270 | 1,990 | 910 |
| £25,000 but under £35,000 | 370 | 2,630 | 180 | 1,200 | 390 | 380 | 710 | 2,100 |
| £35,000 but under £45,000 | 190 | 3,230 | 90 | 1,260 | 210 | 430 | 310 | 3,060 |
| £45,000 or more | 230 | 4,290 | 120 | 1,400 | 280 | 510 | 370 | 4,520 |
| **Directors** | | | | | | | | |
| Below £25,000 | 110 | 2,920 | 80 | 1,260 | 60 | 660 | 240 | 3,000 |
| £25,000 but under £35,000 | 70 | 3,270 | 50 | 1,370 | 40 | 650 | 100 | 4,150 |
| £35,000 but under £45,000 | 50 | 3,850 | 40 | 1,490 | 30 | 670 | 70 | 5,430 |
| £45,000 or more | 140 | 5,530 | 110 | 1,650 | 120 | 830 | 190 | 9,600 |
| **All employees[1] and directors** | 1,680 | 2,970 | 930 | 1,240 | 1,920 | 410 | 3,980 | 2,320 |

1 Employees with gross earnings of at least £8,500 a year, but excluding directors - except for 'Any benefit or expenses payment', as some benefits and expenses are taxable regardless of income.
2 Estimates for 1998-99 are based on projections from the 1997-98 survey.
3 The taxable value of company cars is based on the list price of the car subject to reductions for age and business mileage.
4 The taxable value of free fuel is based on a scale charge which depends on both the car engine size and the type of fuel.
5 The cost to the employer of providing the benefit.
6 Includes other benefits not shown separately. Some recipients receive more than one type of benefit.

*Source: Survey of Expenses and Benefits, Inland Revenue*

## Taxes

# 5.12

Table 5.2 showed that in 1999, 11 per cent of household income was paid out in taxes on income and 16 per cent in social contributions. Since every taxpayer is entitled to a personal allowance, which in 2000-01 is £4,385, those with income below this do not pay any tax. If they are aged over 65 they may be entitled to further allowances. The income tax regime for 2000-01 includes three different rates of tax. Taxable income of up to £1,520 (ie after the deduction of allowances and any other tax relief to which the individual may be entitled) is charged at 10 per cent. Taxable income above £1,520 but less than £28,400 is charged at 22 per cent, while income above this level is charged at 40 per cent. Special rates apply to savings income.

**Women's gross lifetime earnings**

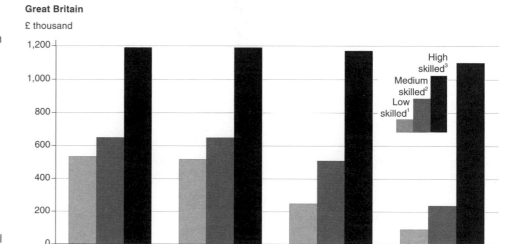

Great Britain
£ thousand

1 No qualifications.
2 At least one 'O' level or GCSE equivalent.
3 Degree.

*Source: Women's Unit, Cabinet Office*

# 5.13

## Income tax payable: by annual income[1], 2000-01[2]

**United Kingdom**

| | Number of taxpayers (millions) | Total tax payable (£ million) | Average rate of tax payable (percentages) | Average amount of tax payable (£) |
|---|---|---|---|---|
| £4,385-£4,999 | 0.8 | 20 | 1 | 30 |
| £5,000-£7,499 | 3.8 | 800 | 3 | 200 |
| £7,500-£9,999 | 3.5 | 2,400 | 7 | 650 |
| £10,000-£14,999 | 6.3 | 9,100 | 11 | 1,400 |
| £15,000-£19,999 | 4.6 | 11,500 | 14 | 2,460 |
| £20,000-£29,999 | 5.0 | 19,600 | 16 | 3,880 |
| £30,000-£49,999 | 2.7 | 19,200 | 19 | 7,020 |
| £50,000-£99,999 | 0.9 | 15,300 | 27 | 17,600 |
| £100,000 and over | 0.3 | 19,700 | 34 | 72,800 |
| All incomes | 27.9 | 97,500 | 17 | 3,470 |

1 Total income of the individual for income tax purposes including earned and investment income. Figures relate to taxpayers only.
2 Based on projections from 1998-99 data.

**Source: Survey of Personal Incomes, Inland Revenue**

# 5.14

## Indirect taxes as a percentage of disposable income: by income grouping[1] of household, 1998-99

**United Kingdom**

Percentages

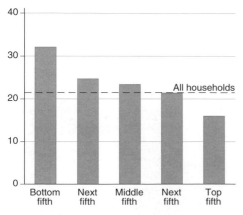

1 Equivalised disposable income has been used for ranking the households. See Appendix, Part 5: Equivalisation scales.

**Source: Office for National Statistics**

**Equivalisation** – in analysing the distribution of income, household disposable income is usually adjusted to take account of the size and composition of the household. This is in recognition of the fact that, for example, to achieve the same standard of living a household of five would require a higher income than would a single person. This process is known as equivalisation (see Appendix, Part 5: Equivalisation scales). Adjustments may also be made to deduct housing costs but these have not been made in the estimates in this chapter.

The Inland Revenue estimates that in 2000-01 there will be around 27.9 million taxpayers in the United Kingdom, over half the adult population (Table 5.13). Of these, 2.7 million pay tax only at the lowest rate and the same number are higher rate taxpayers. Because of the progressive nature of the income tax system, the amount of tax payable increases both in cash terms and as a proportion of income as income increases, averaging £30 per year for taxpayers with taxable incomes under £5,000 and £72,800 for those with incomes of £100,000 and above.

In addition to income tax, households also pay indirect taxes through their expenditure. Indirect taxes include value added tax (VAT), customs duties and excise duties and are included in the prices of consumer goods and services. These taxes are specific to particular commodities: for example, in 2000-01 VAT was payable on most consumer goods at 17.5 per cent of their value, though not on most foods nor on books and newspapers and at a reduced rate on heating and lighting. Customs and excise duties, on the other hand, tend to vary by the volume rather than value of goods purchased. Because high income households are more likely to devote a larger proportion of their income to investments or repaying loans, and low income households may be funding their expenditure through taking out loans or drawing down savings, the proportion of income paid in indirect taxes tends to be higher for those on low incomes than for those on high incomes (Chart 5.14).

National insurance (NI) contributions are paid according to an individual's earnings rather than their total income, and for employees payments are made both by the individual and by their employer. Employees' contributions tend to be slightly smaller as a proportion of earnings for those on higher weekly earnings compared with those on lower earnings because there is a ceiling on contributions: in 2000-01 contributions were levied only on the first £535 of weekly earnings. Chart 5.15 shows NI contributions and income tax

# 5.15

each as a percentage of household income. NI contributions fell from 16.7 per cent of household income in 1989 to 14.5 per cent in 1993, but have since risen to 16.2 per cent in 1998 and 16.0 per cent 1999. Income tax was above 11 per cent of income between 1987 and 1992, reaching a peak of 11.5 per cent in 1990 and 1991. It then fell to 9.5 per cent in 1997 and has since risen to 10.9 per cent.

## Income distribution

We have already seen how the various components of income differ in importance for different household types and how the levels of earnings vary between individuals. The result is an uneven distribution of total income between households, though the inequality is reduced to some extent by the deduction of taxes and social contributions and their redistribution to households in the form of social security benefits and other payments from government.

During the 1970s, there was relatively little change in the distribution of disposable income among households (Chart 5.16). However, the 1980s were characterised by a large increase in inequality: between 1981 and 1989, whereas average (median) income rose by 27 per cent when adjusted for inflation, income at the ninetieth percentile rose by 38 per cent and that at the tenth percentile rose by only 7 per cent. During the first half of the 1990s, the income distribution appeared to stabilise, but in the most recent period there appears to have been a further small increase in inequality.

The Institute for Fiscal Studies has investigated some of the possible explanations for the changes in inequality seen over the last two decades, and in particular why the trends are different over the economic cycles of the 1980s and 1990s. They found that wage growth played a part: inequality tends to rise during periods of rapid wage growth because the poorest households are the most

**Quintile groups** – the main method of analysing income distribution used in this chapter is to rank units (households, individuals or adults) by a given income measure, and then to divide the ranked units into groups of equal size. Groups containing 20 per cent of units are referred to as 'quintile groups' or 'fifths'. Thus the 'bottom quintile group' is the 20 per cent of units with the lowest incomes.

**Percentiles** – an alternative method also used in the chapter is to present the income level above or below which a certain proportion of units fall. Thus the ninetieth percentile is the income level above which only 10 per cent of units fall when ranked by a given income measure. The median is then the midpoint of the distribution above and below which 50 per cent of units fall.

### Taxes and social security contributions as a percentage of household income

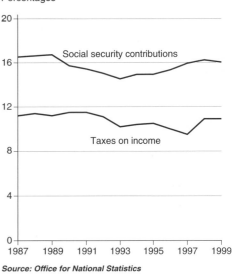

**United Kingdom**

Percentages

*Source: Office for National Statistics*

# 5.16

### Distribution of real[1] household disposable income[2]

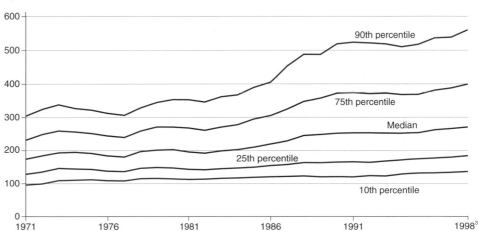

**United Kingdom**

£ per week

1 Before housing costs adjusted to February 2000 prices using the retail prices index less local taxes.
2 Equivalised disposable household income has been used for ranking the individuals. See Appendix, Part 5: Equivalisation scales.
3 Data from 1993 onwards are for financial years; data for 1994-95 onwards exclude Northern Ireland.
*Source: Institute for Fiscal Studies*

# 5.17

## Distribution of equivalised disposable income[1]: by household type, 1998-99

**Great Britain**        Percentages

| | Bottom fifth | Next fifth | Middle fifth | Next fifth | Top fifth | All (=100%) (millions) |
|---|---|---|---|---|---|---|
| Two adults one or both over pensionable age, no children | 25 | 27 | 20 | 15 | 13 | 6.8 |
| One adult above pensionable age, no children | 28 | 35 | 19 | 11 | 6 | 3.4 |
| Two adults below pensionable age | | | | | | |
| No children | 11 | 10 | 16 | 24 | 38 | 8.9 |
| One or more children | 20 | 19 | 22 | 20 | 18 | 17.8 |
| One adult below pensionable age | | | | | | |
| No children | 19 | 16 | 16 | 19 | 29 | 3.5 |
| One or more children | 42 | 36 | 13 | 6 | 3 | 3.9 |
| Other households | 14 | 17 | 23 | 27 | 19 | 12.3 |
| All individuals | 20 | 20 | 20 | 20 | 20 | 56.6 |

1 Equivalised household disposable income, before housing costs, has been used for ranking the individuals into quintile groups. See Appendix, Part 5: Equivalisation scales.

**Source: Family Resources Survey, Department of Social Security**

# 5.18

## Adults moving within the income distribution[1] between 1991 and 1998

**Great Britain**        Percentages

| | 1998 income grouping | | | | | |
|---|---|---|---|---|---|---|
| | Bottom fifth | Next fifth | Middle fifth | Next fifth | Top fifth | All adults |
| **1991 income grouping** | | | | | | |
| Bottom fifth | 49 | 27 | 14 | 7 | 4 | 100 |
| Next fifth | 26 | 35 | 21 | 11 | 7 | 100 |
| Middle fifth | 13 | 21 | 30 | 24 | 13 | 100 |
| Next fifth | 6 | 15 | 21 | 31 | 26 | 100 |
| Top fifth | 4 | 6 | 12 | 23 | 55 | 100 |

1 Equivalised household gross income has been used for ranking the adults. See Appendix, Part 5: Equivalisation scales.

**Source: British Household Panel Survey, Institute for Social and Economic Research**

likely to contain non-working individuals (see Chart 4.10, Workless households). The economic recovery in the 1980s was characterised by large increases in wages in each of the years from 1984 to 1988 (see Chart 5.7 above) matching the period when inequality increased rapidly. In contrast, wage growth was very slow to return in the recovery of the 1990s – a time of stable or falling inequality. Growth in self-employment income and in unemployment were also found to be associated with periods of increased inequality. However, this research did not examine the role of tax and benefit policy or the contribution of changing household composition and demographic factors.

Lone parents were more than twice as likely as the average individual to be in the bottom quintile group of disposable income in 1998-99 (Table 5.17). Also over-represented in this group were those over pensionable age, whether living on their own or with another adult. The section below on low incomes examines the characteristics of those at the lower end of the income distribution in more depth. At the other end of the distribution, non-pensioner couples with no children were nearly twice as likely as the average individual to be in the top quintile group. Couples with children were fairly evenly spread across the income distribution.

The Department of Social Security's Households Below Average Income analysis, from which Table 5.17 is derived, provides an annual cross-sectional snapshot of the distribution of income based on the Family Resources Survey. The British Household Panel Survey (BHPS) complements this by providing longitudinal information about how the incomes of a fixed sample of individuals change from year to year. This enables us to track how people move through the income distribution over time, and to identify the factors associated with changes in their position in the distribution.

# 5.19

Around 55 per cent of those adults in the top quintile group of gross income in 1991 were in the same group in 1998, though they did not necessarily remain in that group throughout the period (Table 5.18). A similar proportion of people (49 per cent) were in the bottom quintile group in both years. There is more movement in and out of the three middle quintile groups, simply because it is possible to move out of these groups through either an increase or a decrease in income. Movement out of the top group generally only occurs if income falls – an individual will remain in the group however great an increase in income is experienced. The converse is true at the bottom of the distribution. Nevertheless, the table shows that there is a considerable degree of turnover within each income group.

As discussed earlier in this chapter, households initially receive income from various sources such as employment, occupational pensions, investments, and transfers from other households. The state then intervenes both to raise taxes and national insurance contributions from individuals and to redistribute the revenue thus raised in the form of cash benefits to households and in the provision of services which are free or subsidised at the point of use. Some households will pay more in tax than they receive in benefits, while others will benefit more than they are taxed. Overall, this process results in a redistribution of income from households with higher incomes to those on lower incomes.

The average taxes paid and benefits received by each quintile group in 1998-99 are set out in Table 5.19. The distribution of 'original' income – before any state intervention – is highly unequal, with the average income of the top quintile group nearly 17 times greater than that of the bottom quintile group. Payment of cash benefits reduces this disparity so that the ratio of gross income in the top group compared with the bottom is 7:1, and deduction of direct taxes reduces the ratio further to around 6:1. Based on people's expenditure patterns it is then possible to calculate an

estimated payment of indirect taxes such as VAT and excise duties, which are deducted to produce a measure of post-tax income. Finally, an estimate is made for value of the benefit they receive from government expenditure on services such as education and health. (It is not possible to estimate the benefit to households of some items of government expenditure, for example defence and road-building.) Addition of these estimates gives a household's final income. The ratio of average final income in the top quintile group to

## Redistribution of income through taxes and benefits[1], 1998-99

United Kingdom £ per year

| | Quintile group of households[2] | | | | | All house-holds |
| --- | --- | --- | --- | --- | --- | --- |
| | Bottom fifth | Next fifth | Middle fifth | Next fifth | Top fifth | |
| **Average per household** | | | | | | |
| Wages and salaries | 1,820 | 5,100 | 12,490 | 21,380 | 38,830 | 15,930 |
| Imputed income from benefits in kind | 10 | 20 | 140 | 310 | 1,010 | 300 |
| Self-employment income | 410 | 690 | 1,380 | 1,830 | 5,540 | 1,970 |
| Occupational pensions, annuities | 370 | 990 | 1,700 | 2,010 | 2,820 | 1,580 |
| Investment income | 230 | 340 | 600 | 920 | 2,800 | 980 |
| Other income | 100 | 120 | 250 | 240 | 220 | 190 |
| **Total original income** | 2,940 | 7,260 | 16,570 | 26,700 | 51,220 | 20,940 |
| *plus* Benefits in cash | | | | | | |
| Contributory | 2,160 | 2,690 | 1,810 | 1,130 | 700 | 1,700 |
| Non-contributory | 2,640 | 2,490 | 1,640 | 900 | 420 | 1,620 |
| **Gross income** | 7,740 | 12,430 | 20,010 | 28,720 | 52,340 | 24,250 |
| *less* Income tax[3] and NIC[4] | 410 | 1,130 | 2,950 | 5,300 | 11,680 | 4,290 |
| *less* Local taxes[5] (net) | 500 | 580 | 740 | 840 | 980 | 730 |
| **Disposable income** | 6,830 | 10,730 | 16,330 | 22,590 | 39,680 | 19,230 |
| *less* Indirect taxes | 2,190 | 2,650 | 3,820 | 4,840 | 6,340 | 3,970 |
| **Post-tax income** | 4,630 | 8,070 | 12,500 | 17,750 | 33,340 | 15,260 |
| *plus* Benefits in kind | | | | | | |
| Education | 1,880 | 1,200 | 1,330 | 980 | 640 | 1,210 |
| National Health Service | 2,110 | 2,050 | 1,910 | 1,560 | 1,350 | 1,800 |
| Housing subsidy | 70 | 60 | 30 | 20 | - | 40 |
| Travel subsidies | 40 | 50 | 50 | 60 | 100 | 60 |
| School meals and welfare milk | 80 | 30 | 10 | - | - | 20 |
| **Final income** | 8,820 | 11,470 | 15,840 | 20,380 | 35,440 | 18,390 |

1 See Appendix, Part 5: Redistribution of income.
2 Equivalised disposable income has been used for ranking the households. See Appendix, Part 5: Equivalisation scales.
3 After tax relief at source on mortgage interest and life assurance premiums.
4 Employees' national insurance contributions.
5 Council tax net of council tax benefits, rates and water charges. Rates net of rebates in Northern Ireland.
**Source: Office for National Statistics**

# 5.20

**Percentage of people whose income is below various fractions of median income[1]**

**United Kingdom**
Percentages

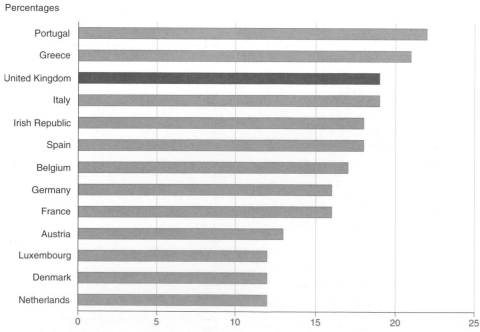

1 Before housing costs. See Appendix, Part 5: Households Below Average Income.
2 Data from 1993 onwards are for financial years; data for 1994-95 onwards exclude Northern Ireland.
**Source: Institute for Fiscal Studies**

# 5.21

**Percentage of people with incomes[1] below 60 per cent of the median: EU comparison, 1996**

Percentages

1 Equivalised disposable income in each country. Data are not available for Finland and Sweden.
**Source: European Community Household Panel, Eurostat**

that in the bottom quintile group is 4:1. Taken together with cash benefits, around 55 per cent of general government expenditure is allocated to households in this analysis.

## Low incomes

The incidence of low incomes, the factors contributing to low income and the ways of mitigating their effects have been an enduring focus of attention of governments from the introduction of the first poor laws in the 16th century up to the present day. The concerns of investigators such as Charles Booth in the latter part of the 19th century were taken up by governments in the 20th century, from the introduction of the first old age pensions in 1909 to the welfare state of Beveridge some 40 years later.

Being disadvantaged, and thus 'excluded' from many of the opportunities available to the average citizen, has often been seen as synonymous with having a low income. While low income is clearly central to poverty and social exclusion, it is now widely accepted that there is a wide range of other factors which are important. People can experience poverty of education, of training, of health, and of environment, as well as poverty in purely cash terms. Nevertheless, the prevalence of low income remains an important indicator of social exclusion and is the focus of this section. Information on many of the other aspects may be found in other chapters of *Social Trends*.

The definition of 'low' income has always been a source of debate and to some extent has to be arbitrary. Only in countries at a very low level of economic development is it sensible to take an absolutist, 'basic needs' approach, which costs the bare essentials to maintain human life and uses this as the yardstick against which incomes are measured. All other approaches are to a greater or lesser extent relative: 'low' income is defined in terms of what is generally considered

# 5.22

adequate to maintain an acceptable standard of living given the norms of a particular society at a particular time. With such approaches, it is possible and indeed perfectly acceptable for 'low' income to differ both temporally and spatially. So, for example, while in one country the possession of sufficient income to pay for central heating might be considered a necessity, this might not have been the case in the same country a generation ago and nor might it be so for a different country today.

In this section, the threshold generally adopted to define low income is 60 per cent of median equivalised household disposable income. This is one of a set of indicators in the *Opportunity for all* report used to monitor the Government's strategy to tackle poverty and social exclusion. In 1998-99, 18 per cent of the population in Great Britain lived in households with income below this level (Chart 5.20). This proportion was fairly static during the 1960s, 1970s and early 1980s, fluctuating between 10 and 15 per cent. It then rose steeply from 1985 to reach a peak of 21 per cent in 1992. There was then a slight drop and the proportion has remained at around 18 per cent over the last three years. This pattern is also reflected in the proportions of people with incomes less than 50 per cent and 40 per cent of the median.

The European Community Household Panel Survey allows us to compare the proportions of people with incomes below 60 per cent of their national median equivalised disposable income throughout the European Union (EU) (Chart 5.21). Across those countries for which data are available, 17 per cent of households had low incomes on this definition in 1996. About half of member states clustered fairly closely around this average. However, Austria, Denmark, Luxembourg and Netherlands stand out as having substantially lower proportions of low income households – only 12 or 13 per cent in each case. In Greece and Portugal more than 20 per cent of households have low incomes. Note that in order to achieve comparability across the EU there are

differences in income concepts used and in methods of measurement compared with national sources, and the relatively small sample sizes in each country may mean that the margin of error around some of the estimates is of the same order of magnitude as the differences between some of them.

Children are disproportionately present in low income households: in 1998-99, 24 per cent of children, or 3.1 million, were living in such households in Great Britain (Chart 5.22). This proportion rose steeply between 1979 and 1981 from 12 per cent to 18 per cent and continued to rise to reach a peak of 27 per cent in 1991-92 and 1992-93.

There is a clear relationship between work and income, illustrated in Table 5.23. Overall, 18 per cent of the population were living in low income households in 1998-99, compared with only 2 per cent of those living in families where all adults were in full-time work. In contrast, 64 per cent of people in families where the head or spouse were

**Proportion of children living in households below 60 per cent of median[1] income**

**United Kingdom**

Percentages

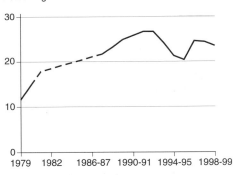

*1 Equivalised household disposable income, before housing costs. Data are not available for 1980 and 1982 to 1986-87. Data from 1979 to 1993-94 are for United Kingdom from the Family Expenditure Survey and a two-year moving average has been used from 1987-88 to 1993-94; from 1994-95 onwards data are for Great Britain from the Family Resources Survey.*

***Source: Department of Social Security***

# 5.23

**Individuals in households with incomes below 60 per cent of median income: by economic activity status**

**United Kingdom and Great Britain[1]**                                   Percentages

|  | 1981 | 1991-92 | 1996-97 | 1998-99 |
|---|---|---|---|---|
| Head or spouse unemployed | 52 | 71 | 62 | 64 |
| Head or spouse aged 60 or over | 19 | 31 | 24 | 26 |
| One or more in part-time work | 24 | 26 | 25 | 24 |
| Self-employed[2] | 13 | 19 | 19 | 20 |
| One in full-time work, one not working | 8 | 12 | 15 | 14 |
| One in full-time, one in part-time work | 2 | 3 | 3 | 4 |
| Single or couple, all in full-time work | 1 | 2 | 2 | 2 |
| Other[3] | 36 | 51 | 42 | 41 |
| All | 13 | 21 | 18 | 18 |

*1 Data for 1981 and 1991-92 are based on the Family Expenditure Survey which covers the United Kingdom. Data for 1996-97 and 1998-99 are based on the Family Resources Survey which covers Great Britain only.*
*2 Those in benefit units which contain one or more adults who are normally self-employed for 31 or more hours a week.*
*3 Includes long-term sick and disabled people and non-working single-parents.*

***Source: Department of Social Security***

# 5.24

**Proportion of adults lacking selected basic necessities[1] through inability to afford them, 1999[2]**

**Great Britain**
Percentages

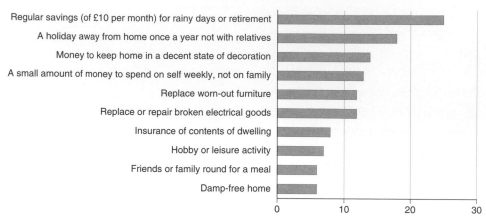

1 Items considered by over 50 per cent of all adults as 'necessary, which all adults should be able to afford and which they should not have to do without'.
2 Fieldwork was carried out in September to October.
**Source: Poverty and Social Exclusion Survey, Joseph Rowntree Foundation**

# 5.25

**Composition of the net wealth[1] of the household sector**

**United Kingdom**                                                                       Percentages

|  | 1987 | 1991 | 1996 | 1997 | 1998 | 1999 |
|---|---|---|---|---|---|---|
| Life assurance and pension funds | 24 | 27 | 35 | 37 | 37 | 35 |
| Residential buildings less loans | 35 | 32 | 23 | 22 | 25 | 26 |
| Securities and shares | 10 | 11 | 15 | 16 | 15 | 16 |
| Currency and deposits | 16 | 17 | 16 | 15 | 15 | 14 |
| Non-marketable tenancy rights | 9 | 8 | 5 | 5 | 5 | 5 |
| Other fixed assets | 6 | 5 | 4 | 4 | 3 | 3 |
| Other financial assets net of liabilities | 1 | 1 | 1 | 1 | 1 | - |
| Total (=100%)(£ billion at 1999 prices[2]) | 2,611 | 2,913 | 3,271 | 3,684 | 3,955 | 4,334 |

1 See Appendix, Part 5: Net wealth of the household sector.
2 Adjusted to 1999 prices using the expenditure deflator for the household sector.
**Source: Office for National Statistics**

unemployed had low incomes. This proportion has fallen since the 1991-92 estimate of 71 per cent. About a quarter of people in families where the head or spouse were aged 60 or over had low incomes in 1998-99.

However, the existence of income from employment is not always sufficient to lift a household out of low income. For people in some occupations and industries, wage rates may be so low that their household income may still be insufficient for them to support a family adequately. The aim of the Working Families' Tax Credit, which replaced Family Credit from 5 October 1999, is to guarantee a minimum income of £208 per week to working families with children, increasing to £214 per week in April 2001.

Low income may lead to material deprivation. The 1999 Poverty and Social Exclusion Survey, commissioned by the Joseph Rowntree Foundation, sought to identify the items that a majority of the general public perceive to be necessities which all adults should be able to afford and which they should not have to do without. The next step was to find out how many people lacked these because they could not afford them rather than because they did not want them. About 28 per cent of people said that they were unable to afford two or more of the items considered by the general population as being necessities. Chart 5.24 shows those items which the highest proportions of people do not have because they cannot afford them. A quarter of people are unable to 'have regular savings of £10 a month for rainy days or retirement', although this will include younger people whose propensity to save is in any case low. Nearly a fifth cannot afford a 'holiday away from home once a year not staying with relatives'. Other 'one-off' larger items of expenditure which more than one in ten people cannot afford are 'replace or repair broken electrical goods', 'replace worn-out furniture', and 'money to keep home in a decent state of decoration'.

# 5.26

## Wealth

Although the terms 'wealthy' and 'high income' are often used interchangeably, in fact they relate to quite distinct concepts. 'Income' represents a flow of resources over a period, received either in cash or in kind. 'Wealth' on the other hand describes the ownership of assets valued at a particular point in time. These assets may provide the owner with a flow of income, for example interest payments on a building society account, or they may not, for example the ownership of works of art – unless of course the asset is sold. However, not all assets can be sold and their value realised. In particular, an individual's stake in an occupational pension scheme often cannot be 'cashed in'. The distinction is therefore usually made between 'marketable wealth' which the owner can sell if they so desire, and 'non-marketable wealth'. Wealth may be accumulated either by the purchase of new assets, or by the increase in value of existing assets.

The wealth of the household sector in the United Kingdom, net of any loans outstanding on the purchase of assets such as housing, has shown strong growth in recent years, increasing by an average of 4 per cent per year between 1987 and 1999 after adjusting for inflation (Table 5.25). Holdings in life assurance and pension funds formed the most important component of the net wealth of the household sector in 1999, followed by the value of residential buildings net of mortgage and loan debt on them. This is a reversal of the position twelve years ago, a result partly of strong growth in the take-up of private pensions and partly the fall in value of owner-occupied housing during the early 1990s.

### Distribution of wealth[1]

| United Kingdom | | | | | | | Percentages |
|---|---|---|---|---|---|---|---|
| | 1976 | 1981 | 1986 | 1991 | 1996 | 1997 | 1998 |
| **Marketable wealth** | | | | | | | |
| Percentage of wealth owned by[2]: | | | | | | | |
| Most wealthy 1% | 21 | 18 | 18 | 17 | 20 | 22 | 23 |
| Most wealthy 5% | 38 | 36 | 36 | 35 | 40 | 43 | 44 |
| Most wealthy 10% | 50 | 50 | 50 | 47 | 52 | 55 | 56 |
| Most wealthy 25% | 71 | 73 | 73 | 71 | 74 | 75 | 75 |
| Most wealthy 50% | 92 | 92 | 90 | 92 | 93 | 93 | 94 |
| | | | | | | | |
| Total marketable wealth (£ billion) | 280 | 565 | 955 | 1,711 | 2,092 | 2,280 | 2,543 |
| **Marketable wealth less value of dwellings** | | | | | | | |
| Percentage of wealth owned by[2]: | | | | | | | |
| Most wealthy 1% | 29 | 26 | 25 | 29 | 26 | 30 | 26 |
| Most wealthy 5% | 47 | 45 | 46 | 51 | 49 | 55 | 50 |
| Most wealthy 10% | 57 | 56 | 58 | 64 | 63 | 67 | 65 |
| Most wealthy 25% | 73 | 74 | 75 | 80 | 81 | 84 | 86 |
| Most wealthy 50% | 88 | 87 | 89 | 93 | 94 | 95 | 95 |

1 See Appendix, Part 5: Distribution of personal wealth. Estimates for individual years should be treated with caution as they are affected by sampling error and the particular pattern of deaths in that year.
2 Adults aged 18 and over.

**Source: Inland Revenue**

Wealth is considerably less evenly distributed than income. Life cycle effects mean that this will almost always be so: people build up assets during the course of their working lives and then draw them down during the years of retirement with the residue passing to others at their death. It is estimated that the most wealthy 1 per cent of individuals owned between a fifth and a quarter of the total wealth of the household sector in recent years (Table 5.26). In contrast, half the population shared between them only 6 per cent of total wealth. If the value of housing is omitted from the wealth estimates, the resulting distribution is even more skewed, indicating that this form of wealth is rather more evenly distributed than the remainder.

# 5.27

**Household savings: by ethnic group of head of household and amount, 1998-99**

Great Britain                                                                                           Percentages

| | No savings | Less than £1,500 | £1,500 but less than £10,000 | £10,000 but less than £20,000 | £20,000 or more | All households |
|---|---|---|---|---|---|---|
| White | 27 | 22 | 26 | 10 | 15 | 100 |
| Black | 54 | 28 | 15 | 2 | 1 | 100 |
| Indian | 30 | 16 | 25 | 12 | 16 | 100 |
| Pakistani/Bangladeshi | 59 | 23 | 14 | 3 | 1 | 100 |
| Other ethnic minorities | 44 | 22 | 21 | 6 | 8 | 100 |
| All ethnic groups | 28 | 22 | 25 | 10 | 14 | 100 |

*Source: Family Resources Survey, Department of Social Security*

# 5.28

**Annual growth in gross domestic product at constant prices**

**United Kingdom**
Percentages

*Source: Office for National Statistics*

This analysis of the aggregate data available on the distribution of wealth is borne out by information available from the Family Resources Survey based on individuals' own estimates of their savings. In 1998-99, 50 per cent of households in Great Britain reported having less than £1,500 in savings, with 28 per cent reporting no savings at all (Table 5.27). Savings patterns vary with ethnic group. In particular, 59 per cent of Pakistani and Bangladeshi households and 54 per cent of Black households had no savings. White and Indian households were much more likely to have savings, and in fact had very similar savings patterns.

The term 'financial exclusion' has been coined to describe those people who do not use financial services at all. Data from the Family Resources Survey indicate that, in 1998-99, 8 per cent of households did not have any kind of current account (including Post Office account) or investments such as savings accounts or premium bonds. This proportion rises to 16 per cent of households whose total weekly income is less than £100. Since the options for operating a household budget without mainstream financial services are more expensive and often unregulated, this is of policy concern. Qualitative research commissioned by the Joseph Rowntree Foundation has suggested that the largest group of those who have never made use of financial services are householders who have never had a secure job. Other groups affected are people aged 70 and over who are part of a cash-only generation, women who became single mothers at an early age, and some ethnic minority groups, particularly Pakistani and Bangladeshi households.

## 5.29

## National income and expenditure

Gross domestic product (GDP) measures, in accordance with international conventions, the level of income generated by economic activity in the United Kingdom. Chart 5.1 at the beginning of this chapter showed that when adjusted for inflation, the trend in GDP per head since 1971 has generally been one of steady growth. However, within this long-term trend the United Kingdom is nevertheless subject to cycles of weaker and stronger growth usually referred to as the economic or business cycle.

The year on year growth rates for GDP, adjusted to remove the effects of inflation, shown in Chart 5.28 suggest that the United Kingdom's economy contracted in the mid-1970s, at the time of the OPEC oil crisis, and again in the early 1980s and early 1990s. However, growth has exceeded 4 per cent per year 11 times in the post-war period, most recently in 1994. The long-term average annual growth rate was 2.5 per cent between 1948 and 1999.

GDP per head shows marked variations between the regions of the United Kingdom. During the 1990s, GDP per head was lower in Northern Ireland than anywhere else in the United Kingdom, at around a fifth below the United Kingdom average, followed by the North East and Wales (Table 5.29). GDP per head in London has remained considerably higher than the United Kingdom average. The South East and the East have also maintained above average levels of GDP per head over the same period.

A comparison of GDP per head across the countries of the European Union (EU) in 1998 shows that Luxembourg had the highest level of economic activity, around 75 per cent higher than

the EU average (Table 5.30). This is because of the importance of the financial sector in the Luxembourg economy. At the other end of the scale, Portugal and Greece had GDP per head of a quarter and a third below the EU average respectively, though in Portugal it has grown relative to the EU average since 1995. Other countries were clustered more closely around the EU average, with the United Kingdom, France, Finland, Italy and Sweden all lying within two percentage points of the average. The most dramatic increase between 1995 and 1998 in GDP per head was for the Irish Republic, which rose from 93 per cent of the EU average in 1995 to 8 per cent above average in 1998. These estimates have been converted to a common basis making adjustments for the relative purchasing power of national currencies.

### Gross domestic product per head at basic prices[1]: by region

Indices (UK[2]=100)

| | 1991 | 1992 | 1993 | 1994 | 1995 | 1996 | 1997 | 1998 |
|---|---|---|---|---|---|---|---|---|
| North East | 84 | 84 | 84 | 82 | 82 | 81 | 79 | 79 |
| North West | 91 | 91 | 90 | 91 | 90 | 89 | 89 | 88 |
| Yorkshire and the Humber | 89 | 88 | 88 | 87 | 88 | 89 | 89 | 88 |
| East Midlands | 95 | 94 | 94 | 93 | 93 | 95 | 96 | 95 |
| West Midlands | 93 | 93 | 93 | 93 | 94 | 93 | 92 | 92 |
| East | 112 | 113 | 111 | 113 | 112 | 112 | 115 | 114 |
| London | 129 | 130 | 130 | 130 | 127 | 127 | 129 | 130 |
| South East | 111 | 111 | 112 | 113 | 112 | 114 | 114 | 117 |
| South West | 91 | 92 | 92 | 92 | 93 | 93 | 93 | 92 |
| England | 102 | 102 | 102 | 102 | 102 | 102 | 102 | 103 |
| Wales | 84 | 83 | 83 | 83 | 84 | 82 | 80 | 79 |
| Scotland | 99 | 99 | 99 | 99 | 101 | 99 | 96 | 96 |
| Northern Ireland | 75 | 76 | 77 | 78 | 79 | 78 | 78 | 76 |

1 Excludes Extra-Regio and statistical discrepancy.
2 United Kingdom less that part of GDP that cannot be allocated to a specific region.
**Source: Office for National Statistics**

## 5.30

### Gross domestic product[1] per head: EU comparison, 1995 and 1998

Index (EU=100)

| | 1995 | 1998 |
|---|---|---|
| Luxembourg | 173 | 176 |
| Denmark | 118 | 119 |
| Netherlands | 109 | 113 |
| Austria | 110 | 112 |
| Belgium | 112 | 111 |
| Irish Republic | 93 | 108 |
| Germany | 110 | 108 |
| United Kingdom | 96 | 102 |
| Finland | 97 | 102 |
| Sweden | 103 | 102 |
| Italy | 104 | 101 |
| France | 104 | 99 |
| Spain | 78 | 81 |
| Portugal | 71 | 75 |
| Greece | 66 | 66 |

1 Gross domestic product at current market prices using current purchasing power standard and compiled on the basis of the European System of Accounts 1995.
**Source: Eurostat**

# 5.31

## Expenditure of general government in real terms[1]: by function

**United Kingdom**

£ billion at 1999 prices[1]

| | 1987 | 1991 | 1996 | 1997 | 1998 | 1999 |
|---|---|---|---|---|---|---|
| Social protection | 102 | 115 | 140 | 140 | 137 | 137 |
| Health | 35 | 39 | 47 | 46 | 48 | 50 |
| Education | 33 | 35 | 39 | 39 | 39 | 40 |
| Defence | 32 | 32 | 25 | 25 | 26 | 26 |
| Public order and safety | 12 | 16 | 17 | 18 | 18 | 20 |
| | | | | | | |
| General public services | 10 | 14 | 16 | 16 | 17 | 18 |
| Housing and community amenities | 11 | 12 | 7 | 7 | 5 | 5 |
| Recreation, culture and religion | 4 | 5 | 5 | 4 | 5 | 3 |
| Other economic affairs and environmental protection[2] | 26 | 27 | 29 | 24 | 23 | 25 |
| Gross debt interest | 32 | 23 | 30 | 32 | 31 | 26 |
| | | | | | | |
| All expenditure | 297 | 319 | 355 | 350 | 349 | 350 |

1 Adjusted to 1999 prices using the GDP market prices deflator.
2 Includes expenditure on transport and communication, agriculture, forestry and fishing, mining, manufacture, construction, fuel and energy and services.

**Source: Office for National Statistics**

# 5.32

## First priority for extra government spending[1]

**Great Britain**

Percentages

| | 1986 | 1991 | 1996 | 1999 |
|---|---|---|---|---|
| Health | 47 | 48 | 54 | 47 |
| Education | 27 | 29 | 28 | 34 |
| Housing | 7 | 8 | 4 | 4 |
| Public transport | - | 1 | 2 | 4 |
| Help for industry | 8 | 4 | 4 | 3 |
| | | | | |
| Police and prisons | 3 | 2 | 3 | 3 |
| Roads | 1 | 1 | 1 | 3 |
| Social security benefits | 5 | 5 | 3 | 2 |
| Overseas aid | 1 | 1 | - | 1 |
| Defence | 1 | 2 | 1 | 1 |
| | | | | |
| All[2] | 100 | 100 | 100 | 100 |

1 Respondents aged 18 and over were asked to select from a list of items of government spending 'which of them, if any, would be their highest priority for extra spending?'
2 Includes don't know/not answered/none of these.

**Source: British Social Attitudes Survey, National Centre for Social Research**

Government receives income primarily through transfers from individuals, companies and other organisations in the form of taxes, national insurance contributions and other payments, though they may also engage in economic activity from which income is derived. This revenue is then spent on the provision of goods and services such as health care and education, on servicing government debt, and on transfer payments such as social security benefits. The sum of all such expenditure and transfer payments net of requited receipts is known as general government expenditure (GGE) and it is this measure which until recently has been used to analyse trends in public expenditure. The present Government's main measure of public expenditure is however Total Managed Expenditure: one of the main differences between this aggregate and GGE is that it excludes privatisation proceeds.

Although the way in which public expenditure is allocated to different purposes depends on government policy priorities, significant shifts in expenditure patterns tend only to be discernible over a relatively long time period. Over the last ten years, by far the most important category of expenditure in the United Kingdom both in cash terms and as a percentage of total expenditure has been social protection – for example, social security payments (Table 5.31). Government expenditure on social protection rose by over a third in real terms between 1987 and 1999, and accounted for 39 per cent of expenditure in 1999 compared with 34 per cent in 1987. Expenditure on defence and on housing and community amenities fell in real terms during the 1990s.

The British Social Attitudes Survey asks people what their top priority is for additional government spending. Table 5.32 shows that consistently since 1986, the most popular area for additional spending is the health service, followed by education: four out of five people questioned chose one of these two services as their first

# 5.33

priority. None of the other areas of government expenditure was the first priority for more than one in 20 people in 1999. This includes social security benefits which include retirement pensions, though it seems likely that in peoples' minds they are synonymous with means-tested benefits. This is confirmed by the fact that 76 per cent of people thought that 'more' or 'much more' should be spent on old age pensions in 1996 when the question was last asked.

As well as expenditure for purely domestic purposes, GGE also includes the contributions made by the United Kingdom to the European Community (EC) budget. In 1998 the United Kingdom contributed £8.4 billion and had receipts amounting to £4.6 billion (Table 5.33). Germany was the largest net contributor, with contributions exceeding receipts by £7 billion. The only net recipients from the EC budget in 1998 were the Irish Republic, Portugal, Greece and Spain.

**Contributions to and receipts[1] from the EC budget[2], 1998**

|  | | | £ billion |
|---|---|---|---|
|  | Contri-bution | Receipts | Net receipts |
| Germany | 13.8 | 6.8 | -7.0 |
| United Kingdom | 8.4 | 4.6 | -3.8 |
| Netherlands | 3.4 | 1.4 | -2.0 |
| Italy | 7.1 | 5.7 | -1.4 |
| France | 9.1 | 8.0 | -1.1 |
| Belgium | 2.1 | 1.1 | -1.0 |
| Sweden | 1.6 | 0.8 | -0.8 |
| Austria | 1.4 | 0.8 | -0.6 |
| Finland | 0.8 | 0.6 | -0.2 |
| Luxembourg | 0.1 | 0.1 | -0.1 |
| Denmark | 1.1 | 1.0 | -0.1 |
| Irish Republic | 0.7 | 2.1 | 1.4 |
| Portugal | 0.7 | 2.6 | 1.9 |
| Greece | 0.9 | 3.9 | 3.0 |
| Spain | 3.9 | 8.2 | 4.3 |

1 Excludes gains from spending on administration or other institutions.
2 See Appendix, Part 5: Contributions to and receipts from the EC budget.

**Source: European Court of Auditors**

## Websites

| | |
|---|---|
| National Statistics | www.statistics.gov.uk |
| Department of Social Security | www.dss.gov.uk |
| Inland Revenue | www.inlandrevenue.gov.uk |
| Eurostat | www.europa.eu.int\comm\eurostat\ |
| Institute for Fiscal Studies | www.ifs.org.uk |
| Institute for Social and Economic Research | www.iser.essex.ac.uk |
| National Centre for Social Research | www.natcen.ac.uk |

## Contacts

| | |
|---|---|
| **Office for National Statistics** | |
| Chapter author | 020 7533 5783 |
| Effects of taxes and benefits | 020 7533 5770 |
| National accounts | 020 7533 6003 |
| New Earnings Survey | 01633 819011 |
| Regional accounts | 020 7533 5790 |
| **Department for Education and Employment** | 020 7273 5971 |
| **Department of Social Security** | |
| Family Resources Survey | 020 7962 8092 |
| Households Below Average Income | 020 7962 8232 |
| Individual Income | 020 7712 2258 |
| Pensioners' Incomes | 020 7962 8223 |
| **Inland Revenue** | 020 7438 7370 |
| **Eurostat** | |
| Data Shop Luxembourg | 00 352 4335 2251 |
| Data Shop London | 020 7533 5676 |
| **Institute for Fiscal Studies** | 020 7291 4800 |
| **Institute for Social and Economic Research** | 01206 872957 |
| **National Centre for Social Research** | 020 7549 9571 |

# Chapter 6 Expenditure

### Household and personal expenditure

- In the United Kingdom, total household expenditure in real terms in 1999 was nearly three and a half times higher than in 1951. (Chart 6.1)

- In 1999, £1.0 billion was spent on postal services in the United Kingdom, a third less than the amount in real terms in 1963. Expenditure on telecommunications doubled over the same period, to £12.1 billion. (Chart 6.4)

- In 1999-00 girls spent double the proportion spent by boys on clothing and footwear. Conversely, boys spent one and a half times the proportion spent by girls on leisure goods and services. (Table 6.5)

- In 1997-2000, Londoners spent over 50 per cent more than households in the North East region on leisure goods and services, and a fifth more than the UK average. (Table 6.9)

### Prices

- Only three EU countries would have appeared more expensive to someone from the United Kingdom in 1998 and they were all in Scandinavia. (Chart 6.13)

### Transactions and credit

- The amount of consumer credit outstanding in the United Kingdom increased to £115 billion in 1999, almost double the 1987 level in real terms. (Table 6.15)

- Around one in five debit card purchases in supermarkets involve cash-back, with an average value of £24. (Page 125)

- Food and drink purchases accounted for a third of all debit card expenditure in 1999. (Chart 6.17)

# 6.1

**Household expenditure at constant prices[1]**

**United Kingdom**
£ billion

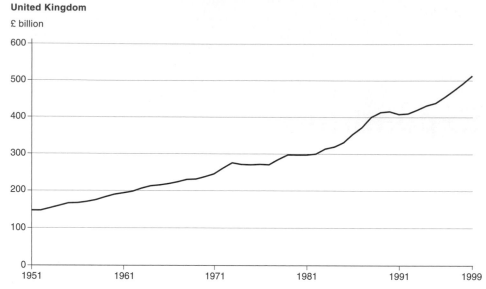

1 At constant 1995 prices. See Appendix, Part 6: Household expenditure.
**Source: Office for National Statistics**

# 6.2

**Household expenditure[1]: by type of product**

**United Kingdom**
Percentages

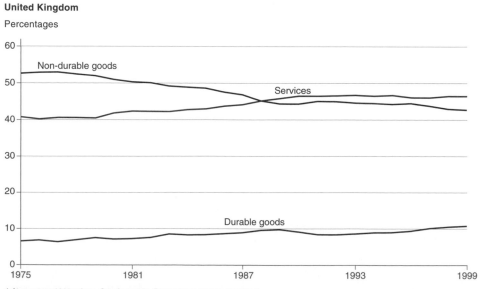

1 At constant 1995 prices. See Appendix, Part 6: Household expenditure.
**Source: Office for National Statistics**

How and where people chose to spend their income has changed considerably over the past 40 years, reflecting both the way that society has evolved and the consumer choices available. Expenditure patterns also vary within society: age, gender, income, economic status and the region in which people live can all influence expenditure patterns.

## Household and personal expenditure

In real terms, that is, after allowing for inflation, household expenditure has increased in most years over the past 50 years or so. Years when household expenditure showed less than buoyant growth are generally linked to downturns in the economic cycle. Despite the occasional blip, long-term growth has been remarkably steady: total household expenditure in real terms in 1999 was nearly three and a half times the equivalent figure in 1951 (Chart 6.1).

Long-term comparisons of expenditure patterns over the course of the 20th century are made difficult by two factors: scarcity of reliable information collected at the start of the century and the major disruption to the economy caused by the Second World War. *Britain, An Official Handbook*, noted in 1952 that 'changes in relative prices, in the quality and character of goods and services supplied and in the relative importance of different types of expenditure, make any precise statistical comparisons of the volume of consumption before and after the Second World War unrealistic, especially as it is clear that at least a part of the change in spending habits has been caused by controls (rationing) which restrict consumers' choice and therefore lessen their satisfaction'. Official collection of a wider range of economic statistics started in the immediate post-war years.

# 6.3

In 1999 total household expenditure in the United Kingdom was £564 billion, which was more than double the amount in real terms – that is, after allowing for inflation – on the 1971 level. Over the past three decades there have been marked shifts in household expenditure patterns. The proportions spent on both services and durable goods have gradually increased while the proportion on non-durable goods has declined (Chart 6.2). Since 1988 more has been spent on services than non-durable goods (such as food and fuel and power).

Since 1971 household expenditure has increased in real terms in all the broad categories of expenditure shown in Table 6.3, with the exception of tobacco. This decreased by more than half between 1971 and 1999 and can be explained by the fall in the number of people smoking. Some categories of goods and services have grown faster than others. For example, spending on financial services and UK tourists' expenditure abroad was almost five times and almost six times higher respectively in 1999 than in 1971. This latter increase is reflected in the increase in the number of visits abroad (see Table 12.17 on page 218 in the Transport chapter). In contrast, expenditure on food increased by only a quarter in real terms over the period.

Since the early 1960s, there has also been a decline in real terms in expenditure on postal items: at its lowest point in 1980, £691 million were spent on postal services in the United Kingdom, half the amount spent in real terms in 1963 (Chart 6.4). In part this reflects the move from paper to electronic services such as telephones, mobile phones, email and fax technology. Since the early 1980s, there has been a general upturn in spending on postal services, but at £1,004 million in 1999, this is still a third less than in 1963. Expenditure on telecommunications (telephone, fax and computer transmission charges including mobile and cable) increased twentyfold in real terms over the same period, from £619 million to £12,077 million.

## Household[1] expenditure

| United Kingdom | | | | | | Indices[2] (1971=100) | |
|---|---|---|---|---|---|---|---|
| | Indices at constant prices[2] | | | | | | £ billion (current prices) |
| | 1971 | 1981 | 1986 | 1991 | 1998 | 1999 | 1999 |
| Household goods | 100 | 132 | 171 | 201 | 270 | 288 | 143.0 |
| Rent, water and sewerage charges[3] | 100 | 121 | 131 | 140 | 152 | 155 | 77.9 |
| Food | 100 | 104 | 109 | 115 | 126 | 128 | 54.9 |
| Transport and communication | 100 | 143 | 183 | 214 | 279 | 303 | 54.4 |
| Clothing and footwear | 100 | 129 | 178 | 200 | 290 | 309 | 33.5 |
| Alcohol | 100 | 127 | 134 | 132 | 132 | 137 | 32.6 |
| Recreational and cultural activities | 100 | 142 | 156 | 182 | 221 | 220 | 28.1 |
| Financial services | 100 | 136 | 256 | 369 | 452 | 478 | 25.9 |
| Fuel and power | 100 | 110 | 120 | 126 | 123 | 123 | 13.6 |
| Tobacco | 100 | 89 | 74 | 72 | 51 | 47 | 12.0 |
| Other services | 100 | 108 | 205 | 267 | 308 | 311 | 84.4 |
| Less expenditure by foreign tourists, etc | 100 | 152 | 197 | 187 | 248 | 242 | -14.5 |
| Household expenditure abroad | 100 | 193 | 229 | 298 | 504 | 579 | 18.6 |
| All household expenditure | 100 | 121 | 144 | 166 | 200 | 209 | 564.4 |

1 See Appendix, Part 6: Household expenditure.
2 At constant 1995 prices.
3 Includes rents, rates and water charges, but excludes expenditure on home improvements, insurance, community charge and council tax.

*Source: Office for National Statistics*

# 6.4

## Household expenditure on post and telecommunications at constant prices[1]

**United Kingdom**
£ billion

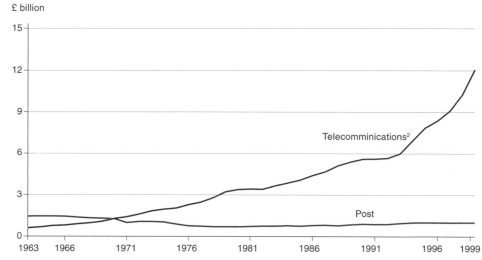

1 At constant 1995 prices.
2 Includes telephone, fax and computer transmission charges including mobile and cable.

*Source: Office for National Statistics*

# 6.5

### Children's[1] expenditure: by gender and type of purchase, 1999-00

| United Kingdom | | | Percentages |
|---|---|---|---|
| | Males | Fe-males | All aged 7-15 |
| Food and soft drinks | 37 | 36 | 36 |
| Leisure goods | 29 | 17 | 23 |
| Clothing and footwear | 8 | 16 | 12 |
| Leisure services | 11 | 8 | 10 |
| Household goods and services | 5 | 8 | 7 |
| Transport and fares | 7 | 4 | 6 |
| Other goods and services | 4 | 10 | 7 |
| | | | |
| All expenditure (=100%) (£ per week) | 10.60 | 10.80 | 10.70 |

1 Children aged 7 to 15.

*Source: Family Expenditure Survey, Office for National Statistics*

# 6.6

### Student[1] expenditure, 1995/96 and 1998/99

| United Kingdom | Percentages | |
|---|---|---|
| | 1995/96 | 1998/99 |
| **Essential expenditure** | | |
| Accommodation | 23 | 20 |
| Food, bills, household goods | 20 | 18 |
| Course expenditure | 10 | 7 |
| Essential travel | 3 | 6 |
| Children | 1 | - |
| | | |
| All essential expenditure | 57 | 51 |
| **Other expenditure** | | |
| Entertainment | 26 | 31 |
| Non-essential travel | 4 | 3 |
| Other[2] | 12 | 16 |
| | | |
| All other expenditure | 43 | 49 |
| | | |
| **All expenditure** (=100%) (£ per student per year at July 1999 prices[3]) | 5,031 | 5,403 |

1 Students under the age of 26 in higher education.
2 Includes non-essential consumer items and credit repayments.
3 Adjusted to July 1999 prices using the retail prices deflator (excluding mortgage interest payments).

*Source: Student Income and Expenditure Survey, Department for Education and Employment*

As well as spending proportionately more on services and less on goods than we did 40 years ago, we also spend proportionately more on non-essential items (such as leisure goods and services) and less on essential items (such as fuel light and power). The emergence of new products and services on the market mean that consumers are given a wider choice of what to spend their money on. The expansion of cable, satellite and digital television has contributed to the continuing longer-term increase in expenditure on home entertainment equipment. Average household expenditure on buying (ie excluding rental) television, video, computers and audio rose in real terms from £2 per household per week in the late 1960s to about £8 per household per week in 1999-00. Our higher levels of disposable income (see Chart 5.1 in the Income and Wealth chapter on page 94) have enabled us to spend more on non-essential items and essential items.

Information from the Family Expenditure Survey (FES) illustrates differences in the types of goods and services bought by different households. In 1999-00 'staple' products, such as fruit and vegetables and fresh milk, were bought by over 90 per cent of households in the two week diary-keeping period. A smaller proportion of households buy other products. Three-fifths of households spent money on beer and lager and two-fifths bought wine, but under a quarter of households spent money on participant sports and a sixth paid for domestic help.

One way of illustrating increasing relative prosperity for those in employment is to compare the increase in prices as measured by the retail prices index (RPI) with the increase in wages as measured by the average earnings index (AEI) (see Chart 5.7 on page 98). Generally, earnings have increased at a faster rate than prices, and thus the length of time required to work to pay for goods has decreased.

The income of those primarily dependent on state benefits is linked to RPI increases and has therefore not kept pace with the AEI. However, as the previous chapter also reveals, the savings and other income sources of some economically inactive groups (particularly retired households holding private pension arrangements) has also increased in recent years, indicating that the higher 'spending power' of particular groups in society has not been confined to those in work.

Different age groups in society also spend their money in different ways. As young people gain access to money, they are able to make choices in the way that they spend it. The FES collects information about children's expenditure patterns in the United Kingdom. Like adults, children aged 7 to 15 are asked to keep diaries to record their spending over a two-week period. In 1999-00, more than a third of the expenditure of children aged 7 to 15 years was on food and soft drinks and a similar proportion was spent on leisure goods and leisure services (Table 6.5). Only 7 per cent of their expenditure was on household goods and services, reflecting the fact that most young people under the age of 16 live in the family home. Transport and fare costs accounted for only 6 per cent of children's expenditure, as children's fares tend to be paid for by parents and guardians, and public transport fares for young people are subsidised. It is important to note that young people will usually have access to items that they do not buy themselves as parents will still be purchasing many of the items that their children need.

There are differences in the spending patterns of boys and girls. Girls spent double the proportion on clothing and footwear compared with boys. Conversely, boys spent one and a half times more than girls on leisure goods and leisure services.

## 6.7

Even when children get older, many are still financially reliant on their parents, especially if they become students. Students have very specific spending patterns. For instance, they are required to buy items that other people would not buy, such as text books. According to the Student Income and Expenditure Survey, around half of the expenditure by students under the age of 26 in higher education in 1998/99 was on what could be termed 'essential items', such as accommodation, food, bills and household goods and course expenditure (Table 6.6). Students who lived at home with their parents spent on average a quarter of the amount paid by students living independently on housing as they were subsidised by their parents.

Some student spending has changed over the last few years. By 1998/99, proportional expenditure on accommodation had decreased by 3 percentage points since 1995/96, while entertainment had increased by 5 percentage points. In 1995/96, course expenditure (which includes text books, personal computers and special equipment) was 10 per cent of expenditure; by 1998/99 this had decreased to 7 per cent. Student's income is shown in Table 5.4 on page 96. It was not possible to balance exactly a student's incomings and outgoings in the survey. Although the Student Income and Expenditure Survey attempted to isolate income and expenditure for the student, most of the excess expenditure represents spending within couples or families which would be met by the student's partner's income.

The average expenditure of households varies according to the economic activity status of the household head. Households where the head is self-employed tend to have higher than average expenditure: £500 per week in 1999-00, nearly two-fifths higher than the average for all households (Table 6.7). Average weekly expenditure by households where the head was retired was, at £201, under three-fifths the average expenditure for all households. Households headed by a retired person or an unemployed person spent the greatest proportion (a fifth) of their expenditure per week on food and non-alcoholic drink. On the other hand, these households also spent the lowest proportion on motoring and fares compared with other household groups – an eighth of their expenditure per week. Households headed by an unemployed person spent the smallest proportion of all households on leisure goods and services, but they also spent a higher proportion than other households on tobacco.

**Household expenditure[1]: by economic activity status of head of household, 1999-00**

United Kingdom — Percentages

| | In employ-ment[2] | Self-employed | Un-employed | Retired | Un-occupied | All house-holds |
|---|---|---|---|---|---|---|
| Food and non-alcoholic drink | 16 | 16 | 20 | 20 | 19 | 17 |
| Leisure goods and services | 17 | 19 | 13 | 18 | 18 | 17 |
| Motoring and fares | 18 | 18 | 12 | 13 | 15 | 17 |
| Housing | 17 | 16 | 13 | 14 | 13 | 16 |
| Household goods and services | 13 | 13 | 15 | 16 | 14 | 14 |
| | | | | | | |
| Clothing and footwear | 6 | 6 | 8 | 5 | 6 | 6 |
| Alcohol | 4 | 4 | 5 | 4 | 5 | 4 |
| Fuel, light and power | 3 | 3 | 5 | 5 | 4 | 3 |
| Tobacco | 1 | 1 | 4 | 1 | 3 | 2 |
| Other goods and services | 4 | 4 | 5 | 5 | 4 | 4 |
| | | | | | | |
| All household expenditure (=100%)(£ per week) | 457 | 500 | 212 | 201 | 260 | 359 |

1 See Appendix, Part 6: Household expenditure.
2 Excludes the self-employed.

**Source: Family Expenditure Survey, Office for National Statistics**

As has been described, the economic activity status of the head of household affects expenditure patterns. This is linked to the level of income that a household has at its disposal. There are some notable differences between the expenditure patterns of households with different levels of equivalised income (that is, income after the size and composition of the household has been taken into account in order to recognise differing demands on resources – see page 102 in the Income and Wealth chapter for a fuller definition). In 1998-99 the households in the bottom fifth of the equivalised income distribution spent over a quarter of their expenditure on the essentials of food, fuel, light and power – a higher proportion than those households in the top fifth of incomes (Table 6.8). Conversely, those with the highest incomes spent a greater proportion of their income than those with low incomes on motoring and fares, and leisure goods and services.

There are also distinct regional variations in patterns of expenditure. In the period 1997-98 to 1999-00 average household expenditure was highest in London, followed by the South East; it was lowest in the North East. At around £71.20 per household per week, households in the South East spent almost 70 per cent more than households in the North East region on motoring and fares, and a fifth more than the UK average (Table 6.9).

Households in Northern Ireland spent around two-fifths less than the UK average on housing, while households in London spent around a third more than the UK average. Households in Northern Ireland spent 15 per cent more than the UK average on food and non-alcoholic drink, while households in the North East region spent 14 per cent less.

## Prices

Price changes have long been of interest. Records of the changes in the prices of basic items can be traced to medieval times as people tried to observe the effects on their lives of the 'cost of living'. The forerunner of the modern retail prices index (RPI) began in 1914 when the government decided it needed to understand the impact of the First World War on the prices of goods bought by the 'working classes'. These included items such as bread, tobacco and candles. The usefulness of such a socio-economic measure was widely recognised and work was begun on producing a more comprehensive and universally relevant price measurement index. The outbreak of the Second World War meant that its final implementation had to be postponed, and the modern RPI was introduced in 1947.

The RPI is not strictly a 'cost of living' index, a concept which means different things to different people, primarily because it is difficult to decide which 'essentials' should or should not be included. The index simply gives an indication of

# 6.8

**Household expenditure[1]: by income grouping, 1998-99**

United Kingdom          Percentages

| | Bottom fifth | Next fifth | Middle fifth | Next fifth | Top fifth | All house-holds |
|---|---|---|---|---|---|---|
| | Quintile groups of households[2] | | | | | |
| Motoring and fares | 13 | 13 | 17 | 18 | 19 | 17 |
| Leisure goods and services | 13 | 14 | 17 | 17 | 19 | 17 |
| Food and non-alcoholic drink | 22 | 21 | 18 | 16 | 13 | 17 |
| Housing | 17 | 16 | 15 | 16 | 17 | 16 |
| Household goods and services | 13 | 14 | 13 | 13 | 15 | 14 |
| Clothing and footwear | 6 | 6 | 6 | 6 | 6 | 6 |
| Alcohol | 3 | 4 | 4 | 4 | 4 | 4 |
| Fuel, light and power | 5 | 5 | 4 | 3 | 2 | 3 |
| Tobacco | 3 | 3 | 2 | 1 | 1 | 2 |
| Other goods and services | 4 | 4 | 4 | 4 | 4 | 4 |
| All household expenditure (=100%)(£ per week) | 189 | 223 | 327 | 420 | 601 | 352 |

1 See Appendix, Part 6: Household expenditure.
2 Equivalised disposable income has been used for ranking the households into quintile groups. See Appendix, Part 5: Equivalisation scales.

**Source: Family Expenditure Survey, Office for National Statistics**

**6.9**

### Household expenditure[1]: by region, 1997-2000

£ per week

| | Leisure goods and services | Motoring and fares | Food and non-alcoholic drink | Housing | House-hold goods and services | Clothing and footwear | Alcohol and tobacco | Fuel, light and power | Other goods and services | All expend-iture |
|---|---|---|---|---|---|---|---|---|---|---|
| United Kingdom | 59.70 | 59.20 | 58.50 | 55.20 | 47.60 | 21.00 | 20.50 | 11.90 | 14.50 | 348.20 |
| North East | 47.10 | 42.30 | 50.10 | 43.50 | 39.20 | 19.70 | 20.60 | 12.00 | 10.90 | 285.40 |
| North West | 57.90 | 57.30 | 56.00 | 49.00 | 42.30 | 22.50 | 23.50 | 12.40 | 13.80 | 334.60 |
| Yorkshire and the Humber | 57.80 | 56.10 | 54.70 | 48.70 | 44.70 | 20.20 | 22.20 | 11.70 | 13.40 | 329.60 |
| East Midlands | 57.80 | 60.00 | 58.00 | 51.50 | 47.30 | 18.30 | 20.50 | 11.90 | 13.50 | 338.70 |
| West Midlands | 58.60 | 58.00 | 57.30 | 50.30 | 46.60 | 19.80 | 19.80 | 12.40 | 13.30 | 336.20 |
| East | 59.60 | 65.40 | 60.10 | 57.60 | 49.70 | 21.00 | 17.30 | 11.30 | 15.80 | 357.90 |
| London | 72.00 | 62.80 | 65.90 | 74.50 | 54.60 | 24.50 | 21.00 | 10.90 | 17.70 | 403.90 |
| South East | 67.60 | 71.20 | 61.40 | 67.70 | 56.00 | 21.40 | 18.90 | 11.30 | 17.10 | 392.50 |
| South West | 55.80 | 58.00 | 55.40 | 54.80 | 47.10 | 17.30 | 18.00 | 11.20 | 14.70 | 332.20 |
| England | 61.10 | 60.80 | 58.60 | 57.50 | 48.70 | 20.90 | 20.20 | 11.60 | 15.00 | 354.30 |
| Wales | 56.60 | 48.20 | 55.20 | 44.70 | 43.70 | 20.50 | 20.60 | 12.60 | 13.60 | 315.60 |
| Scotland | 51.70 | 51.80 | 57.70 | 46.70 | 41.00 | 21.00 | 23.00 | 12.90 | 11.50 | 317.30 |
| Northern Ireland[2] | 48.00 | 53.20 | 67.30 | 30.60 | 43.50 | 25.30 | 21.20 | 15.20 | 12.60 | 316.90 |

1 See Appendix, Part 6: Household Expenditure. Combined data from the 1997-98, 1998-99 and 1999-00 surveys.
2 Northern Ireland data are calculated from an enhanced sample for 1998-99 and 1999-00, but the United Kingdom figures are calculated from the main Family Expenditure Survey sample. The data from the main Family Expenditure Survey include expenditure by children; the Northern Ireland data relate to adults only.
*Source: Family Expenditure Survey, Office for National Statistics and Northern Ireland Statistics and Research Agency*

what we would need to spend in order to purchase the same things we chose to buy in an earlier period. The current RPI collects prices for around 600 specified types of goods and services. The majority are collected from retail outlets in 146 different areas of the United Kingdom. The remainder (over 100) are collected by the ONS centrally. These prices are then computed to produce a monthly figure usually referred to as the 'all items' inflation rate. This figure is used to uprate many payments such as pensions and social security benefits, wages and allowances, rent and alimony payments. Consequently, it affects the lives of nearly everyone in the country. Inflation rates are usually expressed as an annual change figure. There have been periods of both high and low inflation and Chart 6.10 shows these fluctuations over the last 40 years in the United Kingdom. Over this period, inflation was at its

**6.10**

### Retail prices index[1]

**United Kingdom**
Percentage change over 12 months

1 See Appendix, Part 6: Retail prices index.
*Source: Office for National Statistics*

# 6.11

## Retail prices index: 12 month change, 1999[1]

**United Kingdom**

Percentages

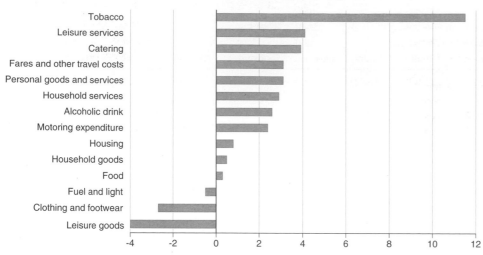

1 Annual average percentage change on the previous year.

**Source: Office for National Statistics**

and 4.0 per cent respectively, reflecting 'price wars' over items within these groups in the high street.

The types of items for which prices are collected alter over the years, to keep up to date with consumer tastes, trends and developments. Every year in February, new items are added to a number of groups while others are removed to reflect changes in people's spending and consumption. For example, in 2000, PC printers were introduced in the leisure goods category, and in food and catering, broccoli, pre-packed salad and takeaway/delivered pizza were included for the first time. In the light of increasing use of the Internet, it was decided to incorporate a couple of items, books and toys, commonly bought on the Internet.

lowest level in July 1963 at 0.8 per cent. It reached its highest level in August 1975 when it was 26.9 per cent. Since then, there has been an overall decline so that by September 2000, inflation stood at 3.3 per cent. This rate is one of several that are used in measuring price changes.

The movement of the inflation rate reflects the price movements of its components, such as food, clothing and footwear, housing and fuel and light, among others. Each part is given a different weight, to represent the amount of expenditure by households on them. For example, in 2000, housing had the largest weight of 195 parts per 1,000 whereas fares and other travel carried the lowest with 21. Chart 6.11 shows the annual average percentage changes for the main parts of the RPI in 1999 on the previous year in the United Kingdom. The largest change was in tobacco, which was mainly due to increases in duty in the Budget. Housing rose by less than 1 per cent, largely as a result of lower mortgage interest rates. The biggest decreases were in clothing and footwear and leisure goods, falls of 2.7 per cent

Although some items alter in the RPI, others remain over the years. Some of these 'staple goods' are shown in Table 6.12. To buy the 'basket' of goods illustrated would have cost 6 shillings in 1914, the equivalent of 30 pence. The same basket today would cost £10.73.

Another measure of inflation is the Harmonised Index of Consumer Prices (HICP). It is often useful to be able to compare price changes in one country with another, particularly when countries belong to a trading group such as the European Union (EU). The HICPs are constructed on a comparable basis in each member state of the EU and have been published monthly by Eurostat since March 1997 (see Appendix, Part 6: Harmonised index of consumer prices).

Another way of looking at the difference between price levels in different countries is by measuring Purchasing Power Parities (PPPs). A PPP between the United Kingdom and another country is the exchange rate that would be required to purchase the same quantity of goods and services

# 6.12

## Cost of groceries

| United Kingdom | | | Pence |
|---|---|---|---|
| | 1914[1] | 1950[1] | 2000 |
| 500g streaky bacon | 5 | 11 | 220 |
| 500g beef (brisket without bone) | 5 | 6 | 211 |
| 250g cheddar cheese | 2 | 3 | 118 |
| 500g margarine | 3 | 5 | 87 |
| 250g butter (home produced) | 6 | 6 | 83 |
| Half dozen eggs (size 2) | 3 | 11 | 82 |
| 125g loose tea | 2 | 5 | 79 |
| 1 kg granulated sugar | 2 | 5 | 56 |
| 800g white sliced bread | 1 | 2 | 52 |
| 1 kg old potatoes | 1 | 1 | 51 |
| 1 pint pasteurised milk | 1 | 2 | 34 |
| Total of above items | 30 | 57 | 1,073 |

1 Prices and weights are given to the nearest decimal equivalents.

**Source: Office for National Statistics**

# 6.13

costing £1 in the UK. PPPs represent the purchasing power of currencies better than official exchange rates, as the latter do not always fully reflect the price level differences which exist between countries. Chart 6.13 shows how much more expensive or cheaper goods and services would have appeared to someone from the United Kingdom in 1998 in any other country within the EU. Expressed as an index, those countries which were below 100 would have appeared to have been cheaper, and those above more expensive. The two countries that would have seemed cheapest were Portugal and Greece. The countries that would have seemed cheaper were also among the most popular holiday destinations for UK holidaymakers (see Table 13.15 in the Lifestyles and Social Participation chapter). The three EU states that would have appeared most expensive were all in Scandinavia.

**Relative price levels[1]: EU comparison, 1998**

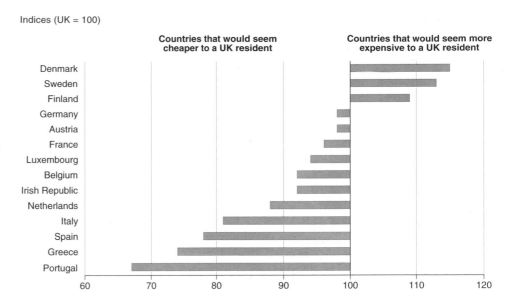

1 Price level indices for private consumption - the ratio of purchasing power parities to the official exchange rates.
*Source: Eurostat*

## Transactions and credit

Some purchases are paid for over a period of time using one of the many forms of credit available. New borrowing by consumers, net of repayments, provides the best measure of current growth in consumer credit in the United Kingdom and its movements clearly mirror the effects of the economic cycle. For example, a rise in interest rates which makes borrowing comparatively more expensive, and the decreasing job security which can be associated with a downturn in the economic cycle, may result in a decrease in borrowing levels. Net borrowing by consumers fell in real terms from around £3 billion in the fourth quarter of 1987 to a small net repayment in the second quarter of 1992 (Chart 6.14). Borrowing has followed an upward trend between 1992 and 1998 in real terms, although there was some fluctuation during the period, and then it stabilised. In the second quarter of 2000 consumers borrowed around £3.5 billion.

# 6.14

**Net borrowing by consumers in real terms[1]**

**United Kingdom**
£ billion at 1999 prices[1]

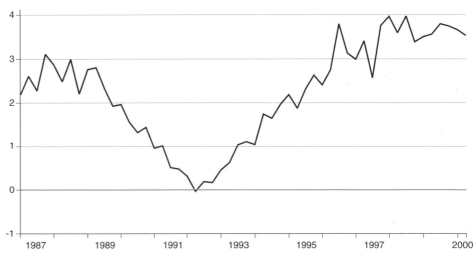

1 Seasonally adjusted. Adjusted to 1999 prices using the RPI deflator; excludes lending secured on dwellings.
*Source: Bank of England*

# 6.15

## Composition of consumer credit[1] in real terms[2]

**United Kingdom**          Percentages

| | 1987 | 1989 | 1991 | 1993 | 1995 | 1997 | 1999 |
|---|---|---|---|---|---|---|---|
| Bank loans | 80 | 81 | 81 | 78 | 73 | 74 | 72 |
| Retailers | 6 | 5 | 5 | 5 | 4 | 3 | 3 |
| Insurance companies | 2 | 2 | 2 | 3 | 2 | 2 | 1 |
| Building society loans[3] | - | 1 | 1 | 1 | 2 | - | - |
| Other specialist lenders[4] | 12 | 11 | 11 | 13 | 19 | 21 | 24 |
| Credit outstanding at end of year (=100%)(£ billion at 1999 prices[2]) | 58.9 | 69.8 | 66.9 | 62.3 | 75.0 | 91.9 | 114.9 |

1 Excludes mortgage borrowing. See also Appendix, Part 6: Consumer credit.
2 Adjusted to 1998 prices using the retail prices index.
3 Building society unsecured loans to individuals or companies (ie Class 3 loans as defined in the Building Societies Act 1986).
4 Includes new non-bank credit granters from 1995.

**Source: Bank of England; Office for National Statistics**

Table 6.15 shows the total indebtedness of consumers after allowing for inflation. This definition of consumer credit excludes mortgage borrowing. The amount of consumer credit outstanding in the United Kingdom in real terms increased sharply between 1987 and 1989, and then fell to 1993. Since then it has increased again to £115 billion in 1999, almost double in real terms the 1987 level. Bank loans, while still accounting for the majority of consumer credit, represented a smaller share of outstanding credit in 1999 (72 per cent) than in 1987 (80 per cent).

A continuing trend in the payment market has been the declining share of all payments made by cash. Data from the Association for Payment Clearing Services (APACS) shows cash payment

# 6.16

## Volume of transactions

**United Kingdom**      Millions

| | 1991 | 1992 | 1993 | 1994 | 1995 | 1996 | 1997 | 1998 | 1999 |
|---|---|---|---|---|---|---|---|---|---|
| **Non-cash payments** | | | | | | | | | |
| Plastic cards purchases | | | | | | | | | |
|   Debit card | 359 | 522 | 659 | 808 | 1,004 | 1,270 | 1,503 | 1,736 | 2,062 |
|   Credit and charge card | 699 | 724 | 748 | 815 | 908 | 1,025 | 1,128 | 1,224 | 1,344 |
|   Store card | 46 | 70 | 82 | 100 | 109 | 118 | 128 | 134 | 131 |
|   All plastic card purchases | 1,104 | 1,316 | 1,488 | 1,723 | 2,023 | 2,413 | 2,759 | 3,094 | 3,537 |
| Withdrawals at ATMs and counters | 1,112 | 1,199 | 1,277 | 1,372 | 1,512 | 1,656 | 1,809 | 1,917 | 2,025 |
| Direct debits, standing orders, direct credits and CHAPS | 1,848 | 1,962 | 2,047 | 2,196 | 2,402 | 2,613 | 2,826 | 3,056 | 3,255 |
| Cheques | | | | | | | | | |
|   For payment | 3,450 | 3,332 | 3,163 | 3,074 | 2,938 | 2,901 | 2,838 | 2,757 | 2,641 |
|   For cash acquisition | 432 | 396 | 396 | 356 | 345 | 302 | 245 | 229 | 213 |
|   All cheques | 3,882 | 3,728 | 3,559 | 3,430 | 3,283 | 3,203 | 3,083 | 2,986 | 2,854 |
| Total non-cash | 7,946 | 8,205 | 8,371 | 8,721 | 9,220 | 9,885 | 10,477 | 11,053 | 11,672 |
| **Cash payments** | 28,022 | 27,845 | 27,273 | 26,179 | 26,270 | 26,318 | 25,540 | 25,309 | 25,596 |
| **Post office order book and passbook withdrawals** | 1,056 | 1,108 | 1,144 | 1,127 | 1,163 | 1,114 | 1,066 | 1,017 | 962 |
| **Total transactions** | 37,025 | 37,158 | 36,788 | 36,026 | 36,654 | 37,318 | 37,083 | 37,379 | 38,230 |

**Source: Association of Payment Clearing Services**

# 6.17

volumes fell to around £25.6 billion in 1999 but still accounted for two-thirds of all payments (Table 6.16). Direct debits, standing orders, direct credits and payments through CHAPS (Clearing House Automated Payment System) have increased by more than three-quarters between 1991 and 1999 while cheque payments have declined by around a quarter over the same period.

Reliable information on e-commerce and Internet transactions is difficult to obtain, but indications are that Internet usage accounts for around 2 per cent of card turnover value. Although exact data are not available, there is evidence that cardholders' use of different payment card types (such as debit and credit cards) for Internet transactions is similar to that for ordinary (ie face-to-face) card transactions.

Increased availability and awareness of cash-back facilities saw the number of this type of transaction grow by 20 per cent in 1999 to 164 million. Figures from APACS indicate that about one in five debit card purchases in supermarkets now involve cash-back, with an average value of £24. There has also been an increase in the number of Automated Teller Machines (ATMs), particularly in non-bank locations such as supermarkets, convenience stores, pubs, petrol stations and railway stations.

Figures from the Credit Card Research Group indicate that the core areas for debit card usage remain supermarkets, petrol stations and retail stores – particularly department stores – while credit and charge cards are used more for travel

and entertainment. Credit cards tend to be used for larger transactions than debit cards. The average purchase value on debit cards in 1999 was £31, compared with £88 on charge cards and £51 on credit cards. This difference is reflected in the types of purchases which are more likely to be made with each type of card (Chart 6.17). For example, in 1999, credit cards were used for £3.5 billion of expenditure on hotels, compared with only £0.7 billion by debit cards. Food and drink purchases dominated in debit card expenditure, accounting for £21.8 billion in 1999, a third of all debit card expenditure. Not all of this reflects spending as such, as it also includes the impact of cash-back services offered by supermarkets mentioned earlier.

**Credit[1] and debit[2] card spending: by type of purchase, 1999**

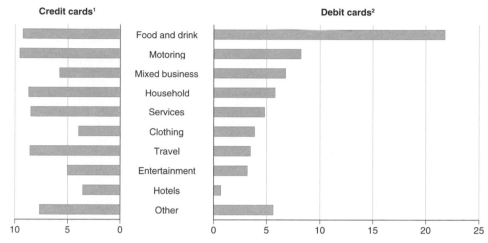

**United Kingdom**
£ billion

1 Mastercard and Visa cards only.
2 Visa and Switch cards only.
**Source: Credit Card Research Group**

## Websites

| | |
|---|---|
| National Statistics | www.statistics.gov.uk |
| Association for Payment Clearing Services | www.apacs.org.uk |
| Bank of England | www.bankofengland.co.uk |
| Credit Card Research Group | www.ccrg.org.uk |
| National Centre for Social Research | www.natcen.ac.uk |

## Contacts

| | |
|---|---|
| **Office for National Statistics** | |
| Chapter author | 020 7533 5776 |
| Family Expenditure Survey | 020 7533 5756 |
| Harmonised index of consumer prices | 020 7533 5818 |
| Household expenditure | 020 7533 5999 |
| Purchasing power parities | 020 7533 5819 |
| Retail prices index | 020 7533 5874 |
| Retail sales | 01633 812609 |
| **Department for Education and Employment** | 020 7273 5971 |
| **Association for Payment Clearing Services** | 020 7711 6235 |
| **Bank of England** | 020 7601 4878 |
| **Credit Card Research Group** | 020 7436 9937 |

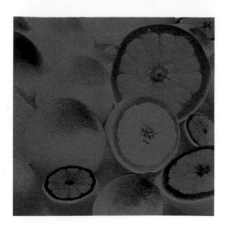

# Chapter 7 Health

### The nation's health

- In 1841, life expectancy at birth was 41 years for males and 43 for females in England and Wales; by 1998, in Great Britain, these had reached 75 and 80 respectively. (Table 7.1)

- In 1999, 5.8 children per 1,000 died before the age of one in the United Kingdom, compared with 83.8 in 1921. (Chart 7.2)

### Diet and lifestyle

- The amount of fresh fruit eaten in the home in Great Britain has risen over a third since the mid-1980s, to around 700 grams per person per week in 1999. However, in 1997, a fifth of children aged 4 to 18 reported not having eaten any fruit (excluding fruit juice) during the seven day dietary record. (Chart 7.12 and page 134)

- In 1998-99, around a half of men aged 16 to 24 and two-fifths of women of the same age in the United Kingdom had consumed in excess of the recommended amount of alcohol (four units for men and three for women) on their heaviest drinking day in the week prior to being interviewed. (Table 7.15)

- Among people aged 16 to 24 in England, almost a fifth of males and one in 20 females took part in more than seven hours of sport or exercise per week in 1998. (Table 7.18)

### Causes of death

- Among 15 to 74 year olds in 1911, deaths from respiratory diseases and infections together made up nearly a third of all deaths for males and a quarter of those for females in Great Britain. By 1999 respiratory disease and infections were the cause of only around one in ten deaths in the same age range. (Page 137)

- In 1996, there were 34 deaths per 100,000 females from breast cancer in the United Kingdom; only four other countries in the European Union had a higher death rate. (Chart 7.20)

### Prevention

- In 1998-99, 89 per cent of children in the United Kingdom had been immunised against measles, mumps and rubella by their second birthday, compared with 54 per cent in England, Wales and Northern Ireland in 1981. (Table 7.26)

# 7.1

### Life expectancy and healthy life expectancy at birth[1]: by gender

| Great Britain | | | | | | | | | Years |
|---|---|---|---|---|---|---|---|---|---|
| | 1841 | 1901 | 1931 | 1961 | 1981 | 1986 | 1991 | 1997 | 1998 |
| **Males** | | | | | | | | | |
| Life expectancy | 41.0 | 45.7 | 58.1 | 67.8 | 70.9 | 72.0 | 73.2 | 74.6 | 74.9 |
| Healthy life expectancy | .. | .. | .. | .. | 64.4 | 65.4 | 66.2 | 66.9 | .. |
| **Females** | | | | | | | | | |
| Life expectancy | 43.0 | 49.6 | 62.1 | 73.7 | 76.8 | 77.7 | 78.8 | 79.6 | 79.8 |
| Healthy life expectancy | .. | .. | .. | .. | 66.7 | 67.6 | 68.6 | 68.7 | .. |

1 Data for 1841 and 1901 are for England and Wales only. See also Appendix, Part 7: Expectation of life and Healthy life expectancy.

**Source: Government Actuary's Department; Office for National Statistics**

# 7.2

### Infant mortality[1]

**United Kingdom**

Rate per 1,000 live births

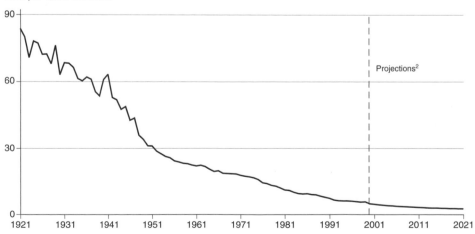

1 Deaths within one year of birth.
2 1998-based projections.

**Source: Office for National Statistics; General Register Office for Scotland; Northern Ireland Statistics and Research Agency; Government Actuary's Department**

The last 200 years have seen huge improvements in the nation's health. Many factors have contributed towards this, such as advances in medical and scientific knowledge and services, screening, and improved standards of living. As a result, infant mortality has fallen and people live longer.

## The nation's health

Mortality is one way of measuring health, and life expectancy provides a useful age standardised measure of mortality. Since the middle of the 19th century the expectation of life at birth for both females and males has almost doubled (Table 7.1). Neither men nor women born in England and Wales in 1841 had an average life expectancy from birth much beyond 40, although those who survived to the age of 15 could expect another 45 years of life. However, by 1998 the life expectancy at birth of females in Great Britain had almost reached 80, and males nearly 75 years.

Despite its use as a general indicator of health, life expectancy takes no account of the quality of life. 'Healthy life expectancy' overcomes this limitation by combining mortality and morbidity data into a single index. Recent research by the Office for National Statistics (ONS) into healthy life expectancy, defined as expected years of life in good or fairly good self-assessed general health, has shown that since 1981 healthy life expectancy has increased in Great Britain – but it has not risen as much as life expectancy. Both males and females born in 1997 can therefore expect to live more years in poor health: males, at birth, could expect 66.9 years of life in good or fairly good health, and females could expect 68.7 years.

A major cause of the rise in life expectancy has been the decrease in infant mortality. This has fallen since the early years of the 20th century (Chart 7.2). In 1921, 83.8 children per 1,000 live births died before the age of one in the United

Kingdom. There was a sharp fall after the Second World War, from 48.8 deaths before the age of one per 1,000 live births to exactly half that only 11 years later in 1956. This decline has continued, so that in 1999 the rate was 5.8. This is likely to have been largely due to improvements in the nutritional intake of children, in sanitary and hygiene improvements, better antenatal and postnatal care, the development of an immunisation programme and other improvements in medical care, and, more recently, the fall in the rate of cot deaths. In addition, changes in medical technology over the past two decades have played a large part in improving the survival and life chances of premature and very low birthweight babies.

Given the failure of healthy life expectancy to rise as fast as life expectancy over the last 20 years, it is perhaps little surprise that there has been increased reporting of morbidity (Chart 7.3). The most notable rise has been among the older age groups. In 1972, 8 per cent of females and 7 per cent of males in Great Britain had reported some restricted activity in the 14 days prior to being interviewed for the General Household Survey (GHS); by 1979 both of these figures had almost doubled, to 14 and 12 per cent respectively. The rates of increase then levelled off and, in 1998-99, 16 per cent of females and 14 per cent of males reported restricted activity.

Although reporting of restricted activity rose across all age categories between 1972 and 1998-99, the rise was most notable among older people. Among those aged 65 to 74, the proportion rose from 10 per cent to 21 per cent, and among those 75 and over it increased from 13 per cent to 26 per cent. There are other measures of morbidity, and the trends for these are similar to those for restricted activity. The proportion of all people reporting a longstanding illness rose from a fifth in 1972 to a third in 1998-99; and reporting of a limiting longstanding illness increased by 5 percentage points over the same period, to 20 per cent. However, with all of these measures, the

**Self-reported restricted activity[1]: by gender**

Great Britain

Percentages

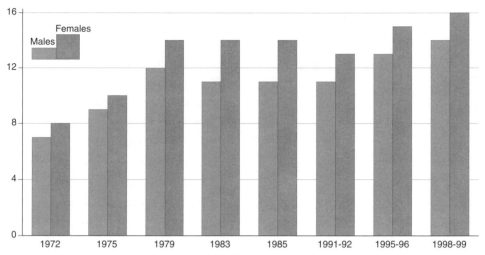

1 Percentage of people of all ages reporting restricted activity in the 14 days prior to interview.
*Source: General Household Survey, Office for National Statistics*

**Standardised incidence rates[1] of selected cancers: by gender**

Great Britain

Rates per 100,000 population

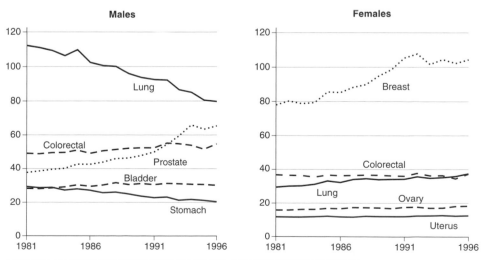

1 Age-standardised to the European population. See Appendix, Part 7: Standardised incidence rates.
*Source: Office for National Statistics*

# 7.5

### Prevalence of treated coronary heart disease and stroke: by age and gender, 1998

| England & Wales | | Rates per 1,000 patients[1] | | |
| --- | --- | --- | --- | --- |
| | Heart disease | | Stroke | |
| | Males | Fe-males | Males | Fe-males |
| Under 35 | - | - | - | - |
| 35-44 | 5 | 2 | 1 | 0 |
| 45-54 | 30 | 13 | 1 | 1 |
| 55-64 | 95 | 49 | 4 | 2 |
| 65-74 | 184 | 112 | 8 | 5 |
| 75-84 | 231 | 167 | 16 | 11 |
| 85 and over | 224 | 180 | 21 | 20 |
| All ages[2] | 37 | 22 | 2 | 1 |

1 Data are recorded in general practice.
2 Age standardised to the European population. See Appendix, Part 7: Standardised prevalence rates.

**Source: Office for National Statistics; Medicines Control Agency**

# 7.6

### Prevalence of treated depression: by type of area[1] and gender, 1994-1998

| England & Wales | Rates per 1,000 patients[2] | |
| --- | --- | --- |
| | Males | Females |
| Deprived industrial areas | 34 | 77 |
| Mature populations | 29 | 67 |
| Metropolitan professionals | 28 | 60 |
| Industrial areas | 27 | 71 |
| Lower status owner-occupier | 26 | 62 |
| Rural fringe | 23 | 56 |
| Established owner-occupier | 23 | 58 |
| Rural areas | 23 | 57 |
| Inner/deprived city | 23 | 53 |
| Middling Britain | 22 | 58 |
| Prosperous areas | 22 | 57 |
| Suburbia | 21 | 55 |
| All areas | 25 | 61 |

1 ONS area classification (ward level). See Appendix, Part 7: The ONS area classification.
2 All ages. Age standardised to the European population. See Appendix, Part 7: Standardised prevalence rates.

**Source: Office for National Statistics; Medicines Control Agency**

rises may be a result of people's perceptions of illness changing as well as a real increase in morbidity.

The nation's health is affected by many factors including social conditions, people's lifestyles and the availability of healthcare. The Government's NHS Plan, published in July 2000, set out its priorities for health care in England. Its overall aim is to meet the challenge 'to use the resources available to achieve real benefits for patients and to ensure that the NHS is modernised to meet modern public expectations'. Among the key focuses are cancer, coronary heart disease, mental health and health inequalities.

About a third of the population develop cancer at some time in their life and cancer is responsible for around a quarter of all deaths. The incidence of cancer has changed since the early 1980s (see Chart 7.4 on the previous page). Lung cancer among males in Great Britain fell dramatically between 1981 and 1996, mainly as a result of the decline in smoking. (Information on smoking is shown in more detail in Table 7.16.) However, breast and prostate cancer have both risen considerably. In 1981 there were 78 cases of breast cancer per 100,000 women in Great Britain, and 38 cases of prostate cancer per 100,000 men. By 1996 these rates had risen to 104 and 65 respectively. This may be due in part to the screening systems put in place, as more cases of cancer are now diagnosed than would have been previously; information on these systems is provided later in this chapter in Table 7.24 and Table 7.25. The incidence of breast cancer peaked in 1992 following the introduction of the NHS screening programme in the late 1980s, but has since fallen slightly.

A reduction in premature deaths from circulatory diseases is another of the areas that the Government intends to target. One of these diseases is coronary heart disease (CHD), which is much more common among men than women.

According to data from the General Practice Research Database, in 1998 the proportion of males in England and Wales who had received treatment for CHD during the year was 70 per cent higher than for females (Table 7.5). The proportion of patients with treated CHD generally increases with age – people aged 75 and over are most at risk. Similarly, the proportion of patients having a stroke rises with age although the differential between men and women is less than for CHD. The key lifestyle risk factors for CHD are now well established, and include smoking, poor nutrition, obesity and physical inactivity. Information on some of these topics is contained in the Diet and lifestyle section of this chapter which begins on page 133.

A third focus of the NHS Plan is mental health. In 2000 the Department of Health commissioned a survey on attitudes to mental illness in Great Britain. Three-quarters of adults thought that 'mental illness was an illness like any other'. In addition, despite the controversy surrounding the issue, three-quarters of the population agreed with the statement that 'the best way to treat the mentally ill' was via care in the community.

Mental illness is strongly linked to several aspects of social inequality. People living in England and Wales in deprived industrial areas are more likely to be treated for depression than people living in any other type of area (Table 7.6). Over the period 1994-1998, 34 per 1,000 male patients and 77 per 1,000 female patients in deprived industrial areas had been treated for depression, compared with rates of 21 and 55 respectively in suburban areas. The gender variation is very evident in all types of areas, and in England and Wales overall the rate for females was two and a half times that for males.

In 1999 ONS carried out the first nationally representative survey of the mental health of children and adolescents. Results indicate that there are inequalities in children's mental health depending on their household's income. Children from households with lower gross weekly incomes were more likely than those from households with higher incomes to display a mental disorder of some kind (Table 7.7). For most income brackets, children aged 11 to 15 were more likely to have a mental disorder than those aged five to ten. In addition, children were more likely to suffer from poor mental health if their parents were unemployed, and if their parents had few or no educational qualifications.

Asthma is a condition with particular relevance to young people, as it is far more prevalent among children of school age than in any other age group. In 1998, 132 per 1,000 boys aged between five and 15 were treated for the condition in England and Wales; the rate for girls of the same age was slightly lower at 104 per 1,000.

The mean weekly incidence rate for new episodes of asthma peaked in 1993 for males and a year later for females (Chart 7.8). In 1999 the rate was 29 cases per 100,000 population for males and 35 cases per 100,000 population for females. These are considerable drops, of nearly 42 per cent for males and 33 per cent for females, from the peak years. Research by the Royal College of General Practitioners has concluded that changes in the number of cases of asthma cannot be explained by either changes in consulting patterns in primary care or doctors' diagnostic preferences. Since 1993 the rate for new episodes of asthma among males was lower than among females, a reversal

of what was historically the case, though higher rates persist for males in the under five and five to 14 year old age groups.

Another illness that has increased is insulin-treated diabetes (see Table 7.9 on the next page). Between 1994 and 1998 the prevalence rate for the 55 to 74 age group showed particularly large increases. Children under 16 had low rates of insulin-treated diabetes in 1998: for both males and females, there were fewer than two cases per 1,000 patients.

One illness to have received publicity over the last 20 years is Human Immunodeficiency Virus (HIV), which causes Acquired Immune Deficiency Syndrome (AIDS). Figures from the Public Health

**Prevalence of mental disorders[1] among children: by gross weekly household income and age of child, 1999**

| Great Britain | | | Percentages |
|---|---|---|---|
| | | | All aged |
| | 5-10 | 11-15 | 5-15 |
| Under £100 | 14 | 19 | 16 |
| £100-£199 | 13 | 20 | 16 |
| £200-£299 | 10 | 14 | 12 |
| £300-£399 | 8 | 11 | 9 |
| | | | |
| £400-£499 | 7 | 6 | 7 |
| £500-£599 | 4 | 8 | 6 |
| £600-£770 | 5 | 6 | 5 |
| Over £770 | 5 | 7 | 6 |
| | | | |
| All | 8 | 11 | 10 |

1 Percentage with a disorder.

*Source: Survey of the Mental Health of Children and Adolescents, Office for National Statistics*

**7.8**

**New episodes[1] of asthma: by gender**

**England & Wales**

Rates per 100,000 population

1 Mean weekly incidence. A diagnosis for the first time or a previously diagnosed asthmatic person having a new attack.

*Source: The Royal College of General Practitioners*

# 7.9

## Prevalence of insulin treated diabetes: by gender and age

**England & Wales**                                                  Rates per 1,000 patients[1]

|  | 1994 | 1995 | 1996 | 1997 | 1998 |
|---|---|---|---|---|---|
| **Males** | | | | | |
| Under 16 | 1 | 1 | 1 | 1 | 1 |
| 16-34 | 4 | 4 | 4 | 4 | 4 |
| 35-54 | 6 | 6 | 6 | 6 | 7 |
| 55-74 | 8 | 9 | 9 | 10 | 11 |
| 75 and over | 8 | 9 | 9 | 10 | 10 |
| | | | | | |
| All ages[2] | 5 | 5 | 5 | 5 | 6 |
| **Females** | | | | | |
| Under 16 | 1 | 1 | 1 | 1 | 2 |
| 16-34 | 3 | 4 | 4 | 4 | 4 |
| 35-54 | 4 | 5 | 5 | 5 | 5 |
| 55-74 | 8 | 9 | 9 | 10 | 11 |
| 75 and over | 7 | 7 | 8 | 8 | 8 |
| | | | | | |
| All ages[2] | 4 | 4 | 5 | 5 | 5 |

1 Data are recorded in general practice.
2 Age-standardised to the European population. See Appendix, Part 7: Standardised prevalence rates.
**Source: Office for National Statistics; Medicines Control Agency**

# 7.10

## HIV infections[1]: by year of diagnosis and route of tranmission

**United Kingdom**
Thousands

1 Numbers of diagnoses recorded, particularly for recent years, will rise as further reports are received. Those where the probable route of infection was not known, particularly for recent years, will fall as follow-up continues.
**Source: Public Health Laboratory Service**

Laboratory Service (PHLS) indicate that 41 thousand diagnoses of HIV infection had been reported in the United Kingdom by March 2000, among whom 17.0 thousand had developed AIDS and 13.5 thousand had died. London has been the main focus of the epidemic, and two-thirds of the 3 thousand infections diagnosed in 1999 were reported from that region. The number of diagnosed HIV cases has increased each year since 1994, when there were just over 2.5 thousand cases in the United Kingdom, to over 2.9 thousand in 1999. However, this rise may be partly due to an increasing awareness of the disease and the consequent increase in testing. The way that those with HIV contracted the infection has also changed. In the late 1990s, diagnoses of infections acquired through sex between men were overtaken by diagnoses of infections due to sex between men and women (Chart 7.10). Forty-five per cent of the people who were diagnosed with HIV in 1999 contracted the virus through heterosexual sex. Three-quarters of these heterosexually acquired infections probably occurred abroad, with over 800 attributed to infection in Africa. Meanwhile, the number of people becoming infected as a result of the use of injected drugs has more than halved since 1993, to less than 100. However, it should be noted that numbers for all of these categories for recent years are likely to rise as delayed reports come in.

Data on sexually transmitted infections (STIs) are produced by the PHLS. As Chart 7.11 shows, between 1998 and 1999 there was a 25 per cent rise in the number of new cases of gonorrhoea – a disease which can cause infertility – diagnosed at genito-urinary medicine clinics in the United Kingdom. Although more men than women were diagnosed with gonorrhoea, the rise in incidence occurred across both genders. The rise in genital uncomplicated chlamydia has also been dramatic over the last five years – 80 per cent more women and 70 per cent more men were diagnosed with chlamydia in 1999 than in 1995. The rises in STIs (not including HIV) are likely to be associated with increasing unsafe sexual behaviour among young heterosexuals and among men who have sex with men, although the substantial rise in genital chlamydial infection may also reflect increased testing for this infection. STIs also display a marked regional variation: for example, two-fifths of new syphilis cases in 1999 were in London.

## Diet and lifestyle

Increasingly, dietary concerns have shifted from the early 20th century problems of under-nutrition towards the problems of over-nutrition, and hence obesity, and the health-related properties of particular foods. Sedentary lifestyles also have a significant role to play in the increasing prevalence of obesity. Many other aspects of people's lives and lifestyles can also affect their overall health.

Results from the National Food Survey (NFS) provide some evidence that people in Great Britain are eating more healthily at home. They are, for example, consuming more reduced-fat milks and low-fat spreads at the expense of full-fat milk and butter. The amount of fresh fruit eaten at home has risen steadily since the mid-1980s, to around 700 grams per person per week in 1999; consumption of processed fruit (mainly fruit juice) also rose over the period. However, the move towards healthier eating is not universally true either in terms of all food types or population sub-groups. The consumption of processed potatoes (mainly chips and crisps) at home has risen at a time when the consumption of fresh potatoes, a key source of carbohydrates and vitamin C, has fallen steadily from around 1,300 grams per person per week in 1974 to less than 700 grams in 1999 (Chart 7.12). (The sudden dip in 1976 was

**Gonorrhoea cases[1]: by year of diagnosis and gender**

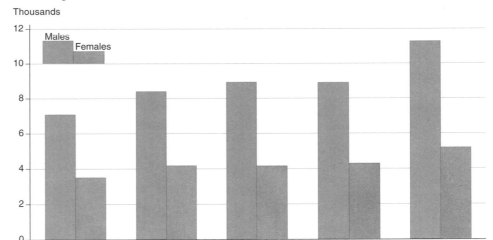

**United Kingdom**
Thousands

1 Uncomplicated gonorrhoea, diagnosed in genitourinary medical clinics.
2 Data not available for Northern Ireland.
**Source: Public Health Laboratory Service; National Health Service in Scotland**

**Changing patterns in the consumption of fruit and vegetables at home**

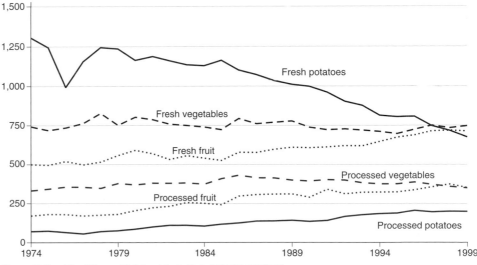

**Great Britain**
Grams per person per week

**Source: National Food Survey, Ministry of Agriculture, Fisheries and Food**

# 7.13

**Percentage of people aged 16 and over who are obese[1]: by ethnic group and gender, 1999**

| England | | Percentages |
|---|---|---|
| | Males | Females |
| Irish | 20 | 21 |
| Black Caribbean | 18 | 32 |
| Pakistani | 13 | 26 |
| Indian | 12 | 20 |
| Chinese | 6 | 4 |
| Bangladeshi | 5 | 10 |
| | | |
| Whole population[2] | 19 | 21 |

1 See Appendix, Part 7: Body mass index.
2 Whole population refers to all people, whether from an ethnic minority group or not.
**Source: Health Survey for England, Department of Health**

a result of the atypically poor potato crops in 1975 and 1976.) The consumption of ready-cooked, easy to prepare food has also risen. Results from the National Diet and Nutrition Survey (NDNS) indicate that children are still not eating enough of some important foods. In 1997, a fifth of children aged 4 to 18 had not eaten any fruit (excluding fruit juice) during the seven day dietary record, and three-fifths had not eaten any leafy green vegetables. They also found that among 15 to 18 year olds, 16 per cent of girls and 3 per cent of boys reported that they were dieting to lose weight.

The NHS Plan highlighted the inequalities in health that existed for ethnic groups, and this is reflected in the figures for obesity, an important risk factor for cardiovascular disease. The body mass index (BMI) measures people's weight relative to their height, and a BMI score of over 30 is taken as the definition of obesity (Table 7.13). Among people aged 16 and over in England, Black Caribbean women are far more likely to be

obese than members of any other ethnic group, while the likelihood of Chinese women being obese is very low. Being seriously underweight relative to one's height can also be a health risk – people with a BMI of 20 or less are classed as underweight. Several ethnic minority groups contained a higher proportion of underweight adults than the national average of 3.6 per cent of men and 6.6 per cent of women in 1999. According to the BMI score, one in five Bangladeshi men, and around one in seven women of Bangladeshi and Chinese origin, were underweight.

Another indicator of a healthy lifestyle is dental health. According to the NDNS, more than half of children aged 4 to 18 in Great Britain had some form of dental decay in 1997. Up until they reach the 7 to 10 age group, children's intake of sugary foods rises significantly. According to the Adult Dental Health Survey, in 1998, two-fifths of adults had reported some oral pain in the previous 12 months. Also in 1998 around a third of dentate males (those with at least one natural tooth) did not clean their teeth last thing at night, compared with a fifth of dentate females (Chart 7.14).

The consumption of alcohol in excessive amounts can lead to ill health, and an increased likelihood of problems such as high blood pressure, cancer and cirrhosis of the liver. The current Department of Health advice on alcohol is that consumption of between three and four units a day for men and two to three units a day for women will not accrue significant health risks, but consistently drinking four or more units a day for men (three units or more for women) is not advised because of the progressive health risks. In 1998-99, around two-fifths of men aged 16 and over and a fifth of women aged 16 and over in the United Kingdom had exceeded the recommended amount of alcohol on their heaviest drinking day in the week prior to being interviewed (Table 7.15). However, the proportions for 16 to 24 year olds were much

# 7.14

**Time of day dentate adults[1] clean their teeth: by gender, 1998**

**United Kingdom**
Percentages

1 People aged 16 and over who have one or more natural teeth.
**Source: Adult Dental Health Survey, Office for National Statistics**

## 7.15

**Percentage of adults consuming over specified levels of alcohol[1]: by gender and age, 1998-99**

higher, with half of young men having consumed more than four units and two-fifths of young women having consumed more than three units.

More cancer deaths in the United Kingdom can be attributed to smoking tobacco than to any other single risk factor. The Health Education Authority estimated that smoking caused 120 thousand deaths in 1995. The prevalence of smoking varies by social class. For both men and women, the proportion of smokers is higher among those in the manual socio-economic groups than among those in the non-manual groups. Over a quarter of people aged 16 and over in the United Kingdom were smokers in 1998-99, but while only 13 per cent of male professionals and 14 per cent of female professionals smoked, over two-fifths of unskilled males and a third of unskilled females did so (Table 7.16). Smoking during pregnancy can have harmful effects on the health of the child. Between 1985 and 1995 the proportion of women who smoked during pregnancy in the United Kingdom fell from 30 per cent to 24 per cent.

According to research by the General Household Survey (GHS) in 1998-99, 69 per cent of smokers in Great Britain wanted to give up, much the same proportion as in 1992. However, between 1992-93 and 1998-99 the proportion of both men and women who are ex-regular smokers has remained virtually the same.

Another focus of increasing public attention is drug misuse. Findings from the 1998 British Crime Survey indicate that nearly 500 thousand 16 to 24 year olds in England and Wales had used Class A drugs in the previous 12 months, and 200 thousand in that age group had done so during the last month. These figures represent 8 per cent and 3 per cent of 16 to 24 year olds respectively. Young people are more likely than older people to misuse drugs. The most commonly used illegal drug in 1998 among both young men and young women was cannabis, which had been used by

| United Kingdom | | | | | Percentages |
|---|---|---|---|---|---|
| | 16-24 | 25-44 | 45-64 | 65 and over | All aged 16 and over |
| **Males** | | | | | |
| More than 4 units and up to 8 units | 13 | 18 | 20 | 12 | 17 |
| More than 8 units | 37 | 28 | 17 | 4 | 21 |
| **Females** | | | | | |
| More than 3 units and up to 6 units | 18 | 17 | 12 | 3 | 13 |
| More than 6 units | 23 | 11 | 4 | 1 | 8 |

1 On the heaviest drinking day last week. See Appendix, Part 7: Alcohol consumption.

*Source: General Household Survey, Office for National Statistics; Continuous Household Survey, Northern Ireland Statistics and Research Agency*

## 7.16

**Smoking status: by gender and socio-economic group[1], 1998-99**

| United Kingdom | | | | Percentages |
|---|---|---|---|---|
| | Smokers | Ex-smokers[2] | Non-smokers[3] | All |
| **Males** | | | | |
| Professional | 13 | 29 | 58 | 100 |
| Employers and managers | 20 | 36 | 44 | 100 |
| Intermediate and junior non-manual | 23 | 30 | 47 | 100 |
| Skilled manual | 34 | 32 | 34 | 100 |
| Semi-skilled manual | 39 | 31 | 30 | 100 |
| Unskilled manual | 44 | 25 | 30 | 100 |
| All aged 16 and over | 28 | 30 | 41 | 100 |
| **Females** | | | | |
| Professional | 14 | 13 | 73 | 100 |
| Employers and managers | 24 | 22 | 54 | 100 |
| Intermediate and junior non-manual | 23 | 21 | 56 | 100 |
| Skilled manual | 28 | 24 | 48 | 100 |
| Semi-skilled manual | 34 | 20 | 46 | 100 |
| Unskilled manual | 33 | 24 | 43 | 100 |
| All aged 16 and over | 26 | 20 | 53 | 100 |

1 Socio-economic group based on current or last job. Members of the armed forces, full-time students, persons in inadequately described occupations and all persons who have never worked have not been shown in separate categories but are included in the figures shown as totals.
2 Includes only ex-smokers who smoked regularly.
3 Those who never or only occasionally smoked cigarettes.

*Source: General Household Survey, Office for National Statistics; Continuous Household Survey, Northern Ireland Statistics and Research Agency*

# 7.17

### Young people who had used selected drugs in the last year: by age, 1998

| England & Wales | | | Percentages |
|---|---|---|---|
| | | | All aged |
| | 16-19 | 20-24 | 16-24 |
| Cannabis | 28 | 26 | 27 |
| Amphetamine | 9 | 10 | 10 |
| Ecstasy | 4 | 6 | 5 |
| Poppers | 4 | 5 | 5 |
| Magic mushrooms | 4 | 3 | 4 |
| Cocaine | 1 | 5 | 3 |
| LSD | 2 | 3 | 3 |
| Any drug | 31 | 28 | 29 |

*Source: British Crime Survey, Home Office*

more than a quarter of young people aged 16 to 24 in England and Wales in the previous year (Table 7.17). Along with age, lifestyles are a good indicator of likely drug use. In particular, young people who go out more than three times a week, those who visit pubs and bars and those who go clubbing are all much more likely to use drugs than other young people. However, the use of more harmful drugs, such as heroin and crack, appears to be linked more with indicators of relative deprivation.

Some drug use also occurs among those under the age of 16. According to the 1999 survey of drug use among young teenagers carried out by ONS, 12 per cent of children aged 11 to 15 in England said that they had taken an illegal drug in the last year. Cannabis was again the most commonly taken drug: 10 per cent of this age group had taken cannabis, 3 per cent had tried any stimulant and 2 per cent had sniffed glue.

Education to increase young people's awareness of the dangers of drug use is being seen as increasingly important. The Government has set a target for all secondary schools and 80 per cent of primary schools to have a policy on drugs education in line with Department for Education and Employment guidance by 2003. The United Kingdom Anti-Drugs Co-ordination Unit reported that in 1999/00, 75 per cent of primary schools and 93 per cent of secondary schools in the United Kingdom had met this target. Ninety-five per cent of all Scottish schools provided some form of drugs education in 1999/00.

Physical activity helps give protection against coronary heart disease and stroke. It also has beneficial effects on weight control, blood pressure and diabetes, all of which are cardiovascular disease risk factors in their own right. Regular exercise also protects against brittle bones, maintains muscle power and increases people's general sense of well being. Among males aged 16 to 24 in England, almost a fifth said they took part in seven or more hours of sport or exercise per week in 1998 (Table 7.18). However, almost two-fifths engaged in less than an hour's sport or exercise. The story was worse for females, with three-fifths of women aged 16 to 24 taking part in less than an hour's sport or exercise per week. Only one in 20 young women took part in more than seven hours per week. By the age of 45, the gap between the genders more or less disappeared. As people get older, they engage in less physical activity. The vast majority of people aged 65 and above did not take any exercise or play any sport.

# 7.18

### Time spent participating in sports and exercise[1]: by gender and age, 1998

| England | | | | | | | | Percentages |
|---|---|---|---|---|---|---|---|---|
| | | | | | | | | All aged |
| | | | | | | | 75 and | 16 and |
| | 16-24 | 25-34 | 35-44 | 45-54 | 55-64 | 65-74 | over | over |
| **Males** | | | | | | | | |
| No time | 23 | 38 | 50 | 64 | 77 | 83 | 93 | 58 |
| Less than 1 hour | 14 | 20 | 17 | 14 | 9 | 8 | 3 | 13 |
| 1 hour but less than 3 | 22 | 20 | 20 | 14 | 7 | 5 | 2 | 14 |
| 3 hours but less than 5 | 13 | 10 | 7 | 4 | 3 | 2 | - | 6 |
| 5 hours but less than 7 | 9 | 5 | 3 | 2 | 2 | - | - | 3 |
| 7 or more hours | 18 | 7 | 4 | 3 | 1 | 1 | 1 | 5 |
| All | 100 | 100 | 100 | 100 | 100 | 100 | 100 | 100 |
| **Females** | | | | | | | | |
| No time | 42 | 50 | 57 | 64 | 74 | 84 | 96 | 64 |
| Less than 1 hour | 18 | 19 | 17 | 15 | 11 | 5 | 1 | 13 |
| 1 hour but less than 3 | 22 | 19 | 17 | 14 | 10 | 8 | 2 | 14 |
| 3 hours but less than 5 | 10 | 8 | 6 | 4 | 4 | 1 | - | 5 |
| 5 hours but less than 7 | 4 | 3 | 2 | 1 | 1 | 1 | - | 2 |
| 7 or more hours | 5 | 2 | 2 | 1 | 1 | 1 | - | 2 |
| All | 100 | 100 | 100 | 100 | 100 | 100 | 100 | 100 |

1 Number of hours spent participating in sports or exercise each week.
*Source: Health Survey for England, Department of Health*

## Causes of death

In the early part of the 20th century, infectious and respiratory diseases were major causes of death for both males and females. Over the last century the broad trend has been that the proportion of deaths due to infectious diseases has fallen, while the proportion due to circulatory diseases and cancer has risen, as people are generally living longer. Medical advances, including the advent of the National Health Service in 1948, appear to have contributed to a decline in overall mortality. The fall is generally regarded as a consequence of a number of major social and economic trends, including an increase in real incomes, improvements in nutrition and housing, higher levels of education, improved health services and developments in medicines and their wider availability to the population.

In 1911 there were nearly 3 thousand deaths per million population of males aged 15 to 74 from respiratory diseases in Great Britain, and just under 2 thousand deaths per million population among females in the same age group (Chart 7.19). Deaths from respiratory diseases and infections together made up nearly a third of all deaths for males aged 15 to 74 and a quarter of those for females of the same age group. By 1999 respiratory disease and infections caused only one in ten deaths. Having peaked at being the cause of 5 thousand male deaths per million population in 1963 and 1969, in 1999 circulatory illnesses caused just over 2 thousand deaths per million for males.

Mortality from cancer also rose over the period. In 1911 cancers were responsible for 11 per cent of male deaths and 16 per cent of female deaths. By 1999 these proportions had increased to 32 and 42 per cent of male and female deaths respectively, although the number of deaths from cancer has been falling in recent years. In 1983 cancers overtook circulatory illnesses as the main cause of death among females.

In 1996 there were 34 deaths per 100,000 females from breast cancer in the United Kingdom, and 27 deaths per 100,000 males from prostate cancer. Chart 7.20 compares these figures with those from the other member states of the European Union (EU). Women in only four countries – Denmark, the Netherlands, the Irish Republic and Belgium – had higher mortality rates from breast

**Mortality[1]: by gender and major cause**

**Great Britain**

Rates per million population

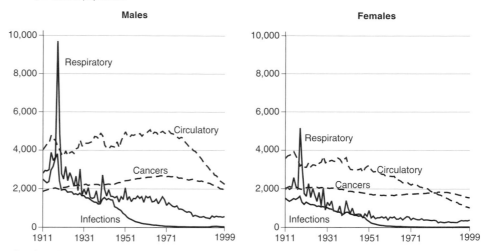

1 People aged 15 to 74. Data have been age-standardised to the European population. See Appendix, Part 7: Standardised death rates and International Classification of Diseases.

**Source: Office for National Statistics**

**Death rates[1] from breast and prostate cancer: EU comparison, 1996**

Rates per 100,000 population

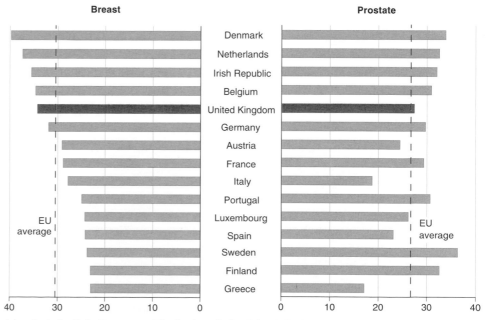

1 Age-standardised to the European population. See Appendix, Part 7: Standardised death rates. Per 100,000 females for breast cancer and per 100,000 males for prostate cancer.

**Source: European Network of Cancer Registries**

# 7.21

## Accidental deaths: by cause

**United Kingdom** Numbers

| | 1971 | 1981 | 1991[1] | 1998 |
|---|---|---|---|---|
| Road accident[2] | 8,302 | 5,133 | 5,276 | 3,501 |
| Railway accident | 213 | 97 | 90 | 47 |
| Other transport accident | 235 | 146 | 115 | 87 |
| Other accident | | | | |
|   At home or in communal | | | | |
|     establishments | 7,224 | .. | 4,865 | 3,763 |
|   Elsewhere | 3,930 | .. | 2,569 | 4,319 |
| All other accidents[3] | 11,207 | 10,414 | 7,493 | 8,519 |
| All accidental deaths[3] | 19,957 | 15,790 | 12,974 | 12,154 |

*1 Excludes deaths under 28 days.*
*2 These figures are not comparable with those issued by the Department of the Environment, Transport and the Regions. See Appendix, Part 7: Accidental deaths.*
*3 Late effects of accidental injury are not available by place of occurrence for England and Wales but are included in the totals for other accidents and total accidental deaths.*
***Source: Office for National Statistics; General Register Office for Scotland; Northern Ireland Statistics and Research Agency***

# 7.22

## Death rates from suicide[1]: by gender and age

**United Kingdom**
Rates per 100,000 population

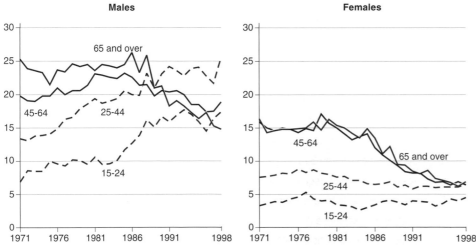

*1 Figures are based on suicides registered in the year. Includes deaths undetermined whether accidentally or purposely inflicted.*
***Source: Office for National Statistics; General Register Office for Scotland; Northern Ireland Statistics and Research Agency***

cancer. For both cancers the United Kingdom had a higher death rate than the EU average. Greece had the lowest mortality from both breast and prostate cancers. Sweden, despite having a very low death rate from breast cancer (24 deaths per 100,000 females), had the highest rate for prostate cancer, at 36 deaths per 100,000 males.

It is not just ill health that causes death. In 1998 there were more than 12 thousand accidental deaths in the United Kingdom (Table 7.21); this represents a fall of almost two-fifths since 1971. Moreover, the number of deaths caused by road accidents has fallen at an even faster rate – almost three-fifths – to 3.5 thousand. Further information on road accidents is contained in Table 12.19 on page 219 in the Transport chapter.

Trends in suicide rates by age group and gender have shown some marked differences in the last 30 years. For males aged 15 to 24, there were 17 suicides per 100,000 population in 1998, compared with a rate of only seven in 1971 and 11 a decade later (Chart 7.22). The suicide rate for males aged 25 to 44 doubled between 1971 and 1998, to reach a peak of almost 26 per 100,000 population. Conversely, the suicide rate for males older than this has fallen since the mid-1980s. For females, the suicide rate in 1998 for those aged 15 to 24 was similar to that for the previous two years, but higher than for the first half of the 1990s. The rates for females in all other age groups were lower in 1998 than 20 years previously.

There is a distinct gender difference in suicide rates. In 1998 the rate for males aged 15 and over was three times that for females. This gap has widened considerably since 1971, when around one and half times more males than females committed suicide. There are also very large differences in suicide rates by marital status. In

1995 the suicide rate for widowed and divorced men aged 15 to 44 was 352 per million population, more than double the rate for married men. The rate for single men has risen markedly since 1983, from 151 per million population to 217 per million population in 1995. For females the figures are much lower, but it is still those who are widowed and divorced who have the highest rate.

Deaths defined as being related to drug poisoning have also increased during the 1990s. The ONS maintains a database of these, containing data from 1993 onwards, which allows identification of specific substances involved in these deaths. The number of deaths in England and Wales where heroin or morphine were mentioned on the death certificate more than trebled between 1993 and 1998 (Table 7.23). There have also been rises in the number of deaths with mentions of cocaine and methadone, although the latter fell for the first time in 1998. Deaths with a mention of antidepressants or paracetamol show a much less marked increase.

An important avoidable cause of death in the young is volatile substance abuse. More than half of these deaths since 1995 have been caused by butane cigarette lighter refills. According to figures released by St. George's Hospital Medical School, there were 70 deaths from volatile substance abuse in the United Kingdom in 1998. This represents a large fall since the peak year of 1990, when there were 152 deaths.

## Prevention

The NHS provides screening programmes for breast and cervical cancer with the aims of early treatment and improved survival. There are no known primary prevention measures that men can take to minimise the risk of developing prostate

**Drug-related poisoning deaths[1]: by selected type of drug**

| England & Wales | | | | | | Numbers |
| --- | --- | --- | --- | --- | --- | --- |
| | 1993 | 1994 | 1995 | 1996 | 1997 | 1998 |
| Heroin and morphine[2] | 187 | 276 | 355 | 464 | 445 | 632 |
| Paracetamol[3] | 463 | 468 | 526 | 480 | 562 | 517 |
| Antidepressants | 459 | 476 | 489 | 540 | 539 | 502 |
| Methadone | 230 | 269 | 310 | 368 | 421 | 363 |
| Temazepam | 173 | 163 | 138 | 98 | 104 | 110 |
| Cocaine | 12 | 24 | 19 | 18 | 38 | 65 |
| Barbiturates | 44 | 46 | 46 | 30 | 20 | 35 |
| MDMA/Ecstasy | 8 | 27 | 10 | 16 | 11 | 15 |
| Cannabis | 14 | 18 | 17 | 11 | 13 | 5 |
| LSD | 0 | 1 | 1 | 0 | 1 | 1 |

1 Deaths where selected drugs were mentioned on the death certificate.
2 As heroin breaks down in the body into morphine, the latter may be detected at post mortem and recorded on the death certificate.
3 Includes deaths with any mention of paracetamol or any paracetamol containing compounds.
**Source: Office for National Statistics**

cancer. However, a prostate cancer risk management programme is to be introduced in 2001, including a standardised testing system and a systematic and standardised follow-up procedure. In addition, a pilot study into the feasibility of screening for colorectal cancer is due to be completed in 2002, and trials into ovarian cancer screening are also under way.

More than a quarter of all cancer cases and just under a fifth of cancer deaths in women are due to breast cancer (see incidence rates in Chart 7.4 and death rates in Chart 7.20). Around two-thirds of women in England and Wales with breast cancer survive for at least five years after diagnosis. At present, breast cancer screening is offered to all women aged between 50 and 64 (and women aged 65 and over on request) in the United Kingdom; this is likely to be extended to all 65 to 70 year olds, and those above 70 on request. The proportion of those who are actually invited for screening who attend has remained approximately constant over the last three years.

# 7.24

### Breast cancer screening[1]: by region

| | | | | | Percentages |
|---|---|---|---|---|---|
| | 1991-92 | 1993-94 | 1995-96 | 1997-98 | 1998-99 |
| United Kingdom | 71 | 72 | 76 | 75 | 76 |
| Trent | 78 | 78 | 81 | 81 | 81 |
| Anglia & Oxford | 79 | 76 | 82 | 79 | 80 |
| South West | 77 | 75 | 79 | 79 | 79 |
| Northern & Yorkshire | 74 | 73 | 77 | 79 | 78 |
| West Midlands | 72 | 72 | 78 | 76 | 77 |
| North West | 71 | 74 | 77 | 75 | 76 |
| South Thames | 69 | 69 | 74 | 73 | 74 |
| North Thames | 59 | 60 | 66 | 66 | 65 |
| England | 72 | 72 | 76 | 75 | 76 |
| Wales | 77 | 75 | 77 | 77 | 77 |
| Scotland | 72 | 71 | 72 | 71 | 74 |
| Northern Ireland | 63 | 64 | 72 | 74 | 72 |

1 As a percentage of women aged 50 to 64 invited for screening.

**Source: Department of Health; National Assembly for Wales; National Health Service in Scotland; Department of Health, Social Services and Public Safety, Northern Ireland**

# 7.25

### Cervical screening[1]: by age[2] and country, March 1999

| | | | Percentages |
|---|---|---|---|
| | England | Wales | Scotland |
| 25-34 | 82 | 78 | 81 |
| 35-44 | 87 | 87 | 91 |
| 45-54 | 86 | 86 | 92 |
| 55-64 | 80 | 78 | 86 |
| All aged 25 to 64 | 84 | 82 | 87 |

1 Women in the target age group who are within five years of their most recent cervical screening test. Target population in England excludes those no longer eligible for clinical reasons.
2 For Wales, the age groups are 20-34, 35-44, 45-54, 55-64 and 20-64 respectively. For Scotland they are 20-34, 35-44, 45-54, 55-59 and 20-59 respectively.

**Source: Department of Health; National Assembly for Wales; National Health Service in Scotland**

In 1998-99, around three-quarters of the women invited from the target population in the United Kingdom underwent screening for breast cancer (Table 7.24). The NHS region with the highest breast cancer screening rate was the Trent region, where uptake reached 81 per cent. However, the proportion was almost as high in several other regions, and only in North Thames was it below 70 per cent.

National policy for cervical screening is that women should be screened every three to five years (three and a half to five and a half years in Scotland). In order to prevent cervical cancer at an early stage, a system is in place whereby women are screened for cervical intraepithelial neoplasia, as cervical cancer is most commonly preceded by a long developmental stage which may proceed to invasive cancer. The programme invites women aged 20 to 64 (20 to 59 in Scotland) for screening. However, since many women are not invited immediately when they reach their 20th birthday, the age group 25 to 64 is used to give a more accurate estimate of coverage of the target population in England. At 31st March 1999, more than four-fifths of women

in the target population had been screened in England, Wales and Scotland (Table 7.25). This is a considerable improvement on the figures for 1989, when 44 per cent of the target population in England had undergone a smear test in the previous five years.

One of the main factors contributing to the fall in deaths from infectious disease (see Chart 7.19) has been the introduction of immunisation. For example, diphtheria was a leading cause of death in children until 1941 when immunisation was introduced; by the end of the 1950s the disease had almost disappeared and in the 1980s only 30 cases were reported.

Many children are immunised against a variety of diseases before their second birthday. There have been a number of campaigns to encourage parents to have their children immunised against major infectious diseases. Virtually every child under the age of two is now immunised against diphtheria, tetanus, whooping cough and polio (Table 7.26).

Pertussis (whooping cough) immunisation started in the 1950s, and this led to a sharp decline in deaths and notifications. In 1970, however, a study suggested that encephalopathy and brain damage might be a rare complication of immunisation. By 1978, only 30 per cent of children under two years were immunised and large outbreaks of whooping cough followed in 1978 and 1982. New evidence showed that the association between immunisation and encephalopathy was not causative; vaccine coverage rates have increased and, by 1998-99, 94 per cent of children in the United Kingdom had been immunised by their second birthday against whooping cough.

Measles immunisation was introduced in 1968 and, although immunisation was slow to gain general acceptance, notifications fell by about two-thirds to an average of about 90 thousand per year in the early 1980s in the United Kingdom. In

1988, the measles/mumps/rubella (MMR) vaccine was introduced and a higher coverage of immunisation was achieved as it became widely available. Notifications of measles fell to their lowest recorded annual total of under 4 thousand in 1997. Adverse publicity about the MMR combined vaccine has led to a fall in the number of children immunised against MMR by their second birthday, from 91 per cent in 1994-95 to 89 per cent in 1998-99.

In November 1999 a vaccination programme for Meningitis C was initiated in the United Kingdom, aimed primarily at young people aged between 15 and 17 and babies under one year of age. In the three months up to the beginning of September 2000 there were seven cases of Meningitis C in the target age groups, compared with 45 in the same period in 1999. By the end of 2000, all people under 18 years of age should have been offered the Meningitis C vaccine.

Tuberculosis (TB) has been rising in incidence in recent years, and after a year's gap the TB immunisation scheme has been resumed. Research continues into preventing, or at least minimising the effects of, various diseases and conditions, such as HIV and cancer.

**Immunisation of children[1] by their second birthday**

**United Kingdom** Percentages

| | 1981[2] | 1991-92 | 1994-95[3] | 1997-98 | 1998-99 |
|---|---|---|---|---|---|
| Tetanus | 83 | 94 | 93 | 96 | 96 |
| Diphtheria | 83 | 94 | 95 | 96 | 95 |
| Poliomyelitis | 82 | 94 | 95 | 96 | 95 |
| Whooping cough | 45 | 88 | 95 | 94 | 94 |
| Measles, mumps, rubella[4] | 54 | 90 | 91 | 91 | 89 |

1 See Appendix, Part 7: Immunisation.
2 Data exclude Scotland.
3 Data for Scotland are for calendar years.
4 Includes measles only vaccine for 1981. Combined vaccine was not available prior to 1988.
*Source: Department of Health; National Assembly for Wales; National Health Service in Scotland; Department of Health, Social Services and Public Safety, Northern Ireland*

## Websites

| | |
|---|---|
| National Statistics | www.statistics.gov.uk |
| Department of Health | www.doh.gov.uk |
| Department of Health, Social Services and Public Safety, Northern Ireland | www.dhsspsni.gov.uk/hpss/statistics |
| Food Standards Agency | www.foodstandards.gov.uk |
| General Register Office for Scotland | www.gro-scotland.gov.uk |
| Government Actuary's Department | www.gad.gov.uk |
| Ministry of Agriculture, Fisheries and Food | www.maff.gov.uk |
| National Assembly for Wales | www.assembly.wales.gov.uk |
| National Health Service in Scotland | www.show.scot.nhs.uk/isd |
| Northern Ireland Statistics and Research Agency | www.nisra.gov.uk |
| European Network of Cancer Registries | www-dep.iarc.fr |
| Public Health Laboratory Service | www.phls.co.uk |
| St George's Hospital Medical School | www.sghms.ac.uk |

## Contacts

**Office for National Statistics**

| | |
|---|---|
| Chapter author | 020 7533 5081 |
| Adult Dental Health Survey | 020 7533 5303 |
| Cancer statistics | 020 7533 5230 |
| Child health and mortality statistics | 020 7533 5641 |
| Drug related poisoning deaths | 020 7533 5243 |
| General Household Survey | 020 7533 5444 |
| Healthy life expectancy | 020 7533 5223 |
| Mental Health | 020 7533 5416 |
| Morbidity and healthcare | 020 7533 5244 |
| Mortality statistics | 01329 813758 |
| **Department of Health** | |
| Health Survey for England | 020 7972 5675/5660 |
| National Diet and Nutrition Survey | 020 7972 1367 |
| Smoking, misuse of alcohol and drugs | 020 7972 5551 |
| **Department of Agriculture for Northern Ireland** | 028 9052 4594 |
| **Department of Health, Social Services and Public Safety, Northern Ireland** | 028 9052 2800 |
| **Food Standards Agency** | 020 7267 8000 |
| **General Register Office for Northern Ireland** | 02890 252031 |
| **General Register Office for Scotland** | 0131 314 4243 |
| **Government Actuary's Department** | 020 7211 2667 |
| **Health and Safety Executive** | 0151 951 3819/3431 |
| **Home Office** | 020 7273 2084 |
| **Ministry of Agriculture, Fisheries and Food** | 020 7270 8547 |
| **National Assembly for Wales** | 029 20825080 |
| **National Health Service in Scotland** | 0131 551 8899 |
| **Northern Ireland Statistics and Research Agency** | 028 9034 8132 |
| Continuous Household Survey | 028 9034 8243 |
| **Eurostat** | 00352 43 35 22 51 |
| **Public Health Laboratory Service** | 020 8200 6868 |
| **St George's Hospital Medical School** | 020 8725 5491 |
| **The Royal College of General Practitioners** | 0121 426 1125 |

# Chapter 8 Social Protection

### Overview

- Between 1977-78 and 1999-00, social security benefit expenditure more than doubled in real terms, to almost £103 billion. (Chart 8.3)

- Between 1981 and 1999, the number of GPs in Great Britain rose by a third. The number of direct care staff employed in the NHS hospital and community health service fell by 4 per cent over the same period. (Table 8.9)

### Sick and disabled people

- Between 1981 and 1998-99, the number of finished consultant episodes for acute in-patient cases in the United Kingdom rose by more than 2 million to 7.9 million – an increase of 40 per cent. (Table 8.12)

- The number of long-term sick and disabled people receiving incapacity benefit (and its predecessors) or severe disablement allowance increased rapidly in Great Britain, from 0.8 million in 1981-82 to peak at 2.0 million in 1996-97, before falling slightly in the following three years to 1.8 million in 1999-00. (Table 8.14)

### Elderly people

- Between 1989 and 1999 the number of places in residential and nursing homes intended for elderly people in England, Scotland and Northern Ireland rose by 11 per cent, to 410 thousand. (Table 8.16)

- In 1998-99, household members provided the necessary help to 68 per cent of elderly people who needed help getting in or out of bed and 56 per cent of elderly people who needed help walking down the road. (Table 8.17)

### Families

- In 1981, the mean duration of stay in hospital for maternity visits in England was 5.5 days; by 1998-99 it had more than halved to 2.1 days. (Chart 8.22)

- The number of children looked after by local authorities in England, Wales and Northern Ireland was 61 thousand in 1999, 11 per cent more than five years earlier. (Chart 8.24)

Social protection encompasses the various ways in which central government, local authorities, private companies, the voluntary sector and individuals provide help for people who are in need or are at some sort of risk. Such need or risk may arise through a variety of circumstances, such as ill health, disability or inadequate income. Generally, people who are in need of help are identified in other chapters of *Social Trends*. This chapter focuses on the support provided for groups such as elderly people, those who are sick or disabled, and families.

## Overview

Two hundred years ago, when census records began, social protection was only provided voluntarily. While unpaid carers still play a large part in the provision of social protection in the United Kingdom today, over the last 60 years state social care and welfare services have developed significantly. At the beginning of the 20th century these services hardly existed, with the exception of the Poor Law which provided some assistance to those with very low incomes. The major development in social security came in 1942 with the Beveridge report which introduced the concept of the welfare state. This included the development of family allowances and a universal health service. A large proportion of expenditure on social protection today is funded by the Government on similar programmes, including social security benefits, training programmes and the NHS. These are designed specifically to protect people against common sources of hardship such as the problems associated with old age, sickness, unemployment and disability. Benefits can be direct cash payments, such as jobseeker's allowance; payments in kind, for example free prescriptions; or provision of services, such as National Health Service (NHS) GP consultations. Non-government expenditure is aimed principally at elderly people or survivors (for example, widows) in the form of occupational pensions, but also at sick and disabled people in the form of sick pay and compensation for occupational accidents or diseases, and expectant mothers in the form of maternity pay.

In order for spending on social protection to be compared across the member countries of the European Union (EU), Eurostat has designed a framework for the presentation of information on such expenditure which has been adopted by member states as the European System of Integrated Social Protection Statistics (ESSPROS). For this purpose, programmes specifically designed to protect people against common sources of hardship are collectively

# 8.1

**Expenditure on social protection benefits in real terms[1]: by function, 1993-94 and 1998-99**

**United Kingdom**

£ billion at 1998-99 prices[1]

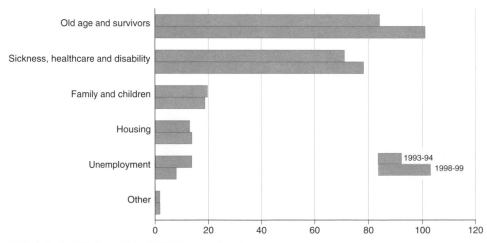

1 Adjusted to 1998-99 prices using the GDP market prices deflator.

**Source: Office for National Statistics**

# 8.2

described as expenditure on social protection benefits, and are those from which households can readily perceive a direct benefit, whether in cash or kind.

A total of £221 billion was spent in the United Kingdom on social protection benefits in 1998-99. Approaching half of this was expenditure specifically for 'elderly people and survivors (widows and widowers)', on whom spending had increased by 20 per cent in real terms (after allowing for inflation) since 1993-94 (Chart 8.1). Expenditure on 'sickness, healthcare and disability' (for people of all ages) also rose. Spending on 'unemployment', however, fell by 43 per cent in real terms, to £7.9 billion in 1998-99.

Despite the rises in expenditure for some of the main components of social protection benefits, spending in the United Kingdom was roughly the same as the average for the EU (Chart 8.2). To compare expenditure between countries, expenditure must be expressed in the same currency. However, this takes no account of differences in the general level of prices of goods and services within each country. Thus in order to make direct real terms comparisons between countries, expenditure is expressed in purchasing power standards. The differences shown in the chart between countries reflect differences in the social protection systems, demographic structures, unemployment rates and other social, institutional and economic factors. In Luxembourg, social protection benefit expenditure per head in 1997 was £6.1 thousand. In the United Kingdom, expenditure per head was £3.7 thousand – twice as much as Portugal, the country which spent the least on social protection benefits. Expenditure on

**Expenditure[1] on social protection benefits per head: EU comparison, 1997**

£ thousand per head

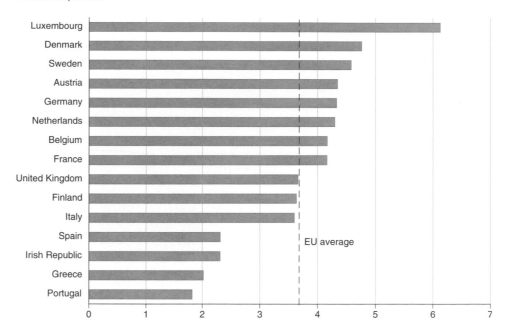

1 Before deduction of tax, where applicable. Figures are Purchasing Power Parities per inhabitant.
**Source: Eurostat**

social protection benefits as a proportion of gross domestic product (GDP) in 1997 ranged from 18 per cent in the Irish Republic to 34 per cent in Sweden. The figure for the United Kingdom was 27 per cent.

A large proportion of social protection expenditure in the United Kingdom is taken up by spending on the social security programme and on the NHS. Between 1977-78 and 1999-00 social security expenditure more than doubled in real terms, to almost £103 billion (see Chart 8.3 overleaf). Spending on social security has tended to be cyclical, in line with the general economic pattern. NHS expenditure, on the other hand, rose steadily in real terms to £53 billion in 1999-00. This

# 8.3

**Real[1] growth in social security benefits and National Health Service expenditure**

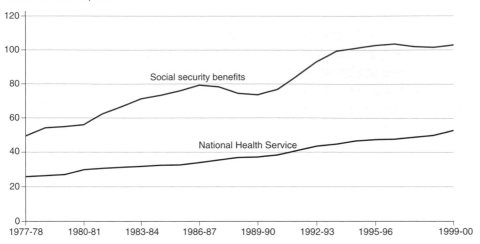

**United Kingdom**
£ billion at 1999-00 prices[1]

1 Adjusted to 1999-00 prices using the GDP market prices deflator.

*Source: Department of Health; Department of Social Security; Department for Social Development, Northern Ireland*

represents a doubling since 1977-78. The amount spent on the NHS in 1999-00 was half the amount spent on social security benefits.

Benefits of one type or another are received by most people at some point in their lives. Information from the Family Resources Survey shows that around three in five families in Great Britain received some sort of social security benefit in 1998-99 (Table 8.4). All pensioners are eligible to receive a state pension (from the age of 65 for men and currently from the age of 60 for women), and most pensioners take it up. Single pensioners were much more likely than those living as a couple to also receive income support, housing benefit and council tax benefit. Virtually all lone parents receive some sort of benefit. In 1998-99, almost three-quarters of single people

# 8.4

**Receipt of selected social security benefits: by family type[1], 1998-99**

Great Britain — Percentages

| | Family credit or income support | Housing benefit | Council tax benefit | Job-seeker's allowance | Retirement pension | Incapacity or disablement benefits[2] | Child benefit | Any benefit |
|---|---|---|---|---|---|---|---|---|
| **Pensioners[3]** | | | | | | | | |
| Couple | 5 | 11 | 20 | 0 | 99 | 24 | 1 | 100 |
| Single | | | | | | | | |
| Male | 13 | 29 | 34 | 0 | 97 | 21 | - | 100 |
| Female | 24 | 31 | 45 | 0 | 96 | 20 | - | 100 |
| **Couples** | | | | | | | | |
| Dependent children | 11 | 9 | 11 | 4 | - | 9 | 98 | 99 |
| No dependent children | 4 | 5 | 7 | 2 | 8 | 16 | . | 28 |
| **Single person** | | | | | | | | |
| Dependent children | 72 | 57 | 64 | 1 | 0 | 8 | 98 | 99 |
| No dependent children | | | | | | | | |
| Male | 7 | 11 | 11 | 8 | - | 9 | . | 24 |
| Female | 8 | 9 | 12 | 5 | 0 | 9 | . | 23 |
| **All family types[4]** | 13 | 15 | 18 | 3 | 24 | 13 | 23 | 59 |

1 See Appendix, Part 8: Benefit units.
2 Incapacity benefit, disability living allowance (care and mobility components), severe disablement allowance, industrial injuries disability benefit, war disablement pension, attendance allowance and disability working allowance.
3 Females aged 60 and over, males aged 65 and over; for couples, where head is over pension age.
4 Components do not add to the total as each benefit unit may receive more than one benefit.

*Source: Family Resources Survey, Department of Social Security*

## 8.5

with dependent children were in receipt of family credit or income support, almost three-fifths received housing benefit and nearly two-thirds received council tax benefit. In October 1999 a series of tax credits (such as the Working Families' Tax Credit (WFTC), which replaced family credit) were introduced in the United Kingdom. These tax credits are available to people or families who work. In February 2000, just under one million people in the United Kingdom were receiving at least the basic WFTC of £53.15 per week. Families can be awarded more than this minimum level, and in February 2000 the average WFTC award was £71.45 per week, compared with an average of £65.32 for family credit. Just over half of the WFTC's recipient families were lone parent families.

In 1998-99, nearly two-fifths of hospital and community health service expenditure in England, around £10 billion, went towards people aged 65 and over. Expenditure per head on that age group was £1,300 per head of population (Chart 8.5). Just over £1,000 per head was spent on children aged 0 to 4. However, the amounts for the age groups in between the youngest and the oldest in the population were much lower. Expenditure on children aged 5 to 15 was £160 per head.

As well as the more established health services, such as hospitals and GPs, the NHS has introduced new initiatives over the past few years. NHS Direct, a telephone helpline, was launched in England in 1999. The scheme was designed to provide people at home with faster advice and information about health, illness and the NHS, so that they were better able to care for themselves and their families. Most NHS Direct call centre sites are staffed by expert call handlers, who pass the caller to a nurse advisor if they need advice or clinical information, or transfer the caller direct to the 999 emergency service if they need an

emergency ambulance. In 1999-00, the first full year of the service, 1.6 million calls were made to NHS Direct (Table 8.6). Of those calls that received advice from a nurse, 36 per cent resulted in self-care advice being given over the telephone, 29 per cent of callers were advised to seek an urgent GP visit within 24 hours, and another 9 per cent were advised to visit an accident and emergency department. A further new healthcare initiative is NHS walk-in centres, which are currently being piloted – 30 had opened by the end of November 2000. They are being set up to help improve access to healthcare information, advice and treatment for minor ailments and injuries such as coughs, colds, strains and sprains. They are intended to complement GP surgeries and help to reduce pressure on GPs by diverting minor problems away.

**Hospital and community health service expenditure: by age of recipient, 1998-99**

England

£ per head of population

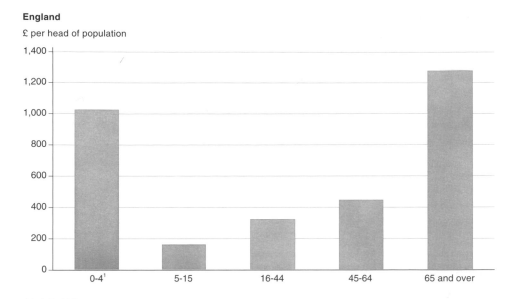

1 Includes birth.

*Source: Department of Health*

## 8.6

**Outcomes of calls to NHS Direct, 1999-00**

| England | Percentages |
| --- | --- |
| | 1999-00 |
| **Nurse advice given** | |
| Gave self-care advice | 36 |
| Advised an urgent GP visit (within 24 hours) | 29 |
| Advised a routine GP visit | 12 |
| Advised a visit to accident and emergency | 9 |
| Advised patient to contact other professionals | 9 |
| Arranged for an emergency ambulance | 3 |
| Other/call aborted | 2 |
| | |
| All calls receiving nurse advice (=100%)(millions) | 1.2 |
| **Other calls (millions)** | 0.4 |
| **All calls (millions)** | 1.6 |

*Source: Department of Health*

# 8.7

## Use of health services: by gender and age, 1998-99

| United Kingdom | | | | | | | | Percentages |
|---|---|---|---|---|---|---|---|---|
| | 16-24 | 25-34 | 35-44 | 45-54 | 55-64 | 65-74 | 75 and over | All aged 16 and over |
| **Males** | | | | | | | | |
| Consultation with GP[1] | 7 | 9 | 10 | 12 | 16 | 17 | 21 | 12 |
| Outpatient visit[2] | 12 | 14 | 13 | 15 | 20 | 25 | 29 | 17 |
| Casualty visit[2,3] | 7 | 7 | 5 | 4 | 3 | 3 | 3 | 5 |
| **Females** | | | | | | | | |
| Consultation with GP[1] | 15 | 18 | 16 | 19 | 17 | 19 | 21 | 18 |
| Outpatient visit[2] | 13 | 13 | 12 | 17 | 19 | 21 | 26 | 17 |
| Casualty visit[2,3] | 6 | 4 | 3 | 3 | 3 | 3 | 3 | 4 |

1 Consultations with an NHS GP in the last two weeks.
2 In the last three months; includes visits to casualty in Great Britain only.
3 The question was only asked of those who said they had an outpatient visit.

**Source: General Household Survey, Office for National Statistics; Continuous Household Survey, Northern Ireland Statistics and Research Agency**

# 8.8

## Satisfaction with hospital and community health services[1]

| Great Britain | | | | Percentages |
|---|---|---|---|---|
| | 1987 | 1991 | 1996 | 1999 |
| **Hospital services** | | | | |
| Quality of medical treatment | 67 | 65 | 66 | 66 |
| Time spent waiting for an ambulance after a 999 call | .. | .. | 58 | 60 |
| General condition of hospital buildings | 44 | 40 | 48 | 53 |
| Time spent waiting in out-patient departments | .. | 17 | 29 | 28 |
| Time spent waiting in accident and emergency departments before being seen by a doctor | .. | 24 | 24 | 20 |
| Waiting lists for non-emergency operations | 10 | 13 | 21 | 20 |
| Waiting time before getting appointments with hospital consultants | 14 | 14 | 19 | 17 |
| **GP services** | | | | |
| Quality of medical treatment by GPs | 72 | 73 | 76 | 76 |
| Being able to choose which GP to see | 70 | 72 | 71 | 71 |
| Amount of time GP gives to each patient | 66 | 65 | 68 | 69 |
| GPs' appointment systems | 51 | 54 | 56 | 54 |

1 Percentage of respondents who said that each service was 'very good' or 'satisfactory' when asked 'From what you know or have heard, say whether you think the NHS in your area is, on the whole, satisfactory or in need of improvement'.

**Source: British Social Attitudes Survey, National Centre for Social Research**

According to the 1998-99 General Household Survey (GHS) and Continuous Household Survey (CHS), use of GP and out-patient services rose with age, but the use of accident and emergency (A&E) departments fell (Table 8.7). Among 16 to 24 year olds, 7 per cent of males and 15 per cent of females had visited an NHS GP in the last two weeks, and 12 per cent of males and 13 per cent of females had had an out-patient appointment in the last three months. For those aged 75 and over, 21 per cent of both males and females had visited an NHS GP, and 29 per cent of males and 26 per cent of females had had an out-patient appointment. Seven percent of males aged 16 to 24 had used A&E, compared with 3 per cent of males aged 75 and over. The form of consultations with GPs has also changed. In 1971, 22 per cent of GP consultations in Great Britain were home visits. By 1998-99 this had fallen to 6 per cent, and meanwhile the proportion of consultations which were conducted by telephone had more than doubled, to 10 per cent.

An important measure of the services delivered by the NHS is people's perception of them. According to the British Social Attitudes Survey, satisfaction with many hospital and community health services has slowly risen since the mid-1980s (Table 8.8). In 1999, around two-thirds of people said that the quality of medical treatment in hospitals was 'very good' or 'satisfactory' and a higher proportion, just over three-quarters, said the same about the quality of medical treatment by GPs. People were least satisfied with waiting times in accident and emergency departments before being seen by a doctor, waiting times before getting an appointment with a hospital consultant, and waiting lists for non-emergency operations. However, some of these services have seen considerable rises in satisfaction levels. For instance, 28 per cent of people in 1999 felt that waiting times in out-patient departments were 'very good' or 'satisfactory', whereas in 1991 only 17 per cent felt that way. Similarly, the proportion of people who were satisfied with the waiting lists for non-emergency operations rose from 10 per

# 8.9

cent in 1987 to 20 per cent in 1999. At the end of August 2000, around 1.0 million English residents were waiting to be admitted to NHS hospitals, and 50 thousand of these had been waiting for over a year.

Between 1981 and 1999, the number of GPs in Great Britain rose by a third, from 27 thousand to 36 thousand (Table 8.9), and the number of general dental practitioners increased by two-fifths, from 15 thousand to 21 thousand. Conversely, the number of direct care staff (excluding GPs) employed in the NHS hospital and community health sector fell by 4 per cent over the same period: the number of nurses, midwives and health visitors fell by 9 per cent, and the number of other non-medical direct care staff fell by 3 per cent. This is largely because student nurses are no longer counted in the figures. But it is also due in part to the growth of the private sector as a provider of healthcare. For the last 10 years in England and Scotland, the number of public sector nurses has remained reasonably constant, fluctuating around 380 thousand (excluding nurses who are agency nurses working in NHS hospitals). However, the number of nurses employed in the private sector has risen from 81 thousand in 1990 to 151 thousand in 1999, an increase of 86 per cent.

Another aspect of the private sector's involvement in the nation's health provision is private medical insurance, the coverage of which increased considerably in the late 1970s and the 1980s. The number of people covered in the United Kingdom in 1971 was 2.1 million and by 1990 this had tripled, to 6.7 million (Chart 8.10). Since then, the number of people covered has stabilised and 11 per cent of the population were covered by private medical insurance in 1999. The total amount paid in 1999 in benefits to people who had a private medical insurance policy was £1,794 million, which represents a real terms rise of 5 per cent on the previous year after adjusting for inflation as measured by the retail prices index.

## Health and personal social services staff[1]

| Great Britain | | | | | Thousands |
|---|---|---|---|---|---|
| | 1981 | 1986 | 1991 | 1994 | 1999 |
| **NHS hospital and community health service** | | | | | |
| Direct care staff | | | | | |
| Medical and dental | 48 | 51 | 56 | 60 | 72 |
| Nursing, midwifery and health visitors | 457 | 472 | 470 | 426 | 414 |
| Other non-medical staff | 473 | 436 | 429 | 432 | 457 |
| All direct care staff | 978 | 959 | 955 | 918 | 943 |
| **General medical practitioners** | 27 | 29 | 31 | 32 | 36 |
| **General dental practitioners** | 15 | 17 | 18 | 19 | 21 |
| **Personal social services** | 240 | 270 | 289 | 294 | 274 |

1 See Appendix, Part 8: Health and personal social services staff.
**Source: Department of Health; National Assembly for Wales; National Health Service in Scotland**

# 8.10

## People insured by private medical insurance[1]

**United Kingdom**
Millions

1 Data from 1977 to 1984 are from BUPA, PPP and WPA; 1985 onwards are from the Laing & Buisson survey of private medical insurance.
2 The apparent decrease in the number of people insured in 1986 and 1993 is an artefact of re-estimation of BUPA's multiplier which converts subscribers to persons covered.
**Source: BUPA; PPP; WPA; Laing & Buisson**

# 8.11

## Places available in residential care homes: by sector

**United Kingdom**        Thousands

| | 1994 | 1995 | 1996[1] | 1997 | 1998 | 1999 |
|---|---|---|---|---|---|---|
| **Public sector** | | | | | | |
| Older people | 81.2 | 75.7 | 67.4 | 66.2 | 64.3 | 60.5 |
| People with physical or sensory or | | | | | | |
|   learning disabilities | 13.6 | 13.0 | 11.9 | 11.1 | 11.3 | 10.2 |
| People with mental health problems | 5.6 | 5.2 | 5.0 | 5.3 | 4.9 | 3.8 |
| Other people | 0.5 | 0.4 | 0.4 | 0.5 | 0.6 | 0.6 |
| All places | 100.9 | 94.3 | 84.7 | 83.2 | 81.1 | 75.1 |
| **Independent sector** | | | | | | |
| Older people | 202.7 | 204.1 | 196.8 | 212.0 | 219.1 | 219.5 |
| People with physical or sensory or | | | | | | |
|   learning disabilities | 40.0 | 43.9 | 45.7 | 53.1 | 55.9 | 57.6 |
| People with mental health problems | 20.9 | 21.0 | 22.7 | 34.1 | 36.5 | 37.1 |
| Other people | 3.1 | 4.3 | 3.9 | 4.4 | 5.5 | 4.5 |
| All places | 266.8 | 273.2 | 269.1 | 303.6 | 316.9 | 318.7 |

1 Data for 1996 are for England, Scotland and Northern Ireland only.

*Source: Department of Health; National Assembly for Wales; Scottish Executive; Department of Health, Social Services and Public Safety, Northern Ireland*

The provision of residential care is another area of healthcare where the independent sector is a significant service provider. In 1999, four-fifths of the places available in residential care homes in the United Kingdom were in independent sector homes (that is, the private sector plus the voluntary sector) (Table 8.11). Between 1994 and 1999 the total number of places in residential homes increased by 7 per cent. However, this comprised an increase of 52 thousand places in independent sector homes and a partially offsetting fall of 26 thousand places in public sector homes. Particularly sharp increases in independent sector places have been for people other than the elderly who need residential care. There was an increase of four-fifths in the provision of residential places for people with mental health problems, and a rise of more than two-fifths in provision for people with physical, sensory or learning difficulties. The number of such places provided by the public sector fell over the period for both categories.

# 8.12

## National Health Service activity for sick and disabled people[1]: in-patients

**United Kingdom**

| | 1981 | 1986 | 1991-92 | 1996-97 | 1998-99 |
|---|---|---|---|---|---|
| **Acute[2]** | | | | | |
| Finished consultant episodes[3] (thousands) | 5,693 | 6,239 | 6,729 | 7,260 | 7,946 |
| In-patient episodes per available bed | | | | | |
|   (numbers) | 31.1 | 36.9 | 45.9 | 52.9 | 58.5 |
| Mean duration of stay (days) | 8.4 | 7.2 | 6.0 | 5.2 | 4.9 |
| **Mentally ill** | | | | | |
| Finished consultant episodes[3] (thousands) | 244 | 265 | 281 | 300 | 276 |
| In-patient episodes per available bed | | | | | |
|   (numbers) | 2.2 | 2.7 | 4.0 | 5.8 | 5.7 |
| Mean duration of stay (days) | .. | .. | 114.8 | 61.0 | 75.2 |
| **People with learning disabilities[4]** | | | | | |
| Finished consultant episodes[3] (thousands) | 34 | 59 | 62 | 63 | 65 |
| In-patient episodes per available bed | | | | | |
|   (numbers) | 0.6 | 1.2 | 2.2 | 4.4 | 4.0 |
| Mean duration of stay (days) | .. | .. | 544.1 | 200.6 | 101.9 |

1 Excludes NHS beds and activity in joint-user and contractual hospitals.
2 Wards for general patients, excluding elderly, maternity and neonate cots in maternity units.
3 See Appendix, Part 8: In-patient activity.
4 Excludes mental handicap community units.

*Source: Department of Health; National Assembly for Wales; National Health Service in Scotland; Department of Health, Social Services and Public Safety, Northern Ireland*

## Sick and disabled people

The nature of health and ill health among the population is discussed in Chapter 7: Health; this section focuses on the support provided for sick and disabled people.

Between 1981 and 1998-99 the number of finished consultant episodes for acute cases in the United Kingdom rose by more than 2 million to 7.9 million – an increase of 40 per cent. The fastest rate of increase has been for people with learning disabilities (Table 8.12), among whom there was a 91 per cent increase in the number of finished consultant episodes over the same period to 65 thousand. An overall decline in the mean

# 8.13

duration of stay in NHS hospitals has occurred across all specialities. For acute cases, for example, the mean duration of stay was just over eight days in 1981, compared with five days in 1998-99.

As well as an increase in the number of in-patients, the number of people being treated as an accident and emergency patient or an out-patient or day case has also increased (Table 8.13). The number of day case episodes was more than five times as high in 1998-99 as in 1981. The total number of out-patient attendances also increased – by over a quarter – over the same time period.

Some help provided by the government for sick and disabled people comes in the form of cash benefits. The number of long-term sick and disabled people receiving incapacity benefit (and its predecessors, sickness and invalidity benefits) or severe disablement allowance increased rapidly in Great Britain from 1981-82, to peak at 2.0 million in 1996-97, before falling slightly in the following three years to 1.8 million in 1999-00 (Table 8.14). This more recent decrease occurred after the replacement of invalidity benefit (IVB) by incapacity benefit (IB). People who were in receipt of IVB when they reached state pension age were allowed to carry on receiving the benefit for five more years, whereas with IB the benefit is stopped when the recipient reaches pension age. On the other hand, the number receiving incapacity benefit for short-term sickness declined rapidly after the introduction of statutory sick pay in 1983. By 1999-00 the number receiving these benefits was just 28 per cent of those receiving the equivalent benefits in 1981-82. The rise in the number receiving the long-term invalidity benefits is partly due to an increase in the duration of claims rather than an increase in new claims.

**National Health Service activity for sick and disabled people: accident and emergency, and acute out-patients and day cases**

United Kingdom                                                    Thousands

|                                      | 1981   | 1986   | 1991-92 | 1996-97 | 1998-99 |
|--------------------------------------|--------|--------|---------|---------|---------|
| **Accident and emergency services**  |        |        |         |         |         |
| New attendances                      | 11,321 | 12,663 | 13,397  | 15,191  | 15,603  |
| Total attendances                    | 15,957 | 16,606 | 16,289  | 17,308  | 17,492  |
| **Out-patient services**             |        |        |         |         |         |
| New attendances                      | 8,619  | 9,495  | 9,862   | 12,431  | 13,173  |
| Total attendances                    | 36,160 | 38,822 | 38,944  | 43,602  | 46,148  |
| **Day case finished consultant**     |        |        |         |         |         |
| episodes[1]                          | 817    | 1,204  | 1,772   | 3,585   | 4,195   |

1 Excludes Northern Ireland in 1981 and 1986. Data for Northern Ireland from 1991-92 are for day case admissions.
**Source: Department of Health; National Assembly for Wales; National Health Service in Scotland; Department of Health, Social Services and Public Safety, Northern Ireland**

# 8.14

**Recipients of benefits[1] for sick and disabled people**

Great Britain                                                            Thousands

|                                                      | 1981-82 | 1986-87 | 1991-92 | 1996-97 | 1998-99 | 1999-00 |
|------------------------------------------------------|---------|---------|---------|---------|---------|---------|
| **Long-term sick and people with disabilities**      |         |         |         |         |         |         |
| Incapacity benefit/severe disablement allowance      | 826     | 1,228   | 1,741   | 1,996   | 1,832   | 1,781   |
| One of the above benefits plus income support        | 103     | 136     | 240     | 366     | 403     | 402     |
| Income support only                                  | ..      | ..      | 229     | 498     | 560     | 593     |
| **Short-term sick**                                  |         |         |         |         |         |         |
| Incapacity benefit only                              | 393     | 110     | 138     | 117     | 95      | 91      |
| Incapacity benefit and income support                | 24      | 16      | 28      | 48      | 25      | 27      |
| Income support only                                  | ..      | ..      | 79      | 174     | 159     | 157     |
| **Disability living allowance**                      | 582     | 1,113   | 1,758   | 3,020   | 3,274   | 3,353   |

1 See Appendix, Part 8: Recipients of benefits.
**Source: Department of Social Security**

# 8.15

**Hospital and community health service expenditure on the elderly: by sector[1]**

England     Percentages

|  | 1994-95 | 1995-96 | 1996-97 | 1997-98 | 1998-99 |
|---|---|---|---|---|---|
| Acute | 50 | 51 | 54 | 57 | 57 |
| Elderly | 24 | 23 | 22 | 21 | 20 |
| Mental health | 11 | 10 | 11 | 10 | 10 |
| Other community | 2 | 3 | 2 | 2 | 3 |
| Learning disability | 1 | 1 | 1 | 1 | 1 |
| Other | 8 | 8 | 5 | 5 | 7 |
| HQ Admin | 4 | 4 | 4 | 3 | 3 |
| All expenditure (=100%) | | | | | |
| (£ million in 1998-99 prices)[2] | 10,330 | 10,505 | 9,563 | 9,347 | 9,927 |

1 Consultant's specialist area.
2 Adjusted to 1998-99 prices using the market prices deflator.

**Source: Department of Health**

# 8.16

**Places or registered beds in residential and nursing homes intended for older people[1]**

England, Scotland & Northern Ireland     Percentages

|  | Nursing homes[2] | Dual registered homes[3] | Local authority staffed homes | Small homes[4] | Voluntary homes | Private homes | All homes (=100%) (thousands) |
|---|---|---|---|---|---|---|---|
| 1989[5] | 22 | .. | 32 | .. | 9 | 37 | 369.6 |
| 1990[5] | 25 | .. | 29 | .. | 9 | 37 | 393.7 |
| 1991[5] | 29 | .. | 25 | .. | 8 | 37 | 418.4 |
| 1992[5] | 32 | .. | 22 | .. | 9 | 37 | 431.1 |
| 1993[5] | 32 | 5 | 20 | .. | 8 | 35 | 423.5 |
| 1994 | 31 | 7 | 18 | 1 | 9 | 34 | 416.3 |
| 1995 | 32 | 8 | 17 | 1 | 9 | 34 | 416.4 |
| 1996 | 30 | 10 | 16 | 1 | 9 | 34 | 414.4 |
| 1997 | 26 | 16 | 15 | 1 | 9 | 34 | 410.8 |
| 1998 | 24 | 19 | 14 | 1 | 8 | 33 | 428.1 |
| 1999 | 24 | 18 | 14 | 1 | 8 | 35 | 409.9 |

1 Intended for those aged 65 and over. Excludes older mentally infirm. Data refer to places in residential care homes and registered beds in private nursing homes and hospitals and clinics.
2 England and Scotland only. For England, excludes registered beds in dual registered nursing homes and hospitals and clinics.
3 England only. Homes registered with the local authority and health authority.
4 England only. Homes with fewer than four places.
5 For Scotland, 1989 to 1993 data for Nursing Homes are for all available beds. Specific data for older people were not collected during this period.

**Source: Department of Health; Scottish Executive; Department of Health, Social Services and Public Safety, Northern Ireland**

## Elderly people

Nearly a fifth of the UK's population is over state pension age. The provision and type of services for elderly people has changed significantly since the early 1900s. Formally provided care at the beginning of the century was mainly carried out in institutions, with the Poor Law representing almost all of the cost of welfare services. By the time of the *National Insurance Act* in 1946, there had been a general shift from the provision of care in institutions to those provided in the community, such as meals on wheels and other services, and the replacement of workhouses by old people's homes. The number of older people in public residential accommodation has increased dramatically since 1900, reflecting the changing age structure of the population (see Table 1.3 on page 31 in the Population chapter).

The total amount of hospital and community health services expenditure on the elderly in England was £9,927 million in 1998-99 (Table 8.15). Almost three-fifths of this was spent on acute care, spending on which rose by an average of 2 per cent per year between 1994-95 and 1998-99. One area of health that affects many elderly people is eye care. In April 1999 eye tests were made free for all people aged 60 and over. In 1999-00, around 9.4 million NHS eye tests were performed, of which more than a third were for people on the basis of them being aged 60 or above.

A major part of expenditure on the elderly is residential care. Between 1989 and 1999 the number of places in residential and nursing homes intended for elderly people in England, Scotland and Northern Ireland rose by 11 per cent to 410 thousand. However, this was 5 per cent lower than the peak year of 1992 (Table 8.16). The proportion of these places which were staffed by local authorities has fallen considerably, from 32 per cent in 1989 to 14 per cent in 1999.

# 8.17

Another part of social protection for the elderly is community and home care. In the survey week in September 1999, 2.7 million contact hours were provided to around 424 thousand households in the form of home help and home care services by local authorities in England. Around a third of these households received either six or more visits and more than five hours of care. However, while the average number of contact hours per household almost doubled between 1992 and 1999, from 3.2 hours to 6.3 hours, the total number of households receiving services decreased by 20 per cent. In fact, for a variety of tasks which people aged 65 or over need help with, the help is often provided informally. In 1998-99, household members provided the necessary help to 68 per cent of the elderly people who needed help getting in or out of bed and 56 per cent of the elderly people who needed help walking down the road (Table 8.17). The NHS and personal social services provided help for a fifth of people who received help getting in or out of bed, but much lower proportions for elderly people who were helped with mobility, walking and using public transport.

According to the General Household Survey (GHS), in 1995-96 there were 5.7 million carers in Great Britain; and it has been estimated using Continuous Household Survey data and mid-year population estimates that there were a quarter of a million carers in Northern Ireland in the same year. Some charities provide help and advice specifically for elderly people and their carers. For example, Age Concern acts as a network of local organisations intended to help elderly people. Help the Aged provides, among other things, a free welfare rights service, SeniorLine, and a transportation campaign called SeniorMobility. SeniorLine dealt with more than 49 thousand calls in the first six months of 2000, and at 31 October 2000, 1.4 thousand groups had taken delivery of specially adapted vehicles through the SeniorMobility service.

**Usual source of help for those aged 65 and over able to do various tasks only with help, 1998-99**

| United Kingdom | | | | Percentages |
|---|---|---|---|---|
| | Mobility[1] | Getting in/out of bed | Walking down the road | Using public transport |
| Spouse/partner | 57 | 54 | 46 | 48 |
| Other household member | 19 | 14 | 10 | 7 |
| Non-household relative | 11 | 9 | 25 | 24 |
| Friend/neighbour | 3 | 0 | 12 | 9 |
| Paid help | 3 | 2 | 1 | 1 |
| NHS or personal social services | 2 | 20 | 4 | 3 |
| Other | 5 | 1 | 2 | 7 |
| All | 100 | 100 | 100 | 100 |

1 Getting around the house, getting to the toilet, using stairs.

*Source: General Household Survey, Office for National Statistics; Continuous Household Survey, Northern Ireland Statistics and Research Agency*

Virtually all pensioners receive the state retirement pension (see also Table 8.4 on page 146). In addition, in 1999-00, 12 per cent of pensioners were also receiving income support along with their basic state pension. This represents a fall of six percentage points since 1981-82. The basic state pension rose by £21 for single people and £33 for married couples between April 1990 and April 2000, to £67.50 and £107.90 per week respectively and the equivalent of 44 per cent (Table 8.18). However, after allowing for inflation (as measured by the retail prices index), these changes represent rises of £6 for single people and less than £7 for married couples. Over the same period, average earnings in Great Britain (as measured by the average earnings index) have risen by 62 per cent. In April 1999 the Government introduced the Minimum Income Guarantee. People aged 60 or over who do not have savings of £8 thousand or more and are not on income support are entitled to receive a top-up to their pension so as to take them to the minimum weekly levels. The Minimum Income Guarantee levels vary depending on whether the person is single or married, and their age.

# 8.18

**State retirement pensions**

| United Kingdom | | £ per week |
|---|---|---|
| | Single person | Married couple |
| 1989-90 | 43.60 | 69.80 |
| 1990-91 | 46.90 | 75.10 |
| 1991-92 | 52.00 | 83.25 |
| 1992-93 | 54.15 | 86.70 |
| 1993-94 | 56.10 | 89.80 |
| 1994-95 | 57.60 | 92.10 |
| 1995-96 | 58.85 | 94.10 |
| 1996-97 | 61.15 | 97.75 |
| 1997-98 | 62.45 | 99.80 |
| 1998-99 | 64.70 | 103.40 |
| 1999-00 | 66.75 | 106.70 |
| 2000-01 | 67.50 | 107.90 |

*Source: Department of Social Security*

## 8.19

**Meal provision[1] for elderly people[2] unable to cook a meal on their own: by type of household, 1998-99**

United Kingdom                                    Percentages

|                                | Lived alone | Lived with other(s) | All[2] |
|--------------------------------|-------------|---------------------|--------|
| Local authority home help[3]   | 50          | 12                  | 25     |
| Visited a day centre for the elderly | 22    | 10                  | 14     |
| Meals-on-wheels                | 21          | 1                   | 8      |
| Visited a lunch club           | 11          | 2                   | 5      |
| At least one of the above      | 61          | 20                  | 34     |

1 In the month prior to interview.
2 People aged 65 and over.
3 Health and social services home help or home care workers in Northern Ireland.

*Source: General Household Survey, Office for National Statistics; Continuous Household Survey, Northern Ireland Statistics and Research Agency*

Another source of income for some elderly people is through a private or occupational pension. Just before the Second World War 15 per cent of the workforce were members of an occupational pension scheme but during the 1950s and 1960s the number of people with these schemes grew rapidly. Data from the Family Resources Survey (FRS) show that in 1998-99, 59 per cent of single male pensioners aged under 70 were in receipt of an occupational pension, compared with 58 per cent of single male pensioners aged 80 and over. For single female pensioners, 53 per cent of those aged under 70 were in receipt of an occupational pension, compared with 38 per cent of those aged 80 and over. From April 2001, employers will be obliged to provide a new type of pension, a

Stakeholder Pension, especially to any employee who is not eligible to join an occupational pension scheme. Stakeholder Pensions will also be available to people who are self-employed.

An important task that some elderly people need help with is cooking meals. According to GHS and the CHS, in 1998-99, 5 per cent of elderly people living in private households could not cook a main meal. Of these, a quarter received the necessary help from local authority home helps, and one in 12 received a meals-on-wheels service (Table 8.19). Such help was much more likely to be received by elderly people who lived alone: three-fifths of elderly people who were unable to cook a meal and who lived alone used services such as a local authority home help, meals-on-wheels, a lunch club or a day centre, compared with a fifth of those who lived with others.

## 8.20

**Recipients of benefits for families**

Great Britain                                                        Thousands

|                                         | 1981-82 | 1986-87 | 1991-92 | 1996-97 | 1998-99 | 1999-00 |
|-----------------------------------------|---------|---------|---------|---------|---------|---------|
| **Child benefit**                       |         |         |         |         |         |         |
| Children                                | 13,079  | 12,217  | 12,401  | 12,752  | 12,716  | 12,867  |
| Families                                | 7,174   | 6,816   | 6,852   | 7,009   | 6,978   | 7,108   |
| **Lone parent families**                |         |         |         |         |         |         |
| One parent benefit/child benefit (lone parent)[1] only | 469 | 607 | 475 | 1,011 | 1,735 | .. |
| One parent benefit/child benefit (lone parent)[1] and income support | 146 | 253 | 340 | 394 | 362 | 311 |
| Income support only[2]                  | 222     | 376     | 531     | 639     | 583     | 614     |
| **Other benefits**                      |         |         |         |         |         |         |
| Maternity allowance[2]                  | 115     | 109     | 11      | 11      | 11      | 11      |
| Statutory maternity pay                 | .       | .       | 85      | 90      | ..      | ..      |
| Family credit[2]                        | 139     | 218     | 356     | 734     | 789     | ..      |

1 From April 1997 the supplement for the eldest or only child where someone brings up children alone, formally known as one parent benefit, was incorporated into the main child benefit rates.
2 See Appendix, Part 8: Recipients of benefits.

*Source: Department of Social Security*

## Families

Families and children may receive social protection in a number of different ways. All families with dependent children are eligible to receive child benefit; and families on low incomes receive other benefits. Children may be the victims of abuse and have to be moved into local authority accommodation, or they may have parents who are unable to look after them and consequently need to be fostered or adopted.

Around £19 billion of social protection benefit expenditure was spent on children and families in 1998-99 in the United Kingdom, which represents 8 per cent of all social protection benefit expenditure (see Chart 8.1). The main social security benefits and tax credits received by families with children are child benefit, one parent benefit, family credit (which has now been replaced by the working families' tax credit),

# 8.21

income support and maternity allowance. The most widely received benefit in this group is child benefit, which was received by just over 7 million families in Great Britain in 1999-00 (Table 8.20). The most notable change has been in the number of one parent families receiving benefits. The number of families receiving child benefit for lone parents (or its predecessor, one parent benefit) without income support rose by 1.3 million between 1981-82 and 1998-99, reflecting the increase in lone parent families (see Table 2.2 on page 42 in the Households and Families chapter).

An important part of the social protection provided for families is maternity care. In 1998-99, an estimated 71 thousand deliveries were performed by Caesarean section. This represents 18 per cent of all deliveries, which is a large rise since 1989-90, when 11 per cent of deliveries were performed by Caesarean (Chart 8.21).

Another notable trend in maternity care has been the fall in the mean duration of stay for maternity visits when mothers are in hospital to give birth. In 1981, new mothers in England stayed in hospital for 5.5 days on average (Chart 8.22) . By 1998-99, this had more than halved, to 2.1 days. Over the same period, the number of beds available for maternity care fell by 42 per cent.

Day care is provided for young children by childminders, voluntary agencies, private nurseries and local authorities as well as nannies and relations. In 1999 there were over 1.1 million places with childminders, in playgroups, in day nurseries and in out of school clubs for children under the age of eight in England and Wales and under the age of 12 in Northern Ireland (see Table 8.23 overleaf). In 1999 there were four times as many day nursery places as there were in 1987,

and the number of childminder places more than doubled over the same period. Looking at day care places by type of provider, the story is one of a decrease in state provision. The number of places in day nurseries, with childminders and in playgroups combined which were provided by local authorities fell by 21 per cent between 1987 and 1999. Out of school clubs have been introduced in recent years and in 1999 there were 119 thousand such places in England, Wales and Northern Ireland (further information is provided in Chart 3.8 on page 62 in the Education and Training chapter).

**Percentage of births performed by Caesarean section**

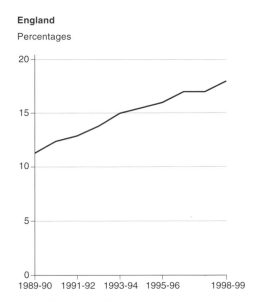

England
Percentages

Source: Department of Health

# 8.22

**Mean duration of in-patient maternity episodes[1]**

**England**
Days

1 Finished consultant episodes include all episodes not resulting in a birth, all delivery episodes and those birth episodes not resulting in well babies. Data for 1981 relate to deaths and discharges. See Appendix, Part 8: In-patient activity.

Source: Department of Health

# 8.23

### Day care places for children[1]

England, Wales & Northern Ireland                                                           Thousands

|  | 1987 | 1992 | 1997 | 1998 | 1999 |
|---|---|---|---|---|---|
| **Day nurseries** | | | | | |
| Local authority provided[2] | 29 | 24 | 20 | 19 | 16 |
| Registered | 32 | 98 | 184 | 216 | 235 |
| Non-registered[3] | 1 | 1 | 2 | 1 | 12 |
| All day nursery places | 62 | 123 | 206 | 236 | 262 |
| **Childminders** | | | | | |
| Local authority provided[2] | 2 | 2 | 4 | 4 | 9 |
| Other registered | 159 | 275 | 398 | 403 | 360 |
| All childminder places | 161 | 277 | 402 | 407 | 369 |
| **Playgroups** | | | | | |
| Local authority provided | 4 | 2 | 2 | 2 | 3 |
| Registered | 434 | 450 | 424 | 423 | 383 |
| Non-registered[2] | 7 | 3 | 3 | 1 | 3 |
| All playgroup places | 444 | 455 | 429 | 426 | 389 |
| **Out of school clubs**[2] | .. | .. | .. | 97 | 119 |

1 Under the age of eight. Under the age of twelve in Northern Ireland.
2 England and Wales only.
3 England only.

**Source: Department for Education and Employment; National Assembly for Wales; Department of Health, Social Services and Public Safety, Northern Ireland**

# 8.24

### Children looked after by local authorities[1]: by type of accommodation, 1994 and 1999

England, Wales & Northern Ireland
Thousands

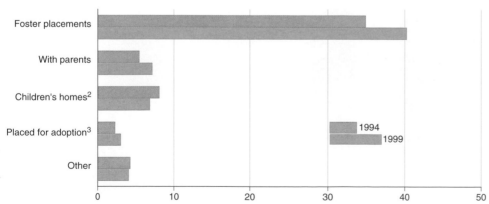

1 In England, excludes children looked after under an agreed series of short-term placements.
2 In England includes local authority, voluntary sector and private children's homes.
3 Not collected for Northern Ireland.

**Source: Department of Health; National Assembly for Wales; Department of Health, Social Services and Public Safety, Northern Ireland**

Local authorities must provide accommodation for children who have no parent or guardian, who have been abandoned, or whose parents are unable to provide for them. If local authorities think that taking a child into their care would promote the child's welfare, they may apply to a court for a care order. The number of children looked after by local authorities in England, Wales and Northern Ireland was 61 thousand in 1999, an increase of 11 per cent on five years earlier (Chart 8.24). Of the children looked after by local authorities, 40 thousand were in foster homes – this represents a rise of more than 5 thousand since 1994. The proportion of children looked after who were in foster homes also rose over the period, from 64 per cent to 66 per cent. A Government campaign to recruit 7 thousand more foster carers was launched in July 2000. The average duration of foster placements in England which ended in the year 1998-99 was 230 days, and 15 thousand placements lasted for seven days or less.

Scotland has a different definition of children looked after which means data are not comparable with the rest of the United Kingdom. In Scotland, children who have committed offences or are in need of care and protection may be brought before a Children's Hearing, which can impose a supervision requirement if it thinks that compulsory measures are appropriate. Under these requirements, most children are allowed to remain at home under the supervision of a social worker, but some may live with foster parents or in a residential establishment while under supervision. Those under supervision are considered to be looked after while in the rest of the United Kingdom those under a supervision order are not. Supervision requirements are reviewed at least once a year until ended by a Children's Hearing. In 1998 there were around 11 thousand children looked after in Scotland.

In addition, social services help children who are considered to be at risk of abuse. All local authority social services departments hold a central register of such children. Registration

# 8.25

takes place following a case conference in which decisions are made about the level of risk to the child. Subsequently, the child's name may be placed on the register and a plan set out in order to protect the child. In 1999, around 37 thousand children in England, Wales and Northern Ireland were on such a register (Table 8.25). This represents a drop of around 12 thousand, or 25 per cent, since 1991. This fall followed the implementation in October 1991 of the *Children Act*, the overriding purpose of which was to promote and protect children's welfare by enabling local authorities to work with families to provide help to keep the family together.

It is not just the state that offers protection for children who are considered to be at risk. Many charities also play a role. The National Society for the Prevention of Cruelty to Children (NSPCC) offers help to children with a variety of problems, and of all the non-governmental organisations in this field it is the only one authorised in law to conduct investigations and initiate care proceedings. In 1998-99, the NSPCC received around 82 thousand requests for assistance of which 5 per cent were sexual abuse cases, 3 per cent were physical abuse cases and 3 per cent were neglect cases.

**Children on child protection registers: by gender**

| England, Wales & Northern Ireland | | | Thousands |
|---|---|---|---|
| | Males | Females | All children |
| 1991 | 24 | 25 | 49 |
| 1992 | 21 | 21 | 42 |
| 1993 | 18 | 18 | 36 |
| 1994 | 19 | 19 | 38 |
| 1995 | 19 | 19 | 38 |
| 1996 | 18 | 18 | 35 |
| 1997 | 18 | 17 | 35 |
| 1998 | 18 | 17 | 35 |
| 1999 | 18 | 19 | 37 |

*Source: Department of Health; National Assembly for Wales; Department of Health, Social Services and Public Safety, Northern Ireland*

# Websites

| | |
|---|---|
| National Statistics | www.statistics.gov.uk |
| Department of Health | www.doh.gov.uk |
| Department of Social Security | www.dss.gov.uk |
| Department for Social Development, Northern Ireland | www.dsdni.gov.uk |
| Department of Health, Social Services and Public Safety, Northern Ireland | www.dhsspsni.gov.uk/hpss/statistics/ |
| General Register Office for Scotland | www.gro-scotland.gov.uk |
| National Assembly for Wales | www.wales.gov.uk |
| National Health Service in Scotland | www.show.scot.nhs.uk/isd |
| Northern Ireland Statistics and Research Agency | www.nisra.gov.uk |
| Scottish Executive | www.scotland.gov.uk |
| Eurostat | www.europa.eu.int/comm/eurostat/ |
| Laing & Buisson | www.laingbuisson.co.uk |
| National Centre for Social Research | www.natcen.ac.uk |
| The National Society for the Prevention of Cruelty to Children | www.nspcc.org.uk |

## Contacts

**Office for National Statistics**

| | |
|---|---|
| Chapter author | 020 7533 5081 |
| General Household Survey | 020 7533 5444 |

**Department of Health**

| | |
|---|---|
| Acute services activity | 0113 254 5522 |
| Adults' services | 020 7972 5585 |
| Children's services | 020 7972 5581 |
| Community and Cross-sector services | 020 7972 5533 |
| General dental and community dental service | 020 7972 5392 |
| General medical services statistics | 0113 254 5911 |
| General ophthalmic services | 020 7972 5507 |
| General pharmacy services | 020 7972 5504 |
| Mental illness/handicap | 020 7972 5546 |
| NHS expenditure | 0113 254 6012 |
| NHS non-medical manpower | 0113 254 5744 |
| Non-psychiatric hospital activity | 020 7972 5529 |
| Personal social services budget data | 020 7210 5699 |
| Prescription analysis | 020 7972 5515 |
| Social services staffing and finance data | 020 7972 5595 |
| Waiting lists | 0113 254 5555 |

| | |
|---|---|
| **Department of Social Security** | 020 7962 8000 |
| Family Resources Survey | 020 7962 8092 |
| Number of benefit recipients | 0191 22 57373 |

| | |
|---|---|
| **Department for Social Development, Northern Ireland** | 028 9052 2280 |

**Department of Health, Social Services and Public Safety, Northern Ireland**

| | |
|---|---|
| Health and personal social services activity | 028 9052 2800 |
| Health and personal social services manpower | 028 9052 2008 |

| | |
|---|---|
| **General Register Office for Scotland** | 0131 314 4243 |
| **National Assembly for Wales** | 029 2082 5080 |
| **National Health Service in Scotland, Common Services Agency** | 0131 551 8899 |
| **Northern Ireland Statistics and Research Agency** | 028 9034 8243 |

**Scottish Executive**

| | |
|---|---|
| Adult community care | 0131 244 3777 |
| Children's social services | 0131 244 3551 |
| Social work staffing | 0131 244 3740 |

| | |
|---|---|
| **Eurostat** | 00 352 4301 34122 |
| **Laing & Buisson** | 020 78339123 |
| **National Centre for Social Research** | 020 7250 1866 |

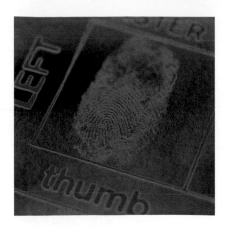

# Chapter 9 Crime and Justice

### Offences

● In 1999 there were nearly 15 million incidents of crime reported in the British Crime Survey in England and Wales, a third higher than in 1981 but 23 per cent lower than in 1995. (Chart 9.2)

● In 1999-00 there were 5.3 million crimes recorded by the police in England and Wales, an increase of 4 per cent on the previous year. (Table 9.3)

● Alcohol was a factor in 53 per cent of violent incidents in England and Wales in 1999 where the perpetrator was unknown to the victim. (Page 163)

● There were almost 152 thousand drug seizures in the United Kingdom in 1998, the highest figure ever recorded. (Table 9.6)

### Victims

● One in five males aged 16 to 24 in England and Wales was a victim of violence in 1999. (Table 9.7)

### Prevention

● The proportion of homes in England and Wales with burglar alarms doubled between 1992 and 2000, from 13 per cent to 26 per cent. (Table 9.10 )

### Civil justice

● The number of applications of civil legal aid granted in England and Wales has fallen in each of the past five years, to 228 thousand in 1999-00. (Table 9.22)

Crimes, and fear of crime, affect many people during their lives. Dealing with crime and its impact is a continual problem for both society and government. England and Wales, Scotland and Northern Ireland are often shown separately in this chapter because of their differing legal systems.

A formal legal system designed to administer justice and deal with offenders has existed in some form in Britain since the Middle Ages. However, it was only comparatively recently, in 1829, that the passing of the *Metropolitan Police Act* made provision for a regular police force in the metropolitan London area, and even then it excluded the City of London and provinces. This was followed by further legislation eventually establishing 43 county and borough forces maintained by local police authorities throughout England and Wales. The first public policing Act in Scotland was passed in 1833. The Royal Ulster Constabulary in Northern Ireland was established in 1922.

## Offences

Figures were collected on crime in the 19th century, based on information passed to the local police. *Criminal Statistics*, published in 1866, notes that there were '2,734 Known Thieves at large, 14,766 crimes committed and 5,823 persons apprehended in the Metropolis'. It also notes that the 'Proportion of persons apprehended declined to 39.4 per cent in 1865-66 from 41.5 per cent in 1864-65'.

Although Victorian crime statistics gave a good estimate of 'Known Thieves at large', they were often rudimentary in that they took little account of the population. It is not unreasonable to expect crime levels to rise and fall broadly in line with population fluctuations. For this reason crime rates – the number of crimes committed per head of population – give a more sophisticated indication of whether crime is becoming more or less prevalent.

The rate of recorded offences in England and Wales more than doubled between 1977 and 1992, when it reached 109 per 1,000 population (Chart 9.1). It then decreased steadily to a rate of 86 in 1998-99. Major changes in methods of recording crime were adopted by the police in England, Wales and Northern Ireland from April 1998. The new rules have increased the coverage of offences and have also increased the emphasis on measuring one crime per victim rather than one crime per offender. A detailed explanation of these changes is contained in Appendix: Part 9, Types of offences in England and Wales – recorded crime statistics. Under these new counting rules, recorded crime rates rose from 98 per 1,000 population in 1998-99 to 101 per 1,000 population in 1999-00.

In Northern Ireland the rate of recorded crime has been affected substantially by the changes in recording methods and the rate also rose between 1998-99 and 1999-00, from 65 to 71 per 1,000 population. The recorded crime rate in Scotland

# 9.1

**Recorded crime**[1]

Rates per 1,000 population

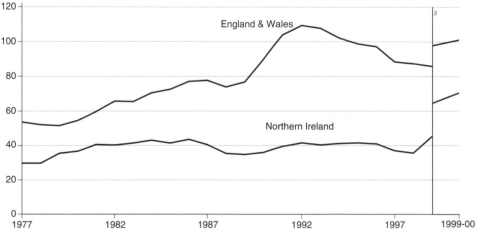

1 Indictable offences up to and including 1978. See also Appendix, Part 9: Types of offences in England, Wales and Northern Ireland. Includes possession of controlled drugs in Northern Ireland.
2 There was a change in counting rules on 1 April 1998. See Appendix, Part 9: Counting rules. Data from 1998-99 are on a financial year basis.

**Source: Home Office; Royal Ulster Constabulary**

# 9.2

decreased each year from the peak rate of 112 per 1,000 population 1991 to a rate of 82 in 1997. It then rose again slightly to 84 per 1,000 population in 1998, and to 85 per 1,000 population in 1999.

An additional consideration when measuring the true level of crime is that, consistently, surveys of victims, most notably the British Crime Survey (BCS), indicate a higher rate of crime than is recorded by the police. This is because the BCS measures include not only reported crime but also unrecorded and unreported crimes against individuals. There are some differences in the coverage of police recorded crime and BCS measured crime. The BCS is restricted to crimes against adults (aged 16 or more) living in private households and their property and does not include some types of crime (for example, fraud, murder and so-called victimless crimes). Since 1991 the BCS has been carried out in England and Wales every two years but is moving to an annual cycle from 2001. Similar surveys are conducted in Scotland and Northern Ireland periodically. Crime data collected by the police are a by-product of the administrative procedure of completing a record for crimes which they investigate. While this provides detailed data on crime, many crimes are never reported to the police and some that are reported are not recorded.

Between 1997 and 1999, the police recorded a 5 per cent fall in crimes that can be compared with BCS categories. The number of comparable BCS crimes fell by 10 per cent. For the second time (the first being between 1995 and 1997), both measures suggested a fall in crime. Patterns in recorded crime are influenced by variations in people's willingness to report crime to the police, and in police recording practice. Between 1997 and 1999 the greater fall in BCS crime than recorded crime is consistent with more reported crimes being recorded by the police. According to the British Crime Survey, there were nearly 15 million incidents of crime in 1999, a third higher

## Crimes[1]

**England & Wales**

Millions

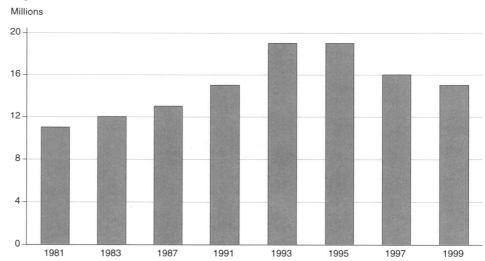

1 All incidents measured by the survey, whether or not they were recorded by the police. Surveys were not carried out in 1985 or 1989.

**Source: British Crime Survey, Home Office**

than the figure of 11 million in 1981, but 23 per cent lower than the 19 million incidents of crime in 1995 (Chart 9.2).

One of the factors that affects the relationship between BCS and recorded crime figures is the proportion of crimes reported to the police. This has changed over time. For those offences that are comparable between police records and BCS offences, the proportion reported to the police increased during the 1980s but fell slowly through the 1990s to 44 per cent in both 1997 and 1999. In Scotland, 53 per cent of crimes were reported to the police in 1999.

Reasons for the increase in the proportion of crimes reported to the police in the past decade are complex. More victims became insured during this period and this could have led to higher reporting rates, as reporting to the police may be a necessary step in making a claim. Campaigns in the media, particularly newspapers, against offenders, and the success of television programmes appealing for witnesses to help track down criminals, may have helped to generate a climate where information about crime is more readily passed from the public to the police.

# 9.3

**Recorded crime: by type of offence[1]**

Thousands

| | England & Wales | | | Scotland | | | Northern Ireland | | |
|---|---|---|---|---|---|---|---|---|---|
| | 1981 | 1991 | 1999-00 | 1981 | 1991 | 1999 | 1981 | 1991 | 1999-00[2] |
| Theft and handling stolen goods, | 1,603 | 2,761 | [3] 2,224 | 201 | 284 | 196 | 25 | 32 | [3] 37 |
| of which: theft of vehicles | 333 | 582 | 375 | 33 | 44 | 30 | 5 | 8 | 10 |
| theft from vehicle | 380 | 913 | 669 | .. | .. | 49 | 7 | 7 | 6 |
| Criminal damage[4] | 387 | 821 | 946 | 62 | 90 | 80 | 5 | 2 | 31 |
| Burglary | 718 | 1,220 | 906 | 96 | 116 | 54 | 20 | 17 | 16 |
| Violence against the person | 100 | 190 | 581 | 8 | 16 | 18 | 3 | 4 | 21 |
| Fraud and forgery | 107 | 175 | 335 | 21 | 26 | 24 | 3 | 5 | 8 |
| Drug offences[5] | .. | 11 | 122 | 2 | 3 | 32 | - | - | 2 |
| Robbery | 20 | 45 | 84 | 4 | 6 | 5 | 3 | 2 | 1 |
| Sexual offences, | 19 | 29 | 38 | 2 | 3 | 4 | - | 1 | 1 |
| of which: rape | 1 | 4 | 8 | - | 1 | 1 | - | - | 0 |
| Other notifiable offences[6] | 9 | 23 | 66 | 12 | 28 | 23 | 3 | 1 | 1 |
| All notifiable offences | 2,964 | 5,276 | 5,301 | 408 | 573 | 436 | 62 | 64 | 119 |

1 See Appendix, Part 9: Types of offences in England, Wales and Northern Ireland and Offences and crimes.
2 No longer includes assault on police and communicating false information regarding a bomb hoax. These offences have been removed from the categories 'Violence against the person' and 'Other notifiable offences'.
3 The counting rules were revised on 1 April 1998.
4 Northern Ireland data for 1981 and 1991 exclude criminal damage valued at less than £200.
5 From 1 April 1998 a new 'drug offence' group was created. Included within it are drug trafficking, possession of controlled drugs and other drugs offences. The 1991 England and Wales figure is trafficking in controlled drugs only.
6 In Northern Ireland includes 'offences against the state'. In Scotland excludes 'offending while on bail' from 1991 onwards.
**Source: Home Office; Scottish Executive; Royal Ulster Constabulary**

# 9.4

**Theft**

**England & Wales** Thousands

| | 1995-96 | 1996-97 | 1997-98 | 1998-99 | 1999-00 |
|---|---|---|---|---|---|
| Theft of vehicle | 817 | 778 | 695 | [1] 686 | 669 |
| Theft from vehicle | 514 | 467 | 401 | 392 | 375 |
| Theft from shops | 282 | 278 | 274 | 282 | 292 |
| Theft of pedal cycle | 168 | 147 | 140 | 129 | 131 |
| Theft from the person | 60 | 59 | 58 | 63 | 76 |
| Vehicle tampering | .. | .. | .. | 48 | 57 |
| Other theft | 624 | 594 | 578 | 592 | 623 |
| All theft and handling stolen goods | 2,466 | 2,324 | 2,145 | 2,191 | 2,224 |

1 The counting rules were revised on 1 April 1998. See Appendix, Part 9: Types of offences in England & Wales.
**Source: Home Office**

Not all crimes that are reported to the police will be recorded by them. A little over half of the crimes reported to the police in England and Wales in 1999 were recorded. The police may choose not to record a reported crime for a number of reasons. They may consider that the report of a crime is too trivial or that there is insufficient evidence. Relying on the discretion of individual forces has led to inconsistencies in police data covering recorded crime. Following a recent review of crime statistics a number of changes are under consideration which would have the effect of promoting greater consistency.

While the police figures for the total amount of recorded crime do not cover the complete picture, these data do allow quite detailed analyses to be carried out. Due to differences in the legal systems, recording practices and classifications, comparisons between England and Wales,

# 9.5

Scotland and Northern Ireland should only be made with care. In Scotland the term 'crimes' is used for the more serious criminal acts (roughly equivalent to 'indictable' and 'triable-either-way' offences in England and Wales). Less serious crimes are termed 'offences'. Scottish figures are given for crimes only, unless otherwise stated. In Northern Ireland the definitions used are broadly comparable with those in England and Wales.

Trends in the total number of offences recorded by the police in England and Wales show steady increases from the early 1950s, when there were less than half a million per year, to a peak of 5.6 million in 1992. They then decreased to 4.5 million in 1998-99 under the old counting rules. Under the new rules 5.1 million offences were recorded by the police in England and Wales in 1998-99. Most recent figures, for 1999-00, show a 4 per cent increase over the previous year in the number of crimes recorded by the police, to 5.3 million (Table 9.3). Recorded crime in Scotland rose slightly from 432 thousand offences in 1998 to 436 thousand in 1999. In Northern Ireland, 119 thousand offences were recorded in 1999-00 under the new counting rules.

Alcohol is an important factor in the incidence of violent crime – around 40 per cent of violent crimes are committed when the victim believes the offender is under the influence of alcohol. According to the British Crime Survey, alcohol in 1999 was a factor in 53 per cent of violent incidents in England and Wales where the perpetrator was unknown to the victim, and 17 per cent of muggings. The same survey estimated drugs to have been a factor in 18 per cent of violent incidents.

The MacPherson report, an official inquiry into policing methods, helped to highlight how issues connected with race were handled within the criminal justice system. Partly out of a concern to attach more importance to the seriousness of

racially motivated crime and partly out of a wish to extend the scope of what is considered criminal to include more anti-social acts or offensive behaviour, *The Crime and Disorder Act* of 1998 created new categories of 'racially aggravated offences' which hitherto had not been counted separately in police statistics. Over 21 thousand racially aggravated offences were recorded by the police in England and Wales in 1999-00. Around half of all racially aggravated offences involved some form of harassment.

In 1999-00, over 2 million crimes of theft were notified to the police in England and Wales, making up half of all recorded property crime. While the total number of theft-related offences was 10 per cent lower in 1999-00 than in 1995-96, theft of and from vehicles declined by around 18 per cent and 27 per cent respectively (Table 9.4). Shoplifting remained roughly constant over the same period, and theft from the person rose by around a quarter. Increasing use of security measures for cars (such as car alarms, which were used by 49 per cent of car owners in 2000 compared with 23 per cent in 1992) may help to explain the continuing decline in car-related theft.

There are striking regional variations in recorded crime. In general, those police force areas that include large urban conurbations have higher rates of recorded crime than those in suburban or rural locations. Recent increases in recorded crime have varied across England and Wales, with metropolitan forces recording 7.2 per cent more crimes in 1999-00 than the previous year, and non-metropolitan forces recording a much smaller overall increase of 0.9 per cent. Excluding the City of London (which has a small resident population), Greater Manchester had the highest rate of all the police force areas in England and Wales for vehicle-related theft in 1999-00, at 341 crimes per 10,000 vehicle-owning households (Chart 9.5). The police force area with the next highest rate was the West Midlands, at 293 crimes per 10,000

**Recorded vehicle theft[1] crimes: by police force area, 1999-00**

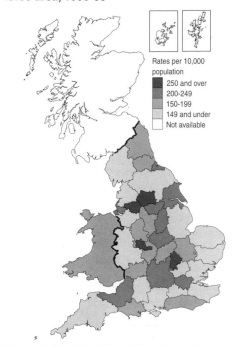

1 Comprises theft of vehicles, theft from vehicles and associated attempts. Based on vehicle-owning households only.
**Source: Home Office**

# 9.6

## Seizures[1] of selected drugs

| United Kingdom | | | | | Numbers |
|---|---|---|---|---|---|
| | 1981 | 1991 | 1994 | 1996 | 1998 |
| Cannabis | 17,227 | 59,420 | 88,540 | 91,736 | 114,666 |
| Amphetamines | 1,076 | 6,821 | 12,970 | 18,261 | 18,629 |
| Heroin | 819 | 2,640 | 4,480 | 9,828 | 18,269 |
| Cocaine | 503 | 1,984 | 2,992 | 4,097 | 5,207 |
| Ecstasy type | .. | 1,735 | 3,574 | 6,206 | 4,849 |
| Crack | .. | 583 | 1,320 | 1,332 | 2,488 |
| Methadone | 402 | 427 | 729 | 1,357 | 1,584 |
| LSD | 384 | 1,636 | 2,289 | 1,141 | 623 |
| Morphine | 243 | 119 | 135 | 118 | 159 |
| Opium | 137 | 49 | 35 | 23 | 35 |
| Pethidine | 135 | 33 | 23 | 7 | 18 |
| All seizures | 19,428 | 69,805 | 107,629 | 122,119 | 151,718 |

1 Seizures by the police and HM Customs. A seizure can include more than one type of drug. See Appendix, Part 9: Drugs seizures.
**Source: Home Office**

# 9.7

## Victims of violent crime[1]: by gender and age, 1999

| England & Wales | | | | | Percentages |
|---|---|---|---|---|---|
| | Domestic | Acquain-tance[2] | Stranger | Mugging | All violence |
| **Males** | | | | | |
| 16-24 | 1.8 | 8.2 | 8.3 | 4.3 | 20.1 |
| 25-44 | 0.6 | 1.9 | 2.6 | 0.5 | 5.4 |
| 45-64 | 0.2 | 1.0 | 1.1 | 0.3 | 2.5 |
| 65-74 | - | 0.1 | 0.4 | 0.3 | 0.7 |
| 75 and over | - | 0.2 | 0.3 | 0.2 | 0.7 |
| All aged 16 and over | 0.5 | 2.0 | 2.3 | 0.8 | 5.3 |
| **Females** | | | | | |
| 16-24 | 3.4 | 3.6 | 2.3 | 1.4 | 9.1 |
| 25-44 | 1.5 | 1.4 | 0.8 | 0.4 | 3.9 |
| 45-64 | 0.3 | 1.1 | 0.4 | 0.2 | 2.0 |
| 65-74 | - | 0.4 | 0.2 | 0.5 | 1.0 |
| 75 and over | - | 0.1 | 0.1 | 0.6 | 0.7 |
| All aged 16 and over | 1.0 | 1.3 | 0.7 | 0.5 | 3.3 |

1 Percentage victimised once or more.
2 Assaults in which the victim knew one or more of the offenders at least by sight.
**Source: British Crime Survey, Home Office**

vehicle-owning households. Surrey had the lowest rate at 95. In Scotland, the vehicle theft rate for 1999 was 153 per 1,000 vehicle owners.

Drug taking and drug-related crime are current topics of debate. Almost eight times more drugs seizures were made in the United Kingdom in 1998 than in 1991 (Table 9.6). There were almost 152 thousand drugs seizures in 1998, the highest figure ever recorded. Cannabis accounted for three-quarters of the number of seizures, and 94 per cent of the total volume of drugs seized in 1998. The number of seizures involving heroin almost doubled between 1996 and 1998 and those involving cocaine rose by around a quarter. Conversely, there were declines in the number of seizures of ecstasy and LSD. The type of action taken against drug offenders is shown in Table 9.16, while information on drug use is contained in Table 7.17 on page 136 in the Health chapter.

## Victims

Some individuals and households are more at risk than others of being on the receiving end of crime. When assessing how people's lives are affected in a broader sense by crime, it is also useful to look at people's perceptions, concerns and fears about crime.

Generally, young men run a higher risk of being victims of violent crime than any other group. According to the British Crime Survey, one in five males aged 16 to 24 in England and Wales were the victims of violence in 1999, more than twice the rate for females of the same age, who were the next highest 'at risk' group (Table 9.7). For all people aged 45 and over there was far less risk of being a victim of any sort of violence. The type of housing people live in is one of the many factors associated with the likelihood of them suffering from violent crime. In 1999 almost one in ten

# 9.8

private renters in England and Wales suffered some form of violent attack compared with less than one in 30 owner-occupiers. Around 6 per cent of adults living in flats or maisonettes suffered some form of violent attack compared with around 3 per cent of adults living in detached houses. These comparisons, while useful, should be interpreted with a degree of caution. Some risk factors overlap. For instance, proportionately more young people than older people are private renters, and a higher proportion of younger people than older people tend to live in flats. The most common reaction to violent incidents in 1999 was one of anger, displayed by around two-thirds of BCS respondents in England and Wales. A smaller proportion reported that being a victim of violent crime meant they had difficulty sleeping. Fear and shock were also common reactions for some.

Women worried more than men about most types of crime in 2000, and were particularly worried about violent crime (Table 9.8). There were some age differences in people's fear of crime. In general, a higher proportion of young people than older people were afraid of rape or physical attack. Within each gender, similar proportions of each age group feared being a victim of burglary. Around two-fifths of Black or Asian people surveyed by the BCS expressed worry about burglary, compared with under a fifth of White people.

People's concerns about crime have altered little over the last 16 years. Fifty-seven per cent of BCS respondents said that they were very or fairly worried about burglary in 2000, compared with 58 per cent in 1984. For mugging, the percentage who were very or fairly worried about crime was 44 per cent in 2000. Fear of crime can have implications on the quality of people's lives. Six per cent of BCS respondents in 2000 indicated

that the fear of crime had a substantial effect on the quality of their lives; 55 per cent said it had minimal effect.

Measures such as street lighting and the presence of police on the beat can alter people's perceptions of their safety. Findings from the British Crime Survey reveal some important differences in how safe people feel. In 2000, women in England and Wales were more likely than men to feel insecure walking alone after dark, and being alone in their home at night (Table 9.9). Feelings of insecurity among females tended to increase with age, with nearly one in three women aged 60 and over feeling 'very unsafe' in 1999 walking alone in their area after dark compared with less than one in five women of all ages.

## Prevention

Issues relating to crime prevention have been prominent in recent initiatives to combat crime. Neighbourhood watch schemes, established in 1982, encouraging members of the public to assist in crime surveillance, have increased in number

**Fear of crime[1]: by gender and age, 2000**

| England & Wales | | | | | | | | Percentages |
|---|---|---|---|---|---|---|---|---|
| | Males | | | | Females | | | |
| | 16-29 | 30-59 | 60 and over | All aged 16 and over | 16-29 | 30-59 | 60 and over | All aged 16 and over |
| Theft of car[2] | 22 | 18 | 19 | 19 | 27 | 21 | 21 | 22 |
| Theft from car[2] | 19 | 16 | 15 | 16 | 18 | 15 | 15 | 16 |
| Burglary | 17 | 16 | 15 | 16 | 23 | 21 | 22 | 22 |
| Mugging | 12 | 10 | 12 | 11 | 24 | 21 | 25 | 23 |
| Physical attack | 11 | 8 | 8 | 9 | 33 | 26 | 23 | 27 |
| Rape | 12 | 7 | 4 | 7 | 37 | 29 | 24 | 29 |

1 Percentage of people who were 'very worried' about each type of crime.
2 Percentage of car owners.
**Source: British Crime Survey, Home Office**

# 9.9

**Feelings of insecurity[1]: by gender and age, 2000**

| England & Wales | Percentages | |
|---|---|---|
| | Walking alone in area after dark | Alone at home at night |
| **Males** | | |
| 16-29 | 2 | 1 |
| 30-59 | 2 | 1 |
| 60 and over | 9 | 1 |
| All aged 16 and over | 4 | 1 |
| **Females** | | |
| 16-29 | 14 | 4 |
| 30-59 | 13 | 2 |
| 60 and over | 30 | 3 |
| All aged 16 and over | 18 | 3 |

1 Percentage feeling 'very unsafe'.
**Source: British Crime Survey, Home Office**

# 9.10

**Types of security used in the home**

England & Wales | | | | | Percentages

| | 1992 | 1994 | 1996 | 1998 | 2000 |
|---|---|---|---|---|---|
| Double/deadlocks[1] | 61 | 70 | 70 | 72 | 75 |
| Window locks | 52 | 62 | 68 | 71 | 75 |
| Light timers/sensors | 22 | 32 | 40 | 48 | 50 |
| Security chains/bolts | .. | .. | .. | 59 | 48 |
| Burglar alarm | 13 | 18 | 20 | 24 | 26 |
| Window bars | .. | 7 | 9 | 8 | 7 |
| Dummy alarm | .. | .. | .. | 3 | 4 |

1 On the outside doors of the house.

**Source: British Crime Survey, Home Office**

# 9.11

**Offenders found guilty of, or cautioned for, indictable offences[1]: by gender, type of offence and age, 1999**

England & Wales | | | | Rates per 10,000 population

| | 10-15 | 16-24 | 25-34 | 35 and over | All aged 10 and over (thousands) |
|---|---|---|---|---|---|
| **Males** | | | | | |
| Theft and handling stolen goods | 125 | 223 | 91 | 17 | 151.5 |
| Drug offences | 14 | 159 | 63 | 9 | 87.1 |
| Violence against the person | 29 | 69 | 31 | 7 | 48.7 |
| Burglary | 36 | 60 | 18 | 2 | 35.0 |
| Criminal damage | 13 | 18 | 7 | 1 | 12.5 |
| Robbery | 5 | 11 | 3 | - | 5.7 |
| Sexual offences | 3 | 4 | 3 | 2 | 5.7 |
| Other indictable offences | 12 | 102 | 57 | 12 | 71.7 |
| | | | | | |
| All indictable offences | 237 | 648 | 271 | 51 | 417.8 |
| **Females** | | | | | |
| Theft and handling stolen goods | 64 | 76 | 31 | 7 | 55.2 |
| Drug offences | 2 | 17 | 10 | 1 | 11.0 |
| Violence against the person | 10 | 11 | 5 | 1 | 8.2 |
| Burglary | 3 | 3 | 1 | - | 2.0 |
| Criminal damage | 1 | 2 | 1 | - | 1.4 |
| Robbery | 1 | 1 | - | - | 0.5 |
| Sexual offences | - | - | - | - | 0.1 |
| Other indictable offences | 3 | 21 | 13 | 2 | 15.1 |
| | | | | | |
| All indictable offences | 84 | 130 | 61 | 12 | 93.4 |

1 See Appendix, Part 9: Types of offences in England, Wales and Northern Ireland.

**Source: Home Office**

over the past 10 years. There are now 160 thousand schemes in operation, covering roughly one in ten of the population in England and Wales. Public investment in closed circuit television cameras (£153 million in 1999) has provided greater surveillance of high street shopping areas and other public places. Seventy Youth Inclusion schemes have been sent up as a crime prevention initiative to try and tackle specific problems associated with young offenders. There is also evidence that, increasingly, individuals and households are taking more preventative measures to combat crime. The proportion of houses fitted with a burglar alarm doubled between 1992 and 2000 from 13 to 26 per cent of respondents (Table 9.10). The proportion of houses with window locks rose from just over half to three-quarters over the same period.

## Offenders

In 1999, 511 thousand people were found guilty, or cautioned, for an indictable offence in England and Wales (Table 9.11). The vast majority of these, around eight in ten, were male. In order to provide a straightforward comparison of offending rates by age of offender, the information shown in the table is expressed as offenders per 10,000 population in each age group. For both males and females it was young adults who offended the most. In 1999, 648 per 10,000 population of 16 to 24 year old men were found guilty of, or cautioned for, an indictable offence, compared with a rate of 130 per 10,000 women in the same age group. For each offence group, men aged 16 to 24 were the most likely to have committed an offence. Over half of all female offenders were found guilty or cautioned for theft-related offences. Theft was the most common offence for males to have

# 9.12

committed as well; but the proportion of all male offenders committing it was lower (36 per cent) and male offenders were more evenly distributed among the other main offence groups.

Nearly half of all females and approaching two-thirds of males who were convicted in England and Wales in 1998 had already been convicted previously (Table 9.12). Eighteen per cent of males convicted and 7 per cent of females had 10 or more previous convictions. Compared with other age groups, higher proportions of males and females aged 55 and over found guilty of offences had no previous convictions. Males and females convicted for theft were more likely to re-offend than those convicted for other offences.

## Police and courts action

In England, Wales and Northern Ireland, following an arrest the police may release the suspect without further action, caution (either formally or informally), or charge. The new counting rules introduced on 1 April 1998 had an effect on the clear-up figures, although their precise extent cannot be quantified. A number of the newer offences, such as drug possession, common assault and dangerous driving have relatively high clear-up rates, which have increased the overall clear-up rate. However, all offences of criminal damage are now included in the clear-up rate, whereas previously only those where the damage was valued at over £20 were included – this will have reduced the overall clear-up rate.

Clear-up rates vary according to the type of offence. Of the main categories of offence, drug offences were the most likely to be cleared up in the United Kingdom in 1999-00 and theft from

**People convicted: by gender, age and number of previous convictions[1], 1998**

England & Wales          Percentages

| | Number of previous convictions | | | | | All people convicted |
|---|---|---|---|---|---|---|
| | 0 | 1 | 2 | 3-9 | 10 or more | |
| **Males** | | | | | | |
| 10-17 | 49 | 18 | 10 | 21 | 2 | 100 |
| 18-34 | 34 | 12 | 8 | 28 | 18 | 100 |
| 35-54 | 34 | 11 | 7 | 22 | 26 | 100 |
| 55 and over | 58 | 11 | 5 | 14 | 12 | 100 |
| | | | | | | |
| All aged 10 and over | 37 | 12 | 8 | 26 | 18 | 100 |
| **Females** | | | | | | |
| 10-17 | 61 | 20 | 8 | 11 | - | 100 |
| 18-34 | 49 | 14 | 8 | 20 | 8 | 100 |
| 35-54 | 62 | 12 | 5 | 13 | 9 | 100 |
| 55 and over | 69 | 8 | 2 | 13 | 7 | 100 |
| | | | | | | |
| All aged 10 and over | 54 | 14 | 7 | 17 | 7 | 100 |

1 Based on a sample of people convicted in the first 15 days of March and November 1998 for standard list offences only. For a definition of standard list offences see Appendix, Part 9: Types of offences in England, Wales and Northern Ireland.
**Source: Home Office**

vehicles the least likely (see Table 9.13 overleaf). In England and Wales, overall clear-up rates were 25 per cent in 1999-00, under the new counting rules. Additional guidelines clarifying precisely what is meant by offences being 'cleared up' were introduced in England and Wales in 1999. Under these guidelines, evidence given by convicted prisoners is no longer counted in police clear up rates. Scotland had a 'clear-up' rate of 43 per cent in 1999 and Northern Ireland had a clear up rate of 30 per cent in 1999-00.

In England and Wales, when an offender has admitted their guilt, there is sufficient evidence for a conviction and it does not seem in the public interest to institute criminal proceedings, a formal caution may be given by a senior police officer. In

# 9.13

**Clear-up rates for notifiable offences[1]: by type of offence, 1999-00**

Percentages

| | England & Wales[2] | Scotland[3] | Northern Ireland |
|---|---|---|---|
| Drug offences | 97 | 99 | 90 |
| Violence against the person | 65 | 82 | 64 |
| Sexual offences, | 59 | 77 | 75 |
| of which: rape | 54 | 79 | 76 |
| Fraud and forgery | 30 | 76 | 44 |
| Robbery | 18 | 38 | 19 |
| | | | |
| Theft and handling stolen goods, | 18 | 33 | 22 |
| of which: theft of vehicles | 13 | 32 | 13 |
| theft from vehicles | 6 | 17 | 7 |
| Criminal damage[4] | 15 | 24 | 15 |
| Burglary | 13 | 23 | 16 |
| Other notifiable offences[5] | 74 | 98 | 75 |
| | | | |
| All notifiable offences | 25 | 43 | 30 |

1 See Appendix, Part 9: Types of offences in England and Wales, Types of offences in Northern Ireland, and Offences and crimes.
2 No longer includes detections obtained by the interview of a convicted prisoner.
3 Scottish figures refer to 1999 crimes.
4 In Northern Ireland, under new counting rules all criminal damage is recorded.
5 In Northern Ireland includes 'offences against the state'.
**Source: Home Office; Scottish Executive; Royal Ulster Constabulary**

# 9.14

**Offenders cautioned for indictable offences[1]: by type of offence**

**England & Wales**

Thousands

| | 1971[2] | 1981 | 1991 | 1992 | 1997 | 1998 | 1999 |
|---|---|---|---|---|---|---|---|
| Theft and handling stolen goods | 53.5 | 79.2 | 108.5 | 130.3 | 82.8 | 83.6 | 75.4 |
| Drug offences[2] | .. | 0.3 | 21.2 | 27.6 | 56.0 | 58.7 | 49.4 |
| Violence against the person | 2.3 | 5.6 | 19.4 | 23.5 | 23.6 | 23.5 | 21.2 |
| Burglary[3] | 12.4 | 11.2 | 13.3 | 14.4 | 9.4 | 8.4 | 7.7 |
| Fraud and forgery | 1.0 | 1.4 | 5.6 | 7.5 | 7.2 | 7.4 | 7.2 |
| | | | | | | | |
| Criminal damage | 3.6 | 2.1 | 3.8 | 4.0 | 2.8 | 2.7 | 3.0 |
| Sexual offences | 3.9 | 2.8 | 3.3 | 3.4 | 1.9 | 1.7 | 1.5 |
| Robbery | 0.2 | 0.1 | 0.6 | 0.6 | 0.7 | 0.6 | 0.6 |
| Other | 0.3 | 1.3 | 4.1 | 4.8 | 5.0 | 5.0 | 4.6 |
| | | | | | | | |
| All offenders cautioned | 77.3 | 103.9 | 179.9 | 216.2 | 189.4 | 191.7 | 170.6 |

1 Excludes motoring offences.
2 Adjusted to take account of the Criminal Damage Act 1971. Drug offences data for 1971 are included in 'Other'.
3 See Appendix, Part 9: Offenders cautioned for burglary.
**Source: Home Office**

1999, 171 thousand people were given such a caution for an indictable offence in England and Wales – a fall from the peak of 216 thousand in 1992 (Table 9.14). Prior to this the number had risen steadily from 1971 when only 77 thousand offenders were cautioned. The number of cautions for drug offences rose sharply in the 1980s and continued to a peak of 59 thousand in 1998. Between 1998 and 1999 the number of people cautioned for drug offences fell to 49 thousand. Around a quarter of all offenders who were cautioned were young offenders (aged 10 to 18) of theft-related offences. Adult offenders, responsible for 70 per cent of all theft-related offences, received a quarter fewer cautions than younger people for such offences.

When an offender has been charged, or summoned and then found guilty, the court will impose a sentence. Sentences in England, Wales and Northern Ireland can include immediate custody, a community sentence, a fine or, if the court considers that no punishment is necessary, a discharge. In 1999, 342 thousand people were sentenced for indictable offences in England and Wales (Table 9.15). The form of sentence varied according to the type of offence committed. Those sentenced for motoring offences were the most likely to be fined, with 53 per cent receiving this form of sentence. Offenders sentenced for robbery were the most likely to be sentenced to immediate custody while those sentenced for fraud and forgery were the most likely to receive a community sentence. Tagging, where the whereabouts of the offender is made known to the relevant authorities by means of an electronic device, has been piloted since 1995 as an alternative means of sentencing, principally to monitor prisoners released early from prison.

Certain powers under the *Police and Criminal Evidence Act, 1984* were implemented in January 1986, covering stops and searches of people or vehicles, road checks, detention of people and intimate searches of people. In 1998-99 the police

# 9.15

### Offenders sentenced for indictable offences[1]: by type of offence and type of sentence[2], 1999

**England & Wales**                                                                                                                  Percentages

| | Discharge | Fine | Community sentence | Fully suspended sentence | Immediate custody | Other | All sentenced (=100%) (thousands) |
|---|---|---|---|---|---|---|---|
| Theft and handling stolen goods | 24 | 24 | 31 | - | 19 | 2 | 130.6 |
| Drug offences | 15 | 47 | 18 | 1 | 18 | 1 | 48.9 |
| Violence against the person | 14 | 12 | 38 | 1 | 31 | 3 | 36.0 |
| Burglary | 7 | 4 | 38 | 1 | 49 | 1 | 29.3 |
| Fraud and forgery | 18 | 17 | 41 | 2 | 20 | 2 | 20.2 |
| | | | | | | | |
| Criminal damage | 27 | 17 | 36 | - | 12 | 7 | 10.7 |
| Motoring | 6 | 53 | 21 | 1 | 20 | 1 | 8.3 |
| Robbery | 2 | - | 23 | 1 | 72 | 1 | 5.7 |
| Sexual offences | 4 | 4 | 27 | 2 | 61 | 2 | 4.3 |
| Other offences | 12 | 45 | 16 | 1 | 16 | 10 | 47.6 |
| | | | | | | | |
| All indictable offences | 17 | 27 | 29 | 1 | 23 | 3 | 341.7 |

1 See Appendix, Part 9: Types of offences in England and Wales.
2 See Appendix, Part 9: Sentences and orders.
**Source: Home Office**

stopped and searched over one million people or vehicles in England and Wales, roughly the same as in the previous year and over nine times the number in 1987 (Table 9.16). Suspicion of stolen property and possession of drugs are the two biggest reasons why individuals are stopped and searched, followed by suspicion of 'going equipped' to commit an offence. Just over a quarter of all stops and searches made in 1998-99 took place in the Metropolitan police area.

## Probation and prisons

Prisons have been a part of the criminal justice system as long as courts. Early prisons were often dangerous and unhygienic. Conditions in the prison system were improved significantly by the pioneering work of Elizabeth Fry (1780-1845), a leading prison reformer who advocated separation of the sexes in prisons and female supervision of women prisoners.

# 9.16

### Stops and searches made by the police: by reason

**England & Wales**                                                                     Thousands

| | 1987 | 1991 | 1995 | 1997-98 | 1998-99 |
|---|---|---|---|---|---|
| Stolen property | 49 | 114 | 253 | 398 | 436 |
| Drugs | 38 | 110 | 232 | 343 | 362 |
| Going equipped | 14 | 51 | 126 | 169 | 151 |
| Offensive weapons | 9 | 16 | 40 | 60 | 56 |
| Firearms | 1 | 2 | 6 | 7 | 7 |
| Other | 8 | 11 | 34 | 73 | 69 |
| | | | | | |
| All | 118 | 304 | 690 | 1,051 | 1,081 |

**Source: Home Office**

# 9.17

**Prison population**[1]

**Great Britain**
Thousands

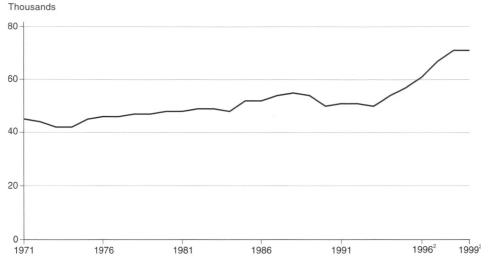

1 Includes those held in police cells up to June 1995. Includes non-criminal prisoners.
2 From 1996 onwards the Scottish prison population is for financial years.

**Source: Home Office; Scottish Executive**

# 9.18

## Prison population: by type of establishment

| England & Wales | | Thousands | |
| --- | --- | --- | --- |
| | 1980 | 1990 | 1999[1] |
| Local prisons | 17.3 | 15.5 | 25.1 |
| Closed training prisons | 13.0 | 17.1 | 24.3 |
| Young offender institutions[2] | . | 5.3 | 5.2 |
| Remand centres | 2.4 | 2.3 | 4.5 |
| Open prisons | 3.7 | 3.7 | 3.9 |
| Juvenile institutions | . | 0.3 | 1.6 |
| | | | |
| Closed borstal institutions | 3.9 | . | . |
| Open borstal institutions | 1.6 | . | . |
| Senior detention centres | 1.3 | . | . |
| Junior detention centres | 0.7 | . | . |
| Short sentence institutions | . | 0.3 | . |
| Police cells | . | 0.9 | . |
| | | | |
| All prisons | 43.9 | 45.5 | 64.5 |

1 Based on population at 30 June.
2 See Appendix, Part 9: Young offender institutions.

**Source: Home Office**

The total prison population in Great Britain fell in the late 1980s, but grew again between 1993 and 1998 to peak at 71 thousand. The prison population in 1999 remained unchanged at 71 thousand (Chart 9.17). In Northern Ireland the prison population fell throughout most of the 1980s before rising in the early 1990s. However, since 1994 the prison population of Northern Ireland has been decreasing. As a result of the Good Friday Agreement in 1998 over 300 prisoners have been released early. The majority of prisoners in Northern Ireland have been convicted of offences which are not related to terrorism.

The proportion of prisoners serving life sentences in England and Wales has fluctuated over time. In 1981, 4 per cent of prisoners were serving a life sentence. This proportion rose steadily to 7 per cent in 1992 to 1994, but then fell slightly to 6 per cent in 1995 to 1997, and remained at 6 per cent in 1999. Almost one person in five of the total prison population of England and Wales is from an ethnic minority group, a higher proportion than ethnic minorities make up of the population as a whole. The kind of establishment prisoners are in has varied over time (Table 9.18). Borstals and detention centres, established to house young offenders, were replaced in the 1980s by young offender institutions. The numbers in remand centres, local and closed prisons and juvenille insitutions have increased over the past two decades, reflecting increases in the overall prison population. Numbers of offenders in open prisons have remained roughly constant over the same period.

Increasingly greater flexibility is being introduced into the way prisoners are sentenced. The Home Detention Curfew scheme, introduced in 1999, enabled those serving sentences of three months or over but less than four years to be considered for release up to two months early. In its first year of operation 45 thousand prisoners were eligible for the scheme, and 14 thousand were released.

While custodial sentences are given for some of the more serious offences, other crimes are more likely to result in the offender receiving a criminal supervision order. In 1999, some 126 thousand people started a criminal supervision order in England and Wales; this compares with 79 thousand people in 1981 (Table 9.19). Males outnumbered females by five to one. As the same people may receive more than one order, the number of orders exceeds the number of people receiving orders. In 1999, 41 per cent of the orders issued were community service orders, while a slightly higher proportion, 44 per cent, were probation orders.

**9.19**

## Civil justice

While this chapter has so far looked at cases where a charge has been made as part of the official legal system, for example by the Crown Prosecution Service in England and Wales, a case may also be brought under civil law by others, including an individual or a company. The majority of these cases are handled by the county courts and High Court in England, Wales and Northern Ireland and by the Sheriff Court and Court of Session in Scotland. The High Court and Court of Session deal with the more substantial and complex cases. Civil cases may include consumer problems, claims for debt, negligence and recovery of land.

Following the issuing of a claim, many cases are settled without the need for a court hearing. Around 95 per cent of cases were settled at county court level in 1999 (Chart 9.20). The total number of claims issued in county courts in England and Wales rose sharply from just under 2.0 million in 1981 to peak at 3.7 million in 1991. This rise may be explained, in part, by the increase in lending as a consequence of financial deregulation. This led to an increase in cases concerned with the recovery and collection of debt, so that in 1999 such claims accounted for over half the total number of 2 million claims issued in 1999. After debt recovery, the second and third most common types of claims related to recovery of land and personal injury. In 1999 there were 136 thousand cases initiated in the Sheriff Court and 5 thousand in the Court of Session in Scotland.

### People commencing criminal supervision orders[1]

**England & Wales**                                                     Thousands

|  | 1981 | 1986 | 1991 | 1997 | 1998 | 1999 |
|---|---|---|---|---|---|---|
| Probation | 36 | 40 | 45 | 52 | 56 | 56 |
| Community service | 28 | 35 | 42 | 48 | 50 | 51 |
| Combination | . | . | . | 19 | 21 | 21 |
| Under the Children and Young Persons Act 1969 | 12 | 6 | 2 | 3 | 3 | 2 |
| Other | 8 | 7 | 8 | 8 | 7 | 6 |
| All[2] | 79 | 83 | 91 | 120 | 127 | 126 |

1 Supervised by the probation service. See Appendix, Part 9: Sentences and orders.
2 Individual figures do not sum to the total because each person may have more than one type of order.
**Source: Home Office**

**9.20**

### Writs and summonses issued[1]

**England & Wales**
Millions

1 See Appendix, Part 9: Civil courts.
2 Queen's Bench Division.
**Source: Court Service**

# 9.21

## Complaints against the police[1]: by outcome

**England & Wales**                                                                                        Thousands

|  | Substantiated | Unsub-stantiated | Informally resolved | Withdrawn/not proceeded with | All complaints |
|---|---|---|---|---|---|
| 1981 | 1.5 | 14.7 | . | 16.2 | 32.4 |
| 1986 | 1.1 | 12.7 | 4.0 | 11.3 | 29.2 |
| 1991 | 0.8 | 11.3 | 9.0 | 14.2 | 35.3 |
| 1995-96 | 0.7 | 7.9 | 11.7 | 15.5 | 35.8 |
| 1996-97 | 0.8 | 10.0 | 11.6 | 14.3 | 36.7 |
| 1997-98 | 0.9 | 9.0 | 12.3 | 13.7 | 35.8 |
| 1998-99 | 0.7 | 8.5 | 11.0 | 11.4 | 31.7 |
| 1999-00 | 0.7 | 7.3 | 11.1 | 11.7 | 30.8 |

1 Complaints are counted in the year in which they are completed.
**Source: Home Office**

# 9.22

## Civil legal aid[1]: applications received and granted

**England & Wales**

Thousands

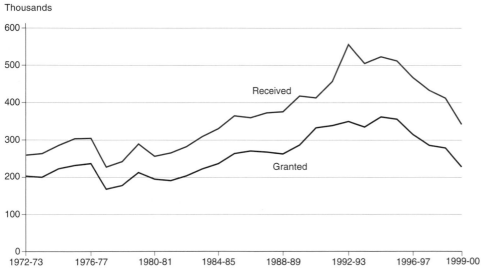

1 See Appendix, Part 9: Legal aid.
**Source: Lord Chancellor's Department**

Individuals and organisations may also make a complaint against the police. In England and Wales there were 31 thousand complaints completed in 1999-00, slightly fewer than in the previous year (Table 9.21). The proportion of complaints which were substantiated is small – only 2 per cent of complaints were substantiated in 1999-00.

The number of applications granted and received for legal aid is another measure of activity levels within the civil justice system. The number of applications granted in England and Wales has fallen in each of the past five years to 228 thousand in 1999-00. The number of applications received fell at a similar rate to 343 thousand in 1999-00 (Chart 9.22). Roughly two-thirds of applications received were granted. Around £1.6 billion was made available for legal aid in 1999-00, a 6 per cent decrease in real terms on the previous year. Over two-thirds of the decline was in the field of personal injury and other negligence, where the use of conditional fee agreements has been increasing. There were marked reductions too in the areas of contract and landlord and tenant proceedings.

## Resources

A large share of expenditure in the criminal justice system has traditionally been spent on the police force, with smaller amounts being spent on prisons and the courts (administered in England and Wales by the Lord Chancellor's Department.) In 1999-00, around £12 billion was spent on the criminal justice system. Changes in accounting systems mean that it is difficult to make comparisons with expenditure in previous years.

However, official estimates show that spending on the main elements of the criminal justice system (excluding the prison service) more than doubled in real terms between 1977 and 1997 compared with a 45 per cent rise in overall public expenditure.

Labour costs form the largest component of police force expenditure. At 31 March 2000, 53 thousand civilians were employed in the police service in England and Wales, in addition to the 124 thousand police officers (Table 9.23). The overall total represents an increase of 42 per cent on 1971 and a slight decline from 1997-98 when 180 thousand people were employed in the police service. The proportion of police service employees who were civilians rose from 22 per cent in 1971 to 30 per cent in 1999-00. Numbers working in the probation service remained fairly constant in the 1990s, although there was a drop in the number between 1998-99 and 1999-00.

There were the equivalent of 124 thousand police officers in England and Wales at 31 March 2000 (Table 9.24). The figures in the table exclude the 2 thousand on secondment. Excluding those on secondment, 17 per cent of officers were female. Constables formed the majority of officers, representing 78 per cent of police officer strength.

While 75 per cent of male police officers were constables, the proportion was 89 per cent for female officers. Over 2.7 thousand police officers in England and Wales belonged to an ethnic minority group. Eighty five per cent of police officers belonging to ethnic minority groups were constables. Seventy police officers in Scotland belonged to minority ethnic groups, less than 1 per cent of the total number of officers.

# 9.23

**Employment in the criminal justice system**

| England & Wales | | | | | | Thousands |
|---|---|---|---|---|---|---|
| | 1971 | 1981 | 1991 | 1997-98 | 1998-99 | 1999-00 |
| **Police service[1]** | | | | | | |
| Police | 97 | 120 | 127 | 127 | 126 | 124 |
| Civilian staff[2] | 28 | 38 | 46 | 53 | 53 | 53 |
| All police service | 125 | 157 | 174 | 180 | 179 | 178 |
| **Prison service[3]** | 17 | 24 | 33 | 41 | 43 | 43 |
| **Probation service[4]** | .. | 13 | 18 | 17 | 17 | 15 |

1 1971 and 1981 as at December each year; from 1991 as at 31 March each year.
2 Excludes traffic wardens and cadets.
3 For 1991 and earlier years excludes headquarters staff and prison officer class trainees.
4 Full-time plus part-time workers and includes some temporary officers and also some trainees from 1981 onwards. Excludes non-probation officer grade hostel staff. Data for 1997-98 onwards are for calendar years.
**Source: Home Office**

# 9.24

**Police officer strength[1]: by rank and gender, at 31 March 2000**

| England & Wales | | Numbers |
|---|---|---|
| | Males | Females |
| Chief Constable | 44 | 3 |
| Assistant Chief Constable | 137 | 12 |
| Superintendent | 1,164 | 62 |
| Chief Inspector | 1,465 | 109 |
| Inspector | 5,553 | 388 |
| Sergeant | 16,867 | 1,633 |
| Constable | 76,570 | 17,948 |
| All ranks | 101,800 | 20,155 |

1 Full-time equivalents employed in the 43 police force areas in England and Wales. With officers on secondment, the total police strength was 123,593.
**Source: Home Office**

## Websites

| | |
|---|---|
| National Statistics | www.statistics.gov.uk |
| Home Office | www.homeoffice.gov.uk/rds |
| Home Office (Criminal Justice System) | www.criminal-justice-system.gov.uk |
| Court Service | www.courtservice.gov.uk |
| Lord Chancellor's Department | www.open.gov.uk/lcd |
| National Assembly for Wales | www.wales.gov.uk |
| Northern Ireland Executive Information Service | www.nics.gov.uk |
| Northern Ireland Office | www.nio.gov.uk |
| Royal Ulster Constabulary | www.ruc.police.uk |
| Scottish Executive | www.scotland.gov.uk |

## Contacts

**Office for National Statistics**

| | |
|---|---|
| Chapter author | 020 7533 5776 |
| **Home Office** | 020 7273 2084 |
| **Lord Chancellor's Department** | 020 7210 8781 |
| **Northern Ireland Office** | 028 9052 7534/8 |
| **Royal Ulster Constabulary** | 028 9065 0222 ext. 24135 |
| **Scottish Executive Justice Department** | 0131 244 2598 |

Social Trends 31, © Crown copyright 2001

# Chapter 10 Housing

### Housing stock and housebuilding

- During the last two centuries the number of dwellings in Great Britain increased substantially, from almost 2 million at the start of the 19th century to nearly 25 million at the beginning of the 21st century. (Chart 10.1)

- A fifth of dwellings in England were built before the end of the First World War and almost two-fifths since 1965. (Table 10.2)

- In the United Kingdom private enterprises were the main providers of new dwellings in 1999-00 and Registered Social Landlords dominated building by the social sector. (Chart 10.3)

### Types of tenure and accommodation

- Between 1981 and 2000, the number of owner-occupied dwellings in Great Britain increased by more than two-fifths to 1.2 million. The number of homes rented from a Registered Social Landlord more than doubled over the same period. (Chart 10.5 and page 179)

- In 1999-00 almost half of all households headed by someone under the age of 25 in England were living in privately rented accommodation compared with one in seven households headed by someone aged 25 to 44. (Table 10.7)

- Between 1994-95 and 1999-00, the proportion of householders in England who said crime was a problem in their area fell by almost 20 percentage points to 56 per cent. (Table 10.15)

### Housing costs and expenditure

- In 1999 the average dwelling price in England and Wales was £94,600. (Table 10.21)

- The popularity of endowment mortgages continues to decline. In 1988, 83 per cent of house purchases were with an endowment; by 1999 the figure had fallen to 27 per cent. (Chart 10.22)

# 10.1

## Stock of dwellings[1]

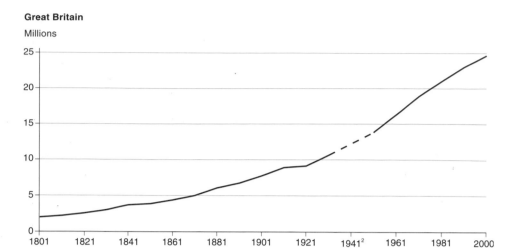

**Great Britain**

Millions

1 See Appendix, Part 10: Dwelling stock. Data for 1801 to 1981 are census outputs. Data for 1991 and 2000 for England and Wales are at 31 March, and for Scotland at 31 December of the previous year.
2 No census was undertaken in 1941.

**Source: Census; Department of the Environment, Transport and the Regions; National Assembly for Wales; Scottish Executive**

The need for adequate shelter is regarded as a basic human requisite. The condition of our homes and the nature of the surrounding area may have an impact on the quality of our daily lives, both directly and indirectly. Poor quality housing may be harmful to health and is often associated with other social problems.

## Housing stock and housebuilding

During the last two centuries the number of dwellings in Great Britain increased substantially, from almost 2 million at the start of the 19th century to nearly 25 million at the beginning of the 21st century (Chart 10.1). The increase in the population over the past two centuries (see Table 1.1 on page 30 in the Population chapter) has had a direct impact on the level of demand for accommodation. In 1801, and in all subsequent censuses up to and including 1951, there were fewer houses than households, whereas from 1971 onwards there were more separate dwellings than households. A higher proportion of households had a house or a flat to themselves in 1991 and far fewer shared – about 2 per cent in 1991 compared with 15 per cent in 1911. The composition of the population also influences accommodation requirements. The number of households tripled in Great Britain during the 20th century, partly as a result of decreasing household and family sizes and, in the latter part of the century, partly as a result of the increase in the numbers of people living on their own (see Table 2.2 on page 42 in the Households and Families chapter).

The numbers of households are projected to increase further (see page 42 in the Households and Families chapter), with the largest increase being projected in one-person households. These are factors planning authorities are expected to take into account when planning future housing provision. The revised *Planning Policy Guidance Note 3 on Housing*, providing national planning guidance on the future of housebuilding and

# 10.2

## Type of accommodation: by construction date, 1999-00

**England**                                                                    Percentages

|  | Before 1919 | 1919-1944 | 1945-1964 | 1965-1984 | 1985 or later | All |
|---|---|---|---|---|---|---|
| **House or bungalow** | | | | | | |
| Detached | 13 | 15 | 18 | 31 | 23 | 100 |
| Semi-detached | 10 | 30 | 30 | 21 | 9 | 100 |
| Terraced | 36 | 20 | 17 | 19 | 8 | 100 |
| **Flat or maisonette** | | | | | | |
| Purpose-built | 4 | 8 | 25 | 44 | 20 | 100 |
| Other | 64 | 17 | 6 | 7 | 6 | 100 |
| **All dwellings[1]** | 20 | 21 | 22 | 25 | 13 | 100 |

1 Includes other types of accommodation, such as mobile homes.
**Source: Survey of English Housing, Department of the Environment, Transport and the Regions**

regional development in England, was issued by the Department of the Environment, Transport and the Regions in March 2000. This guidance includes proposals for planning authorities to recycle 'brownfield' – previously developed sites – and empty properties in preference to 'greenfield' sites; for using land more efficiently; for assisting with the provision of affordable housing in both rural and urban areas; and for promoting mixed-use developments which integrate housing with shops, local services and transport.

The Government's target for England is that, by 2008, 60 per cent of additional housing should be provided on previously developed land or by re-using existing buildings. In 1998, the proportion of new dwellings built on previously developed land or provided by conversions of existing buildings was 57 per cent. Over the period 1994 to 1998, the average density on previously developed land was 28 dwellings per hectare compared with 22 dwellings per hectare on land not previously developed. London continues to have a higher density of dwellings built per hectare than anywhere else in England.

Much of the current housing stock reflects over 100 years of housebuilding, with a fifth of dwellings in England having been built before the end of the First World War (Table 10.2). The type of dwellings that are built, however, has changed during this time. Over a third of the current stock of terraced houses was built before 1919. Between the two World Wars there was a shift in the emphasis in the type of home that was being built in favour of semi-detached dwellings and, since 1965, there has been a shift towards the building of detached houses and purpose-built flats. Almost two-thirds of the current stock of purpose-built flats or maisonettes were built after 1964, and very few before 1919.

Chart 10.3 shows trends in housebuilding in the United Kingdom since 1949. In the early post-war years most dwelling construction was undertaken by local authorities while private enterprise

**Housebuilding completions[1]**

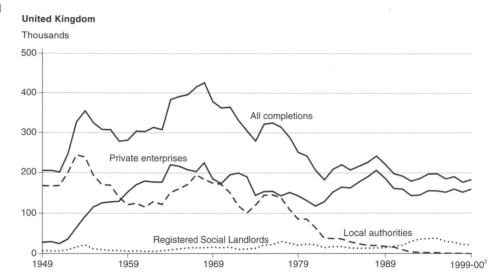

**United Kingdom**
Thousands

1 See Appendix, Part 10: Dwelling stock and Dwellings completed.
2 From 1990–91 data are financial year.

**Source: Department of the Environment, Transport and the Regions; National Assembly for Wales; Scottish Executive; Department for Social Development, Northern Ireland**

building began to take off during the 1950s. There have been more completions by private enterprises than by either Registered Social Landlords (RSLs) or local authorities in most years since 1959. Total completions over the last 50 years peaked in 1968, when 226 thousand dwellings were built by private enterprises and a further 200 thousand by the remaining sectors. Since the early 1990s the local authority housebuilding programme has been minimal. RSLs now dominate building by the social sector, accounting for an eighth of all completions in 1999-00.

The average usable floor area for all dwellings in England in 1996 was 85 square metres, which was virtually the same as for France (85 square metres) and Germany (86 square metres), but only half that of the USA (152 square metres). An alternative means of assessing dwelling size is by the number of bedrooms. There were changes in the number of bedrooms that dwellings are constructed with in England and Wales during the last 30 or so years of the 20th century. One in 14 houses completed in 1971 had four or more bedrooms; by 1997 this had increased to almost

# 10.4

### Housebuilding completions: by number of bedrooms

| England & Wales | | | | Percentages |
| --- | --- | --- | --- | --- |
| | 1971 | 1981 | 1991 | 1997 |
| 1 bedroom | 14 | 22 | 19 | 7 |
| 2 bedrooms | 23 | 25 | 31 | 27 |
| 3 bedrooms | 55 | 40 | 30 | 38 |
| 4 or more bedrooms | 7 | 13 | 20 | 28 |
| All houses and flats (=100%) (thousands) | 323 | 189 | 165 | 156 |

*Source: Department of the Environment, Transport and the Regions; National Assembly for Wales*

# 10.5

### Stock of dwellings[1]: by tenure

**Great Britain**

Millions

1 See Appendix, Part 10: Dwelling stock. Data for England and Wales are at 31 December until 1990 and from 31 March thereafter. Data for Scotland are as at 31 December of the previous year throughout.

*Source: Department of the Environment, Transport and the Regions; National Assembly for Wales; Scottish Executive*

three in ten (Table 10.4). At the same time there was a reduction in the proportion of one bedroom homes that were completed. The apparent anomaly of the decrease in the proportion of larger families (see Table 2.2 on page 42 in the Households and Families chapter) can be explained by householders' aspiration to purchase the largest house that they are able to afford, regardless of the household or family size.

## Types of tenure and accommodation

The increase in owner-occupation has been a notable feature of the 20th century. At the start of the century, almost all dwellings in England – 89 per cent – were privately rented and only a small proportion – 10 per cent – were owner-occupied. The 1950s saw a period of growth in prosperity alongside initiatives to improve housebuilding; this was accompanied by deregulation in both planning and the building industry. Thus, owner-occupation increased from 29 per cent in 1951 to 45 per cent in 1964. Between 1981 and 2000 the number of owner-occupied dwellings in Great Britain increased by more than two-fifths, while the number of rented dwellings fell by a seventh (Chart 10.5). By 2000, at over 16.6 million, the number of owner-occupied dwellings was more than double the number of rented dwellings. This was partly due to legislation introduced in October 1980 which allowed public sector tenants to buy their own homes.

The 1998-99 Survey of English Housing estimated that about 250 thousand households with their main residence in England (1 per cent of the total) had a second home in England. Over four in ten had the second property as a holiday home, while almost three in ten had it as an investment.

# 10.6

Dwellings can be rented either from local authorities, RSLs, or from private landlords. In Scotland and Northern Ireland, dwellings can also be rented from Scottish Homes and the Northern Ireland Housing Executive respectively. Although the number of dwellings rented from local authorities has declined since 1981, they still dominate the rented sector. More than 50 per cent of all rented homes were rented from a local authority in Great Britain in 2000. The number of those rented from RSLs more than doubled to 1.2 million between 1981 and 2000.

Tenure varies according to type of household. Data combined from the General Household Survey in Great Britain and the Continuous Household Survey in Northern Ireland show that, in 1998-99, households comprised of lone parents with dependent children were more likely to rent their property than to own it (Table 10.6). Households containing dependent children (whether couple or lone parent households) were less likely to own their property outright than any other household type.

That tenure of housing also varies with the age of the head of household in part reflects people's life cycle transitions. In 1999-00 almost half of households headed by someone under 25 in England were living in privately rented accommodation, which was more than three times the proportion for those aged 25 to 44 and far greater than for any other age group (Table 10.7). Private renters in furnished accommodation were particularly likely to be young, male and single. Heads of households aged 65 and over were most likely to own their property outright, as by the time they retire many will have repaid their mortgage in its entirety. A third of all social sector renters in England were aged 65 or over compared with a quarter of owner-occupiers and one in eight

## Household type: by tenure, 1998-99

United Kingdom                                                                                              Percentages

| | Owned outright | Owned with mortgage | Rented from social sector | Rented privately[1] | All tenures |
|---|---|---|---|---|---|
| **One person** | 35 | 22 | 31 | 12 | 100 |
| **Two or more unrelated adults** | 25 | 20 | 18 | 37 | 100 |
| **One family households[2]** | | | | | |
| Couple | | | | | |
| No children | 42 | 39 | 12 | 7 | 100 |
| Dependent children[3] | 6 | 72 | 15 | 8 | 100 |
| Non-dependent children only | 37 | 51 | 11 | 2 | 100 |
| Lone parent | | | | | |
| Dependent children[3] | 6 | 27 | 54 | 13 | 100 |
| Non-dependent children only | 35 | 29 | 32 | 4 | 100 |
| **Multi-family households** | 18 | 49 | 29 | 4 | 100 |
| **All households** | 28 | 41 | 22 | 9 | 100 |

1 Includes rent-free accommodation.
2 Other individuals who were not family members may also be included.
3 May also include non-dependent children.

**Source: General Household Survey, Office for National Statistics; Continuous Household Survey, Northern Ireland Statistics and Research Agency**

# 10.7

## Age of head of household: by tenure, 1999-00

England                                                                                                     Percentages

| | 16-24 | 25-44 | 45-64 | 65-74 | 75 and over | All aged 16 and over |
|---|---|---|---|---|---|---|
| **Owner-occupied** | | | | | | |
| Owned outright | 1 | 4 | 31 | 64 | 56 | 27 |
| Owned with mortgage | 22 | 62 | 49 | 9 | 3 | 42 |
| **Rented from social sector** | | | | | | |
| Council | 19 | 14 | 11 | 17 | 26 | 15 |
| Registered Social Landlord | 11 | 6 | 4 | 6 | 8 | 6 |
| **Rented privately[1]** | | | | | | |
| Furnished | 28 | 4 | 1 | - | 1 | 3 |
| Unfurnished[2] | 19 | 10 | 4 | 4 | 6 | 7 |
| **All tenures** | 100 | 100 | 100 | 100 | 100 | 100 |

1 Includes rent-free accommodation.
2 Includes partly furnished accommodation.

**Source: Survey of English Housing, Department of the Environment, Transport and the Regions**

# 10.8

## Percentage of households living in houses: EU comparison, 1996

Percentages

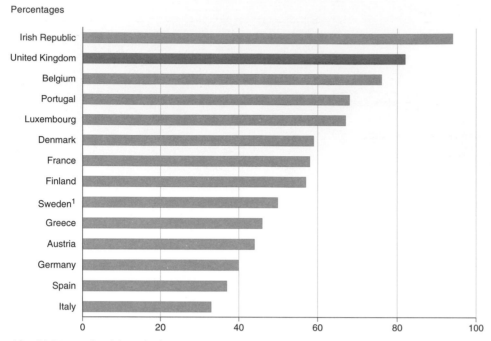

1 Swedish data are collected via a national source.

**Source: European Community Household Panel, Eurostat**

# 10.9

## Tenure: by type of accommodation, 1999-00

England | | | | | | Percentages

| | House or bungalow | | | Flat or maisonette | | |
| --- | --- | --- | --- | --- | --- | --- |
| | Detached | Semi-detached | Terraced | Purpose-built | Converted | All dwellings[1] |
| **Owner-occupied** | | | | | | |
| Owned outright | 34 | 37 | 23 | 5 | 1 | 100 |
| Owned with mortgage | 26 | 39 | 29 | 4 | 2 | 100 |
| **Rented from social sector** | | | | | | |
| Council | 1 | 32 | 27 | 37 | 3 | 100 |
| Registered Social | | | | | | |
| Landlord | 1 | 19 | 32 | 37 | 11 | 100 |
| **Rented privately[2]** | | | | | | |
| Furnished | 6 | 12 | 25 | 19 | 37 | 100 |
| Unfurnished[3] | 12 | 23 | 31 | 16 | 18 | 100 |
| **All tenures** | 21 | 34 | 27 | 13 | 5 | 100 |

1 Excludes those living in mobile homes.
2 Includes rent-free accommodation.
3 Includes partly furnished accommodation.

**Source: Survey of English Housing, Department of the Environment, Transport and the Regions**

private renters in 1999-00. This age difference is reflected in the high proportions of household heads who were widowed or retired and contributes to the high proportion of one-person households: 41 per cent of social sector households compared with 28 per cent of all households across all tenures.

Life cycles are not the only explanation for the age differences in tenure. Different generations have had different tenure patterns. An analysis for the Department of the Environment, Transport and the Regions, undertaken using data from the Survey of English Housing 1998-99, showed that among 'mainstream' owner-occupiers in England (those owners who had not come into home-ownership through purchase as sitting tenants from local authorities, new towns or RSLs) a 'cohort' effect was the main reason for the increasing proportion of owner-occupation at older ages over time, rather than moves from renting to owner-occupation at these stages in life. In 1998-99 the proportion of 'mainstream' owner-occupiers was highest for heads of household aged 45 to 54 and then declined with age. With the passage of time it is expected that the relatively higher proportions of current owner-occupiers will increase the proportion of owner-occupation as they reach successively greater ages.

Across the EU, more than half of households lived in houses in 1996 (Chart 10.8). However, the average masks the markedly different situations across the EU; the proportion of households living in houses ranged from a third in Italy to over nine-tenths in the Irish Republic. Differences between countries depend largely on housing stock but also on consumer choice.

In 1999-00 over four-fifths of all households in England lived in a house, whether it was detached, semi-detached or terraced (Table 10.9). Semi-detached houses were the most common type of dwelling, accounting for a third of all dwellings. However, the type of accommodation varies according to tenure and, in general, home-owners were more likely than social renters to live in houses, particularly in detached or semi-detached properties. Almost two-fifths of owner-occupiers lived in a semi-detached house. In comparison, similar proportions of RSL and local authority tenants lived in either a purpose-built flat or a maisonette. Households renting an unfurnished dwelling were more likely to live in a house, particularly a terraced house, compared with those renting a furnished dwelling who were most likely to live in a converted flat or rooms.

Traditionally, housing tenure in the United Kingdom has been closely related to social class and economic status, although the link has become less pronounced in the last 15 years or so. In 1998-99 home-ownership was still, however, generally more common among those in non-manual groups than those in manual groups. Table 10.10 shows that the type of accommodation in which people live also varies with socio-economic group. Among the economically active, more than four in ten of both professional and employer and manager households lived in a detached house, compared with less than one in ten unskilled manual households. The economically inactive were nearly twice as likely as the economically active to live in a purpose-built flat or maisonette.

For a variety of reasons some people may end up homeless. Local authorities have legal duties to provide accommodation or housing assistance for families and vulnerable people who are eligible for assistance, unintentionally homeless and in priority need. The priority need group includes households with dependent children or containing a pregnant woman; people who are vulnerable as a result of old age, youth, mental or physical illness or disability or other special reason; and people who are homeless in an emergency. Local authorities owe lesser duties to people who are homeless but not in priority need, and those who have become homeless intentionally.

**Socio-economic group[1] of head of household: by type of accommodation, 1998-99**

United Kingdom Percentages

| | House or bungalow | | | Flat or maisonette | | |
| --- | --- | --- | --- | --- | --- | --- |
| | Detached | Semi-detached | Terraced | Purpose-built | Other | All dwellings |
| **Economically active** | | | | | | |
| Professional | 44 | 28 | 18 | 7 | 3 | 100 |
| Employers and managers | 41 | 30 | 19 | 7 | 3 | 100 |
| Intermediate non-manual | 21 | 31 | 30 | 11 | 7 | 100 |
| Junior non-manual | 19 | 31 | 28 | 18 | 5 | 100 |
| Skilled manual | 19 | 39 | 30 | 10 | 3 | 100 |
| Semi-skilled manual | 11 | 33 | 32 | 18 | 5 | 100 |
| Unskilled manual | 8 | 34 | 38 | 18 | 3 | 100 |
| | | | | | | |
| All economically active | 25 | 33 | 27 | 11 | 4 | 100 |
| | | | | | | |
| **Economically inactive** | | | | | | |
| Retired | 25 | 33 | 22 | 17 | 3 | 100 |
| Other | 11 | 28 | 31 | 25 | 5 | 100 |
| | | | | | | |
| All economically inactive | 21 | 32 | 25 | 19 | 3 | 100 |
| **All socio-economic groups** | 23 | 32 | 26 | 14 | 4 | 100 |

1 Excludes members of the armed forces, economically active full time students and those who were unemployed and had never worked.

*Source: General Household Survey, Office for National Statistics; Continuous Household Survey, Northern Ireland Statistics and Research Agency*

In 1999-00 local authorities in England made a total of 243.6 thousand decisions on applications for housing from households eligible under the homelessness provisions of the *Housing Acts;* they accepted 105.5 thousand households as homeless.

In 1999 almost three in ten acceptances in England arose because parents, relatives or friends were no longer able or willing to accommodate them; this proportion has been fairly constant since 1995, but was around 40 per cent in the early 1990s. A further quarter of acceptances followed a relationship breakdown. At 5 per cent of acceptances in 1999, mortgage arrears as a cause of homelessness have been steadily declining since a peak of 12 per cent in

# 10.11

### Homeless households in temporary accommodation[1]

**Great Britain**

Thousands

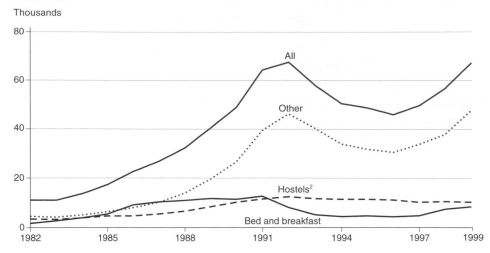

1 Data are at end year and include households awaiting the outcome of homeless enquiries. Households made temporarily homeless through flooding in Wales in 1990 and 1993 are excluded.
2 From 1987 the data for Wales include those households placed in women's refuges.

**Source: Department of the Environment, Transport and the Regions; National Assembly for Wales; Scottish Executive**

# 10.12

### Reasons for declaring dwellings unfit, 1991 and 1996

| England | Percentages | |
| --- | --- | --- |
| | 1991 | 1996 |
| Food preparation | 37 | 33 |
| Disrepair | 36 | 27 |
| Dampness | 23 | 23 |
| Bath/shower/wash-hand basin | 25 | 19 |
| Ventilation | 20 | 17 |
| WC | 20 | 13 |
| Structural stability | 9 | 9 |
| Heating | 14 | 5 |
| Drainage | 6 | 5 |
| Lighting | 7 | 4 |
| Water supply | 2 | 1 |
| All households in unfit dwellings (=100%) (millions) | 1.4 | 1.3 |

**Source: English House Condition Survey, Department of the Environment, Transport and the Regions**

1991. In Wales, three in ten households who were accepted as homeless in 1999 stated that their homelessness was a result of a breakdown of a relationship with a partner. A further three in ten who were homeless gave rent arrears or other reason for loss of rented or tied accommodation. In Scotland, almost a third of households that were assessed as homeless or potentially homeless and in priority need in 1998-99 were so because they were no longer willing or able to remain with parents, relatives or friends, and a similar proportion had experienced a breakdown of relationship with a partner. In Northern Ireland, mortgage arrears accounted for 1 per cent of the reasons of households who presented as homeless.

When a household makes a homelessness application the local housing authority must decide whether the applicant is eligible for assistance (certain persons from abroad are not), unintentionally homeless and in a priority need group. Where all these criteria are met, a main homelessness duty will be owed. In England and Wales, if other suitable accommodation is available in the district (for example, in the private rented sector) the authority must provide sufficient advice and assistance to enable the applicant to obtain this accommodation. Where this is not available, the authority must itself ensure that suitable accommodation is provided for up to two years. The duty, discharged by the provision of temporary accommodation, is likely to recur until a settled housing solution can be found; in most cases this is likely to be the allocation of a secure council tenancy or an assured tenancy with an RSL. The number of such households in temporary accommodation in Great Britain increased rapidly during the 1980s and peaked in 1992 at nearly 68 thousand (Chart 10.11). Between 1992 and 1996 the number of households in temporary accommodation fell by almost a third and since then the number has almost returned to the 1992 level. In England the main reasons for this increase relate to the upturn in the housing market in London and the South East, and to asylum seekers.

Across Great Britain, most households in temporary accommodation in 1999 were placed in privately leased accommodation or dwellings owned or leased by the local authority with a non-secure tenancy. Around one in seven homeless households placed in temporary accommodation were housed in hostels (including women's refuges) and a similar proportion in bed and breakfast accommodation (see Appendix, Part 10: Homeless households).

The Rough Sleepers Unit (RSU), established in April 1999, has responsibility for delivering the target of reducing rough sleeping in England to as near to zero as possible and by at least two-thirds by 2002. This target was set out as part of the 1998 Social Exclusion Unit report. By June 2000, the number of people sleeping rough in England on any single night was estimated to be 1.2 thousand which represented a reduction of around a third since June 1998.

# 10.13

## Housing condition and satisfaction with area

Prior to the advent of social housing provision in the United Kingdom, households with low incomes were unable to afford the private market rents which were demanded for decent housing. People were often forced to live in whatever they could afford, which meant either renting sub-standard, slum housing and/or living in very cramped overcrowded conditions. By the mid-19th century these problems had become particularly acute in the rapidly expanding urban areas of the United Kingdom.

Throughout the latter half of the 19th century, a series of Acts were introduced across the United Kingdom. For example the *Torrens Act* of 1868 included measures to permit local authorities to demolish properties which were unfit for human habitation in Great Britain. In England and Wales and Northern Ireland an attempt was made to address the problems of poor quality building standards with the 1875 *Public Health Act*, which encouraged local by-laws for minimum standards of construction. Although the *Housing of the Working Classes Act* of 1890 permitted local authorities in the United Kingdom to provide local authority housing, no government subsidy was available and the finance had to be found by the local authorities themselves.

These Acts, together with others which were subsequently introduced, largely helped to eradicate many of the problems experienced in housing during the 19th century. Over time the provision of facilities and services inevitably improves as new dwellings are added to the stock with modern facilities and existing dwellings are upgraded or demolished. However, a quantity of sub-standard accommodation remains. Under the current fitness standard in England introduced in 1989 (see Appendix, Part 10: The fitness standard), 1.5 million dwellings were estimated to be unfit for human habitation in 1996, representing 7.5 per cent of the dwelling stock in England. The most common reason for 'unfitness' was facilities for the preparation and cooking of food, accounting for almost four in ten dwellings identified as unfit (Table 10.12). Second in importance was disrepair, followed by dampness. In 1996, over two-thirds of households in dwellings failing the standard were unfit on one item alone. Dwellings failing the standard on one item alone tended to do so more because of the design or usage of dwellings (food preparation, ventilation, bathroom amenities) than because of the deterioration of the fabric (disrepair, instability). Dwellings that were unfit for multiple reasons tended to be run down or unmodernised. Multiple failure dwellings were likely to be older than single failure dwellings and to have higher costs to make fit.

Other important indicators of housing standards are overcrowding and under-occupancy. A Report from the London Statistical Society in 1847 described a street in St Giles in London where in 1841, 27 houses with an average of five rooms had 655 occupants. By 1847, the same houses contained 1,095 people. Some of the increase was attributed, ironically, to 'improvements' such as pulling down dwellings to widen the streets.

The concept of bedroom standard (see Appendix, Part 10: Bedroom standard) is used as an indicator of occupation density and hence of overcrowding and under-occupation. Overcrowding is the difference between the number of bedrooms needed to avoid undesirable sharing (the bedroom standard) and the number of bedrooms the household actually has. In 1999-00, 2 per cent of households in England were below the bedroom standard and hence defined as overcrowded (Table 10.13). Overcrowding was most common among those renting within the social sector. Under-occupation was most common, by far, in the owner-occupied sector and particularly for those who owned their home outright.

### Overcrowding and under-occupation[1]: by tenure, 1999-00

| England | | Percentages |
| --- | --- | --- |
| | Over-crowded[2] | Under-occupied[3] |
| **Owner-occupied** | | |
| Owned outright | 1 | 54 |
| Owned with mortgage | 2 | 36 |
| **Rented from social sector** | | |
| Council | 6 | 13 |
| Registered Social Landlord | 5 | 9 |
| **Rented privately**[4] | | |
| Furnished | 3 | 13 |
| Unfurnished[5] | 4 | 22 |
| **All tenures** | 2 | 34 |

1 See Appendix, Part 10: Bedroom standard.
2 One or more rooms below bedroom standard.
3 Two or more above bedroom standard.
4 Includes rent-free accommodation.
5 Includes partly furnished accommodation.

**Source: Survey of English Housing, Department of the Environment, Transport and the Regions**

# 10.14

**Satisfaction with different aspects of accommodation, 1998-99**

England                                                                                          Percentages

| | Very satisfied | Fairly satisfied | Neither satisfied nor dissatisfied | Slightly dissatisfied | Very dissatisfied | Total |
|---|---|---|---|---|---|---|
| Heating | 62 | 24 | 3 | 6 | 4 | 100 |
| Number of rooms | 60 | 27 | 4 | 8 | 2 | 100 |
| Layout of house/flat | 57 | 33 | 4 | 5 | 2 | 100 |
| Size of rooms | 56 | 31 | 4 | 8 | 2 | 100 |
| General appearance | 50 | 37 | 5 | 6 | 2 | 100 |
| State of repair | 47 | 35 | 5 | 9 | 4 | 100 |
| Insulation and draft proofing | 47 | 31 | 6 | 11 | 5 | 100 |
| Overall satisfaction | 60 | 31 | 3 | 4 | 2 | 100 |

*Source: Survey of English Housing, Department of the Environment, Transport and the Regions*

# 10.15

**Householders[1] saying that there are problems with their area**

England                                        Percentages

| | 1994-95 | 1997-98 | 1999-00 |
|---|---|---|---|
| Crime | 74 | 68 | 56 |
| Litter and rubbish | 46 | 41 | 42 |
| Vandalism and hooliganism | 59 | 55 | 40 |
| Dogs | 42 | 34 | 29 |
| Noise | 25 | 24 | 23 |
| Graffiti | 32 | 29 | 22 |
| Neighbours | 14 | 13 | 13 |
| Racial harassment | 5 | 4 | 4 |

*1 Head of household or partner who replied that they had 'a serious problem' or 'a problem, but not serious'.*
*Source: Survey of English Housing, Department of the Environment, Transport and Regions*

In 1998-99 the Survey of English Housing asked all heads of households or their partners about their satisfaction with their accommodation overall, and more specifically with the heating, insulation/draught proofing, number of rooms, size of rooms, layout, state of repair and general appearance of their dwelling (Table 10.14). Nine in ten household heads were at least 'fairly satisfied' with their accommodation, including six in ten who were very satisfied. Insulation and draft proofing was the aspect of the accommodation with the highest levels of dissatisfaction: 11 per cent were slightly dissatisfied and a further 5 per cent were very dissatisfied. Not surprisingly, those owning their property were less likely to be dissatisfied than those in either the social or private sector.

The 1999-00 Survey of English Housing asked households to identify whether various problems occurred in their area and if so whether they thought that they were serious. Over half of all householders said that crime was a problem, including more than one in ten who thought that it was a serious problem (Table 10.15). Vandalism and hooliganism and litter and rubbish were also common problems that were identified. Between 1994-95 and 1999-00 the proportions reporting that crime and vandalism and hooliganism were a problem each fell by almost 20 percentage points.

## Housing mobility

In 1999-00 the Survey of English Housing estimated that 2.4 million households, 12 per cent of all households, had moved into their present accommodation in the year prior to the interview. Around one in five of these were new households which consisted of people who were previously living as part of someone else's home, such as adult children who had left the parental home. Private renters living in unfurnished accommodation were the most mobile group; 57 per cent had moved during the previous 12 months. In comparison, around 16 per cent who rented from a Registered Social Landlord and 11 per cent who rented from a local authority had moved during the same period. Outright owners were the least mobile group; more than half had been resident for 20 years or more.

Table 10.16 shows the previous tenure of recent movers in 1999-00. The most common types of move were from one owner-occupied home to another or from one privately rented home to another. Of those who had moved and were owner-occupiers after moving, almost three-fifths had owned and around a quarter had rented their previous accommodation. For many, private renting is, to a certain extent, a transitory tenure status, so the shift into owner-occupation is perhaps somewhat unsurprising. There is an apparent two-way flow between owner-occupation and private renting; around a sixth of private renters who had been resident for less than a year had owned their previous home. Once established in an area few households move a significant distance from their original property – seven in ten households moved less than 10 miles in 1999-00.

Of the main reasons for moving given by heads of households, over a fifth of those living in a property owned with a mortgage reported that they wanted a larger house or flat. A similar proportion of those who owned the property outright reported that the main reason for moving had been the desire for a smaller or cheaper house or flat (Table 10.17). Almost three in ten of those who rented privately reported job-related reasons as being the main reason for moving. The knock-on effects of marriage or cohabitation and divorce or separation had both accounted for 8 per cent of all moves during the previous 12 months. Data collected and analysed for the Department of the Environment, Transport and the Regions from the General Household Survey, the Survey of English Housing, the 1991 Census Sample of Anonymised Records and the Office for National Statistics' Longitudinal Study estimated that there were just over 100 thousand divorcing owner-occupier couples a year in England in the early 1990s. Of the 200 thousand or so ex-partners, around 60 thousand left owner-occupation each year. More female than male owner-occupiers remained in the matrimonial home, around 48 thousand compared with 33 thousand.

### Current tenure: by previous tenure[1], 1999-00

England      Percentages

| | New house-holds | Owner-occupied | Rented from council | Rented from Registered Social Landlord | Rented privately | All |
|---|---|---|---|---|---|---|
| | | | | | | |
| **Current tenure** | | | | | | |
| Owner-occupied | 15 | 58 | 3 | 2 | 21 | 100 |
| Rented from council | 20 | 12 | 43 | 7 | 18 | 100 |
| Rented from Registered Social Landlord | 27 | 8 | 13 | 28 | 24 | 100 |
| Rented privately | 22 | 17 | 5 | 3 | 54 | 100 |
| | | | | | | |
| All | 19 | 33 | 10 | 5 | 32 | 100 |

1 All households heads who moved in the year before interview.

**Source: Survey of English Housing, Department of the Environment, Transport and the Regions**

### Tenure: by main reason for moving[1], 1999-00

England      Percentages

| | Owned outright | Owned with mortgage | Rented from council | Rented from Registered Social Landlord | Rented privately | All tenures |
|---|---|---|---|---|---|---|
| Personal reasons | | | | | | |
| Divorce or separation | 7 | 9 | 8 | 7 | 7 | 8 |
| Marriage or cohabitation | 4 | 13 | 7 | 6 | 5 | 8 |
| Other family or personal reasons | 26 | 6 | 24 | 26 | 13 | 14 |
| | | | | | | |
| Wanted larger house or flat | 10 | 22 | 18 | 20 | 11 | 17 |
| Job related reasons | 7 | 11 | 4 | 8 | 28 | 15 |
| To move to a better area | 12 | 10 | 12 | 9 | 10 | 11 |
| Wanted to buy | 3 | 18 | - | 0 | - | 7 |
| | | | | | | |
| Wanted smaller or cheaper house or flat | 22 | 3 | 8 | 4 | 4 | 5 |
| Wanted to live independently | 1 | 5 | 5 | 7 | 5 | 5 |
| Accommodation no longer available | 0 | - | 2 | 4 | 6 | 3 |
| Other reasons | 6 | 3 | 11 | 10 | 11 | 8 |
| | | | | | | |
| All households (=100%)(millions) | 0.2 | 0.9 | 0.3 | 0.2 | 0.8 | 2.4 |

1 Tenure at time of interview, of all household heads who moved in the year before interview.

**Source: Survey of English Housing, Department of the Environment, Transport and the Regions**

# 10.18

**Attitudes towards buying a home as soon as possible[1]: by tenure**

**Great Britain**                                                                                                                            Percentages

|                       | 1986 | 1989 | 1991 | 1996 | 1999 |
|-----------------------|------|------|------|------|------|
| Owner-occupiers       | 83   | 88   | 70   | 62   | 72   |
| Private renters       | 60   | 55   | 36   | 41   | 58   |
| Social sector renters | 54   | 51   | 36   | 31   | 38   |
| All respondents       | 74   | 78   | 60   | 54   | 65   |

1 Respondents, aged 18 and over, were asked the following question: 'Supposing a newly married couple, both with steady jobs, asked advice whether to buy or rent a home. If they had the choice, what would you advise them to do? To buy as soon as possible, to wait a bit, then try to buy a home, not to plan to buy a home at all?' The data are for those that said that the young couple should buy a home as soon as possible.

**Source: British Social Attitudes Survey, National Centre for Social Research**

# 10.19

**Property transactions[1]**

**England & Wales**
Millions

1 See Appendix, Part 10: Property transactions.
**Source: Inland Revenue**

The mobility of owner-occupiers is linked to the housing market. Throughout the post-war period the housing market and the economy have mirrored one another closely, with booms and slumps in one tending to contribute to the other. Attitudes towards home-ownership have also tended to vary accordingly. Since, the 'bubble' burst in 1989, when interest rates rose and the economic recession set in, attitudes towards home-ownership have become less favourable according to the British Social Attitudes Survey. Attitudes do not appear to have responded to the subsequent economic upturn, and now are less positive towards some aspects of home-ownership than they were previously. During the housing boom of the late 1980s around three-quarters of people in Great Britain would have advised a young couple to buy as soon as possible (Table 10.18). This figure dropped during the early 1990s – even by 1996 only just over half took the same view. By 1997 and 1998, there was evidence of a swing back in the direction of more favourable attitudes towards home-ownership, but by 1999 these attitudes remained 13 percentage points lower than their peak in 1989. Not surprisingly, existing home-owners were more likely to advocate home-ownership than those who rented.

In England and Wales the number of housing transactions averaged 1.3 million a year between 1978 and 1982. Over the next six years there was a rapid growth in the number of transactions. This number fell subsequently and recovered to pre-boom levels by 1996 (Chart 10.19). In 1999 there were almost 1.5 million property transactions. The boom-bust cycle coincided with a period of strong economic growth followed by temporary recession. An increase in the number of moving owner-occupiers was the main reason for the boom in transactions from 1983 to 1988. Market activity by first-time buyers and public sector tenants (right to buy purchases) were also factors but contributed to a lesser extent. The housing boom was further amplified by the demographic impact of the coming of age of baby boomers and the liberalisation of the mortgage market in the early 1980s. More new households opted for ownership rather than rental of their first dwelling.

In 1998, the Council of Mortgage Lenders' Housing Finance Survey asked respondents across the United Kingdom how likely they were to buy a home or another home in the next two years. Responses provided some understanding of who was unlikely to enter or move within the market and whether this was a matter of choice or constraint. Over four-fifths of respondents indicated that they were unlikely to move and buy a property in the next two years. While current housing market conditions dominated the decisions about mobility among outright owners and mortgagors, those living in social housing and the private rented sector emphasised the importance of financial factors in their lack of potential mobility.

With few exceptions, public tenants with secure tenancies of at least two years' standing are entitled to buy their own house or flat at a discount under the right to buy scheme. This scheme was introduced across Great Britain in 1980 (introduced in Scotland in 1979). The Northern Ireland Housing Executive is responsible for public sector housing in Northern Ireland and operates a voluntary house sales scheme which is comparable to the right to buy scheme in Great Britain. Another type of scheme which aims to increase low-cost home-ownership across the United Kingdom is shared ownership, in which home-owners buy a share of their property from an RSL and pay rent for the remainder. In Northern Ireland the shared ownership scheme is operated by the Northern Ireland Co-ownership Housing Association. Other schemes include discounted sales of empty properties by local authorities, and interest-free equity loans and cash grants to tenants to help them move out and buy a property on the open market. (This latter scheme is not available in Northern Ireland.) Sales of properties under the right to buy scheme in Great Britain peaked at around 200 thousand in

1982. The following four years saw a decline in the number of sales, but then, more buoyant conditions in the housing market and changes in legislation enabled more tenants to buy, and the number of sales rose again and reached another peak in 1989 at over 180 thousand. In 1999 there were almost 67 thousand sales of right to buy properties (Chart 10.20).

Since the late 1980s, over 400 thousand properties have been transferred from local authority ownership to RSLs, or more recently to Local Housing Companies, via large scale voluntary transfers. In 1999 such transfers accounted for over half of all local authority stock disposals. No large scale voluntary transfers took place in Wales in 1999.

# 10.20

## Sales and transfers of local authority dwellings[1]

**Great Britain**

Thousands

1 Excludes new town and Scottish Homes sales and transfers. See also Appendix, Part 10: Sales and transfers of local authority dwellings.

**Source:** Department of the Environment, Transport and the Regions; National Assembly for Wales; Scottish Executive

# 10.21

**Average dwelling prices[1]: by region and type of accommodation, 1999[2]**

£

| | House or bungalow | | | Flat/ maisonette | All dwellings | Percentage increase 1998-1999 |
|---|---|---|---|---|---|---|
| | Detached | Semi-detached | Terraced | | | |
| England & Wales | 139,760 | 80,599 | 71,367 | 92,567 | 94,581 | 11.6 |
| North East | 101,214 | 55,044 | 42,463 | 44,124 | 59,442 | 6.0 |
| North West | 116,972 | 60,735 | 39,787 | 57,776 | 65,543 | 7.0 |
| Yorkshire and the Humber | 103,493 | 55,694 | 41,987 | 54,101 | 63,524 | 6.8 |
| East Midlands | 101,609 | 54,105 | 43,840 | 47,215 | 69,500 | 7.0 |
| West Midlands | 126,302 | 64,941 | 50,350 | 51,622 | 76,633 | 11.9 |
| East | 142,803 | 84,698 | 70,387 | 58,097 | 94,679 | 8.1 |
| London | 284,789 | 168,159 | 151,204 | 131,475 | 150,094 | 16.7 |
| South East | 196,487 | 106,101 | 84,186 | 68,910 | 118,385 | 12.4 |
| South West | 134,592 | 78,734 | 65,118 | 65,623 | 90,274 | 9.7 |
| England | 146,637 | 84,546 | 74,745 | 96,127 | 98,252 | 14.4 |
| Wales | 92,412 | 55,344 | 42,563 | 51,253 | 62,424 | 6.9 |

1 Excludes those bought at non-market prices. Averages are taken from the last quarter of the year.
2 There is a time lag between the completion of a house purchase and its subsequent lodgement with the Land Registry. Thus data for the final quarter of 1999 are not as complete as those for the final quarter of 1998. The table includes all sales registered up to 31 March 2000.
**Source: HM Land Registry**

# 10.22

**Type of mortgage for house purchase[1]**

**United Kingdom**
Percentages

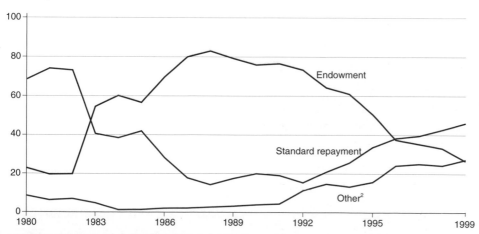

1 Data prior to 1992 are for new mortgages advanced by building societies and Abbey National plc; since 1992 new mortgages advanced by other major lenders have been included. Includes sitting tenants.
2 Includes interest only, PEP/ISA and pension.
**Source: Department of the Environment, Transport and the Regions**

In the April 2000 Housing Green Paper, the Government announced support for the transfer of up to 200 thousand local authority owned homes to RSLs each year in England. There are plans for a new Starter Home Initiative to provide assistance to support home-ownership, including the possibility of interest-free loans for 'key workers' such as nurses and teachers, as well as first-time buyers on modest incomes.

## Housing costs and expenditure

In 1999 the average dwelling price in England and Wales was £94,600, although there were marked regional variations in house prices overall and for the type of accommodation that was purchased. (Table 10.21) House prices in London tended to lead the rest of the country. The amount buyers in London paid for a detached house was over three times the amount paid by buyers in Wales: £285,000 and £92,000 respectively. A terraced house in the North West costs on average £40,000 compared with £151,000 in London. Between 1998 and 1999 house prices in England and Wales increased by over 12 per cent and this ranged from 6 per cent in the North East to almost 17 per cent in London.

Recent house price inflation across the United Kingdom reached a peak of 17.4 per cent in the second quarter of 2000. These levels were not as high as those seen in the late 1980s – with the exception of London. House price inflation fell in the third quarter of 2000.

A feature of home-ownership in the United Kingdom is the relatively large number of homes purchased with a mortgage. Approximately a quarter of all homes are purchased without a mortgage loan facility. In 1999 loans for home purchase were obtained through banks (756 thousand), building societies (304 thousand) and other lenders (122 thousand). Lenders differ in the amount that they are willing to lend relative to annual income and in 1999 the average advance to income ratio for all borrowers was 2.32; 2.39 for first-time buyers and 2.25 for former owner-occupiers. Those who are buying a house can choose from a variety of different types of mortgage; the most common types are repayment, endowment and interest-only. In the early 1980s repayment mortgages, which provide for regular monthly payments so that over the life of the mortgage (usually 25 years) the debt and the interest are entirely repaid, accounted for almost three-quarters of all new mortgages (Chart 10.22). During the 1980s there was a shift in the popularity of endowment policies which peaked in 1988. Endowment policies involve paying off the interest of the loan while contributions are made to an insurance policy designed to repay the outstanding amount at the end of the mortgage term. These types of policies have become increasingly less popular with borrowers because of the possibility that investments may not grow

**New mortgages: average mortgage repayment[1] as a percentage of average household income**

**United Kingdom**
Percentages

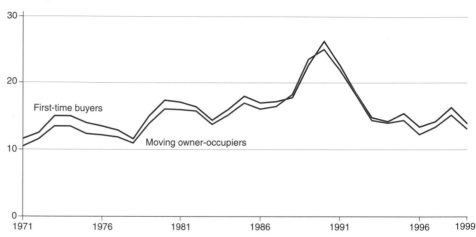

1 Repayments are calculated on the basis of the average advance, after tax relief.
**Source: Department of the Environment, Transport and the Regions**

fast enough to repay the capital borrowed. Interest-only mortgages, which include ISAs (individual savings accounts) and personal pensions, account for the bulk of the other mortgages in Chart 10.22. In addition to the different ways in which mortgage loans can be repaid, there are also a number of different ways that the interest is charged. In 1999 over a third of all bank loans were at a fixed rate.

For most home-owners, their mortgage constitutes a significant proportion of their household budget. In the early 1970s both first-time buyers and former owner-occupiers spent, on average, around a tenth of their household income on their mortgage repayments and by 1990 this proportion had reached more than a quarter (Chart 10.23). In the four years of housing recession between 1990 and 1993 there were declining mortgage interest rates and an increase in real earnings. House prices began stabilising in 1993, and in 1999 both first-time buyers and former owner-occupiers spent around a seventh of their income on mortgage repayments. These were slightly lower proportions than in the previous years.

# 10.24

**Average weekly household expenditure on housing costs[1]: by tenure, 1999-00**

| United Kingdom | £ per week |
|---|---|
| | 1999-00 |
| Owned outright | 30 |
| Owned with mortgage | 84 |
| Rented from council | 30 |
| Rented from Registered Social Landlord | 38 |
| Rented privately | 82 |
| All tenures[2] | 57 |

1 Net of housing benefit, rebates and allowances received.
2 Includes rent-free accommodation.

**Source: Family Expenditure Survey, Office for National Statistics**

Regardless of whether the home is owned or rented, housing constitutes a significant proportion of a household's budget. These costs include, for example, structural insurance, council tax payments and repairs and maintenance, as well as mortgage payments or rent (net of housing benefit). Costs differ across tenures. Results from the Family Expenditure Survey showed that home-owners in the United Kingdom who were repaying a mortgage spent approximately £84 a week on housing costs in 1999-00, which was almost three times more than local authority tenants were paying (Table 10.24). For those who were purchasing their home with a mortgage, three-fifths of their weekly housing expenditure was on their mortgage and a further 15 per cent was spent on council tax. A similar proportion of local authority tenants' weekly housing costs was on council tax.

In 1998-99 the average weekly rent (including housing benefit) for those living in private rented accommodation in England was £91, according to combined data from the Survey of English Housing and the Family Resources Survey. Respondents to the Survey of English Housing between 1997-98 and 1999-00 who were living in privately rented accommodation differed in their attitude towards the value for money of their homes according to the region of England in which they lived (Table 10.25). Almost two-fifths of those living in London, where the average rent was £142 in 1998-99, considered that the price of renting their accommodation was 'very or slightly high considering what you get'. At the same time, the proportion of Londoners who thought that their rent was very or fairly low for what you get was the same as the national proportion.

When people are unable to keep up mortgage payments or fall behind with rent and are unable to reach an alternative payment arrangement with their landlord or mortgage lender, a county court possession summons may be issued, with a view to obtaining a court order. Not all orders will result in possession; it is not uncommon for courts to make suspended orders that provide for arrears to be paid off within a reasonable period. If the court decides not to adjourn the proceedings or suspend a possession order, the warrant will be executed and the home repossessed by the landlord or mortgage lender.

The recession in the economy and the slump in the housing market at the end of the 1980s caused widespread falls in house prices in cash terms. The possibility of the property realising 'negative equity' was of concern to many and the number of home-owners losing their homes through mortgage default rose to unprecedented levels. The number of warrants issued for repossession of properties peaked at 134 thousand in 1991; it then fluctuated but overall declined to 111 thousand in 1996 (Chart 10.26). By 1999, however, the number of warrants issued had reached a new high of 137 thousand.

# 10.25

**Attitudes towards value for money of renting privately[1]: by region, 1997-2000[2]**

| England | Very high for what you get | Slightly high | About right | Slightly low | Very low for what you get | Percentages All |
|---|---|---|---|---|---|---|
| North East | 13 | 17 | 60 | 5 | 5 | 100 |
| North West | 11 | 24 | 51 | 8 | 7 | 100 |
| Yorkshire and the Humber | 10 | 22 | 52 | 10 | 5 | 100 |
| East Midlands | 9 | 19 | 56 | 10 | 5 | 100 |
| West Midlands | 12 | 20 | 51 | 10 | 6 | 100 |
| East | 8 | 19 | 53 | 11 | 8 | 100 |
| London | 15 | 24 | 44 | 10 | 7 | 100 |
| South East | 12 | 21 | 48 | 11 | 9 | 100 |
| South West | 9 | 21 | 54 | 9 | 7 | 100 |
| England | 11 | 22 | 50 | 10 | 7 | 100 |

1 Respondents were asked 'What do you think of the level of the present rent for your accommodation?'
2 Combined data for 1997-98, 1998-99 and 1999-00.

**Source: Survey of English Housing, Department of the Environment and the Regions**

# 10.26

Although the number of warrants executed remained fairly steady at around 50 thousand between 1993 and 1997, by 1999 it had risen by 40 per cent to 71 thousand.

Evictions and repossessions may in many cases be the result of a lengthy spell of financial difficulties, as many households will accumulate arrears prior to being evicted. Households with certain characteristics are more likely to experience financial problems with their housing. For example, households with younger heads are at greater risk of having mortgage arrears. Older people will, in general, have had more time to accumulate savings to cushion against times of unexpected financial hardship.

**Repossession of properties[1]: warrants issued and executed**

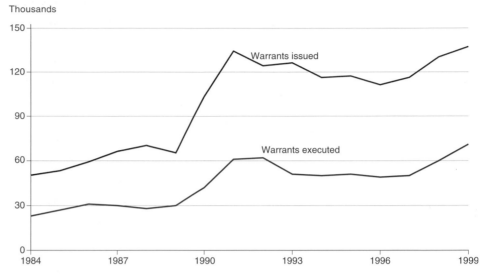

**England & Wales**

Thousands

1 Rented and mortgaged.
*Source: Court Service*

## Websites

| | |
|---|---|
| National Statistics | www.statistics.gov.uk |
| Department of the Environment, Transport and the Regions | www.detr.gov.uk |
| Court Service | www.courtservice.gov.uk |
| Department for Social Development, Northern Ireland | www.doeni.gov.uk |
| Department of Social Security | www.dss.gov.uk |
| National Assembly for Wales | www.wales.gov.uk |
| Northern Ireland Statistics and Research Agency | www.nisra.gov.uk |
| Scottish Executive | www.scotland.gov.uk |
| Social Exclusion Unit | www.cabinet-office.gov.uk/seu |
| Council of Mortgage Lenders | www.cml.org.uk |
| Eurostat | www.europa.eu.int/comm/eurostat |
| Institute for Social and Economic Research | ww.iser.essex.ac.uk |

## Contacts

| | |
|---|---|
| **Office for National Statistics** | |
| Chapter author | 020 7533 6117 |
| Family Expenditure Survey | 020 7533 5754 |
| General Household Survey | 020 7533 5444 |
| **Department of the Environment, Transport and the Regions** | 020 7944 3303 |
| Planning and Land Use Statistics | 020 7944 5533 |
| **Court Service** | 020 7210 1773 |
| **Department for Social Development, Northern Ireland** | 028 9052 2762 |
| **Department of Social Security** | |
| Family Resources Survey | 020 7962 8092 |
| **National Assembly of Wales** | 029 2082 5063 |
| **Northern Ireland Statistics and Research Agency** | 028 9034 8243 |
| **Scottish Executive** | 0131 244 7232 |
| **Council of Mortgage Lenders** | 020 7440 2251 |
| **Eurostat** | 00352 4301 33012 |
| **Institute of Social and Economic Research** | 01206 872957 |

# Chapter 11 Environment

### Air and atmospheric pollution

- Between 1971 and 1998 sulphur dioxide emissions fell by around three quarters, nitrogen oxide emissions fell by 29 per cent and carbon monoxide emissions fell by over two-fifths. (Chart 11.6)

- The United Kingdom was just one of three EU countries – including Luxembourg and Germany – to experience a reduction in carbon dioxide emissions between 1990 and 1998: of 7 per cent, 61 per cent and 13 per cent respectively; whereas emissions for the EU as a whole were unchanged. (Table 11.8)

### Land use and farming

- The number of farm holdings in England and Wales has halved since 1945: from 362 thousand holdings to 175 thousand in June 1999. (Page 200).

- In 1999 almost three-quarters of adults over the age of 18 agreed either definitely or probably that 'growing GM foods poses a danger to other plants and wildlife'. (Page 201).

### Use of resources

- In 1997-98 a third of domestic water was used for the purpose of personal washing, including baths, showers and hand-basins in England and Wales; a quarter – between 35 and 45 litres per head per day – was used for flushing the WC. (Chart 11.17)

- England and Wales produced 28 million tonnes of municipal waste in 1998-99, an increase of 2 per cent since 1997-98. (Page 203)

### Natural resources

- Between 1991 and 1999 domestic energy consumption in the United Kingdom increased by 3 per cent. Over the same period, energy consumption by the industry sector decreased by 7 per cent, despite an increase of 14 per cent in industrial output. (Page 204)

- Two-thirds of all electricity generated in the United Kingdom came from coal and gas in 1998. (Table 11.21)

# 11.1

**Threats to the countryside[1], 1998**

| Great Britain | | Percentages |
|---|---|---|
| | Greatest | Next greatest |
| Land and air pollution, or discharges into rivers and lakes | 32 | 18 |
| New housing and urban sprawl | 20 | 14 |
| Building new roads and motorways | 12 | 14 |
| Industrial development | 11 | 18 |
| Litter and fly-tipping of rubbish | 9 | 9 |
| Changes to traditional ways of farming and of using farmland | 4 | 8 |
| Superstores and out-of-town shopping centres | 3 | 9 |
| Changes to the ordinary natural appearance of the countryside | 3 | 4 |
| Number of tourists and visitors | 1 | 1 |
| None of these[2] | 4 | 5 |
| All | 100 | 100 |

*1 Respondents were asked to indicate which of nine possible threats they believed to be the greatest and the second greatest threats.*
*2 Includes 'other answers', 'don't know', 'not answered' and refusals.*

**Source: British Social Attitudes Survey, National Centre for Social Research**

# 11.2

**Membership of selected environmental organisations**

| United Kingdom | | | | | Thousands |
|---|---|---|---|---|---|
| | 1971 | 1981 | 1991 | 1997 | 1999 |
| National Trust[1] | 278 | 1,046 | 2,152 | 2,489 | 2,643 |
| Royal Society for the Protection of Birds | 98 | 441 | 852 | 1,007 | 1,004 |
| Civic Trust | 214 | .. | 222 | 330 | .. |
| Wildlife Trusts[2] | 64 | 142 | 233 | 310 | 325 |
| World Wide Fund for Nature | 12 | 60 | 227 | 241 | 255 |
| The National Trust for Scotland | 37 | 105 | 234 | 228 | 236 |
| Woodland Trust | .. | 20 | 150 | 195 | 200 |
| Greenpeace | .. | 30 | 312 | 215 | 176 |
| Ramblers Association | 22 | 37 | 87 | 123 | 129 |
| Friends of the Earth[1] | 1 | 18 | 111 | 114 | 112 |
| Council for the Protection of Rural England | 21 | 29 | 45 | 45 | 49 |

*1 Covers England, Wales and Northern Ireland.*
*2 Includes The Royal Society for Nature Conservation.*

**Source: Organisations concerned**

The environment in which we live has changed considerably over the last 200 years. The move from agricultural communities into industrial towns and now urban conglomerates has lead to huge pressures being put on the land, space, wildlife, atmosphere and waters. Attempts to reduce these pressures are reflected in the UK-wide strategy for sustainable development which aims to protect the environment and reduce the impact that human activity has upon it.

## Environmental concern and conservation

Public concern about the environment is high. The Attitudes to the Environment Survey was last conducted by the Department of the Environment, Transport and the Regions in 1996-97. Around nine in ten people aged 18 or over in England and Wales said they were fairly or very concerned about the environment in general.

One of the issues that concerns people is threats to the countryside. Half of the adults who responded to the 1998 British Social Attitudes Survey indicated that out of nine possible environmental concerns, 'land and air pollution or discharges into rivers and lakes' was the greatest or next greatest threat to the countryside (Table 11.1). 'New housing and urban sprawl' was considered to be the greatest or next greatest threat to the countryside by a third of respondents.

Joining an environmental organisation is one example of an action that people can take to pursue their interest in environmental protection. The National Trust has the largest number of members; by 1999 its membership had reached over 2.6 million, more than nine times the number of members in 1971 (Table 11.2).

## 11.3

Although growth continued in the 1990s for many environmental organisations, it has been at a slower rate than in the 1970s and 1980s. Membership of Greenpeace declined between 1991 and 1999 by 136 thousand.

A survey carried out by the British Trust for Ornithology (BTO) is the Common Birds Census, which catalogues the breeding populations of selected birds. Between 1971 and 1999 the breeding populations of common birds such as the starling, song thrush, yellowhammer and skylark more than halved, while the population of woodpigeons nearly doubled, and those of the great tit, chaffinch and robin increased by more than a quarter (Table 11.3). An explanation for the decline of certain bird species – particularly those whose principal breeding habitat is farmland - is changes in farming practices, for example increased use of agro-chemicals and loss of hedgerows, which has led to a decline and deterioration of suitable breeding and feeding areas. Some bird species, such as the blackbird, have more than one nesting site, and although there has been a decline in the blackbird population in general, it seems to be doing less badly in woodland areas which is its preferred breeding location.

**Breeding populations of selected birds**

| Great Britain | | | | | | Indices (1971=100) |
|---|---|---|---|---|---|---|
| | Principal breeding season habitat | 1971 | 1981 | 1991 | 1997 | 1999 |
| Woodpigeon | Farmland | 100 | 122 | 168 | 187 | 198 |
| Great tit | Woodland | 100 | 119 | 119 | 132 | 138 |
| Chaffinch | Woodland | 100 | 117 | 124 | 124 | 126 |
| Robin | Woodland | 100 | 99 | 106 | 119 | 125 |
| Blue tit | Woodland | 100 | 108 | 116 | 123 | 123 |
| Wren | Woodland | 100 | 93 | 117 | 108 | 120 |
| Pheasant | Woodland | 100 | 94 | 126 | 133 | 119 |
| | | | | | | |
| Blackbird | Woodland | 100 | 86 | 75 | 73 | 76 |
| Dunnock | Woodland | 100 | 73 | 58 | 55 | 56 |
| Skylark | Farmland | 100 | 81 | 55 | 48 | 47 |
| Yellowhammer | Farmland | 100 | 94 | 67 | 47 | 44 |
| Song thrush | Woodland | 100 | 61 | 43 | 42 | 42 |
| Starling | Farmland | 100 | 96 | 57 | 38 | 35 |

*Source: British Trust for Ornithology*

## 11.4

Conservation not only relates to animals and nature, but also to the built environment. The extent to which historic buildings and structures are in poor or very bad condition is an indicator of the state of health of the built environment and urban regeneration. In 2000 there were 30 thousand Grade I and Grade II* buildings in England, almost 4 per cent of which were at risk from neglect or decay (Chart 11.4). The percentage at risk is lower in the southern and eastern regions, at around 2 per cent (excluding London), and higher in the north (at nearly

**Grade I and Grade II* listed buildings at risk[1], 2000**

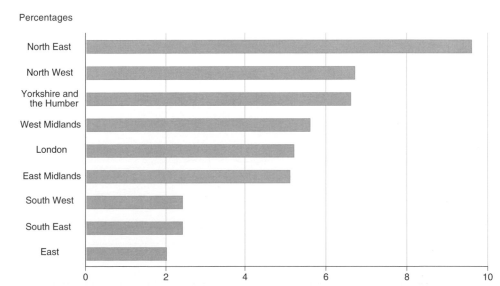

Percentages

1 Historic buildings at risk through neglect and decay (rather than demolition) or vulnerable to becoming so. See Appendix, Part 11: Listed buildings.

*Source: English Heritage*

# 11.5

**Air pollutants: by source, 1998**

**United Kingdom**                                                                 Percentages

|  | Carbon dioxide | Carbon monoxide | Sulphur dioxide | Nitrogen oxides | Volatile organic compounds | PM$_{10}$ |
|---|---|---|---|---|---|---|
| Road transport | 21 | 73 | 1 | 46 | 27 | 24 |
| Electricity supply | 27 | 2 | 66 | 21 | - | 14 |
| Domestic | 16 | 5 | 3 | 4 | 2 | 16 |
| Other | 36 | 20 | 29 | 30 | 71 | 45 |
| | | | | | | |
| All sources (=100%) (million tonnes) | 148.5 | 4.8 | 1.6 | 1.8 | 2.0 | 0.2 |

*Source: National Environmental Technology Centre*

# 11.6

**Air pollutants: emissions of selected gases**

**United Kingdom**
Million tonnes

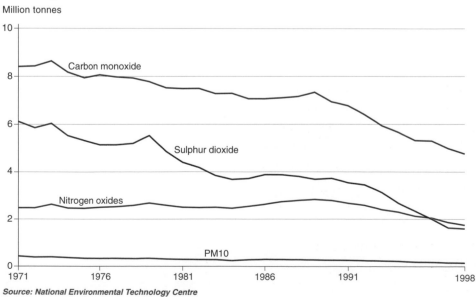

*Source: National Environmental Technology Centre*

10 per cent in the North East) with the Midlands falling between them. In London the aggregate figure of around 5 per cent masks the variety within, with higher rates in the north and east of London offset by lower ones in the centre and west.

## Air and atmospheric pollution

For many years there has been concern about air and atmospheric pollution and its effects on people and ecosystems. The health consequences of localised air pollution include asthma and premature deaths. The Department of Health estimated in 1998 that the premature deaths of between 12 thousand and 24 thousand vulnerable people in the United Kingdom may be brought forward by short-term exposure to air pollution each year.

Localised (urban) air pollution has improved considerably since the late 1950s partly due to the introduction of the first *Clean Air Act* in 1956. Prior to this Act, the burning of coal by domestic premises, factories and power stations resulted in black smoke (dark particulate matter) and sulphur dioxide induced smogs. The *Clean Air Act* created a framework for the reduction of emissions from chimneys in the United Kingdom, and together with subsequent acts – which led to the introduction of smokeless domestic fuels and smokeless zones – has virtually eliminated this type of smog.

The principal forms of UK air pollution are sulphur dioxide, nitrogen oxide and carbon monoxide emissions, fine particles (especially those whose diameter is smaller than 10 mm – indicated by PM$_{10}$) and ground-level ozone. The primary polluters today are the energy sector (particularly the production of electricity) road transport, and domestic users. The production of electricity contributed two-thirds of all sulphur dioxide released into the atmosphere in 1999 and over a quarter of all carbon dioxide. Although power stations do not tend to be located close to communities, they contribute to regional atmospheric pollution (Table 11.5).

In 1998 road users produced three-quarters of all carbon monoxide, over two-fifths of all nitrogen oxides and a quarter of all PM10. Urban road transport emissions of nitrogen oxides and particles rose by over a third from 1971 to peak values in 1989, reflecting the increase in road traffic.

The introduction of cleaner fuels and catalytic converters led to reductions of over 40 per cent in total road traffic emissions for some pollutants (such as particles, nitrogen oxides and volatile organic compounds) between 1989 and 1998, despite a growth of over 13 per cent in road traffic over the same period. However, in the longer term (beyond 2015) increases in traffic volumes could result in a reversal of these trends unless further technological advances are made.

In general, there have been considerable air quality improvements over the past 20 years. Between 1971 and 1998 sulphur dioxide emissions fell by around three-quarters to 1.6 million tonnes, PM$_{10}$ by three-fifths to around 0.2 million tonnes, carbon monoxide emissions fell by over two-fifths to 4.8 million tonnes and nitrogen oxide emissions by 29 per cent to 1.8 million tonnes (Chart 11.6). These reductions are mainly due to EU legislation which requires reductions in sulphur dioxide and nitrogen oxide emissions from large combustion plants; a decline in heavy industries; a switch in power stations from coal to natural gas and nuclear; the move from coal fires to gas in the home; and, as mentioned previously, technical improvements for vehicles.

The new Air Quality Strategy published in January 2000 for England, Scotland, Wales and Northern Ireland sets out national air quality objectives over the next few years up to 2005 for sulphur dioxide,

**Acid rain precursors[1]: by source, 1991 and 1998**

| United Kingdom | | | Thousand tonnes |
|---|---|---|---|
| | 1991 | 1998 | Percentage change 1991-1998 |
| Electricity, gas and water supply | 3,020 | 1,330 | -56 |
| Wholesale and retail trade | 90 | 50 | -44 |
| Manufacturing and construction | 980 | 630 | -36 |
| Domestic | 640 | 440 | -31 |
| Agriculture, mining and quarrying | 770 | 680 | -12 |
| Transport and communication | 570 | 520 | -9 |
| Other[2] | 250 | 160 | -36 |
| All sources | 6,310 | 3,810 | -40 |

1 Acid rain precursor emissions include sulphur dioxide, nitrogen oxides and ammonia, expressed in thousand tonnes of sulphur dioxide equivalent.
2 Includes public administration, financial intermediation, education, health and social work, and other services.
**Source: National Environmental Technology Centre; Office for National Statistics**

PM$_{10,}$ carbon monoxide, ozone and nitrogen oxides, as well as lead, benzene, and 1,3-butadiene.

Gaseous emissions not only result in local and regional air quality issues, they also have a continental effect as pollutants can be carried between countries. Acid rain is one particular problem. This occurs when the artificially produced sulphur and nitrogen in the atmosphere compound in clouds and water particles which finally deposit themselves onto the land and into freshwaters. Members of the United Nations Economic Council for Europe (UNECE) have been working together since 1979 to set targets for reducing emissions of long range transboundary air pollution. The most recent outcome was the 1999 UNECE Gothenburg Protocol which is designed to address acidification, eutrophication and ground level ozone. Emission ceilings have been set for 2010 for sulphur dioxide, nitrogen oxides, volatile organic compounds and ammonia.

Table 11.7 shows reductions of acidifying pollutants within the last decade by polluter. Across all sources, the amount of acidifying pollutants put into the atmosphere between 1991

# 11.8

### Emissions of carbon dioxide[1]: EU comparison, 1990 and 1998

Million tonnes

| | 1990 | 1998 | Percentage change 1990-1998 |
|---|---|---|---|
| Luxembourg | 13 | 5 | -61 |
| Germany | 1,015 | 886 | -13 |
| United Kingdom | 584 | 544 | -7 |
| Sweden | 55 | 57 | 3 |
| France | 388 | 413 | 7 |
| Italy | 430 | 458 | 7 |
| Belgium | 114 | 122 | 7 |
| Austria | 62 | 67 | 7 |
| Finland | 59 | 64 | 8 |
| Netherlands | 161 | 181 | 12 |
| Denmark | 53 | 60 | 14 |
| Greece | 85 | 100 | 18 |
| Spain | 226 | 273 | 21 |
| Portugal | 43 | 54 | 25 |
| Irish Republic | 32 | 40 | 27 |
| EU total | 3,320 | 3,325 | - |

1 $CO_2$ equivalent; excludes land use change and forestry.

**Source: European Environment Agency; Department of the Environment, Transport and the Regions**

and 1998 decreased by two-fifths, while the most considerable reductions have been within the electricity, gas and water supply and wholesale and retail industries: reductions of 56 per cent and 44 per cent respectively.

An example of a global effect of atmospheric pollution is climate change. Over the next century increased temperatures are predicted to cause major adverse effects, including increased incidence of extreme weather events and higher sea levels. Large reductions in the emissions of greenhouse gases (carbon dioxide, methane, nitrous oxide, hydrofluorocarbons, perfluorocarbons and sulphur hexafluoride) will be necessary to stabilise atmospheric greenhouse gas concentrations. Under the internationally agreed Kyoto Protocol, the United Kingdom has a legally binding target to reduce emissions of the 'basket' of six greenhouse gases by 12.5 per cent, relative to the 1990 level by the period 2008 to 2012. Between 1990 and 1998 the 'basket' of greenhouse gases fell by 9 per cent.

Carbon dioxide is the main gas which contributes to climate change. In 1995 the United Kingdom had 1 per cent of the world's population, but emitted 2 per cent of global carbon dioxide. The United Kingdom had the second highest carbon dioxide emission levels in the European Union in 1998 (after Germany) producing 544 million tonnes of carbon dioxide (Table 11.8). At the same time, the United Kingdom was one of just three countries – including Luxembourg and Germany – to experience a reduction in carbon dioxide emissions between 1990 and 1998: a fall of 7 per cent, 61 per cent and 13 per cent respectively. This shows that the United Kingdom is making good progress towards its domestic goal of reducing carbon dioxide emissions by 20 per cent below 1990 levels by 2010. The Irish Republic experienced the greatest percentage increase with carbon dioxide emissions rising by around 27 per cent.

## Land use and farming

Sustained population growth has only occurred in the past 250 years, since the 18th century. This, together with the industrial revolution, was a significant turning point in the history of land development. People moved to urban areas to find work, resulting in a rapidly changing social structure and perception of the countryside. In 1945, 12 million hectares of land was on farm holdings in England and Wales compared with 10.6 million hectares in June 1999. In 1991, almost 90 per cent of people in Great Britain lived in urban areas. These changes have put a number of stresses onto the environment in general, the traditional rural communities and the countryside.

Until the 1960s the majority of people relied on public transport to get them to work and for leisure and shopping journeys. The most convenient place to shop, therefore, was the town or village centre. As car ownership has increased, town centres with their restricted parking facilities and traffic jams have become less attractive. This led to the development of out-of-town supermarkets, shopping centres, leisure complexes and park and ride facilities. This phenomenon first took off during the mid-1980s and, at its peak in 1989, 74 new out-of-town shopping developments, retail warehouse parks and factory outlet centres (whose size were 4,645m[2] and greater (gross)) were completed in Great Britain (Chart 11.9).

Between 1986 and 1998 almost twice as much new floor space was created outside towns than in town centres in the United Kingdom: by September 2000 there were eight regional out-of-town shopping centres (of 100,000m[2] and greater). The latest development of this size is Bluewater near Dartford in Kent, which opened in March 1999. It has 320 shops and parking for 13 thousand cars.

# 11.9

The development of out-of-town shopping centres, retail developments and warehouse parks damages the vitality of the urban areas, diverting trade and future investment in town centres, and can reduce access to facilities, particularly for those without cars. People travelling longer distances to out-of-town centres, often in cars, can cause increased congestion, pollution and noise. Information on the way that people travel to services is contained in Table 12.4 in the Transport chapter (page 210).

In 1996 revised national Policy Planning Guidance 6 was introduced to enable some control over retail developments. All new retail development requires planning permission from the local planning authority, which must consult central government before granting permission for most retail developments of 2,500 sq. m or more. Since this Guidance was introduced the number of large developments has decreased each year. Retailers' attentions are now being turned back to town centres redeveloping existing stores and building smaller outlets.

Land use has changed over the centuries, as land has been converted from ancient woodland to agriculture and developed land. Between the 1950s and 1980s, the amount of woodland increased, mainly due to commercial conifer plantations – especially in upland areas of Scotland. Consequently, the area covered by woodland in the United Kingdom more than doubled during the 20th century, from 5 per cent of land cover in 1900 to more than 11 per cent in 1999. Woodland cover varies throughout the United Kingdom. In March 1999 woodlands covered nearly 17 per cent of Scotland, 14 per cent of Wales, 8 per cent of England, and 6 per cent of Northern Ireland.

Prior to the 1990s, timber production remained the key priority which resulted in the planting of conifer trees which were suitable for timber, but

not necessarily native to the United Kingdom. Since the 1990s the United Kingdom has adopted a sustainable policy of encouraging the planting of trees indigenous to a region. Consequently, there has been an increase in Scotland of native Caledonian Pinewoods, while there has been a gradual growth in the number of broad-leaved trees planted, peaking in 1993-94. In 1998-99, nearly 10 thousand hectares of broad-leaves were planted in Great Britain, compared with around 6 thousand hectares of conifers which is a large decrease from the 41 thousand hectares of conifers planted in 1971-72 (Chart 11.10).

Although land is increasingly becoming urban, agriculture is still the main user of land and still an important industry. The highly modern, fertiliser intensive, agri-businesses of today are unrecognisable from the subsistence farming that occurred 200 years ago.

**Out of town developments[1]**

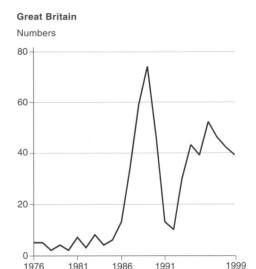

**Great Britain**
Numbers

1 Number of shopping developments, retail warehouse parks and factory outlet centres completed each year over 50,000 square feet (gross).
*Source: CBHillier Parker*

# 11.10

## New woodland creation

**Great Britain**
Thousand hectares

*Source: Forestry Commission*

# 11.11

## Agricultural land use[1]

| United Kingdom[2] | | | | | Thousand hectares |
|---|---|---|---|---|---|
| | 1961 | 1971 | 1981 | 1991 | 1999 |
| Crop areas | | | | | |
| Wheat | 739 | 1,097 | 1,491 | 1,981 | 1,847 |
| Barley | 1,549 | 2,288 | 2,327 | 1,395 | 1,179 |
| Other cereals (excluding maize) | 768 | 424 | 161 | 127 | 115 |
| Rape grown for oil seed | .. | 5 | 125 | 440 | 417 |
| Sugar beet not for stock feeding | 173 | 190 | 210 | 196 | 183 |
| Potatoes (early and main crop) | 285 | 256 | 191 | 177 | 178 |
| Other crops | 761 | 577 | 490 | 643 | 790 |
| All crop areas | 4,276 | 4,838 | 4,995 | 4,957 | 4,709 |
| Bare fallow | 123 | 74 | 76 | 67 | 33 |
| Grasses | 7,999 | 7,240 | 7,013 | 6,935 | 6,675 |
| Sole right rough grazing[3] | 7,359 | 5,550 | 5,021 | 4,950 | 4,575 |
| Common rough grazing | .. | 1,128 | 1,214 | 1,233 | 1,227 |
| Woodland | .. | 154 | 277 | 372 | 501 |
| Set-aside[4] | . | . | . | 97 | 572 |
| All other land on agricultural holdings | .. | 131 | 211 | 242 | 288 |
| All agricultural land[5] | 19,757 | 19,115 | 18,808 | 18,854 | 18,579 |

1 Includes estimates for minor holdings in England, Wales and Northern Ireland for all years and in Scotland prior to 1991.
2 Data are for England and Wales only in 1971 and 1981.
3 Includes common rough grazing in 1961.
4 Data are for England only in 1991.
5 Excludes woodland and all other land on agricultural holdings in 1961.

**Source: Ministry of Agriculture, Fisheries and Food; National Assembly for Wales; Scottish Executive; Department of Agriculture, Northern Ireland**

The number of farm holdings in England and Wales has halved since 1945 and there has been a shift to larger holdings. In 1945 there were 362.5 thousand holdings compared with 175.2 thousand in June 1999 and the average farm size increased from under 40 hectares in 1995 to just over 60 hectares in 1995. The majority of agricultural land in the United Kingdom in 1999 was grasses and sole right rough grazing. Since 1961 there has been a substantial increase in the amount of agricultural land given over to wheat growing: in 1999 wheat covered 1,847 thousand hectares, two and a half times the area in 1961 (Table 11.11).

Larger machinery has meant that farmers have tended to remove field boundaries (such as hedges and stone walls) to create larger, more manageable fields. This, combined with intensive fertiliser usage, has meant that despite the number of farms having decreased, agriculture output has increased, particularly during the 1970s and 1980s. These changes can have a number of impacts upon the countryside. For example: increased field sizes and mechanisation can lead to a loss of wildlife as their habitats, such as hedgerows, disappear; land drainage can lead to loss of wetlands; and intensification of farming can result in soil erosion.

# 11.12

## Attitudes towards farming methods, 1999

| Great Britain | | | | | | Percentages |
|---|---|---|---|---|---|---|
| | Agree strongly | Agree | Disagree | Disagree strongly | Don't know/not answered | All |
| Modern methods of farming have caused damage to the countryside | 17 | 52 | 28 | 1 | 3 | 100 |
| All things considered, farmers do a good job in looking after the countryside | 6 | 70 | 19 | 2 | 3 | 100 |
| Government should withhold some subsidies from farmers and use them to protect the countryside, even if this leads to higher prices | 6 | 50 | 38 | 3 | 4 | 100 |
| If farmers have to choose between producing more food and looking after the countryside, they should produce more food | 3 | 27 | 61 | 6 | 3 | 100 |

**Source: British Social Attitudes Survey, National Centre for Social Research**

In the 1999 British Social Attitudes Survey, seven in ten adults in Great Britain agreed (or strongly agreed) with the statement that 'modern methods of farming have caused damage to the countryside' (Table 11.12). Yet, in the same survey, around three-quarters of respondents agreed with the view that 'all things considered, farmers do a good job in looking after the countryside'. This percentage has stayed reasonably stable since 1985.

One issue where there has been a change in attitude is the balance between conserving the land and the need for more food. In the past few years there has been growing concern about the development of genetically modified (GM) crops and their impact on health and the environment. In 1999 almost three-quarters of the respondents participating in the British Social Attitudes Survey agreed either definitely or probably that 'growing genetically modified (GM) foods poses a danger to other plants and wildlife'.

Anxieties about food safety, combined with concerns about the use of pesticides on crops, have resulted in a heightened interest in organically produced food. Recently, demand for organic products has been outstripping supply in many supermarkets. In 1998 organic food accounted for about 2 per cent of the total UK food market.

The area of land converted, or in conversion, to the production of organic food increased dramatically in the year up to April 1999. In 1999 about 1.5 per cent of agricultural land in the United Kingdom had been converted or was in conversion to organic farming. This was around 276 thousand hectares and six times more land than in 1995 (Chart 11.13). In 1999 there were around 1.5 thousand organic producers in the United Kingdom; this was estimated to have risen to around 4 thousand in 2000.

## Water quality

Water is used in a variety of ways and the quality and quantity of water supplies is important to the health and wellbeing of both society and the natural environment. A number of different things have an impact upon the quality of rivers, including fertiliser run-off, climate, and industrial and sewage discharge.

Since 1990 the Environment Agency (formerly the National Rivers Authority) has monitored the chemical quality of rivers and canals in England and Wales by a system called the General Quality Assessment Scheme. It is estimated that there has been a net upgrading in overall chemical quality of 31 per cent of the total length of rivers and canals in England and Wales between 1990 and 1999. In the period 1997-1999 the proportions of the monitored river networks that were of good or fair quality were 97 per cent in Scotland, 96 per cent in Northern Ireland and 92 per cent in England and Wales (Table 11.14). Improvements are largely the result of water industry investment in cleaning up sewage pollution in more heavily populated areas.

### Area of land converted or in conversion to organic farming

**United Kingdom**
Thousand hectares

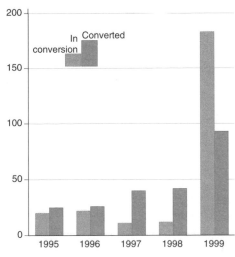

*Source: Ministry of Agriculture, Fisheries and Food*

## 11.14

### River and canal quality[1]: by region[2], 1997-1999

| United Kingdom | | | | | Percentages |
| --- | --- | --- | --- | --- | --- |
| | Good | Fair | Poor | Bad | All |
| Welsh | 92 | 7 | 1 | - | 100 |
| Scotland[3] | 90 | 7 | 2 | - | 100 |
| South West | 81 | 16 | 3 | - | 100 |
| North East | 66 | 25 | 8 | 1 | 100 |
| North West | 61 | 29 | 9 | 1 | 100 |
| Southern | 57 | 34 | 9 | - | 100 |
| Northern Ireland | 56 | 39 | 4 | - | 100 |
| Midlands | 55 | 36 | 9 | 1 | 100 |
| Thames | 52 | 38 | 9 | - | 100 |
| Anglian | 33 | 52 | 14 | 1 | 100 |

1 Chemical water quality based on the General Quality Assessment Scheme (GQA). See Appendix, Part 11: Rivers and canals.
2 The Environment Agency Regions for England and Wales are boundaries based on river catchment areas and not county borders.
3 The system used to assess the chemical quality of rivers and canals in Scotland is not directly comparable with the GQA. See Appendix, Part 11: Rivers and canals.

**Source: Environment Agency; Department of the Environment for Northern Ireland**

# 11.15

## Beaches[1] and marinas receiving the European Blue Flag, 2000

1 Some dots represent more than one beach. See Appendix, Part 11: European Blue Flag Campaign.

**Source: Tidy Britain Group**

Bathing waters, like rivers and canals, can also be affected by discharges from sewage treatment works, storm overflows, rivers, agriculture and diffuse sources. The proportion of bathing waters in the United Kingdom complying with the European Union (EU) mandatory coliform standards increased from 66 per cent in 1988 to 91 per cent in 1999.

In 1987 the Blue Flag Campaign was set up by the Foundation for Environmental Education in Europe in co-operation with the EU. The award covers resort bathing beaches that meet criteria on beach facilities, safety and cleanliness. In 2000 a record number of 57 UK beaches were given the Blue Flag award, an increase of 16 beaches from 1999 and 12 beaches more than in 1998 (Chart 11.15).

The decade to 2000 was characterised by substantial climatic volatility, with rainfall amounts often differing markedly from the seasonal average. This variability is reflected in overall reservoir stocks in England and Wales (Chart 11.16). Within-year variations were commonly large and drought conditions, such as in 1990 and 1995, placed significant stress on water resources in some regions. The period since mid-1997 has seen very healthy overall reservoir stocks, and a switch in the focus of concern from the impact of drought to threat of flooding.

## Use of resources

The implications of varying reservoir stocks will impact upon households' access to water, particularly if household demand for water continues to increase. Average annual unmeasured water consumption per head increased steadily during the early 1990s and reached a peak of 154 litres per head per day in the drought year of 1995. Since then the figure has remained fairly stable at around 150 litres per head per day. As illustrated in Table 2.1 in the Households and Families chapter (page 42), over the last century the number of households has increased and the average size of households decreased. This has put further pressures on water resources, because smaller households use more per person. In 1997-98, a third of domestic water was used for the purpose of personal washing, including baths, showers and hand-basins (Chart 11.17). Between 35 and 45 litres per head per day was used for flushing the WC. Other factors which may lead to increased demand are increasing ownership of domestic appliances (such as dishwashers and washing machines) and increased use of water in gardens during the drier periods.

# 11.16

## Reservoir stocks[1]

**England & Wales**

Percentages

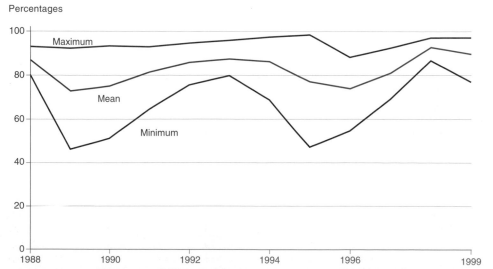

1 For each year, the maximum, mean and minimum percentage of overall net capacity based on a network of large reservoirs.

**Source: Centre for Ecology and Hydrology; from Environment Agency and water service companies data**

## 11.17

There were 28 million tonnes of municipal waste produced in 1998-99 in England and Wales, an increase of almost 2 per cent from 1997-98. Waste from household sources accounted for 90 per cent of municipal waste in 1998-99, amounting to 1.2 tonnes of waste per household per year. In 1998-99 landfill was the most commonly used disposal option for municipal waste – 82 per cent of waste went to landfill – although this was a slight reduction of 3 percentage points since the previous year. There are notable regional differences: in Wales around 95 per cent of waste was sent directly to landfill compared with only 61 per cent in the West Midlands (Table 11.18). The North East experienced the greatest decrease of all regions for waste going to landfill between 1997-98 and 1998-99: a decline of 13 percentage points.

A more environmentally friendly alternative for removing waste is recycling. In 1998-99, England and Wales recycled and composted 9.5 per cent of all municipal waste produced. Of this, around 2.4 million tonnes was household waste, the equivalent of 105 kg of waste per household per year. This was also an increase of 16 per cent since 1997-98. There are regional variations, with the South West and South East regions of England recycling or composting 16 and 14 per cent of their municipal waste respectively, compared with around 4 and 5 per cent in the North East region and Wales. When the regions are compared in respect to the amount of waste recycled, there is a similar split between the north and south. The East, South East and South West recycle the most per household (over 140 kg per year) which was more than double the amount in Wales, the North East and Yorkshire and the Humber (between 38 and 67 kg per year).

Many local authorities run schemes to promote recycling, from the provision of 'drop-off' sites such as bottle banks to kerbside collection schemes. Paper and card make up the bulk of materials recycled by local authorities through kerbside collection schemes: almost two-thirds of all collected waste (see Table 11.19 overleaf). With the exception of paper and card, the majority of household materials is recycled at civic amenity and bring sites. Between 1997-98 and 1998-99 the amount of cans recycled increased by nearly 70 per cent and the amount of co-mingled materials increased by over 40 per cent. Once again, there are regional variations with respect to specific recyclable items. For example, in 1998-99 almost a third of all household waste recycled in the East and South West regions was compost, while this accounted for only a ninth of all waste recycled in London or Wales. The Government's goal is to increase the amount of household waste

**Domestic water use[1], 1997-98**

**England & Wales**
Percentages

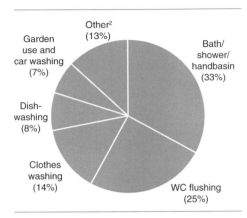

1 Based upon water company resources plans submitted to the Environment Agency.
2 Includes kitchen taps, swimming pools, paddling pool, direct heating systems, general cleaning etc.
*Source: Environment Agency*

## 11.18

**Waste disposal: by region and method, 1998-99**

Percentages

| | Landfill | Incineration without energy recovery | Incineration with energy recovery | RDF[1] manufacture | Recycled /composted | Other | All methods |
|---|---|---|---|---|---|---|---|
| Wales | 95 | 0 | 0 | 0 | 5 | - | 100 |
| North West | 92 | 0 | 0 | 0 | 8 | 0 | 100 |
| Yorkshire and the Humber | 90 | - | 2 | 0 | 8 | 0 | 100 |
| East | 86 | 0 | 1 | 0 | 12 | 0 | 100 |
| South West | 84 | 0 | 0 | 0 | 16 | 0 | 100 |
| South East | 83 | 0 | 0 | 3 | 14 | 0 | 100 |
| East Midlands | 83 | - | 7 | 0 | 10 | 0 | 100 |
| North East | 78 | 0 | 16 | 1 | 4 | 0 | 100 |
| London | 74 | 0 | 19 | 0 | 7 | 0 | 100 |
| West Midlands | 61 | 0 | 31 | 0 | 8 | 0 | 100 |

1 Refuse derived fuel.
*Source: Department of the Environment, Transport and the Regions*

# 11.19

## Recycling of household material[1] by type of scheme, 1998-99

**England & Wales**

Thousand tonnes

| | Kerbside collection schemes[2] | | Civic amenity and bring sites for household waste | All schemes | |
| --- | --- | --- | --- | --- | --- |
| | Integrated | Separate | | (Thousand tonnes) | (Kg per household per year) |
| Paper and card | 26 | 383 | 426 | 835 | 39 |
| Compost | 5 | 28 | 492 | 525 | 24 |
| Glass | 2 | 37 | 324 | 363 | 17 |
| Co-mingled material | 5 | 89 | 25 | 119 | 6 |
| Total cans | 1 | 14 | 17 | 32 | 1 |
| Other[3] | 2 | 19 | 370 | 390 | 18 |
| All | 41 | 571 | 1,654 | 2,264 | 105 |

1 Tonnage data from recycling schemes run by local authorities exclude schemes run by voluntary/private organisations – about 37 thousand tonnes in 1998-99, mostly paper and card.
2 Kerbside collection schemes are split into two categories: those schemes which are carried out as part of the normal waste collection service (integrated) and those collections which are for the purpose of recycling only (separate).
3 Includes scrap metal and white goods, textiles and plastics, and other.

**Source: Department of the Environment, Transport and the Regions; National Assembly for Wales**

# 11.20

## Oil and gas reserves, 1999

**United Kingdom Extra-Regio**

| | Oil (million tonnes) | Gas (billion cubic metres) |
| --- | --- | --- |
| Fields already discovered | | |
| Proven reserves[1] | 665 | 760 |
| Probable reserves | 455 | 500 |
| Possible reserves | 545 | 490 |
| Total remaining reserves in present discoveries | 665-1,665 | 760-1,750 |
| Already recovered | 2,444 | 1,410 |
| Estimates of potential future discoveries | 250-2,600 | 355-1,465 |
| Total recoverable reserves | 3,360-6,710 | 2,525-4,625 |
| Potential additional reserves | 85-370 | 75-245 |

1 Excludes volumes of oil and gas already recovered.
**Source: Department of Trade and Industry**

recycled or composted from 9.4 per cent in 1998-99 to 25 per cent by 2005 and 30 per cent by 2010.

## Natural resources

Although total domestic energy consumption increased during the 1990s, energy consumption per household has been fairly constant. This is due to increased efficiency in the way that energy is used in the domestic sector, for example improved thermal efficiency of housing and improved energy efficiency of individual appliances. Between 1991 and 1999 domestic energy consumption increased by just 3 per cent. Over the same period, energy consumption by the industry sector in the United Kingdom decreased by 7 per cent, despite increases in industrial output of 14 per cent. Once again, this is due to improvements in energy efficiency.

Three of the natural resources available to us are oil, gas and coal, which are used to provide energy and essential chemicals for industry, the transport system and the home. In the early 1970s coal was the main primary fuel produced but it has been overtaken by petroleum and natural gas production. The production of coal has been falling since the 1960s: in 1999, 37 million tonnes of coal was produced, less than a fifth of production in 1960.

For centuries small quantities of oil have been produced in Great Britain. The oil originally came from shale and was produced mainly in the Lothians. The Government tried to encourage oil exploration during the First World War, but interest waned as the war ended and import difficulties eased. During the 1930s concentrated efforts were made, and the first success came in 1937 when an onshore gas field was found in Yorkshire; this was soon followed by the discovery of a small oilfield near Nottingham. The first significant discovery of offshore gas came in 1965 followed by the first discovery of offshore oil in 1969.

By December 1999 there were 209 offshore UK fields in production, comprising 107 oil fields, 86 gas and 16 gas-condensate fields. A total of 137 million tonnes of oil and 105 billion cubic metres of gas were produced in 1999. There were around 665 million tonnes of proven oil reserves and 760 billion cubic metres of gas remaining from discovered oilfields in the United Kingdom Extra-Regio at the end of 1999. These are reserves that have a better than 90 per cent chance of being produced (Table 11.20).

Only a small proportion of the estimated remaining recoverable reserves of oil and gas is known with any degree of certainty. About 8 per cent of the UK's proven, probable and possible oil reserves and about 6 per cent of its gas reserves were consumed in 1999, so that discovered reserves might be expected to last 12 years for oil and 16 years for gas at current production rates. These ratios should not be taken as accurate measures of the future life of UK reserves as additional reserves continue to be discovered and production levels look likely to decline in the near future.

Electricity generation within the United Kingdom is dominated by the use of non-renewable fossil fuels: two-thirds of all electricity generated comes from coal and gas. It is the growth of gas-fired generation – from a negligible amount in 1991 to around a third in the late 1990s – which is a major reason for the decline in greenhouse gas emissions. In the EU as a whole, two-fifths of all electricity was generated by coal and gas in 1998, while a third was from nuclear fuel, another non-renewable source (Table 11.21).

Many countries in the EU – for example, Austria and Luxembourg – have historically obtained a substantial proportion of their electricity from renewable energy sources such as hydro-power. The United Kingdom lags behind many other countries within the EU (particularly northern Europe) in the proportion of electricity obtained from renewable resources. In part this is due to the lack of high mountains, large forests and natural lakes within the United Kingdom (which many other EU countries have in abundance) and also because the United Kingdom has plenty of fossil fuels that it has been economic to recover. However, the United Kingdom is an EU leader in landfill gas and sewage gas use.

In the future it is expected that sources such as biomass, wind and solar will play a larger role in more EU countries, including the United Kingdom, as part of the drive to achieve EC targets for the reduction of greenhouse gas emissions. The UK Government has set a target of 10 per cent of all UK electricity being from renewable sources by 2010, with an interim target of 5 per cent by 2003. The proportion has already increased from 1.7 per cent in 1989 to 2.8 per cent in 1999 (Table 11.22).

### Electricity generation: by fuel used, EU comparison, 1998

Percentages

| | Nuclear | Coal | Oil | Other fossil fuel[1] | Hydro and wind[2] | Other renewable sources[3] | All fuels (=100%) (000 GWh) |
|---|---|---|---|---|---|---|---|
| France | 76 | 6 | 2 | 1 | 13 | 1 | 511 |
| Belgium | 55 | 17 | 3 | 18 | 2 | 5 | 83 |
| Sweden | 46 | 1 | 2 | 0 | 47 | 3 | 158 |
| Finland | 31 | 19 | 1 | 13 | 21 | 15 | 70 |
| Spain | 30 | 28 | 9 | 12 | 19 | 2 | 196 |
| Germany | 29 | 28 | 1 | 35 | 5 | 3 | 557 |
| United Kingdom | 28 | 34 | 2 | 32 | 2 | 2 | 358 |
| Netherlands | 4 | 27 | 4 | 57 | 1 | 7 | 91 |
| Denmark | 0 | 58 | 12 | 20 | 7 | 4 | 41 |
| Irish Republic | 0 | 32 | 23 | 38 | 6 | 0 | 21 |
| Portugal | 0 | 31 | 27 | 5 | 34 | 3 | 39 |
| Italy | 0 | 9 | 41 | 27 | 18 | 4 | 259 |
| Austria | 0 | 6 | 5 | 17 | 67 | 5 | 57 |
| Greece | 0 | 0 | 17 | 74 | 9 | 0 | 46 |
| Luxembourg | 0 | 0 | 0 | 16 | 81 | 3 | 1 |
| EU average | 34 | 20 | 8 | 22 | 14 | 3 | 2,490 |

1 Includes natural gas and brown coal.
2 Includes pumped storage.
3 Includes geothermal, derived gas and biomass and others.
**Source: Eurostat**

**11.22**

### Electricity produced by renewable sources[1]

| United Kingdom | | | Percentages |
|---|---|---|---|
| | 1989 | 1993 | 1999 |
| Hydro power | 87 | 73 | 52 |
| Landfill gas | 3 | 8 | 17 |
| Municipal solid waste combustion | 5 | 7 | 13 |
| Onshore wind | - | 4 | 9 |
| Other | 5 | 9 | 9 |
| All renewable energy sources (=100%)(GWh) | 5,496 | 5,883 | 10,237 |

1 See Appendix, Part 11: Electricity produced by renewable sources.
**Source: Department of Trade and Industry**

## Websites

| | |
|---|---|
| National Statistics | www.statistics.gov.uk |
| Department of the Environment, Transport and the Regions | www.detr.gov.uk |
| Department of Trade and Industry | www.dti.gov.uk/energy/index.htm |
| Environment Agency | www.environment-agency.gov.uk |
| Environment and Heritage Service (NI) | www.ehsni.gov.uk |
| Countryside Agency | www.countryside.gov.uk |
| Forestry Commission | www.forestry.gov.uk |
| Ministry of Agriculture, Fisheries and Food | www.maff.gov.uk |
| National Assembly for Wales | www.wales.org.uk |
| Northern Ireland Department of Environment | www.nics.gov.uk |
| Northern Ireland Statistics and Research Agency | www.nisra.gov.uk |
| OFWAT | www.ofwat.gov.uk |
| Scottish Executive | www.scotland.gov.uk |
| Centre for Ecology and Hydrology, Wallingford | www.nwl.ac.uk |
| National Centre for Social Research | www.natcen.ac.uk |
| Scottish Environment Protection Agency | www.sepa.org.uk |

## Contacts

| | |
|---|---|
| **Office for National Statistics** | |
| Chapter author | 020 7533 5781 |
| **Department of the Environment, Transport and the Regions** | 020 7944 6497 |
| **Department of Trade and Industry** | 020 7215 2697 |
| **Environment Agency** | 0645 333 111 |
| National Water Demand Management Centre | 01903 832 073 |
| **Countryside Agency** | 020 7340 2900 |
| **Environment and Heritage Service (NI)** | 028 9023 5000 |
| **Forestry Commission** | 0131 334 0303 |
| **National Assembly for Wales** | 029 2082 5111 |
| **Northern Ireland Department of Environment** | 028 9054 0540 |
| **Northern Ireland Statistics and Research Agency** | 028 9034 8200 |
| **OFWAT** | 0121 625 1300 |
| **Scottish Environment Protection Agency** | 01786 457 700 |
| **Scottish Executive** | 0131 244 0445 |
| **Centre for Ecology and Hydrology** | 01491 838 800 |
| **Eurostat** | 00 352 4301 37286 |
| **National Centre for Social Research** | 020 7250 1866 |

# Chapter 12  Transport

### Overview

● The distance travelled by car, van and taxi in Great Britain was almost eleven times higher in 1999 than in 1952 and at the end of the century accounted for 85 per cent of all passenger kilometres. (Table 12.1)

● Cars dominated travel to most local services in January and March 2000 in Great Britain, especially those to local hospitals, main food shopping and work. Walking was more common for visiting the post office or going to a chemist for a prescription. (Table 12.4)

### Private transport

● About 2 million cars are newly registered in Great Britain each year; about half of these are company cars. (Table 12.6)

● In 1999, over half of cars on non-urban motorways and dual carriageways in Great Britain exceeded the speed limit and two-thirds of cars exceeded the 30 mile an hour limit on urban roads. (Table 12.9 and page 213)

● Traditionally men are more likely to drive than women – in 1975-76, 69 per cent of men in Great Britain held a car driving licence compared with only 29 per cent of women. By 1997-1999 the proportions were 82 per cent and 59 per cent respectively. (Page 211).

### Public transport

● The proportion of GB households with good access to a bus service (defined as within 13 minutes walk of a bus stop with a service of at least once an hour) rose in rural areas from 35 per cent in 1985-1986 to 42 per cent in 1997-1999. (Table 12.15).

● In 1999-00 there were around 17 thousand kilometres of National Rail route in Great Britain, just over half the length in the peak years of 1919 to 1938. (Page 215).

### Resources

● Motoring costs in the United Kingdom have roughly kept pace with inflation since 1981, but bus and coach and rail fares have increased at a faster rate. (Table 12.22).

# 12.1

## Passenger transport: by mode

**Great Britain**                                                     Billion passenger kilometres

|  | 1952 | 1961 | 1971 | 1981 | 1991 | 1998 | 1999 |
|---|---|---|---|---|---|---|---|
| **Road** | | | | | | | |
| Car and van[1] | 58 | 157 | 313 | 394 | 582 | 617 | 621 |
| Bus and coach | 92 | 76 | 60 | 48 | 44 | 45 | 45 |
| Bicycle | 23 | 11 | 4 | 5 | 5 | 4 | 4 |
| Motorcycle | 7 | 11 | 4 | 10 | 6 | 4 | 5 |
| All road | 180 | 255 | 381 | 458 | 637 | 671 | 675 |
| **Rail**[2] | 38 | 39 | 35 | 34 | 39 | 44 | 46 |
| **Air**[3] | - | 1 | 2 | 3 | 5 | 7 | 7 |
| **All modes** | 218 | 295 | 419 | 495 | 681 | 722 | 728 |

1 Includes taxis.
2 Data relate to financial years.
3 Includes Northern Ireland and Channel Islands.
**Source: Department of the Environment, Transport and the Regions**

# 12.2

## Journeys per person per year: by main mode and journey purpose[1], 1997-1999

**Great Britain**                                                     Percentages

|  | Car | Walk | Bus, coach and rail[2] | Other | All modes |
|---|---|---|---|---|---|
| Social/entertainment | 26 | 19 | 18 | 28 | 23 |
| Shopping | 20 | 24 | 25 | 12 | 21 |
| Commuting | 18 | 7 | 26 | 26 | 16 |
| Education | 3 | 11 | 14 | 11 | 6 |
| Escort education | 4 | 8 | 2 | 1 | 5 |
| Business | 4 | 2 | 2 | 4 | 4 |
| Holiday/day trip | 3 | 1 | 3 | 8 | 3 |
| Other escort and personal business | 21 | 14 | 10 | 10 | 18 |
| Other, including just walk | - | 15 | - | - | 4 |
| All purposes (=100%)(numbers) | 645 | 281 | 78 | 41 | 1,046 |

1 See Appendix, Part 12: Journey purpose.
2 Includes London Underground.
**Source: National Travel Survey, Department of the Environment, Transport and the Regions**

Travel grew enormously in Britain in the 20th century – in the number of journeys, in distance travelled and in terms of access to different kinds of transport, particularly cars and air travel. Public transport – buses, trams, and railways – dominated up to the middle of the century. There was then a general switch to travelling by car during the 1950s and 1960s, which continued throughout the rest of the century. Commercial air flights began and people travelled abroad more. During the 1990s, when the overall levels of travel grew slowly, the shares for the different modes, such as cars, buses and trains, stabilised.

## Overview

During the second half of the 20th century, the distance travelled by bus and coach in Great Britain halved, from 92 billion passenger kilometres a year in 1952 to 45 billion kilometres in 1999 (Table 12.1). The biggest change over the period was the growth of car (including van and taxi) travel, which reached almost 11 times its 1952 value by 1999. At the end of the century cars accounted for 85 per cent of all passenger kilometres. The distance travelled by bicycle halved between 1952 and 1961, and then more than halved again over the next 10 years to 4 billion passenger kilometres in 1971. Since then it has remained around the same level. Domestic air travel increased greatly, from minimal levels in 1952 to 7 billion passenger kilometres in 1999. Rail travel fell from almost 40 billion passenger kilometres a year in the late 1950s to 31 billion kilometres in 1982, as many branch lines were closed in the 1960s, before recovering to the levels of the 1950s in 1991. It fell back in the early 1990s and recovered strongly from 1994 to reach 46 billion passenger kilometres in 1999. As a share of all passenger travel, however, rail travel fell from 18 per cent in 1952 to 6 per cent in 1982 and changed little thereafter. During the 1990s there was little change in the percentage shares held by cars (including vans and taxis), buses and coaches (6 per cent), rail (6 per cent), and air, pedal cycles and motorcycles (1 per cent each).

According to the National Travel Survey in 1997-1999, 62 per cent of all journeys were by car, 27 per cent were on foot and 7 per cent by public transport. This compares with 50 per cent of trips in 1985-86 being by car, 34 per cent on foot and 10 per cent by public transport. Car travel accounted for a lower proportion of journeys made than of distance travelled because people are more likely to use alternative travel modes like walking or buses for short distances. In 1997-1999, 27 per cent of all journeys were under a mile, around 80 per cent of which were on foot. For virtually all long journeys over 50 miles people used either cars (16 trips per person per year) or rail (2 trips per person per year).

People use different forms of transport for different purposes. For example, a quarter of public transport journeys were commuting trips, compared with less than a fifth of car journeys (Table 12.2).

The increase in the use of cars occurred among all age groups and both genders. In Great Britain, around half of all trips by children under 16 were as car or van passengers in 1997-1999 compared with 36 per cent in 1985-86. Half of journeys by 16 to 24 year olds were also by car (as driver or passenger) in 1997-1999, as were seven out of ten journeys by those aged 25 to 59. However, only just over half of journeys by older people were by car.

Journey purposes vary with gender and age, with women making proportionately more shopping trips than men and being more likely to take children to school (Table 12.3). Women also make fewer commuting and business journeys than

men. Most of the gender differences apply to people of working age, however, and reflect different patterns of work. Among children, for example, travel patterns differ little by gender, though girls aged 11 to 15 are slightly more likely than boys of the same age to make shopping or escort and personal business journeys.

### Journeys per person per year: by age, gender and purpose[1], 1997-1999

Great Britain — Percentages

| | Under 5 | 5-10 | 11-15 | 16-25 | 26-59 | 60 and over | All ages |
|---|---|---|---|---|---|---|---|
| **Males** | | | | | | | |
| Social/entertainment | 23 | 26 | 32 | 33 | 20 | 23 | 23 |
| Shopping | 14 | 12 | 12 | 12 | 17 | 33 | 19 |
| Commuting | - | - | 3 | 27 | 27 | 7 | 18 |
| Education | 8 | 37 | 38 | 11 | - | - | 7 |
| Business | - | - | 1 | 3 | 9 | 2 | 5 |
| Escort education | 17 | 3 | - | - | 2 | 1 | 3 |
| Holiday/day trip | 4 | 3 | 3 | 2 | 3 | 4 | 3 |
| Other escort and personal business | 31 | 16 | 8 | 11 | 17 | 21 | 17 |
| Other, including just walk | 3 | 3 | 3 | 2 | 4 | 8 | 4 |
| All journeys (=100%) (numbers per person per year) | 938 | 855 | 893 | 1,030 | 1,184 | 956 | 1,056 |
| **Females** | | | | | | | |
| Social/entertainment | 24 | 28 | 30 | 29 | 20 | 28 | 24 |
| Shopping | 13 | 11 | 15 | 20 | 23 | 37 | 23 |
| Commuting | - | - | 2 | 20 | 18 | 3 | 13 |
| Education | 8 | 36 | 36 | 9 | 1 | - | 6 |
| Business | - | - | - | 2 | 3 | 1 | 2 |
| Escort education | 13 | 2 | 1 | 3 | 10 | 1 | 7 |
| Holiday/day trip | 3 | 3 | 3 | 2 | 2 | 4 | 3 |
| Other escort and personal business | 34 | 16 | 10 | 13 | 19 | 19 | 18 |
| Other, including just walk | 4 | 3 | 3 | 2 | 4 | 7 | 4 |
| All journeys (=100%) (numbers per person per year) | 940 | 885 | 954 | 1,131 | 1,224 | 717 | 1,037 |

1 See Appendix, Part 12: Journey purpose.

**Source: National Travel Survey, Department of the Environment, Transport and the Regions**

# 12.4

**Travel to key services: by mode of transport, January and March 2000**

**Great Britain**  Percentages[1]

| | Car | Foot | Public transport | Other | All |
|---|---|---|---|---|---|
| Main food shopping | 77 | 13 | 8 | 2 | 100 |
| Local hospital | 77 | 6 | 14 | 3 | 100 |
| Work | 72 | 12 | 12 | 5 | 100 |
| Taking children to school or childcare | 55 | 40 | 4 | 1 | 100 |
| GP | 55 | 34 | 8 | 3 | 100 |
| Chemists | 45 | 48 | 4 | 4 | 100 |
| Post Office | 36 | 59 | 3 | 2 | 100 |

1 Percentages of those using service.

**Source: Omnibus Survey, Office for National Statistics**

# 12.5

**Goods moved by domestic freight transport: by mode**

**Great Britain**

Billion tonne kilometres

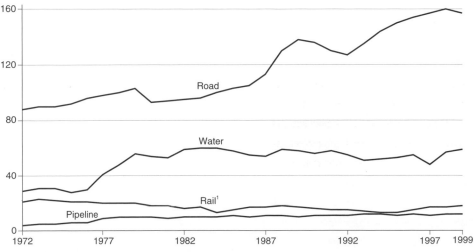

1 From 1991 data for rail are for financial years.

**Source: Department of the Environment, Transport and the Regions**

As people reach state pension age, the number of journeys they make falls. The purposes of their journeys also change. Work journeys decline and shopping accounts for an ever greater proportion of journeys. For example, shopping accounted for 41 per cent of trips by men and for 38 per cent by women aged 80 and over in 1997-1999.

People are, in general, travelling further than they used to – on average they travelled 6.8 thousand miles a year in 1997-1999 compared with 5.3 thousand in 1985-86. There was less change in the number of journeys per person, though the number of journeys made by the over sixties and women aged 26 to 59 increased over the same period.

The National Statistics Omnibus Survey also showed the dominance of cars for travel to most local services in January and March 2000 in Great Britain, especially local hospitals, main food shopping and work (Table 12.4). Walking was more common for visiting the Post Office and going to a chemist for a prescription.

As with personal travel, the end of the 20th century saw major growth of freight travel on the roads (Chart 12.5). The increase in road freight reflects an increase in the distance travelled rather than the amount of goods lifted, which changed little since the early 1970s. The amount of goods moved by rail in Great Britain in 1999 was 18 billion tonne kilometres, half the amount in 1953.

There were 372 thousand kilometres of total road length in Great Britain in 1999, an increase of around a third on the 1909 total of 282 thousand kilometres. The first 13 kilometres of motorway opened in 1959; this had risen to 3.4 thousand kilometres by 1999. Much roads infrastructure work involves improving existing roads rather than building new ones. According to the defects index of road condition in England and Wales (a measure covering non-motorway roads, based on physical defects visible at the surface and their relative costs of repair), the condition of trunk roads has tended to improve since the mid-1980s. At the same time the condition of non-trunk roads has worsened.

## Private transport

About 2 million cars are newly registered each year in Great Britain; about half of these are company cars (Table 12.6). The overall stock of currently licensed motor vehicles increases rather more slowly, as older cars are scrapped as well as new ones registered, and reached 24 million at the end of 1999, reflecting continuing growth in car ownership.

The number of people holding car driving licences increased over the last quarter of the 20th century, for all ages and for both men and women, though the rate of increase was much less after the mid-1990s. In 1997-1999, 18 million men and nearly 14 million women held full car driving licences. Traditionally men were more likely to drive than women – in 1975-76, 69 per cent of men held a driving licence compared with only 29 per cent of women. But women are catching up – by 1997-1999 the proportions with a licence were 82 per cent for men and 59 per cent for women, a much smaller difference.

The proportion of people holding full driving licences is highest among those aged 30 to 49: about nine in ten males and three in four females in this age group held a full car driving licence in 1997-1999. The proportions holding licences then fell with age and were particularly low for females

aged 70 and over – just over one in five held a licence in 1997-1999. This lower proportion of older people holding driving licences was largely because fewer of these people learned to drive when they were younger – very few people gain full licences after the age of 60. As the younger groups grow older, the proportions of those aged 70 and over who hold driving licences can be expected to increase further, even though after the age of 70 drivers have to reapply for their licence at least every three years. In 1995-1997 there were over 2 million licence holders aged 70 or over in Great Britain. Tentative projections suggest that this might double to around 4½ million by 2015.

**Motor cars currently licensed[1] and new registrations**

**Great Britain**

| | Currently licensed | | New registrations | |
|---|---|---|---|---|
| | Total (millions) | Percentage company cars | Total (millions) | Percentage company cars |
| 1987 | 17.9 | 12 | 2.0 | 48 |
| 1988 | 18.9 | 13 | 2.2 | 51 |
| 1989 | 19.7 | 13 | 2.3 | 51 |
| 1990 | 20.2 | 13 | 2.0 | 52 |
| 1991 | 20.3 | 12 | 1.6 | 52 |
| 1992[2] | 20.7 | 11 | 1.6 | 52 |
| 1993 | 20.8 | 11 | 1.8 | 51 |
| 1994 | 21.2 | 10 | 1.9 | 52 |
| 1995[3] | 21.4 | 10 | 1.9 | 53 |
| 1996 | 22.2 | 10 | 2.0 | 52 |
| 1997 | 22.8 | 11 | 2.2 | 52 |
| 1998 | 23.3 | 10 | 2.3 | 52 |
| 1999 | 24.0 | 10 | 2.3 | .. |

1 At 31 December.
2 New methods of estimating vehicle stock were introduced in 1992.
3 Changes to the vehicle taxation system were introduced from July 1 1995.
**Source: Department of the Environment, Transport and the Regions**

# 12.7

**Households with regular use of a car[1]**

**Great Britain**

Percentages

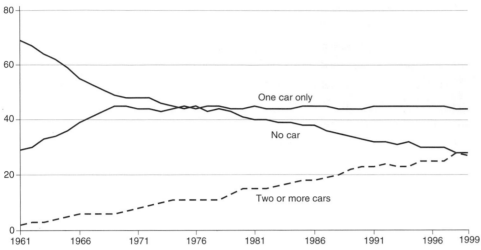

1 See Appendix, Part 12: Car ownership.

**Source: Department of the Environment, Transport and the Regions**

# 12.8

**Average daily flow[1] of motor vehicles: by class of road**

**Great Britain**        Thousands

|  | 1981 | 1991 | 1996 | 1999 |
|---|---|---|---|---|
| Motorways[2] | 30.4 | 53.8 | 62.4 | 68.2 |
| Major roads |  |  |  |  |
|   Built-up | 12.4 | 15.5 | 15.5 | 15.1 |
|   Non built-up | 5.9 | 9.5 | 10.1 | 11.0 |
|   All major roads | 7.9 | 11.2 | 11.7 | 12.2 |
| All minor roads | 1.0 | 1.4 | 1.4 | 1.4 |
| All roads | 2.2 | 3.1 | 3.3 | 3.4 |

1 Flow at an average point on each class of road.
2 Includes motorways owned by local authorities.

**Source: Department of the Environment, Transport and the Regions**

The proportion of households without access to a car has fallen over the last 30 years, while an increasing number have two or more cars (Chart 12.7). In 1999, 28 per cent of households had no car, 23 per cent of households had regular use of two cars, and 5 per cent had three or more. Households headed by a person in the professional and managerial socio-economic group were the most likely to have two or more cars; 54 per cent of such households in 1997-1999, compared with 39 per cent of households headed by people in skilled manual jobs, and 10 per cent of households headed by people who were retired. Almost half of households headed by retired people, and two-thirds of households headed by other economically inactive people, had no car. Older age groups are less likely to have access to a car. In 1997-1999, less than half of households headed by men aged 80 and over, and only one in ten headed by women aged 80 and over, had access to a car.

Cars are the most frequently used mode of transport in Great Britain for reaching services such as doctors and shops (see Table 12.4). People in less densely populated areas are particularly dependent on their cars for access to services. Rural households are more likely to have two or more cars than urban households; in 1997-1999 two in five rural households had two or more cars compared with around one in five for households in large urban, Metropolitan or London areas.

Disabled people are a group for whom access to services may be difficult, and increasing numbers have been issued with orange badges for special parking areas to make access easier. At the end of March 1999, 37 people per thousand population in England had these badges, compared with 14 per thousand in 1987. The person who holds the badge does not have to be the driver, so the vehicle can be driven by a more able-bodied person.

## 12.9

Average traffic flows rose substantially in the 1980s, particularly on motorways, and then grew more slowly in the 1990s (Table 12.8). This partly reflects the opening of some important roads, such as the M25 in the late 1980s. The increase in road traffic is projected to continue over the next decade. The Government has set targets to reduce road congestion over the next ten years by around 5 per cent on 2000 levels across England, with bigger reductions in major cities.

Cars averaged 70 miles an hour on motorways in 1999, compared with 47 miles an hour on single carriageways (Table 12.9). Lorries averaged 55 miles an hour on motorways and 45 miles an hour on single carriageways. Nevertheless, speeding is widespread when roads are not congested, particularly on motorways, dual carriageways and urban roads. In 1999, over half of cars on non-urban motorways and dual carriageways exceeded the speed limit and two-thirds of cars exceeded the 30 mile an hour limit on urban roads. Motorcycles are sometimes used as a way to avoid congestion and have similar average speeds to cars in urban areas. However, a higher proportion (38 per cent) were found to be travelling above the speed limit on 40 mile an hour limit urban roads in 1999 than the proportion of cars (26 per cent).

Excessive or inappropriate speed is estimated to be a major contributory factor in around a third of all road accidents (see also Table 12.19). There were nearly 1 million speed limit offences in England and Wales in 1998, of which 80 per cent were dealt with by fixed penalty notices. Most of the rest were dealt with in magistrates' courts.

While car use has steadily increased since the 1950s, the number of motorcycles had two peaks, in the early 1960s and early 1980s (Chart 12.10). There are signs of a return in interest – the number of currently licensed motorcycles, scooters and mopeds in Great Britain rose by 11

per cent between 1998 and 1999 after a six-year period of little change. The total number licensed has increased since 1995, but in 1999, at 760 thousand, it was still under half the number licensed in the peak years of the 1960s. New motorcycle registrations in Great Britain have increased since 1993 and there were 168 thousand new motorcycle registrations in 1999, more than any year since 1983. The chart covers the motorcycle, scooters and mopeds tax class. In addition, there were around 130 thousand motorcycles in 1999 in other tax classes, for example emergency services and vehicles manufactured before 1973. Men are much more likely than women to hold a motorcycle licence. Estimates for the 1990s suggest that motorcycle ownership is highest among men aged 30 to 39; 4 per cent of this group had a full motorcycle licence and lived in a household with a motorcycle.

**Traffic speeds: by class of road and type of vehicle, 1999**

| Great Britain | | Miles per hour |
| --- | --- | --- |
| | Cars | Buses and coaches |
| **Motorways** | | |
| Average speed | 70 | 61 |
| Speed limit | 70 | 70 |
| Percentage exceeding limit | *56* | *4* |
| **Dual carriageways** | | |
| Average speed | 70 | 59 |
| Speed limit | 70 | 60 |
| Percentage exceeding limit | *53* | *50* |
| **Single carriageways** | | |
| Average speed | 47 | 43 |
| Speed limit | 60 | 50 |
| Percentage exceeding limit | *10* | *23* |

*Source: Department of the Environment, Transport and the Regions*

## 12.10

**Motorcycles[1] currently licensed and new registrations**

**Great Britain**

Millions

1 Includes scooters and mopeds.

*Source: Department of the Environment, Transport and the Regions*

# 12.11

## Average distance walked[1] per child per year: by age

**Great Britain**

Kilometres

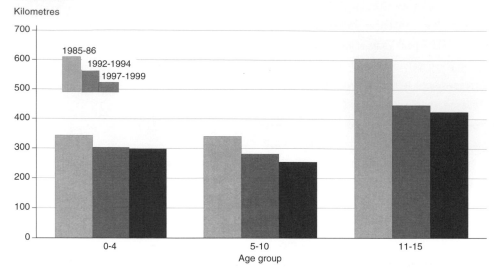

1 On the public highway or other unrestricted areas which are paved or tarred. Includes journeys under one mile.

**Source: National Travel Survey, Department of the Environment, Transport and the Regions**

# 12.12

## Attitudes towards car use

**Great Britain**                                                                 Percentages

| | Many of the short journeys I make by car I could just as easily: | | | | |
| | Go by bus | | Walk | | |
| | 1997 | 1999 | 1993 | 1997 | 1999 |
|---|---|---|---|---|---|
| Agree strongly | 7 | 6 | 12 | 11 | 11 |
| Agree | 24 | 24 | 33 | 30 | 30 |
| Neither agree nor disagree | 10 | 12 | 9 | 11 | 12 |
| Disagree | 33 | 37 | 22 | 28 | 26 |
| Disagree strongly | 15 | 13 | 9 | 10 | 11 |
| Never travel by car | 5 | 4 | 10 | 6 | 5 |
| Don't know/not answered | 6 | 5 | 6 | 5 | 4 |
| | | | | | |
| All respondents | 100 | 100 | 100 | 100 | 100 |

**Source: British Social Attitudes Survey, National Centre for Social Research**

Walking and cycling have declined as modes of transport in recent years. Among both males and females and for all age groups, people walked less far in 1997-1999 than in 1985-86. The fall was greatest among children of secondary school age and males ages 21 to 29. The particularly large falls among school age children (Chart 12.11) have caused concern, in terms of the long-term health implications of less exercise, loss of independence and road congestion. At the morning peak time of 8.50 am, 18 per cent of road traffic in urban areas in term time was generated by the school run in 1997-1999. The proportion of primary schoolchildren walking to school declined from 67 per cent in 1985-86 to 53 per cent in 1997-1999, while the proportion being taken by car increased from 22 to 38 per cent. For secondary school pupils the proportion walking to school declined from 52 to 42 per cent over the same period, and the proportion going by car more than doubled, from 10 to 21 per cent. Bus use increased slightly for older pupils, but there has been a switch from school buses to public bus services. The proportion of secondary school pupils cycling to school fell from 6 per cent in 1985-86 to only 2 per cent in 1997-1999. One factor which may be linked to the decline in children walking or cycling to school is that children have further to travel. The average length of the journey to school increased from 1.1 to 1.5 miles over the same period for primary age children and from 2.3 to 3.1 miles for secondary school pupils.

In contrast to the long-term decline in bicycle use (see Table 12.1) and an average fall of 4 per cent from 1995 to 1998 in cycle traffic, there was an increase of 5 per cent between 1998 and 1999. It is too soon to say whether this could be a change in the trend. Young males aged 11 to 17 cycle the most, averaging 128 miles a year each, over three times the overall average. In all age groups, females cycle much less than males. The Government has set a target to triple the number of cycling trips by 2010, from a 2000 base. The transport charity Sustrans is co-ordinating the development of the National Cycle Network, a linked series of traffic-free paths and traffic-calmed roads providing safe and attractive routes. The first 5 thousand miles of the National Cycle Network officially opened in June 2000, and a further 5 thousand miles are scheduled to be open by 2005. The project is supported by £43.5 million of National Lottery funds from the Millennium Commission.

The British Social Attitudes Survey explored people's attitudes to car use in 1999 and found that around three out of ten adults in Great Britain agreed that many of the short journeys they made by car could just as easily have been done by bus (Table 12.12). Around four in ten agreed they could walk instead of travelling by car. The survey also explored attitudes to measures which people thought might change their car usage. Over half of respondents with regular use of a car thought they might use cars a little or quite a bit less, or give up using the car, for each of the following reasons: gradually doubling the cost of petrol over the next ten years; greatly improving the reliability of public transport; greatly improving long-distance rail and coach services; charging all motorists around £2 each time they enter or drive through a city or town centre at peak times; and cutting in half long-distance rail and coach fares or local public transport fares.

## Public transport

Following the closure of many branch lines in the 1960s, the present rail infrastructure is much smaller than it was in the first part of the 20th century. In 1999-00 there were around 17 thousand kilometres of National Rail route in Great Britain, an amount that has changed little since 1981, and just over half the length in the peak years of 1919 to 1938.

### Rail journeys[1]: by operator

| Great Britain | | | | | | Millions |
|---|---|---|---|---|---|---|
| | 1981-82 | 1991-92 | 1996-97 | 1997-98 | 1998-99 | 1999-00 |
| **Main line/underground** | | | | | | |
| National Rail | 719 | 792 | 801 | 846 | 892 | 947 |
| London Underground | 541 | 751 | 772 | 832 | 866 | 927 |
| Glasgow Underground | 11 | 14 | 14 | 14 | 15 | 15 |
| All main line/underground | 1,271 | 1,557 | 1,587 | 1,692 | 1,773 | 1,889 |
| **Light railways and trams** | | | | | | |
| Tyne and Wear PTE | 14 | 41 | 35 | 35 | 34 | 33 |
| Docklands Light Railway | . | 8 | 17 | 21 | 28 | 31 |
| Greater Manchester Metro | . | . | 13 | 14 | 13 | 14 |
| South Yorkshire Supertram | . | . | 8 | 9 | 10 | 11 |
| West Midlands Metro | . | . | . | . | . | 5 |
| All light railways and trams | 14 | 49 | 73 | 79 | 85 | 94 |
| **All journeys by rail** | 1,285 | 1,605 | 1,660 | 1,771 | 1,858 | 1,983 |

1 Excludes railways operated principally as tourist attractions.
**Source: Department of the Environment, Transport and the Regions**

Rail travel is now above the levels of the 1950s in terms of distance travelled (see Table 12.1) though it has a much smaller share of total travel across all modes, just 6 per cent in 1999 compared with 18 per cent in 1952. The total number of passenger rail journeys in Great Britain, both national main line and underground, continued the increase of recent years in 1999-00 (Table 12.13). Journeys on the London Underground increased by a third between 1950 and 1999-00. A feature of the last 20 years has been the development of light railways and metros: Nexus (Tyne and Wear) from 1980, the Docklands Light Railway from 1988-89, Manchester Metrolink from 1992-93, Sheffield Supertram from 1993-94, Centro (West Midlands Metro) from 1999 and the Croydon Tramlink in 2000. The number of passenger journeys made on light rail systems grew from 14 million in 1981-82 to 94 million in 1999-00. In 2000 the Government set targets for 50 per cent growth in rail passengers, 80 per cent growth in rail freight and 6 thousand new carriages and trains by 2010.

# 12.14

**Bus travel[1]**

**Great Britain**

Indices (1981=100)

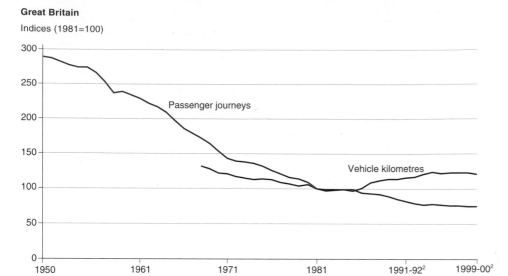

1 Local services only. Includes street-running trams and trolley buses but excludes modern 'supertram' systems.
2 Financial years from 1985-86.

**Source: Department of the Environment, Transport and the Regions**

# 12.15

**Time taken to walk to nearest bus stop: by type of area[1], 1985-1986 and 1997-1999**

**Great Britain**                                                                                                  Percentages

|  | London borough | Metro-politan built-up area | Large urban | Medium urban | Small urban | Rural | All areas |
|---|---|---|---|---|---|---|---|
| **1985-1986** | | | | | | | |
| 6 minutes or less | 86 | 91 | 90 | 90 | 81 | 74 | 86 |
| 7-13 minutes | 12 | 8 | 8 | 8 | 13 | 13 | 10 |
| 14-26 minutes | 1 | 1 | 2 | 1 | 3 | 7 | 2 |
| 27 minutes or more | 0 | - | - | - | 2 | 6 | 1 |
| | | | | | | | |
| Accessibility indicator[2] | 98 | 98 | 96 | 95 | 79 | 35 | 86 |
| **1997-1999** | | | | | | | |
| 6 minutes or less | 88 | 92 | 91 | 90 | 81 | 74 | 87 |
| 7-13 minutes | 11 | 7 | 8 | 8 | 12 | 13 | 10 |
| 14-26 minutes | 1 | 1 | 1 | 2 | 5 | 6 | 2 |
| 27 minutes or more | - | - | - | - | 2 | 6 | 1 |
| | | | | | | | |
| Accessibility indicator[2] | 98 | 99 | 98 | 96 | 77 | 42 | 87 |

1 See Appendix, Part 12: Type of area.
2 Households within 13 minutes walk of a bus stop with a service at least once an hour.

**Source: National Travel Survey, Department of the Environment, Transport and the Regions**

Following privatisation in 1996, passenger rail services on the national network are provided by 25 franchise holders which lease rolling stock and pay access charges to Railtrack plc for use of the track. The franchise holders are regulated through the Franchising Director of the Shadow Strategic Rail Authority (SSRA), which monitors performance and controls fares. In addition, a non-franchised passenger train operator provides a service between central London and Heathrow Airport, and there are an increasing number of privately owned railways for leisure and tourism.

While the numbers of passengers and train services are increasing, so are the number of delays and cancellations. From 1998-99 to 1999-00 passenger numbers in Great Britain grew by 6 per cent and the number of train services rose by 2 per cent. On average, 12 per cent of trains (730 thousand) were either cancelled or seriously delayed (by five minutes or more for London commuter and regional services, or by ten minutes or more for long-distance services) in 1999-00, 3 per cent more than the previous year. These figures used a new public performance measure, which covered all days except those when engineering works were planned or when major incidents occurred. The number of complaints reaching the Rail Passengers Council network declined from nearly 18 thousand to 15 thousand. The Office of the Rail Regulator identified broken rails as an area of major concern; the number of broken rails rose by about a quarter from 1997-98 to 1998-99 and improved marginally in 1999-00.

Buses are the dominant form of public transport in terms of journeys, though not distance, accounting for 4.2 billion passenger journeys in Great Britain in 1998-99, more than twice as many as the number of rail journeys. Bus travel declined steadily from the 1950s, although it has become more stable in recent years (Chart 12.14). The

# 12.16

distance travelled by bus increased between the mid-1980s and the mid-1990s. The distance travelled by non-local bus or coach services has risen since the mid-1990s.

National targets for reliability and investment have been agreed with the bus industry: no more than 0.5 per cent of scheduled bus mileage should be lost for reasons within an operator's control (including predictable peak hour congestion); and the average age of the bus fleet should be reduced to eight years by mid-2001. A bus reliability survey in England in the second quarter of 2000 found some 1.6 per cent of scheduled local bus mileage was lost – in London, the figure was 4.3 per cent. The average age of the bus fleet was 8.6 years at the end of June 2000, continuing a downward trend.

The distance that households live from their nearest bus service changed little over the last decade – 87 per cent of households in Great Britain lived within 6 minutes walk of a bus stop in 1997-1999 (Table 12.15). This proportion was lowest in rural areas – access to public transport is easier in urban areas. The proportion of households with good access to a bus service (defined as within 13 minutes walk of a bus stop with a service of at least once an hour) also changed little, except for those in rural areas where the proportion rose from 35 per cent in 1985-86 to 42 per cent in 1997-1999. The Government has set a target of at least an hourly bus service within about ten minutes walk for a third more rural households by 2010.

Four out of five households in 1998-1999 could walk to their nearest food store in 13 minutes or less. Three-quarters of households could walk to their nearest Post Office, and a third could walk to their nearest shopping centre in this time. A further three out of five households were within 26 minutes of their nearest shopping centre by bus.

Most local authorities offer concessionary fares to groups who are least likely to have access to a car. The March 2000 Budget announced that from April 2001 every pensioner in England and Wales would be entitled to a free bus pass for at least 50 per cent concessionary fares. In 1997-1999, 98 per cent of pensioners in Great Britain had a concessionary fare scheme available. The take-up rate has declined from 60 per cent of those with schemes available in 1989-1991 to 48 per cent in 1997-1999 – car use and driving licence holding has increased among older people in recent years. Take-up was highest in London at 79 per cent, and generally decreased with area size down to 22 per cent in rural areas. Dependence on cars is higher in rural areas, and where there are few buses there is little incentive to use a bus pass.

Domestic air travel grew steadily from minimal levels in the 1950s to 7.3 billion passenger kilometres in 1999. Many regional airports grew faster in terms of passenger numbers in the 1990s than Heathrow (Table 12.16). Stansted and Luton were the fastest growing regional airports between 1991 and 1999. The Department for the Environment, Transport and the Regions has forecast that UK domestic air traffic is expected to grow on average by 3.5 per cent per year from 35 million passengers in 1999 to around 71 million passengers by 2020.

## International travel

Like the number of domestic air passengers, international air travel has also increased greatly since the 1950s, and again regional airports are increasingly important. Heathrow and Gatwick accounted for 74 per cent of all international air passengers in 1981, but this fell to 62 per cent in 1999. Stansted was the fastest growing regional airport over the period. International air traffic is also expected to more than double by 2020.

**Domestic air passengers[1]: by airport**

| United Kingdom | | | Millions |
|---|---|---|---|
| | 1981 | 1991 | 1999 |
| Heathrow | 3.9 | 6.7 | 7.1 |
| Edinburgh | 0.9 | 1.9 | 3.8 |
| Glasgow | 1.4 | 2.3 | 3.5 |
| Gatwick | 1.0 | 1.0 | 2.8 |
| Manchester | 1.0 | 1.9 | 2.7 |
| Belfast International | 1.2 | 1.8 | 2.1 |
| | | | |
| Aberdeen | 1.0 | 1.3 | 1.6 |
| Stansted | - | 0.3 | 1.5 |
| Belfast City | 1.2 | 0.5 | 1.3 |
| Luton | - | 0.2 | 1.3 |
| Birmingham | 0.4 | 0.7 | 1.2 |
| Newcastle | 0.4 | 0.5 | 0.9 |
| | | | |
| East Midlands | 0.2 | 0.3 | 0.4 |
| Leeds/Bradford | 0.1 | 0.4 | 0.4 |
| Bristol | - | 0.1 | 0.4 |
| Cardiff | - | 0.1 | 0.1 |
| Other | 3.4 | 2.9 | 4.1 |
| | | | |
| All airports[2] | 7.0 | 11.5 | 35.0 |

1 Passengers are recorded at both airport of departure and arrival.
2 Adjusted to remove double counting.
**Source: Civil Aviation Authority**

# 12.17

## International travel: by mode[1]

| United Kingdom | | | | | | | Millions |
|---|---|---|---|---|---|---|---|
| | 1981 | 1986 | 1991 | 1996 | 1997 | 1998 | 1999 |
| **Visits to the United Kingdom** | | | | | | | |
| **by overseas residents** | | | | | | | |
| Air | 6.9 | 8.9 | 11.6 | 16.3 | 16.9 | 17.5 | 17.3 |
| Sea | 4.6 | 5.0 | 5.5 | 6.2 | 5.7 | 5.1 | 5.0 |
| Channel tunnel | . | . | . | 2.7 | 2.9 | 3.2 | 3.1 |
| All visits to the United Kingdom | 11.5 | 13.9 | 17.1 | 25.2 | 25.5 | 25.7 | 25.4 |
| **Visits abroad by UK residents** | | | | | | | |
| Air | 11.4 | 16.4 | 20.4 | 27.9 | 30.3 | 34.3 | 37.5 |
| Sea | 7.7 | 8.6 | 10.4 | 10.7 | 11.5 | 10.5 | 10.4 |
| Channel tunnel | . | . | . | 3.5 | 4.1 | 6.1 | 5.9 |
| All visits abroad | 19.0 | 24.9 | 30.8 | 42.1 | 46.0 | 50.9 | 53.9 |

1 Mode of travel from, and into, the United Kingdom.

**Source: International Passenger Survey, Office for National Statistics**

# 12.18

## International travel: by mode of travel and purpose of visit, 1999

| United Kingdom | | | | | | | | Percentages |
|---|---|---|---|---|---|---|---|---|
| | UK residents[1] | | | | Overseas residents[2] | | | |
| | Air | Sea | Channel tunnel | All modes | Air | Sea | Channel tunnel | All modes |
| Holiday | 67 | 66 | 49 | 65 | 33 | 54 | 45 | 39 |
| Business | 17 | 8 | 15 | 15 | 32 | 16 | 24 | 28 |
| Visiting friends and relatives | 13 | 10 | 9 | 12 | 24 | 18 | 22 | 22 |
| Other | 2 | 16 | 27 | 8 | 11 | 12 | 9 | 11 |
| All purposes (=100%) (millions) | 37.5 | 10.4 | 5.9 | 53.9 | 17.3 | 5.0 | 3.1 | 25.4 |

1 Visits abroad by UK residents.
2 Visits to the United Kingdom by overseas residents.

**Source: International Passenger Survey, Office for National Statistics**

Scheduled low cost airlines, like EasyJet and Go, have established themselves in the last few years, offering low fares and tending to operate from relatively uncongested airports. Their traffic is forecast to grow at 6.6 per cent on average between 1998 and 2020 on central assumptions, compared with 4.25 per cent for air traffic as a whole.

There has been a great increase in the last two decades both in the number of visits to the United Kingdom by overseas visitors and in the number of overseas visits by UK residents (Table 12.17). The number of visits by overseas residents to the United Kingdom has changed little since the mid-1990s, though visits abroad by UK residents have continued to grow. The most common method of travel to and from the United Kingdom is by air – two-thirds of all visits are by air.

The Channel Tunnel became fully operational in mid-1995 and accounted for 11 per cent of all visits to and from the United Kingdom in 1999. Measuring the impact of the Tunnel is difficult because no one can say what would have happened without it, but around three in ten visits were by sea before the Tunnel first opened in 1994, compared with around one in five now, while the proportion of air journeys has remained at around two in three.

In 1999, 5.6 million cars entered or left by sea through UK ports, compared with 3.1 million in 1981 and 5.2 million in 1991. France continued to be the most popular destination by sea, accounting for around 4.0 million cars. The Channel Tunnel accounted for a further 3.3 million passenger vehicles using the Shuttle service in 1999.

## 12.19

Two-thirds of UK residents flying abroad in 1999 were on holiday compared with over a third of overseas residents travelling to the United Kingdom by air (Table 12.18). Around half of Channel Tunnel users in 1999 were on holiday. The proportion travelling on business was higher for air and the Channel Tunnel than for sea travel.

## Safety

The United Kingdom has a good record for road safety compared with most European Union (EU) countries. In 1998 the United Kingdom had among the lowest death rates per 100,000 population in the EU, at 7 per 100,000 for adults and 2 per 100,000 for children.

Despite increasing volumes of traffic, UK road casualties fell in 1999 (Table 12.19). This is part of a long-term decline for deaths and serious injuries, but slight injuries had previously been rising (though by less than the rise in the volume of traffic). Within Great Britain there were 221 child deaths, up 7 per cent on 1998, though the numbers of serious child casualties fell. Pedestrian deaths fell by 4 per cent and car user deaths by 1 per cent, but cyclist deaths rose by 9 per cent and the number of motorcyclists (and moped and scooter users) killed rose 10 per cent.

In 1987 the then Government adopted a target to reduce road casualties by a third from the baseline average of casualties in 1981 to 1985 by the year 2000. Deaths and serious injuries were 39 per cent and 48 per cent respectively below the 1981-1985 average by 1999 but slight injuries were 15 per cent above. Pedestrian, cyclist and motorcycle casualties were all below the 1981-

1985 average, by 31 per cent, 20 per cent and 60 per cent respectively. The current Government has set new targets to halve the number of children killed and seriously injured by 2010, and to reduce all age totals by 40 per cent, compared with the 1994-1998 baseline. Measures include creating more 20 mile an hour zones around schools and in residential areas and setting up child pedestrian training schemes in deprived areas, where children are more at risk than in more prosperous areas.

Major contributors to road accidents are excessive speed and too much alcohol or the use of illicit drugs. Over the years there have been many campaigns to discourage drink-driving and the numbers of casualties from road accidents involving illegal alcohol levels have fallen (Chart 12.20). In 1999, 12 per cent of people dying in road accidents in Great Britain tested positive for illegal levels of alcohol.

### Road accident casualties: by severity

| United Kingdom | | | | Thousands |
|---|---|---|---|---|
| | Deaths | Seriously injured | Slightly injured | All casualties |
| 1981 | 6 | 81 | 246 | 333 |
| 1991 | 5 | 53 | 264 | 322 |
| 1996 | 4 | 46 | 283 | 333 |
| 1998 | 4 | 42 | 293 | 339 |
| 1999 | 4 | 41 | 290 | 334 |

*Source: Department of the Environment, Transport and the Regions; Royal Ulster Constabulary*

## 12.20

### Casualties from road accidents involving illegal alcohol levels

**United Kingdom**
Thousands

*Source: Department of the Environment, Transport and the Regions; Royal Ulster Constabulary*

# 12.21

**Passenger death rates[1]: by mode of transport**

| Great Britain | | | | | | Rates per billion passenger kilometres |
|---|---|---|---|---|---|---|
| | 1981 | 1986 | 1991 | 1996 | 1999 | Average 1990-1999 |
| Motorcycle | 115.8 | 100.3 | 94.4 | 98.8 | 112.0 | 104.0 |
| Walk | 76.9 | 75.3 | 75.0 | 54.3 | 49.0 | 62.0 |
| Pedal cycle | 56.9 | 49.6 | 46.8 | 48.0 | 41.0 | 44.0 |
| Car | 6.1 | 5.1 | 3.7 | 3.1 | 2.8 | 3.3 |
| Van | 3.8 | 3.8 | 2.1 | 1.0 | 1.0 | 1.4 |
| Water[2] | 0.4 | 0.5 | 0.0 | 0.8 | 0.3 | 1.0 |
| Rail | 1.0 | 0.9 | 0.8 | 0.4 | 0.9 | 0.5 |
| Bus or coach | 0.3 | 0.5 | 0.6 | 0.2 | 0.2 | 0.4 |
| Air[2] | 0.2 | 0.5 | - | - | - | - |

1 See Appendix, Part 12: Passenger death rates.
2 Data are for United Kingdom.

**Source: Department of the Environment, Transport and the Regions**

# 12.22

**Passenger transport prices[1]**

| United Kingdom | | | | | | Indices (1981=100) |
|---|---|---|---|---|---|---|
| | 1981 | 1986 | 1991 | 1996 | 1998 | 2000 |
| **Motoring costs** | | | | | | |
| Vehicle tax and insurance | 100 | 146 | 220 | 299 | 335 | 400 |
| Maintenance[2] | 100 | 138 | 195 | 251 | 276 | 300 |
| Petrol and oil | 100 | 145 | 156 | 213 | 240 | 285 |
| Purchase of vehicles | 100 | 116 | 144 | 165 | 174 | 158 |
| All motoring expenditure | 100 | 131 | 163 | 205 | 224 | 236 |
| **Fares and other travel costs** | | | | | | |
| Bus and coach fares | 100 | 139 | 198 | 261 | 278 | 299 |
| Rail fares | 100 | 137 | 201 | 262 | 278 | 294 |
| Other | 100 | 107 | 137 | 156 | 167 | 175 |
| All fares and other travel | 100 | 135 | 186 | 229 | 244 | 258 |
| **Retail prices index** | 100 | 137 | 185 | 214 | 227 | 237 |

1 At January each year based on the retail prices index. See Appendix, Part 6: Retail prices index.
2 Includes spares and accessories, repairs and motoring organisation membership fees.

**Source: Office for National Statistics**

Despite the improvements in road safety in recent years, it is still much safer to use public transport than private. Passenger death rates for travel by car, bicycle, on foot and especially motorcycle are higher than deaths on public transport (Table 12.21), even though rail deaths in 1999 included the major accident at Ladbroke Grove, which resulted in 31 deaths and 227 injuries.

## Resources

UK motoring costs have roughly kept pace with inflation since 1981, but bus and coach and rail fares have increased at a faster rate (Table 12.22). Within these general categories the cost of buying vehicles grew at a slower rate than other aspects of motoring, at two-thirds the rate of inflation, while the cost of vehicle tax and insurance ran at two-thirds above inflation.

Household expenditure on motoring almost doubled in real terms over the last 30 years, while expenditure on bus and coach fares fell by almost two-thirds . Nearly half of motoring expenditure in 1999-00 was on the vehicles themselves and spares, rather than running costs. In 1999-00 the average UK household spent 17 per cent of their total weekly expenditure on transport, compared with 13 per cent in 1968. Household expenditure on fares varies little by whether or not the household has a car. Expenditure on motoring is much greater for households with a car than for those without. But the latter households do nevertheless spend some money on motoring – this would include costs like paying for petrol when getting lifts.

These expenditure patterns are also reflected in the variation of distance travelled per person each year by car access for Great Britain. People in households with access to a car travel much further distances in total than others. Main drivers in households with a car used them for 90 per cent of all distance travelled in 1997-1999, and others in households with a car used them for three-quarters of all their travel. People in households without cars still used cars for over a third of all their distance travelled (see also the Private transport section that begins on page 211).

Spending on motoring and fares varies with the age of the head of household. Expenditure on motoring was greatest, at over £60 per UK household a week in 1999-00, for those with household heads aged from 30 to 64. Spending on fares was around £11 for households where the head was aged under 65. Transport expenditure on both motoring and fares fell for older households. Expenditure on transport also varies by income and social class, with households in the highest income bands spending the most in both relative and absolute terms.

Average weekly expenditure in the United Kingdom on rail fares has changed little in real terms since the late 1960s (Chart 12.23). Spending on bus fares decreased sharply between the late 1960s and the mid-1980s and then fell more slowly, reflecting changing bus usage.

**Average weekly expenditure on fares in real terms[1]**

**United Kingdom**

£ per week at 1999-00 prices[1]

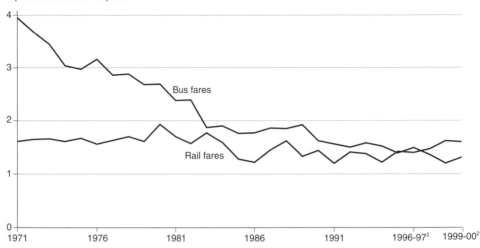

1 Adjusted to 1999-00 prices using the RPI deflator.
2 Financial years from 1994-95.

*Source: Family Expenditure Survey, Office for National Statistics*

## Websites

| | |
|---|---|
| National Statistics | www.statistics.gov.uk |
| Department of the Environment, Transport and the Regions | www.transtat.detr.gov.uk |
| Royal Ulster Constabulary | www.ruc.police.uk |
| Scottish Executive | www.scotland.gov.uk |
| National Centre for Social Research | www.natcen.ac.uk |

## Contacts

**Office for National Statistics**

| | |
|---|---|
| Chapter author | 020 7533 6177 |
| Household expenditure | 020 7533 5756 |
| International Passenger Survey | 020 7533 5765 |
| Retail Prices Index | 020 7533 5853 |

| | |
|---|---|
| **Department of the Environment, Transport and the Regions** | 020 7944 4847 |
| **Department of the Environment for Northern Ireland** | 02890 540807 |
| **Royal Ulster Constabulary** | 028 90650222 ext 24135 |
| **Scottish Executive** | 0131 244 7255/7256 |
| **National Centre for Social Research** | 020 7549 9571 |
| **Office of the Rail Regulator** | 020 7282 2079 |
| **Rail Passenger Council** | 020 7505 9090 |

# Chapter 13 Lifestyles and Social Participation

### Home based activities

- People aged four and over spent, on average, 26 hours per week watching television and 19 hours listening to the radio in 1999. (Table 13.3)

- The number of adult fiction library books issued in the United Kingdom fell from approximately seven per head of population in 1981-82 to around four per head of population in 1998-99. (Page 228)

### Activities outside of the home

- The number of cinema admissions in Great Britain more than doubled between 1984 and 1999, to 128 million. (Page 228)

- In 1998, 25 per cent of people in Great Britian took two or more holidays compared with 15 per cent in 1971. (Chart 13.14)

- In 1999, Spain remained the most popular overseas holiday destination for UK residents; outside Europe, the USA was the most popular destination. (Table 13.15)

### Communication and technology

- Home telephone ownership has increased considerably over the last three decades: 95 per cent of households had a home telephone in 1999-00 compared with 35 per cent in 1970. (Chart 13.17)

- The proportion of households who own a personal computer has almost tripled since 1985, to 38 percent in 1999-00. (Page 233)

- By July 2000, almost half of adults in Great Britain had accessed the Internet at some point in their lives. (Page 233)

# 13.1

**Division of household tasks[1]: by gender, May 1999**

**Great Britain**                                                    Minutes per person per day

|  | Males | Females | All |
|---|---|---|---|
| Cooking, baking, washing up | 30 | 74 | 53 |
| Cleaning house, tidying | 13 | 58 | 36 |
| Gardening, pet care | 48 | 21 | 34 |
| Care of own children and play | 20 | 45 | 33 |
| Maintenance, odd jobs, DIY | 26 | 9 | 17 |
| Clothes, washing, ironing, sewing | 2 | 25 | 14 |
| Care of adults in own home | 4 | 3 | 4 |
| All | 142 | 235 | 191 |

1 Main activities carried out by individuals who are married and living together or co-habiting couples.

**Source: Omnibus Survey, Office for National Statistics**

The way in which people spend their free time has changed considerably over the past few decades. The amount of time people spend doing activities such as sport, watching television, going on holidays or day trips and voluntary work has been affected by both changing working patterns and technological advances.

## Home based leisure activities

The second half of the 20th century saw a considerable increase in the proportion of women in employment, while for males the proportion declined (see Chart 4.1 on page 74 of the Labour Market chapter). Nevertheless, women still, on average, spend longer than men on household tasks. In May 1999 the Omnibus Survey asked couples in Great Britain about the time they spent on household tasks as a main activity. It is

# 13.2

**Households with selected consumer durables: by type of household, 1999-00**

**United Kingdom**                                                                                          Percentages

|  | One adult | One adult with children[1] | Two adults no children[1] | Two adults with children[1] | Two or more adults | All households |
|---|---|---|---|---|---|---|
| Television | 97 | 100 | 99 | 99 | 99 | 99 |
| Telephone | 91 | 86 | 98 | 96 | 98 | 95 |
| Deep freezer/fridge freezer | 81 | 96 | 95 | 98 | 95 | 91 |
| Washing machine | 78 | 97 | 96 | 99 | 97 | 91 |
| Video recorder | 67 | 94 | 91 | 97 | 92 | 86 |
| Microwave | 67 | 86 | 82 | 90 | 83 | 80 |
| Compact disc player | 49 | 84 | 72 | 93 | 76 | 72 |
| Tumble dryer | 33 | 54 | 55 | 68 | 57 | 52 |
| Home computer | 19 | 33 | 35 | 62 | 39 | 38 |
| Satellite TV | 18 | 32 | 30 | 47 | 33 | 32 |
| Dishwasher | 7 | 16 | 26 | 38 | 28 | 23 |

1 Children are unmarried people under 18 years of age.

**Source: Family Expenditure Survey, Office for National Statistics**

important to note that only one 'main' activity could be reported at any one time. For example, a person doing housework at the same time as looking after their children decided which they considered to be the main activity. Women spent more time than men cooking, baking and washing up; cleaning and tidying the house; washing, ironing and sewing clothes; and caring for children (Table 13.1). Men spent more time than women gardening and caring for pets; and on maintenance, odd jobs and DIY.

The amount of time people spend doing household tasks may be affected by advances in technology and the affordability of labour saving devices. Consumer durables, which were once considered luxuries, are now commonplace in many homes. In 1999-00, 91 per cent of households in the United Kingdom had a washing machine compared with around 65 per cent in 1970. Similarly, only 5 per cent of households were without a telephone in 1999-00 compared with around two-thirds at the beginning of the 1970s.

There are, however, sections of the population who are less likely to own certain commodities which others perhaps consider necessities. For example, 99 per cent of households comprising two adults with children owned a washing machine compared with only 78 per cent of households with just one adult (Table 13.2). Such households were also most likely to have a CD player, tumble dryer, satellite TV and, particularly noticeably, a home computer. Almost two-thirds of households comprising two adults with children had a home computer compared with just a third of those comprising one adult with children. Adults living alone were the least likely to have each of the durables. Almost all households have a television and consequently there is little variation in ownership between socio-economic groups or household type. Overall only 1 per cent of households in the United Kingdom are without a television.

**Television viewing and radio listening: by age and gender, 1999**

| United Kingdom | | | | Hours per person per week |
| --- | --- | --- | --- | --- |
| | Television viewing | | Radio listening | |
| | Males | Females | Males | Females |
| 4-15 | 18.6 | 17.9 | 8.4 | 9.2 |
| 16-24 | 17.7 | 22.8 | 19.8 | 18.4 |
| 25-34 | 21.6 | 26.5 | 22.1 | 17.4 |
| 35-44 | 22.5 | 25.4 | 22.6 | 18.0 |
| 45-54 | 25.3 | 26.9 | 23.7 | 20.3 |
| 55-64 | 28.8 | 32.1 | 23.3 | 22.0 |
| 65 and over | 36.4 | 36.5 | 20.9 | 20.4 |
| All aged 4 and over | 24.1 | 26.9 | 19.9 | 17.9 |

*Source: British Broadcasting Corporation; BARB; Taylor Nelson Sofres Ltd; RSMB Ltd; RAJAR/RSL Ltd*

The high ownership of televisions is reflected in the amount of time spent watching television. On average, people aged four and over in the United Kingdom spent 26 hours per week watching television and almost 19 hours listening to the radio in 1999. There are large differences between age groups. Older people watched more television than younger people with those aged 65 and over spending twice as much time watching television as those aged 4 to 15 (Table 13.3). There were also variations across the country: those in the Scotland BBC television region spent the most time watching television, almost five hours more per week than those in the South of England BBC television region. Not only did the amount of television watched vary with age but so too did the type of programme. For example, 17 per cent of programmes watched by those aged 65 and over were news programmes compared with 7 per cent of programmes watched by 4 to 15 year olds.

Overall, drama programmes are the most commonly watched type of television programme in all adult age groups, although children's programmes are as popular among those aged 4 to 15. In a recent poll by the British Film Institute the all time favourite British television programme

# 13.4

**Participation in home-based leisure activities: by gender and socio-economic group[1], 1996-97**

United Kingdom                                                                                                                    Percentages

| | Professional | Employers and managers | Intermediate and junior non-manual | Skilled manual | Semi-skilled manual | Unskilled | All aged 16 and over[2] |
|---|---|---|---|---|---|---|---|
| **Males** | | | | | | | |
| Watching TV | 99 | 99 | 99 | 99 | 98 | 99 | 99 |
| Visiting/entertaining | | | | | | | |
|   friends or relations | 95 | 96 | 96 | 95 | 94 | 88 | 95 |
| Listening to radio | 93 | 92 | 93 | 87 | 85 | 83 | 89 |
| Listening to records/tapes/CDs | 83 | 80 | 85 | 74 | 73 | 67 | 78 |
| Reading books | 81 | 69 | 68 | 48 | 49 | 39 | 58 |
| DIY | 66 | 65 | 59 | 60 | 48 | 40 | 57 |
| Gardening | 62 | 63 | 50 | 52 | 46 | 42 | 52 |
| Dressmaking/needlework/knitting | 4 | 4 | 3 | 3 | 3 | 2 | 3 |
| **Females** | | | | | | | |
| Watching TV | 98 | 99 | 99 | 100 | 99 | 98 | 99 |
| Visiting/entertaining | | | | | | | |
|   friends or relations | 100 | 98 | 97 | 95 | 97 | 96 | 97 |
| Listening to radio | 96 | 89 | 90 | 85 | 82 | 78 | 87 |
| Listening to records/tapes/CDs | 93 | 83 | 80 | 72 | 70 | 64 | 76 |
| Reading books | 91 | 80 | 77 | 63 | 61 | 54 | 71 |
| DIY | 41 | 36 | 32 | 30 | 27 | 22 | 29 |
| Gardening | 49 | 55 | 51 | 42 | 41 | 39 | 45 |
| Dressmaking/needlework/knitting | 30 | 36 | 39 | 40 | 36 | 36 | 36 |

1 Percentage of those aged 16 and over participating in each activity in the four weeks before interview. See also Appendix, Part 13 : Socio-economic group.
2 Includes full-time students, members of the armed forces, those who did not state their socio-economic group, and those whose previous occupation was more than eight years ago, or who have never had a job.

**Source: General Household Survey, Office for National Statistics; Continuous Household Survey, Northern Ireland Statistics and Research Agency**

# 13.5

### Video rentals and purchases

**United Kingdom**

Millions

**Source: British Video Association**

was *Fawlty Towers* which ran for two series made in 1975 and 1979, followed by *Cathy Come Home* (1966) and *Doctor Who* (1963 to 1989 and 1996). While watching television is the most common home-based activity for both men and women in the United Kingdom, participation in other activities varies by gender. For example, almost three-fifths of men had carried out some form of DIY in the four weeks prior to interview in 1996-97 compared with less than a third of women (Table 13.4). Women were more likely to read or do dressmaking, needlework or knitting than men. However, the overall popularity of dressmaking, needlework or knitting among women declined by 14 percentage points between 1977 and 1996-97.

In general, smaller proportions of those in the manual socio-economic groups, such as the unskilled, participated in certain home-based leisure activities than those in the non-manual groups, such as professionals and managers. For example, 81 per cent of professional men said that they had read a book in the four weeks prior to interview compared with 39 per cent of men in the unskilled group. A similarly larger proportion of women from professional backgrounds read books than did women in unskilled occupations. DIY and gardening were also more popular among those from the professional and the employer and manager groups than the unskilled manual.

As the ownership of video players has increased since the mid-1980s, so too has the number of video cassettes purchased (Chart 13.5), although it fell again slightly in 1999. In 1986 around 6 million videos were bought in the United Kingdom with a retail value of £55 million, this increased to 96 million in 1999 with a value of £882 million. In

# 13.6

contrast, the number of videos rented decreased by around 25 per cent between 1986 and 1999, although the value of the rented sector increased from £284 million in 1986 to £408 million in the same period. The best selling video of 1999 was *A Bug's Life* and the most popular rented video was *There's Something About Mary*.

On average, video cassette recorder (VCR) owners rented ten videos in 1999. Just under one in ten VCR owners rented at least one video every week, whereas four in ten said that they never rented a video. Over half of all viewing of rented videos took place at the weekend (Friday, Saturday or Sunday), with Saturday being the most common day for viewing, and over a third of videos were watched between 8 and 10.30 in the evening.

Digital Versatile Disc (DVD), which can play music, video and games, was launched in the United Kingdom in April 1998 and since then both hardware and software sales have rapidly gathered pace. In 1999 almost a quarter of a million DVD players, and more than 4 million discs, were sold in the United Kingdom. The British Video Association suggests that the DVD is the fastest growing consumer electronics format of all time, selling faster than video players and audio compact disc (CD) players did at the same stage during their launch. In 1999 the most popular DVD was *The Matrix* which sold 0.2 million copies in its first month.

Compact disc sales continue to increase, and accounted for 90 per cent of all album sales in 1999, while the sales of cassettes continue to fall (Chart 13.6). In recent years the sales of both LPs and singles appear to have levelled out. Just over 80 million singles were sold in the United Kingdom in 1999 when the best selling single of the year was *One More Time* by Britney Spears, the best selling album was *Come On Over* by Shania Twain. Technological advances saw the introduction of the Minidisc in 1996, and in 1999 over 3 million disks were sold.

**Sales[1] of CDs, LPs, cassettes and singles[2]**

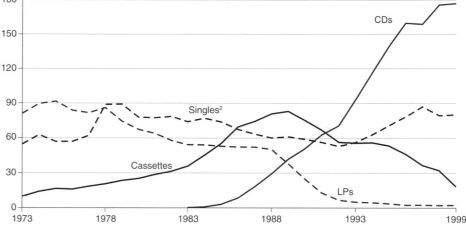

1 Trade deliveries.
2 All formats combined (7", 12", cassette and CD).
**Source: British Phonographic Industry**

# 13.7

Many people enjoy reading as a leisure activity. However, the proportion of people reading a national daily newspaper in Great Britain has fallen since the early 1980s. In the year July 1999 to June 2000 just over half the adult population aged 15 and over read a daily national newspaper, and men were more likely to do so than women (Table 13.7). The most popular national newspaper among adults continues to be *The Sun* with one in five reading this newspaper. *The Sun* is particularly popular among those aged 15 to 24 and especially among young men of this age: 31 per cent of males in this age group read *The Sun*. With one in 20 people reading *The Daily Telegraph,* and a similar proportion reading *The Times*, these were the most popular broadsheet newspapers. *The Times*, founded in 1785, is the oldest surviving national newspaper. *The Daily Telegraph* was most popular among older people, with more than double the proportion of people aged 55 and over reading this particular paper in 1999-00 compared with those aged 16 to 34.

**Reading of national daily newspapers: by gender, 1999-00[1]**

| Great Britain | | | Percentages |
|---|---|---|---|
| | Males | Females | All aged 16 and over |
| The Sun | 24 | 17 | 21 |
| The Mirror | 14 | 12 | 13 |
| Daily Mail | 13 | 12 | 12 |
| The Express | 6 | 5 | 5 |
| The Daily Telegraph | 6 | 4 | 5 |
| The Times | 5 | 3 | 4 |
| Daily Star | 5 | 2 | 3 |
| The Guardian | 3 | 2 | 2 |
| The Independent | 2 | 1 | 1 |
| Financial Times | 2 | 1 | 1 |
| Any national daily newspaper[2] | 59 | 50 | 54 |

1 Data are for July 1999 to June 2000.
2 Includes the above newspapers plus the Daily Record, The Sporting Life and Racing Post.
**Source: National Readership Surveys Ltd**

## 13.8

**Library books issued: by type of book**

**United Kingdom**
Millions

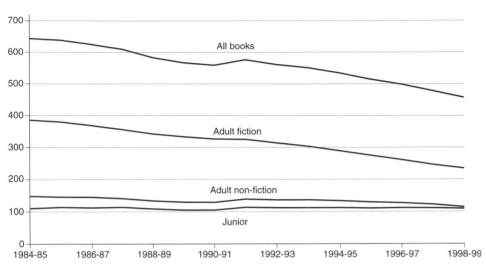

Source: Library & Information Statistics Unit, Loughborough University

## 13.9

**Attendance[1] at cultural events[2]**

| Great Britain | | | Percentages |
| --- | --- | --- | --- |
| | 1987-88 | 1993-94 | 1999-00 |
| Cinema | 34 | 50 | 56 |
| Plays | 24 | 24 | 23 |
| Art galleries/ exhibitions | 21 | 22 | 22 |
| Classical music | 12 | 12 | 12 |
| Ballet | 6 | 7 | 6 |
| Opera | 5 | 7 | 6 |
| Contemporary dance | 4 | 3 | 4 |

1 Percentage of resident population aged 15 and over attending 'these days'.
2 See Appendix, Part 13: Cultural events.

Source: Target Group Index, BMRB International; Cinema Advertising Association

The proportion of people reading Sunday newspapers has fallen over the last three decades and approximately six in ten adults had, on average, read a Sunday newspaper in the year to June 2000 compared with almost nine in ten in 1973. The *News of the World* remains the most popular Sunday newspaper. Only one in 50 adults said that they read *The Observer*, the oldest surviving national Sunday newspaper which was founded in 1791.

As well as a decline in newspaper readership, there has been a general decline in the number of books issued by libraries in the United Kingdom. The number of issues has fallen by 29 per cent since the mid-1980s, from 643 million in 1984-85 to 457 million in 1998-99, with the greatest fall being for adult fiction books (Chart 13.8). The number of junior issues has stayed reasonably constant since 1981-82. The decline in the number of books issued has been greatest in the metropolitan districts and Scotland. The number of books issued per head of population has also

decreased considerably over the same time period. The number of adult fiction books has declined from approximately 7 per head of population in 1981-82 to around 4 per head of population in 1998-99. However, the number of junior books issued per head has remained relatively stable over the last 20 years.

The number of library service points (ie any library, static or mobile, through which the public library authority provides a service to the general public) has fallen by just over 3 thousand between 1994 and 1999 with the majority of these cuts being in institutions, such as old people's homes not covered by agency agreements. As well as a fall in the number of service points there has been a reduction in the number of service points that are open for 60 hours or more. Over the last decade the number of service points open in the United Kingdom for 60 or more hours has fallen by 74 per cent and the number open between 45 and 60 hours has fallen by 19 per cent. Despite that, 59 per cent of the population are library members and, in 1998, 36 per cent of users borrowed from a library more than four times in the two months before interview.

## Activities outside the home

As well as spending leisure time on activities within the home such as watching television and radio listening, attendance at cultural events remains popular. When asked in 1999-00 whether they attended particular types of cultural events 'these days', around one in four adults in Great Britain said they attended plays, roughly the same proportion said that they attended art galleries/ exhibitions and one in eight went to classical music concerts (Table 13.9).

Over the last decade or so the proportion of adults going to particular cultural events has remained relatively constant, with the exception of cinema

## 13.10

going. According to ONS data, going to the cinema has seen quite a revival since its low point in 1984. The number of cinema admissions in Great Britain more than doubled between 1984 and 1999, to 128 million. This up-turn in cinema attendance may be related to the expansion and investment in multiplex cinemas across the country. However, these attendance figures are still significantly less than those in the early 1950s which topped the 1 billion mark.

Cinema attendance varies by age and gender and the increases in cinema attendance are not universal across all age groups. Since 1987-88 there has been a considerable increase in cinema attendance among people of all ages but in particular among those aged 25 and over (Table 13.10). In 1999 the top box office film in the United Kingdom was *Star Wars Episode 1: The Phantom Menace,* followed by *Notting Hill* and *A Bug's Life.*

The 1998 UK Day Visits Survey collected information on round trips made for leisure purposes by GB residents from home to any location in the United Kingdom. The most common reason for a day visit from home for GB residents was to go for something to eat or drink (Table 13.11). Just over a fifth of all day visits made by 15 to 24 years olds were for a meal or drink compared with around an eighth of visits made by those aged 65 and over. Walking and rambling are especially popular among the older age group. Twenty-one per cent of all visits by those aged 45 years and over involved walking or rambling, compared with 7 per cent of those made by people aged 15 to 24

The places that people go for a day trip are often related to the reason for the visit. Of those who went on a day visit to the seaside, more than a quarter did so to walk or ramble, as did a third of those who visited the countryside. Day visits to a town were most commonly for eating or drinking, visiting friends or shopping.

Museums have always been popular places to visit. When the British Museum opened in 1753 potential visitors had to apply in writing to gain entry and by the turn of the 19th century potential visitors had to wait up to two weeks for an admission ticket. The popularity of certain museums in Great Britain has increased considerably over the past two decades. In 1999 the British Museum, Tate Gallery and National Gallery all had approximately twice as many visitors as they did in 1981 (see Table 13.12 overleaf). In contrast, the Natural History Museum and Science Museum, both of which introduced

### Cinema admissions[1]: by age

| Great Britain | | | Percentages |
|---|---|---|---|
| | 1987-88 | 1991-92 | 1998-99 |
| 7-14 | 84 | 87 | 95 |
| 15-24 | 81 | 89 | 96 |
| 25-34 | 64 | 73 | 91 |
| 35 and over | 41 | 46 | 66 |
| All aged 7 and over | 56 | 62 | 78 |

1 Those who reported that they 'Ever go to the cinema'.
**Source: Cinema Advertising Association**

## 13.11

### Day visits from home: by age and main activity, 1998

| Great Britain | | | | | Percentages |
|---|---|---|---|---|---|
| | 15-24 | 25-44 | 45-64 | 65 and over | All aged 15 and over |
| Eat/drink | 22 | 19 | 16 | 13 | 18 |
| Visit friends | 21 | 17 | 15 | 15 | 17 |
| Walk/hill-walk/ramble | 7 | 14 | 21 | 21 | 15 |
| Shop | 13 | 11 | 12 | 13 | 12 |
| Entertainment | 8 | 4 | 6 | 6 | 6 |
| Indoor sport | 6 | 7 | 3 | 3 | 5 |
| Outdoor sport | 7 | 5 | 4 | 4 | 5 |
| Hobby/special interest | 4 | 3 | 6 | 8 | 5 |
| Drive/sightsee | 2 | 2 | 3 | 5 | 3 |
| Swimming | 2 | 4 | 2 | 2 | 3 |
| Leisure attraction | 1 | 2 | 2 | 2 | 2 |
| Watching sport | 2 | 2 | 2 | 1 | 2 |
| Cycling/mountain biking | 1 | 3 | 1 | - | 2 |
| Informal sport/games | 1 | 3 | 1 | 1 | 2 |
| Other | 1 | 3 | 4 | 6 | 3 |
| All visits | 100 | 100 | 100 | 100 | 100 |

**Source: UK Day Visits Survey, National Centre for Social Research**

# 13.12

**Visits to the most popular tourist attractions**

**Great Britain**

Millions

| | 1981 | 1991 | 1999 | | 1981 | 1991 | 1999 |
|---|---|---|---|---|---|---|---|
| **Museums and galleries** | | | | **Historic houses and monuments** | | | |
| British Museum | 2.6 | 5.1 | 5.5 | Tower of London | 2.1 | 1.9 | 2.4 |
| National Gallery | 2.7 | 4.3 | 5.0 | Windsor Castle | 0.7 | 0.6 | 1.3 |
| Tate Gallery, London | 0.9 | 1.8 | 1.8 | Edinburgh Castle | 0.8 | 1.0 | 1.2 |
| Natural History Museum | 3.7 | 1.6 | 1.7 | Roman Baths, Bath | 0.6 | 0.8 | 0.9 |
| Science Museum | 3.8 | 1.3 | 1.5 | Stonehenge | 0.5 | 0.6 | 0.8 |
| **Theme parks** | | | | **Wildlife parks and zoos** | | | |
| Blackpool Pleasure Beach | 7.5 | 6.5 | 7.2 | London Zoo | 1.1 | 1.1 | 1.1 |
| Alton Towers | 1.6 | 2.0 | 2.7 | Chester Zoo | .. | 0.9 | 1.0 |
| Pleasureland, Southport | .. | 1.8 | 2.5 | London Aquarium | . | . | 0.7 |
| Chessington World of Adventure | 0.5 | 1.4 | 1.6 | Edinburgh Zoo | .. | 0.5 | 0.5 |
| Legoland, Windsor | . | . | 1.6 | Knowsley Safari Park | .. | 0.3 | 0.5 |

*Source: National Tourist Boards*

# 13.13

**Participation[1] in selected sports, games and physical activities: by gender, 1996-97**

**United Kingdom**

Percentages

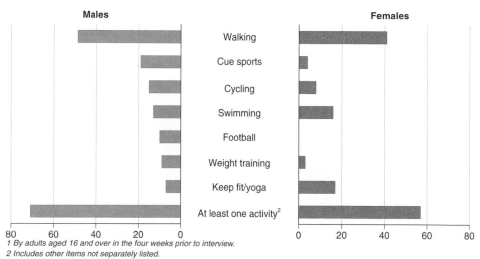

1 By adults aged 16 and over in the four weeks prior to interview.
2 Includes other items not separately listed.

*Source: General Household Survey, Office for National Statistics; Continuous Household Survey, Northern Ireland Statistics and Research Agency*

admission charges in the late 1980s, have seen the number of admissions fall by more than half since 1981. However, they both currently make no admission charge for children (since 1999) or those aged 60 and over (since 2000). In Spring 2000 the Tate Gallery was renamed Tate Britain as a new gallery was opened in London called Tate Modern. During its first six months since opening the Tate Modern attracted 3.2 million visitors. While the British Museum and the National Gallery were among the most popular tourist attractions in 1999, Blackpool Pleasure Beach continued its long tradition of being Britain's most visited tourist attraction with more than 7 million visitors.

A number of attractions were opened in the year 2000 to mark the beginning of the new millennium. The Millennium Dome opened its doors to the public in January 2000 and attracted over half a million visitors each month between February and October, with the exception of August and September. The London Eye, which opened to the public in February, attracted more than a third of a million visitors each month between April and July 2000.

# 13.14

As well as visiting tourist attractions, participation in sporting activities remains a popular way of spending leisure time. In 1996-97 the most common physical or sporting activity in the United Kingdom was walking. Around two-fifths of the population said they had been walking or rambling in the four weeks prior to interview. Although walking was the most popular activity for both men and women, there were considerable gender differences between other activities. Men were more likely than women to play cue sports, such as snooker or pool, and to cycle, whereas women were more likely than men to attend a keep-fit or yoga class, or go swimming (Chart 13.13).

The proportion of people participating in at least one sporting activity decreased with age. Just over two-thirds of people aged 16 to 24 years were involved in at least one activity in the four weeks prior to interview in 1996-97 compared with a third of those aged 65 and over. However, participation in activities such as golf, fishing and bowls differed very little across age groups.

A key way of spending leisure time is to have a break from everyday life and take a holiday, whether it be within the United Kingdom or abroad. Although the proportion of British residents who did not take a holiday of four days or more has remained relatively unchanged over the past three decades (41 per cent in 1998), the proportion taking two or more holidays has increased from 15 per cent in 1971 to 25 per cent in 1998 (Chart 13.14).

In 1999 Spain remained the most popular overseas holiday destination for UK residents. More than a quarter of all holiday visits abroad by UK residents were to Spain. The proportion of holiday visits which were to France has declined since 1981, when around one in four holiday visits abroad by UK residents were across the Channel. In 1999 around over one in five holiday visits were to France (Table 13.15). The most popular destination outside Europe was the United States, which accounted for 7 per cent of all holiday visits.

**Holidays[1] taken by Great Britain residents: by number taken per year**

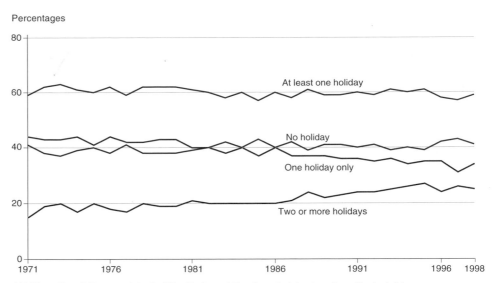

1 Holidays of four nights or more taken by GB residents aged 16 and over. Includes domestic and foreign holidays.
**Source: British National Travel Survey, British Tourist Authority**

# 13.15

**Holidays abroad: by age and destination, 1999**

| United Kingdom | | | | | | | | Percentages |
|---|---|---|---|---|---|---|---|---|
| | Under 16 | 16-24 | 25-34 | 35-44 | 45-54 | 55-64 | 65 and over | All[1] |
| Spain | 32 | 28 | 24 | 26 | 26 | 30 | 31 | 27 |
| France | 29 | 17 | 18 | 21 | 19 | 17 | 17 | 20 |
| USA | 7 | 7 | 9 | 9 | 8 | 6 | 5 | 7 |
| Greece | 4 | 10 | 7 | 6 | 7 | 6 | 3 | 6 |
| Eire | 2 | 5 | 5 | 5 | 5 | 5 | 7 | 6 |
| Italy | 2 | 3 | 5 | 4 | 5 | 5 | 6 | 4 |
| Portugal | 3 | 2 | 3 | 4 | 4 | 5 | 5 | 4 |
| Cyprus | 2 | 3 | 2 | 2 | 3 | 3 | 3 | 2 |
| Netherlands | 2 | 4 | 3 | 2 | 2 | 2 | 2 | 2 |
| Turkey | 2 | 2 | 2 | 3 | 2 | 2 | 2 | 2 |
| Belgium | 2 | 1 | 2 | 2 | 2 | 2 | 2 | 2 |
| Caribbean | 1 | 2 | 3 | 2 | 2 | 1 | 1 | 2 |
| Germany | 3 | 2 | 1 | 1 | 1 | 1 | 2 | 2 |
| North Africa[2] | 1 | 1 | 1 | 1 | 1 | 1 | 1 | 1 |
| Other countries | 8 | 14 | 14 | 11 | 12 | 14 | 13 | 12 |
| All holiday visits (=100%)(millions) | 3.8 | 3.2 | 6.3 | 6.8 | 6.8 | 4.8 | 3.0 | 35.0 |

1 Includes those where age is not known.
2 North Africa excluding Egypt.
**Source: International Passenger Survey, Office for National Statistics**

# 13.16

### Letters posted[1]

**United Kingdom**
Billions

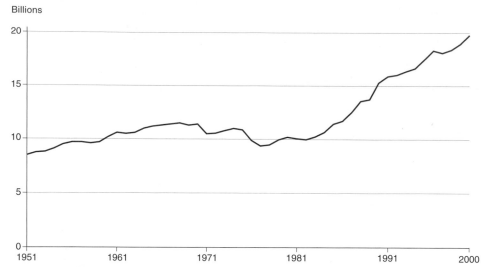

1 As at 31 March each year. Includes printed papers, newspapers, postcards and sample packets.
**Source: Royal Mail; Post Office Counters Limited**

# 13.17

### Households with home telephones[1]

**United Kingdom**
Percentages

1 Fixed line telephones.
2 From 1994-95 onwards, data are for financial years.
**Source: Family Expenditure Survey, Office for National Statistics**

The most popular 14 places visited have changed slightly from 1998 and include a number of destinations further afield such as the Caribbean (2 per cent) and North Africa (1 per cent). However, it is those aged 25 to 34 years who are most likely to venture further afield with almost a quarter of all holidays taken by this group being to destinations outside of Western Europe.

Young people appear to spend about the same amount on their trips to France and Spain as older people, but for all other destinations the amount spent per visit was generally lower than among older adults. Young people take longer trips than people from older age groups. For example, the average trip to Australia was 86 days for 16 to 24 year olds compared with 40 days for those aged 25 and over.

## Communication and technology

The rapid developments in communication and technology have dramatically changed the way in which people both live and work. The number of communication tools available has increased as mobile telephones, email and the Internet have become more affordable. However, there appears to have been little impact on more traditional methods of communication, such as letter writing.

In October 1871 the half-penny postage was introduced in the United Kingdom and in the same year the number of letters delivered stood at 867 million. By the time of the First World War the number of letters, newspapers, halfpenny packets and postcards delivered had almost quadrupled. In 1938, prior to the Second World War, more than 8 billion letters, newspapers and postcards were posted. During the war years the number posted declined to slightly over 6 billion. However, between 1941 and 1944 the number of airmail letters posted increased from 10 million to 224 million. Since then the growth in airmail has been slower and in 1999, 693 million airmail letters were posted. The number of letters posted has increased steadily since 1981 and almost 20 billion were posted in 2000. (Chart 13.16).

The first telegraph system in Great Britain was invented by Sir Charles Wheatstone in 1837 and telecommunications have developed rapidly since Alexander Graham Bell invented the first telephone in 1876. However, home telephones have only become commonplace in the majority of homes over the last two decades. In 1970 around a third of all households in the United Kingdom had a home telephone, and this had risen to 95 per cent by 1999-00 (Chart 13.17). Very few households are now without a home telephone, and mobile telephones are becoming increasingly popular. The proportion of households with at least one mobile telephone almost tripled from 16 per cent in 1996-97, the first year for which data are available, to 44 per cent in 1990-00. Mobile telephones are now more than a communication tool used to talk to other people. Technological advances have allowed people to send and receive email and access the Internet through their mobile telephones.

It was in the late 19th century that Charles Babbage worked out the principles of the modern digital computer and invented the Difference Engine for solving complex mathematical problems. However, it was the mid-1940s before the first modern electronic digital computers were produced. Computers have developed rapidly since then and 38 per cent of all households in the United Kingdom owned a personal computer (PC)

in 1999-00. This was almost triple the proportion that had a computer in 1985. Over the period 1997-98 to 1999-00, the households most likely to have a PC were those in the South East and London (Chart 13.18) and those whose heads work in a professional occupation. Households whose heads worked in professional jobs were four times as likely to own a PC as those in unskilled occupations or those who were retired and unoccupied.

In July 2000 the Omnibus Survey carried a series of questions on Internet usage which included where and how residents of Great Britain aged 16 and over accessed the internet, what they used it for and how often. Overall, 45 per cent of adults have accessed the Internet at some point in their lives. There are a variety of places where people can access the Internet, including at their workplace, school and on the high street through Internet cafes. Over recent years there has been a sizeable increase in the number of schools connected to the Internet and particularly the number of primary schools (see Chart 3.6 on page 61 in the Education and Training chapter). By far the most popular place that people usually accessed the World Wide Web was from their own home (Table 13.19).

## 13.18

**Households with a personal computer: by region, 1997-2000[1]**

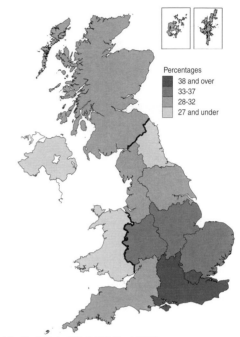

Percentages
- 38 and over
- 33-37
- 28-32
- 27 and under

1 Combined data for 1997-98, 1998-99 and 1999-00.
*Source: Family Expenditure Survey, Office for National Statistics*

## 13.19

**Places where Internet is accessed[1], July 2000**

| Great Britain | Percentages |
|---|---|
| | July 2000 |
| Own home | 59 |
| Another person's home | 14 |
| Workplace | 16 |
| College/university | 6 |
| School | 2 |
| Other[2] | 3 |
| All accessing Internet | 100 |

1 Main place used by those aged 16 and over to access the internet.
2 Includes public libraries, government offices, Internet cafés, community or voluntary organisation.
*Source: Omnibus Survey, Office for National Statistics*

# 13.20

**Internet usage[1]: by age, July 2000**

Great Britain                                                                 Percentages

| | 16-24 | 25-34 | 35-44 | 45-54 | 55 and over | All aged 16 and over |
|---|---|---|---|---|---|---|
| Email | 31 | 29 | 31 | 36 | 47 | 34 |
| Information on goods and services | 12 | 18 | 29 | 30 | 22 | 22 |
| General browsing/surfing | 17 | 23 | 16 | 18 | 15 | 18 |
| Educational | 19 | 6 | 7 | 5 | 3 | 8 |
| Banking, finance and investment | 1 | 7 | 3 | 2 | 5 | 4 |
| Chat rooms/sites | 9 | 2 | 2 | - | .. | 3 |
| Job hunting | 5 | 4 | 2 | 1 | .. | 3 |
| Buying goods and services | .. | 3 | 4 | 2 | 3 | 2 |
| Downloading games | - | 3 | .. | 1 | 2 | 1 |
| Downloading music | 2 | - | .. | 1 | .. | 1 |
| Accessing government services | .. | .. | 1 | 1 | 2 | 1 |
| Other | 3 | 5 | 4 | 4 | 4 | 4 |
| All | 100 | 100 | 100 | 100 | 100 | 100 |

1 Main reason for using the internet.

**Source: Omnibus Survey, Office for National Statistics**

# 13.21

**Frequency of participation in voluntary activities[1]: by gender, 1998**

Great Britain                                                                 Percentages

| | Never | 1 to 5 times | 6 or more times | All[2] |
|---|---|---|---|---|
| **Males** | | | | |
| Charitable activities | 77 | 15 | 5 | 100 |
| Religious and church-related acts | 85 | 7 | 4 | 100 |
| Political activities[3] | 93 | 3 | 1 | 100 |
| Any other kind of voluntary activities | 78 | 11 | 7 | 100 |
| **Females** | | | | |
| Charitable activities | 72 | 17 | 6 | 100 |
| Religious and church-related acts | 80 | 8 | 6 | 100 |
| Political activities[3] | 92 | 2 | - | 100 |
| Any other kind of voluntary activities | 75 | 11 | 8 | 100 |

1 Respondents were asked if they had done any voluntary work in the past 12 months in different areas. Voluntary activity was defined as unpaid work, not just belonging to an organisation or group, of service or benefit to other people or the community and not only to one's family or personal friends.
2 Includes those who did not answer.
3 Includes helping political parties, political movements and election campaigns.

**Source: British Social Attitudes Survey, National Centre for Social Research**

A wide range of information is available to people via the Internet. A third of those who had ever accessed the Internet said that they mainly used it as a tool for sending and receiving email and a fifth used it to gather information on goods and services (Table 13.20).

The main reason given for not using the Internet was a general lack of interest rather than any concerns such as high costs or content. Another reason for not using the Internet was not having access to a computer and this was especially the case for those in the younger age groups.

## Citizenship and social participation

Serving the community through volunteering is a long-established tradition in the United Kingdom. Many people choose to become involved in charitable activities. The Timebank is a new project launched in conjunction with partners such as the BBC on 29 February 2000, the first leap year day of the new millennium. It works with the voluntary sector in order to help more people to get involved across the spectrum of community life.

The 1998 British Social Attitudes Survey asked adults aged 18 and over in Great Britain if they had done any voluntary work in the previous 12 months (that is, any unpaid activity of benefit or service to the community or people other than friends or family). Approximately one in five adults reported that they had done unpaid charitable work in the last year (Table 13.21) and this did not vary significantly by gender: one in five men and about one in four women said that they had volunteered for charitable activities. The least supported were political activities: just 4 per cent of men and 2 per cent of women who responded

## 13.22

participated in these activities in the year before interview. While many adults participated in voluntary activity only a small proportion of the population had done voluntary work on more than five occasions in the previous 12 months.

A survey carried out by the Institute for Volunteering Research in 1997 found that people aged 18 to 24 in Great Britain were less likely to volunteer then those aged 25 to 54 years old. To volunteer was defined as to take part in an activity which involves spending time, unpaid, doing something which aims to benefit someone other than or in addition to close relatives, or to benefit the environment. The survey also found that volunteering by 18 to 24 year olds has declined sharply since 1991, while there has been a correspondingly sharp increase in volunteering among those aged over 65. Over two-fifths of young people volunteered in 1997, with young adults aged 18 to 24 spending an average of 0.7 hours a week volunteering, much lower than other groups.

In addition to voluntary work, many people participate in activities to benefit their community. In 1998 over a quarter of adults aged 18 and over were a member of at least one community organisation, such as a residents association or Parent-Teacher Association. The most common community organisation was the Neighbourhood Watch scheme, of which around one in seven adults were members (Table 13.22).

For some people religion is an important part of their lives – it can provide contact with others as well as participation in the local community. However, in 1999, almost half of all adults aged 18 and over in Great Britain who said they belonged to a religion or were brought up in a religion said that they never or practically never attended a

religious service (Table 13.23). Thirteen per cent of women and 10 per cent of men attended a religious service at least once a week.

Religion clearly plays a more important role in the lives of older people than in those of younger people. In 1999, one in six people aged 65 and over who said they belonged to a religion or were brought up in a religion, attended one or more service a week compared with one in 20 of those aged 18 to 24. Twenty-seven per cent of 18 to 24 year olds said that they had no religion whereas only 2 per cent of those aged 65 and over said this was the case.

### Membership of community organisations[1], 1998

| Great Britain | Percentages |
|---|---|
| | 1998 |
| Neighbourhood Watch scheme | 14 |
| Tenants/residents association | 5 |
| Parent-Teacher Association | 3 |
| Political party | 3 |
| Local conservation/environmental group | 2 |
| | |
| Voluntary group helping sick, elderly, children | 2 |
| Board of school governors | 1 |
| Neighbourhood council | 1 |
| Parish or town council | 1 |
| Other local community/voluntary group | 6 |
| | |
| At least one group | 26 |

1 Adults aged 18 and over.

**Source: British Social Attitudes Survey, National Centre for Social Research**

## 13.23

### Frequency of attending religious services[1]: by gender, 1999

| Great Britain | | | Percentages |
|---|---|---|---|
| | Males | Females | All |
| Once a week or more | 10 | 13 | 12 |
| Less often but at least once in two weeks | 1 | 2 | 2 |
| Less often but at least once a month | 4 | 6 | 5 |
| Less often but at least twice a year | 8 | 10 | 9 |
| Less often but at least once a year | 6 | 7 | 7 |
| | | | |
| Less often | 5 | 5 | 5 |
| Never or practically never | 53 | 44 | 49 |
| Varies too much to say | - | 1 | 1 |
| Not answered | 1 | 2 | 1 |
| No religion | 11 | 10 | 10 |
| | | | |
| All | 100 | 100 | 100 |

1 Respondents aged 18 and over who said they belonged to a religion or were brought up in a religion, were asked how often, apart from special occasions such as weddings, funerals and baptisms, they attended services or meetings connected with their religion.

**Source: British Social Attitudes Survey, National Centre for Social Research**

## Voting

The majority of people in the United Kingdom use their right to vote at general elections even though the proportions doing so have fluctuated considerably over the last century. It can be difficult to compare results from recent elections to those earlier in the 1900s as the eligibility to vote has changed over time. Women aged 30 and over were given the right to vote in 1918 and this was lowered to 21 and over in 1928. In 1910, 87 per cent of the electorate turned out to vote while in 1918 only 59 per cent voted, the lowest turnout in the last century. In the 1997 general election the overall turnout was one of the lowest of all time,

when around 71 per cent voted. The differences in turnout by age were sizeable and there appears to have been particular apathy towards voting among young males, with 56 per cent of those aged 18 to 24 years exercising their right to vote compared with 64 per cent of women of the same age. The difference between the turnout for young men and women was considerably larger than in the elections of 1983 and 1970 (Table 13.24).

This voting behaviour may be linked to young people's attitudes. A third of those aged 18 to 24 interviewed for the 1998 British Social Attitudes Survey felt that 'everyone has an obligation to vote'; this compared with four-fifths of those aged 65 and over. Further analyses suggest that this attitude to voting held by young people may not change as they get older.

According to the Young People's Social Attitudes Survey, political interest among young people was already low in 1994 and had fallen further by 1998. Over a third of young people aged 12 to 19 claimed to have no interest in politics at all in 1998, a rise of 7 percentage points since 1994. A further third had not very much interest in 1998, leaving only one in three teenagers who claimed to have an interest. Although there has also been a fall in interest among adults, they remain substantially more interested in politics than their younger counterparts. Those in education, or who expect to remain there after the age of 19, are more likely to be interested in politics. Teenagers are less likely than older adults to have formed party attachments, with the strongest influence on party identification being that of their parents.

# 13.24

**Voting[1] turnout at general elections: by age and gender**

| Great Britain | | | | | | Percentages |
| --- | --- | --- | --- | --- | --- | --- |
| | 1970 | | 1983 | | 1997 | |
| | Males | Females | Males | Females | Males | Females |
| 18-24 | 67 | 66 | 74 | 73 | 56 | 64 |
| 25-34 | 74 | 77 | 76 | 79 | 67 | 70 |
| 35-44 | 81 | 84 | 87 | 88 | 77 | 78 |
| 45-54 | 86 | 85 | 88 | 90 | 83 | 86 |
| 55-59 | 88 | 86 | 89 | 93 | 90 | 87 |
| 60-64 | 79 | 84 | 82 | 90 | 87 | 88 |
| 65 and over | 93 | 84 | 86 | 82 | 87 | 85 |

1 See Appendix, Part 13: Parliamentary elections.
**Source: British Election Study, National Centre for Social Research**

## Websites

| | |
|---|---|
| National Statistics | www.statistics.gov.uk |
| Department for Culture, Media and Sport | www.culture.gov.uk |
| Northern Ireland Statistics and Research Agency | www.nics.gov.uk |
| British Broadcasting Corporation | www.bbc.co.uk |
| British Film Industry | www.bfi.org.uk |
| British Phonographic Industry | www.bpi.co.uk |
| British Video Association | www.bva.org.uk |
| Centre for Research into Elections and Social Trends | www.crest.ox.ac.uk |
| Cinema Advertising Association | www.carlton.com/mediasales |
| Library & Information Statistics Unit | www.lboro.ac.uk/departments/dils/lisu/lisuhp.html |
| National Centre of Social Research | www.natcen.ac.uk |
| Royal Mail | www.royalmail.com |

## Contacts

| | |
|---|---|
| **Office for National Statistics** | |
| Chapter author | 020 7533 5473 |
| Family Expenditure Survey | 020 7533 5756 |
| General Household Survey | 020 7533 5444 |
| International Passenger Survey | 020 7533 5765 |
| Omnibus Survey | 0207 533 5878 |
| **Department for Culture, Media and Sport** | 020 7211 6409 |
| **Northern Ireland Statistics and Research Agency** | 028 9034 8243 |
| **British Broadcasting Corporation** | 020 8576 4436 |
| **British Phonographic Industry** | 020 7851 4000 |
| **British Tourist Authority** | 020 8846 9000 |
| **British Video Association** | 020 7436 0041 |
| **Cinema Advertising Association** | 020 7534 6363 |
| **Library & Information Statistics Unit** | 0150 922 307 |
| **National Centre for Social Research** | 020 7549 9572 |
| **National Readership Surveys** | 020 7632 2915 |

# Further reading

### General

*Annual Report of the Registrar General for Northern Ireland*, The Stationery Office

*Annual Report of the Registrar General for Scotland*, General Register Office for Scotland

*Britain. The Official Yearbook of the United Kingdom*, The Stationery Office

*British Social Attitudes*, Sage Publishing

*British Social Trends Since 1900*, MacMillan Press

*Family Resources Survey,* Corporate Document Services

*Family Spending,* The Stationery Office

*Living in Britain*, The Stationery Office

*Population Trends*, The Stationery Office

*Regional Trends,* The Stationery Office

*Social Focus on Ethnic Minorities*, The Stationery Office

*Social Focus on Older People*, The Stationery Office

*Social Focus on Women and Men*, The Stationery Office

*Social Focus on Young People,* The Stationery Office

*Social Trends, The Stationery Office*

### 1: Population

*1991 Census Historical Tables: Great Britain,* The Stationery Office

*A Statistical Focus on Wales: Women,* National Assembly for Wales

*Asylum Statistics - United Kingdom*, Home Office

*Birth statistics (Series FM1)*, The Stationery Office

*Control of Immigration: Statistics, United Kingdom*, The Stationery Office

*Demographic Statistics*, Eurostat

*Demographic Yearbook,* United Nations

*Health Statistics Quarterly*, The Stationery Office

*International Migration Statistics (Series MN)*, The Stationery Office

*Key Population and Vital Statistics (Series VS/PP1)*, The Stationery Office

*Mid-year Population Estimates (Series PP1)*, The Stationery Office

*Mid-year Population Estimates, Scotland*, General Register Office for Scotland

*Mortality Statistics for England and Wales (Series DH1, 2, 3, 4)*, The Stationery Office

*National Population Projections (Series PP2)*, The Stationery Office

*Persons Granted British Citizenship - United Kingdom*, Home Office

*Population Projections for the Counties and District Health Authorities of Wales*, National Assembly for Wales

*Population Projections, Scotland (for Administrative Areas)*, General Register Office for Scotland

*Population and Society 1750-1940: Contrasts in Population Growth*, Longman

*The State of World Population*, UNFPA

### 2: Households and Families

*Abortion Statistics (Series AB)*, The Stationery Office

*Birth statistics: historical series, 1837-1983 (Series FM1)*, The Stationery Office

*Housing in England: Survey of English Housing*, The Stationery Office

*Human Fertilisation and Embryology Authority Annual Report*, Human Fertilisation and Embryology Authority

*Key Population and Vital Statistics (Series VS/PP1)*, The Stationery Office

*Marriage, divorce and adoption statistics (Series FM2)*, The Stationery Office

*Marriage and divorce statistics 1837-1983 (Series FM2)*, The Stationery Office

*Personal Relationships and Marriage Expectations: Evidence from the 1998 British Household Panel Study*, ESRC Institute for Social and Economic Research

*Projections of Households in England to 2021*, Department of the Environment, Transport and the Regions

*Teenage Pregnancy, Report by the Social Exclusion Unit*, The Stationery Office

*The British Population*, Oxford University Press

*The Divorced and Who Divorces?* ESRC Research Centre for Analysis of Social Exclusion

*The Fragmenting Family: Does it matter?* The Institute for Economic Affairs

*The Legacy of Parental Divorce*, ESRC Research Centre for Analysis of Social Exclusion

## 3: Education

*Adult Literacy in Britain*, The Stationery Office

*Difficulties with Basic Skills: findings from the 1970 British Cohort Study*, Basic Skills Agency

*Employers Skill Survey: Statistical Report*, DfEE Publications

*Every Pupil Counts: The impact of Class Size at KS1*, NfER

*Statistical Bulletin: Pupil absence and truancy from schools in England: 1998/99, Issue No 15/99*, The Stationery Office

*Statistical Bulletin: Survey of Information and Communications Technology in Schools 2000: Issue No 07/00*, The Stationery Office

*Statistical Bulletin: Youth Cohort Study: Education, Training and Employment of 16-18 year olds in England and the factors associated with non-participation: England and Wales 2000: Issue No 02/00*, The Stationery Office

*Statistical Bulletin: Youth Cohort Study: The Activities and Experiences of 16 year olds: England and Wales 1998: Issue No 4/99*, The Stationery Office

*Statistical Volume: Education and Training Statistics for the United Kingdom 2000*, The Stationery Office

*The Five Giants. A Biography of the Welfare State*. Fontana Press

*Women's attitudes to combining paid work and family life*, The Women's Unit, Cabinet Office

## 4: Labour Market

*Breaking the Long Hours Culture*, Institute of Employment Studies

*How Exactly is Unemployment Measured?*, Office for National Statistics

*Labour Force Survey Historical Supplement*, Office for National Statistics

*Labour Force Survey Quarterly Bulletin*, Office for National Statistics

*Labour Market Quarterly Report*, Office for National Statistics

*Labour Market Trends*, The Stationery Office

*Northern Ireland Labour Force Survey*, Department of Enterprise, Trade and Investment, Northern Ireland

*Northern Ireland Labour Force Survey Historical Supplement*, Department of Enterprise, Trade and Investment, Northern Ireland

*Statistics in Focus, Population and Social Indicators*, Eurostat

## 5: Income and Wealth

*Changing student finances: income, expenditure and the take-up of student loans among full-time higher education students in 1998/99*, The Stationery Office

*Changing Households: The British Household Panel Survey*, ESRC Institute for Social and Economic Research

*Disability in Great Britain,* Department of Social Security

*Economic Trends*, The Stationery Office

*Eurostat National Accounts ESA Aggregates*, Eurostat

*Fiscal Studies*, Institute for Fiscal Studies

*Households Below Average Income*, Corporate Document Services

*Income and Wealth: The latest evidence*, Joseph Rowntree Foundation

*Inland Revenue Statistics*, The Stationery Office

*Inquiry into Income and Wealth*, Joseph Rowntree Foundation

*Labour Market Trends (incorporating Employment Gazette),* The Stationery Office

*Monitoring Poverty and Social Exclusion*, Joseph Rowntree Foundation

*National Accounts, Main Aggregates, Detailed Tables,* OECD

*New Earnings Survey*, The Stationery Office

*Poverty and Social Exclusion in Britain*, Joseph Rowntree Foundation

*Social Security, Departmental Report*, The Stationery Office

*Social Security Statistics*, The Stationery Office

*Tax/Benefit Model Tables*, Department of Social Security

*The Distribution of Wealth in the UK*, Institute for Fiscal Studies

*The Pensioners' Income Series,* Department of Social Security

*United Kingdom National Accounts (The ONS Blue Book)*, The Stationery Office

*United Kingdom National Accounts Concepts, Sources and Methods*, The Stationery Office

*Individual Income, Women's Unit*, Cabinet Office

*Women's Incomes over the Lifetime*, Cabinet Office

## 6: Expenditure

*Business Monitor MM23 (Consumer Price Indices)*, The Stationery Office

*Consumer Trends*, The Stationery Office

*Court of Auditors - Annual report*, European Community

*Economic Situation Report*, Confederation of British Industry

*Economic Trends*, The Stationery Office

*Financial Statistics*, The Stationery Office

*Statistical Yearbook*, Credit Card Research Group

*United Kingdom National Accounts (The ONS Blue Book)*, The Stationery Office

*e-commerce@its.best.uk, A Performance and Innovation Unit Report*, Cabinet Office

## 7: Health

*Adult Dental Health Survey: oral health in the United Kingdom 1998*, The Stationery Office

*Annual Report of the Registrar General for Scotland*, General Register Office for Scotland

*Drug Use, Smoking and Drinking among Young Teenagers in 1999,* The Stationery Office

*Key Health Statistics from General Practice 1998*, Office for National Statistics

*Mental Health of Children and Adolescents in Great Britain*, The Stationery Office

*National Diet and Nutrition Survey: Young People Aged 4 to 18 Years*, The Stationery Office

*On the State of Public Health*, The Stationery Office

*Statistical Publications on Aspects of Health and Personal Social Services Activity in England (various)*,
    Department of Health

*Trends in Deaths Associated with Abuse of Volatile Substances 1971-1998, Report No. 13,* St George's Hospital
    Medical School, London

*The Health of Adult Britain 1841-1994 (Series DS12 and DS13)*, The Stationery Office

*The NHS Plan*, The Stationery Office
*The UK Smoking Epidemic: Deaths in 1995*: Health Education Authority
*Working Together for a Healthier Scotland*, The Stationery Office
*World Health Statistics*, World Health Organisation

## 8: Social Protection

*Annual News Releases (various)*, Scottish Executive
*Community Statistics for Northern Ireland*, Department of Health, Social Services and Public Safety, Northern Ireland
*Department of Health Departmental Report*, The Stationery Office
*Dimensions of the Voluntary Sector*, Charities Aid Foundation
*ESSPROS manual 1996*, Eurostat
*Health and Personal Social Services Statistics for England*, The Stationery Office
*Health Statistics Wales, Welsh Health Survey*, National Assembly for Wales
*Hospital Statistics for Northern Ireland*, Department of Health, Social Services and Public Safety, Northern Ireland
*Hospital Episode Statistics for England*, Department of Health
*Laing's Healthcare Market Review 2000-2001*, Laing & Buisson Publications Ltd.
*Scottish Community Care Statistics*, Scottish Executive
*Scottish Health Statistics,* National Health Service in Scotland, Common Services Agency
*Social Protection Expenditure and Receipts,* Eurostat
*Social Security Departmental Report,* The Stationery Office
*Social Security Statistics,* The Stationery Office
*Statistical Publications on aspects of Health and Personal Social Services Activity in England (various),* Department of Health

## 9: Crime and Justice

*A Commentary on Northern Ireland Crime Statistics,* The Stationery Office
*British Crime Survey,* Home Office
*Chief Constable's Annual Report,* Royal Ulster Constabulary
*Civil Judicial Statistics, Scotland,* The Stationery Office
*Costs, Sentencing Profiles and the Scottish Criminal Justice System,* Scottish Executive
*Crime and the quality of life: public perceptions and experiences of crime in Scotland,* Scottish Executive
*Criminal Statistics, England and Wales,* The Stationery Office
*Crown Prosecution Service, Annual Report,* The Stationery Office
*Digest 4: Information on the Criminal Justice System in England and Wales,* Home Office
*Digest of Information on the Northern Ireland Criminal Justice System 3,* The Stationery Office
*Home Office Annual Report and Accounts,* The Stationery Office
*Home Office Research Findings,* Home Office
*Home Office Statistical Bulletins,* Home Office
*Judicial Statistics, England and Wales,* The Stationery Office
*Local Authority Performance Indicators, Volume 3,* Audit Commission
*Northern Ireland Judicial Statistics,* Northern Ireland Court Service
*Police Statistics, England and Wales,* CIPFA
*Prison Service Annual Report and Accounts,* The Stationery Office
*Prison Statistics, England and Wales,* The Stationery Office

*Prisons in Scotland Report*, The Stationery Office

*Race and the Criminal Justice System*, Home Office

*Report of the Parole Board for England and Wales*, The Stationery Office

*Report on the work of the Northern Ireland Prison Service*, The Stationery Office

*Scottish Crime Survey*, Scottish Executive

*Statistics on the Race and Criminal Justice System*, Home Office

*The Criminal Justice System in England and Wales*, Home Office

*Scottish Executive Statistical Bulletins: Criminal Justice Series*, Scottish Executive

*The Work of the Prison Service*, The Stationery Office

*Young People and Crime*, Home Office

*Review of police forces' crime recording practices*, Home Office

*Review of crime statistics: a discussion document*, Home Office

## 10: Housing

*Becoming a home-owner in Britain in the 1990s. The British Household Panel Survey*, ESRC Institute for Social and Economic Research

*Bringing Britain Together: A National Strategy for Neighbourhood Renewal*, Social Exclusion Unit, Cabinet Office

*Changing Households: The British Household Panel Survey*, ESRC Institute for Social and Economic Research

*Department of the Environment, Transport and the Regions Annual Report*, The Stationery Office

*Divorce, Remarriage and Housing: The Effects of Divorce, Remarriage, Separation and the Formation of New Couple Households on the Number of Separate Households and Housing Demand Conditions*, Department of the Environment, Transport and the Regions

*English House Condition Survey*, The Stationery Office

*Housing Finance*, Council of Mortgage Lenders

*Housing in England: Survey of English Housing*, The Stationery Office

*Housing Statistics*, The Stationery Office

*Living conditions in Europe – statistical pocketbook*, Eurostat

*Local Housing Statistics*, The Stationery Office

*My home was my castle: evictions and repossessions in Britain*, ESRC Institute of Social and Economic Research and Institute of Local Research

*Northern Ireland House Condition Survey*, Northern Ireland Housing Executive

*Northern Ireland Housing Statistics*, CSRB, Department for Social Development, Northern Ireland

*On the move: The housing consequences of migration*, YPS

*Private Renting in Five Localities*, The Stationery Office

*Projections of Households in England to 2021*, Department of the Environment, Transport and the Regions

*Scotland's people: results from the 1999 Scottish Household Survey*, The Stationery Office

*Scottish House Condition Survey 1996*, Scottish Homes

*Social Portrait of Europe*, Eurostat

*Statistical Bulletins on Housing*, Scottish Executive

*Statistics on Housing in the European Community*, Commission of the European Communities

*The social situation in the European Union*, European Commission

*Welsh House Condition Survey*, National Assembly for Wales

*Welsh Housing Statistics*, National Assembly for Wales

## 11: Environment

*A better quality of life*, The Stationery Office

*A Living Environment for Wales*, Countryside Commission for Wales and the Forestry Commission

*A Working Environment for Wales*, Environment Agency, Wales

*Air Quality Strategy for England, Scotland, Wales and Northern Ireland*, The Stationery Office

*Bathing Water Quality in England and Wales*, The Stationery Office

*Biodiversity: The UK Action Plan*, The Stationery Office

*Development of the Oil and Gas Resources of the United Kingdom*, The Stationery Office

*Digest of Environmental Statistics*, The Stationery Office

*Digest of United Kingdom Energy Statistics*, The Stationery Office

*General Quality Assessment*, The Environment Agency

*Hydrological summaries for the United Kingdom*, Centre for Hydrology and British Geological Survey

*National Waste Strategy: Scotland*, Scottish Environment Protection Agency

*OECD Environmental Data Compendium*, OECD

*Organic Farming*, Ministry of Agriculture, Fisheries and Food

*Planning Public Water Supplies*, Environment Agency

*Progress in Water Supply Planning*, Environment Agency

*Quality of life counts*, The Stationery Office

*Scottish Environmental Statistics*, Scottish Executive

*Sustainable Scotland: Priorities and Progress*, Scottish Executive

*The State of the countryside 2000*, The Countryside Agency

*The State of the Environment of England and Wales: The Atmosphere*, The Stationery Office

*The State of the Environment of England and Wales: The Land*, The Stationery Office

*The State of the Environment of England and Wales: Fresh Waters*, The Stationery Office

*The State of the Environment of England and Wales: Coasts*, The Stationery Office

*Waste management strategy for Northern Ireland*, The Stationery Office

*Waste Strategy 2000, England and Wales*, Department of the Environment, Transport and the Regions

*Water Pollution Incidents in England and Wales*, The Stationery Office

*Waterfacts*, Water Services Association

## 12: Transport

*A New Deal for Transport: Better for Everyone*, The Stationery Office

*A Strategy for Sustainable Development for the United Kingdom*, The Stationery Office

*Annual Report*, Rail Passenger Council

*Driving Standards Agency Annual Report and Accounts*, The Stationery Office

*Focus on Personal Travel: 1998 Edition*, The Stationery Office

*Focus on Public Transport: 1999 Edition*, The Stationery Office

*Focus on Roads: 1998 Edition*, The Stationery Office

*International Passenger Transport,* The Stationery Office

*People's Panel*, Cabinet Office

*Rail Complaints*, Office of the Rail Regulator

*Road Accidents Great Britain – The Casualty Report*, The Stationery Office

*Road Accidents, Scotland*, Scottish Executive

*Road Accidents: Wales*, National Assembly for Wales

*Road Traffic Accident Statistics Annual Report*, The Royal Ulster Constabulary

*Scottish Transport Statistics*, Scottish Executive

*Transport Statistics Bulletins and Reports,* Department of the Environment, Transport and the Regions

*Transport Statistical Bulletins,* Scottish Executive

*Transport Statistics Great Britain,* The Stationery Office

*Transport Trends,* The Stationery Office

*Travel Trends,* The Stationery Office

*Vehicle Licensing Statistics,* Department of the Environment, Transport and the Regions

*Vehicle Speeds in Great Britain,* Department of the Environment, Transport and the Regions

*Welsh Transport Statistics,* National Assembly for Wales

### 13: Lifestyles and Social Participation

*Annual Report of Department for Culture, Media and Sport,* The Stationery Office

*BBC Handbook,* BBC

*BPI Statistical Handbook,* British Phonographic Industry

*BVA Yearbook,* British Video Association

*Cinema and Video Industry Audience Research,* CAA

*Consumer and leisure futures,* The Henley Centre

*Cultural Trends in Scotland,* Policy Studies Institute

*Cultural Trends,* Policy Studies Institute

*Digest of Tourist Statistics,* British Tourist Authority

*Film and Television Handbook,* British Film Institute

*LISU Annual Library Statistics,* LISU, Loughborough University

*Religious Trends,* Christian Research

*The UK Tourist,* Tourist Boards of England, Northern Ireland, Scotland and Wales

*Travel Trends,* The Stationery Office

*UK Day Visits Survey,* Countryside Recreation Network, University of Wales

*Young People and Sport in England,* The Sports Council

# Geographical areas of the United Kingdom

### Government Office Regions

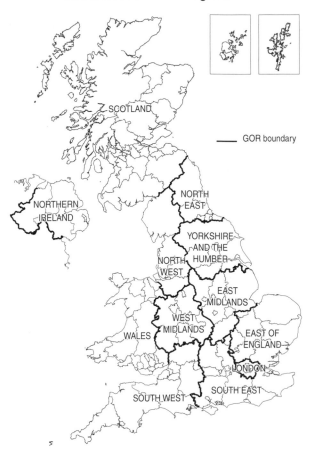

### Standard Statistical Regions

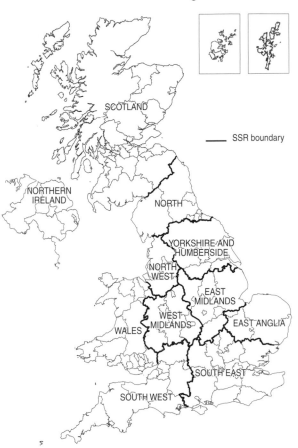

### NHS Regional Office areas
### (from April 1996)

### Environment Agency regions

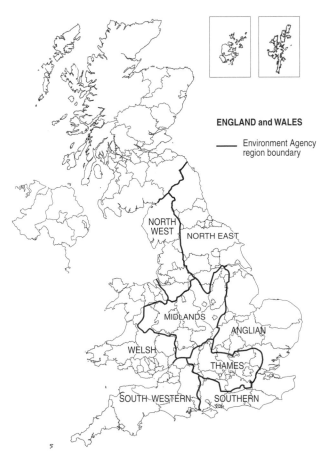

# Geographical areas of the United Kingdom

Police Force areas

Tourist Board regions

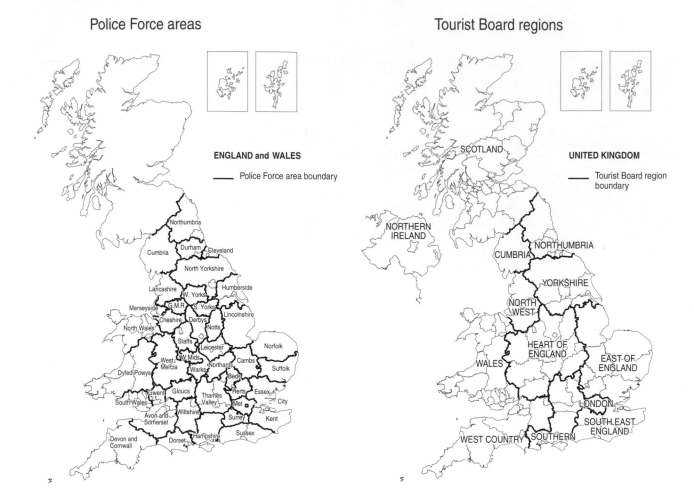

**ENGLAND and WALES**

—— Police Force area boundary

**UNITED KINGDOM**

—— Tourist Board region boundary

# Appendix: major surveys

| | Frequency | Sampling frame | Type of respondent | Coverage | Effective sample size[1] (most recent survey included in *Social Trends*) | Response rate (percentages) |
|---|---|---|---|---|---|---|
| Adult Dental Health Survey | Decennial | Postcode Address File in GB, Rating and Valuation lists in NI | All adults in household | UK | 4,984 households | 74 |
| Agricultural and Horticultural Census | Annual | Farms | Farmers | UK | 238,000 farms | 80 |
| British Crime Survey | Biennial | Postcode Address File | Adult in household | EW | 26,291 addresses | 74 |
| British Household Panel Survey | Annual | Postal Addresses in 1991, members of initial wave households followed in subsequent waves | All adults in households | GB | 5,160 households | 97[2] |
| British Social Attitudes Survey | Annual | Postcode Address File | One adult per household | GB | 5,402 addresses | 58 |
| Census of Population | Decennial | Detailed local | Adult in household | UK | Full count | 98 |
| Continuous Household Survey | Continuous | Valuation and Lands Agency Property | All adults in household | NI | 4,147 addresses | 70 |
| Employers Skills Survey | Annual | BT Database | Employers | E | 26,952 interviews achieved | 59 |
| English House Condition Survey | Quinquennial | Postcode Address File | Any one householder | E | 27,200 addresses | 49[3] |
| European Community Household Panel Survey | Annual | Various | All household members aged 16 and over | EU | 60,000 households | 90[4] |
| Family Expenditure Survey | Continuous | Postcode Address File in GB, Rating and Valuation lists in NI | Household | UK | 11,424 addresses[5] | 63[6] |
| Family Resources Survey | Continuous | Postcode Address File | All adults in household | GB | 34,636 households | 66 |
| General Household Survey | Continuous | Postcode Address File | All adults in household | GB | 11,831 households | 72 |
| Health Education Monitoring Survey | Ad hoc | Postcode Address File | One adult aged 16 and over in household | E | 8,168 households | 71 |
| Health Survey for England | Continuous | Postcode Address File | Adults, children over 2 | E | 12,250 addresses | 74[7] |
| International Passenger Survey | Continuous | International passengers | Individual traveller | UK | 261,000 individuals | 82 |
| Labour Force Survey | Continuous | Postcode Address File | All adults in household | UK | 59,000 addresses | 76[8] |
| National Food Survey | Continuous | Postcode Address File in GB, Valuation and Lands Agency Property in NI | Person responsible for domestic food arrangements | UK | 10,511 addresses | 65 |
| National Readership Survey | Continuous | Postcode Address File | Adults aged 15 and over | GB | 54,074 individuals | 60 |
| National Travel Survey | Continuous | Postcode Address File | All household members | GB | 5,040 households per year | 67[9] |
| New Earnings Survey | Annual | Inland Revenue PAYE records | Employee | GB | [10] | [10] |
| Omnibus Survey | Continuous | Postcode Address File | One adult per household | GB | 3,519 individuals[11] | 65[11] |
| Survey of English Housing | Continuous | Postcode Address File | Household | E | 26,277 households | 71 |
| Survey of Personal Incomes | Annual | Inland Revenue administrative data | Individuals | UK | 125,000 | 95 |
| Youth Cohort Study | Biennial | School records | Young people (Aged 16 to 19) | EW | 22,500 individuals | 65 |

1 Effective sample size includes non-respondents but excludes ineligible households.
2 Wave on wave response rate at wave eight. Around 76 per cent of eligible wave one sample members were respondent in wave eight.
3 The 1996 EHCS response combines successful outcomes from two linked surveys where information is separately gathered about the household and the dwelling for each address.
4 Response rates vary between EU countries.
5 Basic sample only.
6 Response rate refers to Great Britain.
7 Response rate for fully and partially responding households.
8 Response rate to first wave interviews quoted. Response rate to second to fifth wave interviews 91 per cent of those previously accepting.
9 Response rate for the period January 1997 to January 1999.
10 In the New Earnings Survey employers supply data on a 1 per cent sample of employees who are members of PAYE schemes. For the 2000 sample approximately 233 thousand were selected and there was an 87.4 per cent response, but some 53 thousand returned questionnaires were not taken onto the results file for various reasons.
11 The Omnibus Survey changes from month to month. The sample size and response rate are combined for January and March 2000.

# Appendix: definitions and terms

## PART 1: POPULATION

### Population estimates and projections

The estimated and projected populations are of the resident population of an area, i.e. all those usually resident there, whatever their nationality. Members of HM forces stationed outside the United Kingdom are excluded; members of the United States forces stationed in the United Kingdom are included. Students are taken to be resident at their term-time addresses. Figures for the United Kingdom do not include the population of the Channel Islands or the Isle of Man.

The population estimates for mid-1991 were based on results from the 1991 Census of Population and incorporate an allowance for census under-enumeration. Allowances were also made for definitional and timing differences between Census and estimates. Estimates for later years allow for subsequent births, deaths and migration. The estimates for 1982-90 have been revised to give a smooth series consistent with both 1981 and 1991 Census results. Due to definitional changes, there are minor

discontinuities for Scotland and Northern Ireland between the figures for 1971 and earlier years. At the United Kingdom level these discontinuities are negligible.

The most recent set of national population projections published for the United Kingdom are based on the populations of England, Wales, Scotland and Northern Ireland at mid-1998. Further details of these will be found in *1998-based national population projections Series PP2* (The Stationery Office). Subnational projections are also made for constituent countries of the United Kingdom. The latest long-term subnational projections for England are 1996-based. 1998-based short-term subnational projections have also been produced for England. These are produced primarily for the Department of Health and update the 1996-based projections. There are no 1996-based sub-national projections for Wales, but the Office for National Statistics have been asked by the National Assembly for Wales to prepare 1998-based projections.

### Boundaries

Map boundaries showing counties within the United Kingdom are based on Unitary Authorities and counties for 1999. For 1801 densities, county boundaries and areas from the 1851 Census have been used. Densities have been derived using the population data for 1801 given in the 1851 census.

### International migration estimates

Detailed estimates of migration between the United Kingdom and other countries are derived from the International Passenger Survey (IPS).

The IPS provides information on all migrants into the United Kingdom who have resided abroad for a year or more and stated on arrival the intention to stay in the United Kingdom for a year or more and vice versa. Migrants to and from the Irish Republic, diplomats and military personnel are excluded, as are nearly all persons who apply for asylum on entering the country. It is also highly likely that the IPS migration figures exclude persons who enter the country as short term visitors but remain for 12 months or longer after being granted an extension of stay, for example as students, on the basis of marriage or because they applied for asylum after entering the country. Home Office estimates of asylum seekers and 'visitor switches' are added to the IPS figures. Estimates of migrants between the United Kingdom and the Irish Republic are produced using information from the Irish Labour Force Survey and the National Health Service Central Register. They are agreed between the Irish Central Statistics Office and the Office for National Statistics and are also added to the IPS figures.

### Asylum

The basis for recognition as a refugee and hence the granting of asylum is the 1951 United Nations Convention relating to the Status of Refugees, extended in it's application by the 1967 Protocol relating to the Status of Refugees. The United Kingdom is party to both. The Convention defines a refugee as a person who 'owning to a well-founded fear of being persecuted for reasons of race, religion, nationality, membership of a particular social group or political opinion, is outside the country of his nationality and unable, or owing to such fear, is unwilling to avail himself of the protection of that country'. In addition, the United Kingdom is prepared to grant, to applicants who do not meet the requirements of the Convention, exceptional leave to stay here for an appropriate period, if it would be unreasonable, or impracticable, in all circumstances, to seek to enforce their return to their country of origin.

### PART 2: HOUSEHOLDS AND FAMILIES

Although definitions differ slightly across surveys and the census, they are broadly similar.

### Households

*A household*: is a person living alone or a group of people who have the address as their only or main residence and who either share one meal a day or share the living accommodation.

*Students*: living in halls of residence are recorded under their parents household and included in the parents family type in the Labour Force Survey (LFS), although some surveys/projections include such students in the institutional population.

### Families

*Children*: are never-married people of any age who live with one or both parent(s). They also include stepchildren and adopted children (but not foster children) and also grandchildren (where the parents are absent).

*Dependent children*: in the 1961 Census, were defined as children under 15 years of age, and persons of any age in full-time education. In the 1971 Census, dependent children were defined as never-married children in families who were either under 15 years of age, or aged 15 to 24 and in full-time education. However, for direct comparison with the Labour Force Survey (LFS) data, the definition of dependent children used for 1971 in Table 2.3 has been changed to include only never-married children in families who were either under 15 years of age, or aged 15 to 18 and in full-time education. In the 1991 Census, the LFS and the GHS, dependent children are childless never-married children in families who are aged under 16, or aged 16 to 18 and in full-time education.

*A family*: is a married or cohabiting couple, either with or without their never-married child or children (of any age), including couples with no children or a lone parent together with his or her never-married child or children. A family could also consist of grandparent or grandparents with grandchild or grandchildren if there are no apparent parents of the grandchild or grandchildren usually resident in the household. In the LFS, a family unit can also comprise a single person. LFS family units include non-dependent 'children' (who can in fact be adult) provided they are never married and have no children of their own in the household.

*A lone parent family* (in the Census) is a father or mother together with his or her never-married child or children.

*A lone parent family* (in the General Household Survey) consists of a lone parent, living with his or her never-married dependent children, provided these children have no children of their own. Married lone mothers whose husbands are not defined as resident in the household are not classified as lone parents because evidence suggests the majority are separated from their husband either because he usually works away from home or for some other reason that does not imply the breakdown of the marriage (see ONS's *GHS Monitor 82/1*).

*A lone parent family* (in the Labour Force Survey) consists of a lone parent, living with his or her never-married children, provided these children have no children of their own living with them.

### Conceptions

Conception statistics used in Tables 2.12 and 2.13, include pregnancies that result in one or more live or still births, or a legal abortion under the 1967 Act. Conception statistics do not include miscarriages or illegal abortions. Dates of conception are estimated using recorded gestation for abortions and still births, and assuming 38 weeks gestation for live births.

### Average teenage fertility rate

Teenage fertility rates are calculated for each age, summed and then divided by five to obtain the average rate for women aged 15 to 19. In previous editions of Social Trends, the overall teenage rate was calculated as the number of births to women under 20 per 1,000 women aged 15 to 19. This year's methodology is consistent with the Council of Europe publication.

### PART 3: EDUCATION AND TRAINING

**Main categories of educational establishments**
Educational establishments in the United Kingdom are administered and financed in several ways. Most schools are controlled by local education authorities (LEAs), which are part of the structure of local government, but some are 'assisted', receiving grants direct from central government sources and being controlled by governing bodies which have a substantial degree of autonomy. In recent years under the Local Management of Schools initiative all LEA and assisted schools have been given delegated responsibility for managing their own budgets and staff numbers. Since 1988 it has also been possible for LEA schools in England and Wales to apply for grant maintained status, under which they receive direct funding from the Department for Education and Employment or the National Assembly for Wales. The governing bodies of such schools are responsible for all aspects of their management, including use of funds, employment of staff and provision of most educational support services.

Outside the public sector completely are non-maintained schools run by individuals, companies or charitable institutions.

From 1 September 1999, all previous categories of school, including grant-maintained, were replaced by four new categories, all maintained (or funded) by the LEA:

*Community* - schools formerly known as 'county' plus some former GM schools. The LEA is the legal employer of the school's staff, the land owner and the admissions authority.

*Foundation* - most former GM schools. The governing body is the legal employer and admissions authority, as well as landowner unless that is a charitable foundation.

*Voluntary Aided* - schools formerly known as 'aided' and some former GM schools. The governing body is the legal employer and admissions authority, but the landowner is usually a charitable foundation. The governing body contribute towards the capital costs of running the school.

*Voluntary Controlled* - schools formerly known as 'controlled'. The LEA is the legal employer and admissions authority, but the landowner is usually a charitable foundation.

Further Education (FE) courses in FE sector colleges are largely funded through grants from the Further Education Funding Councils in England and Wales. The FEFC in England is responsible for funding provision for FE and some non-prescribed higher education in FE sector colleges; it also funds some FE provided by LEA maintained and other institutions referred to as 'external institutions'. In Wales, the FEFCW also funds FE provision made by FE institutions via a third party or sponsored arrangements. FE colleges in Scotland are funded by the Scottish FEFC (SFEFC) and FE colleges in Northern Ireland are funded by the Northern Ireland Department of Education.

Higher education (HE) courses in higher education establishments are largely publicly funded through block grants from the HE funding councils in England, the National Assembly for Wales, the Scottish Executive and the Northern Ireland Department of Education. In addition, some designated HE (mainly HND/HNC Diplomas and Certificates of HE) is also funded by the HE funding councils. The remainder is funded by FE funding councils.

### Stages of education

Education takes place in several stages: primary, secondary, further and higher, and is compulsory for all children between the ages of 5 (4 in Northern Ireland) and 16. The primary stage covers three age ranges: nursery (under 5), infant (5 to 7 or 8) and junior (up to 11 or 12) but in Scotland and Northern Ireland there is generally no distinction between infant and junior schools. Nursery education can be provided either in separate nursery schools or in nursery classes within primary schools. Most public sector primary schools take both boys and girls in mixed classes. It is usual to transfer straight to secondary school at age 11 (in England, Wales and Northern Ireland) or 12 (in Scotland), but in England some children make the transition via middle schools catering for various age ranges between 8 and 14. Depending on their individual age ranges middle schools are classified as either primary or secondary.

Public provision of secondary education in an area may consist of a combination of different types of school, the pattern reflecting historical circumstance and the policy adopted by the LEA. Comprehensive schools normally admit pupils without reference to ability or aptitude and cater for all the children in a neighbourhood, but in some areas they co-exist with grammar, secondary modern or technical schools. In Northern Ireland, post primary education is provided by secondary and grammar schools.

Special schools (day or boarding) provide education for children who require specialist support to complete their education, for example because they have physical or other difficulties. Many pupils with special educational needs are educated in mainstream schools.

The term further education may be used in a general sense to cover all non-advanced courses taken after the period of compulsory education, but more commonly it excludes those staying on at secondary school and those in higher education, i.e. courses in universities and colleges leading to qualifications above GCE A Level, SCE H Grade, GNVQ/NVQ level 3, and their equivalents.

Higher education is defined as courses that are of a standard that is higher than GCE A level, the Higher Grade of the Scottish Certificate of Education, GNVQ/NVQ level 3 or the Edexcel (formerly BTEC) or SQA National Certificate/Diploma. There are three main levels of HE course: (i) postgraduate courses are those leading to higher degrees, diplomas and certificates (including postgraduate certificates of education and professional qualifications) which usually require a first degree as entry qualification; (ii) first degrees which includes first degrees, first degrees with qualified teacher status, enhanced first degrees, first degrees obtained concurrently with a diploma, and intercalated first degrees; (iii) other undergraduate courses which includes all other higher education courses, for example HNDs and Diplomas in HE.

Figures previously shown in this publication for England related to classes taught by one teacher. In 1999/00, the average Key Stage 1 class, taught by one teacher, had 25.8 pupils, with 8.8 per cent of classes having 31 or more pupils. Further information, including one-teacher class size data for Key Stage 2, primary and secondary schools can be found in DfEE *Statistical First Release 15/2000*.

### Discontinuity in further and higher education statistics

The discontinuity in 1994 in Table 3.11 is due to changes in the data sources. Data prior to 1994 include Further Education Statistical Record data. For 1994 and later years, data include the more recent Individualised Student Record data. This discontinuity also applies in Table 3.12 when comparing 1997/98 (headcounts) with earlier years shown (enrolments).

### The National Curriculum: assessments and tests

Under the *Education Reform Act (1988)* a National Curriculum has been progressively introduced into primary and secondary schools in England and Wales. This consists of mathematics, English and science (and Welsh in Welsh speaking schools in Wales) as core subjects with history, geography, information technology and design and technology, music, art, physical education and (in

secondary schools) a modern foreign language (and Welsh in non-Welsh speaking schools in Wales) as foundation subjects. For all subjects measurable targets have been defined for four key stages, corresponding to ages 7, 11, 14 and 16. Pupils are assessed formally at the ages of 7, 11 and 14 by their teachers and by national tests in the core subjects of English, mathematics and science (and in Welsh speaking schools in Wales, Welsh). Sixteen year olds are assessed by means of the GCSE examination. Statutory authorities have been set up for England and for Wales to advise government on the National Curriculum and promote curriculum development generally. Northern Ireland has its own common curriculum which is similar but not identical to the National Curriculum in England and Wales. Assessment arrangements in Northern Ireland became statutory from September 1996. In Scotland, though school curricula are the responsibility of education authorities and individual head teachers, in practice almost all 14 to 16 year olds study mathematics, English, science, a modern foreign language, a social subject, physical education, religious and moral education, technology and a creative and aesthetic subject.

### Qualifications

In England, Wales and Northern Ireland the main examination for school pupils at the minimum school leaving age is the General Certificate of Secondary Education (GCSE) which can be taken in a wide range of subjects. This replaced the GCE O Level and CSE examinations in 1987 (1988 in Northern Ireland). In England, Wales and Northern Ireland the GCSE is awarded in eight grades, A* to G, the highest four (A* to C) being regarded as equivalent to O level grades A to C or CSE grade 1.

GCE A Level is usually taken after a further two years of study in a sixth form or equivalent, passes being graded from A (the highest) to E (the lowest).

In Scotland pupils study for the Scottish Certificate of Education (SCE) S (Standard) Grade, approximately equivalent to GCSE, in their third and fourth years of secondary schooling (roughly ages 14 and 15). Each subject has several elements, some of which are internally assessed in school, and an award is only made (on a scale of 1 to 7) if the whole course has been completed and examined. The SCE H (Higher) Grade requires one further year of study and for the more able candidates the range of subjects taken may be as wide as at S Grade with as many as five or six subjects spanning both arts and science. Three or more SCE Highers are regarded as being approximately the equivalent of two or more GCE A levels.

After leaving school, people can study towards higher academic qualifications such as degrees. However, a large number of people choose to study towards qualifications aimed at a particular occupation or group of occupations - these qualifications are called vocational qualifications.

Vocational qualifications can be split into three groups, namely National Vocational Qualifications (NVQs), General National Qualifications (GNVQs) and other vocational qualifications.

NVQs are based on an explicit statement of competence derived from an analysis of employment requirements. They are awarded at five levels. Scottish Vocational Qualifications (SVQs) are the Scottish equivalent.

GNVQs are a vocational alternative to GCSEs and GCE A levels . They are awarded at three levels: Foundation, Intermediate and Advanced. General Scottish Vocational Qualifications (GSVQs) are the Scottish equivalent.

There are also a large number of other vocational qualifications which are not NVQs, SVQs, GNVQs or GSVQs , for example, a BTEC Higher National Diploma or a City and Guilds Craft award.

Other qualifications (including academic qualifications) are often expressed as being equivalent to a particular NVQ level so that comparisons can be made more easily.

An NVQ level 5 is equivalent to a Higher Degree.

An NVQ level 4 is equivalent to a First Degree, a HND or HNC, a BTEC Higher Diploma, an RSA Higher Diploma a nursing qualification or other Higher Education.

An NVQ level 3 is equivalent to 2 A levels, an Advanced GNVQ, an RSA advanced diploma, a City & Guilds advanced craft, an OND or ONC or a BTEC National Diploma.

An NVQ level 2 is equivalent to 5 GCSEs at grades A* to C, an Intermediate GNVQ, an RSA diploma, a City and Guilds craft or a BTEC first or general diploma.

**Literacy levels**

| Level | Prose | Document | Quantitative |
|---|---|---|---|
| Level 1 | Locate one piece of information in a text that is identical or synonymous to the information in the question. Any plausible incorrect answer present in the text is not near the correct information. | Locate one piece of information in a text that is identical to the information in the question. Distracting information is usually located away from the correct answer. Some tasks may require entering given personal information on a form. | Perform a single simple operation such as addition for which the problem is already clearly stated or the numbers are provided. |
| Level 2 | Locate one or more pieces of information in a text but several plausible distractors may be present or low level inferences may be required. The reader may also be required to integrate two or more pieces of information or to compare and contrast information. | Tasks at this level are more varied. Where a single match is required more distracting information may be present or a low level inference may be required. Some tasks may require information to be entered on a form or to cycle through information in a document. | Single arithmetic operation (addition or subtraction) using numbers that are easily located in the text. The operation to be performed may be easily inferred from the wording of the question or the format of the material. |
| Level 3 | Readers are required to match information that requires low-level inferences or that meet specific conditions. There may be several pieces of information to be identified located in different parts of the text. Readers may also be required to integrate or to compare and contrast information across paragraphs or sections of text. | Literal or synonymous matches in a wide variety of tasks requiring the reader to take conditional information into account or to match on multiple features of information. The reader must integrate information from one or more displays of information or cycle through a document to provide multiple answers. | At this level the operations become more varied - multiplication and division. Sometimes two or more numbers are needed to solve the problem and the numbers are often embedded in more complex texts or documents. Some tasks require higherorder inferences to define the task. |
| Level 4 | Match multiple features or provide several responses where the requested information must be identified through text based inferences. Reader may be required to contrast or integrate pieces of information sometimes from lengthy texts. Texts usually contain more distracting information and the information requested is more abstract. | Match on multiple features of information, cycle through documents and integrate information. Tasks often require higher order inferences to get correct answer. Sometimes, conditional information in the document must be taken into account in arriving at the correct answer. | A single arithmetic operation where the statement of the task is not easily defined. The directive does not provide a semantic relation term to help the reader define the task. |
| Level 5 | Locate information in dense text that contain a number of plausible answers Sometimes high-level inferences are required and some text may use specialised language. | Readers are required to search through complex displays of information that contain multiple distractors, to make high level inferences, process conditional information or use specialised language. | Readers must perform multiple operations sequentially and must state the problem from the material provided or use background knowledge to work out the problem or operations needed. |

### National Learning Targets

In October 1998, following consultation, the National Learning Targets were announced. They replaced the former National Targets for Education and Training. The Targets state that by 2002:

80% of 11 year olds will reach at least level 4 in the Key Stage 2 English test;
75% of 11 year olds will reach at least level 4 in the Key Stage 2 Mathematics test;
50% of 16 year olds will achieve 5 GCSEs at grades A*- C, or equivalent;
95% of 16 year olds will achieve at least one GCSE grade A*- G, or equivalent;
85% of 19 year olds will be qualified to at least NVQ level 2 or equivalent;
60% of 21 year olds will be qualified to at least NVQ level 3 or equivalent;
28% of economically active adults will be qualified to at least NVQ level 4 or equivalent;
50% of economically active adults will be qualified to at least NVQ level 3 or equivalent;
A learning participation Target is under development;
45% of organisations with 50 or more employees will be recognised as Investors in People; and
10,000 organisations with 10-49 employees will be recognised as Investors in People.

### Learning and Training at Work

Learning and Training at Work 1999 (LATW 1999) is a new multi-purpose survey of employers that investigates the provision of learning and training at work. This information was previously collected in the annual Skill Needs in Britain (SNIB) surveys, along with information on recruitment difficulties, skill shortages and skill gaps.

Due to increasing focus on skills issues on the one hand and employer training on the other, and coupled with the increasing complexity and length of the SNIB questionnaire, the DfEE study decided to replace the single SNIB study with two separate surveys, one covering skills issues and another training. The Learning and Training at Work 1999 report relates to the latter study and includes information about; key indicators of employers' commitment to training, including the volume of off-the-job training provided, awareness of, and participation in, a number of initiatives relevant to training.

The LATW 1999 survey consisted of 4,008 telephone interviews with employers having 1 or more employees at the specific location sampled and covered public and private business and all industry sectors. The main stage of interviewing was carried out between 3 November and 21 December 1999. The overall response rate from employers was 63 per cent, acceptable for a study of this nature. Sample design involved setting separate sample targets for each cell on a Government Office region by industry sector by establishment size matrix. In contrast the SNIB

survey covered employers with 25 or more employees in all business sectors, except agriculture, hunting, forestry and fishing, in Great Britain.

## PART 4: LABOUR MARKET

### Estimates of employment rates

The employment rate series shown in Chart 4.1 uses estimates produced by the Department for Education and Employment for the period 1959 to 1991. Full details of the methodology for these estimates may be found in Labour Market Trends, January 2000 edition. They are provisional and will be replaced by modelled estimates produced by the Office for National Statistics during 2001. Data for 1992 onwards are from the Labour Force Survey (LFS).

### IT occupations

It is not possible from the LFS to estimate the number of people using computers in their work, but the numbers employed in certain occupations most closely linked to IT can be measured. The occupations included in this definition are: computer systems and data processing managers; computer analysts/programmers; computer, data processing and other office operators; computer engineers, installation and maintenance; and software engineers.

### ILO unemployment

The ILO definition of unemployment refers to people without a job who were available to start work within two weeks and had either looked for work in the previous four weeks or were waiting to start a job they had already obtained. Estimates on this basis are not available before 1984, as the Labour Force Survey did not then collect information on job search over a four week period. The former GB/UK Labour Force definition of unemployment, the only one available for estimates up to 1984, counted people not in employment and seeking work in a reference week (or prevented from seeking work by a temporary sickness or holiday, or waiting for the results of a job application, or waiting to start a job they had already obtained), whether or not they were available to start (except students not able to start because they had to complete their education).

### Labour force

Since autumn 1993, the Labour Force had been grossed up using population projections based on 1992 mid year population estimates. Data from autumn 1993 to autumn 1999 have been revised to take account of more up-to-date information on changes in the population (1996-based projections and more up-to date population estimates). The revised data have led to an increase in the size of the growth between 1993 and 1999 in the number of people in employment (from about 1.6 million to

about 2 million), and a very small fall in the size of the decrease in the numbers of ILO unemployed people. Data from winter 1999-2000 have been grossed using the latest population data.

## PART 5: INCOME AND WEALTH

### Household sector

Due to fundamental changes introduced in 1998 to the way that the national accounts are compiled, some of the data in Chapter 5 in this and the last two editions differ from those previously shown in Social Trends. These changes, needed to make better international comparisons, have affected the classification of people and institutions as well as transactions and assets.

The household sector is defined here to include non-profit institutions and individuals living in institutions as well as those living in households. The most obvious example of a non-profit institution is a charity: this sector also includes many other organisations of which universities, trade unions and clubs and societies are the most important. The household sector differs from the personal sector, as previously defined in the national accounts, in that it excludes unincorporated private businesses apart from sole traders. More information is given in United Kingdom National Accounts Concepts, Sources and Methods published by The Stationery Office.

### Disability

The World Health Organisation's International Classification of Impairments, Disabilities and Handicaps was adapted by the Office for National Statistics for use in disability surveys. Respondents are asked to answer a detailed schedule of questions on 13 domains of disability: locomotion; communication; reaching and stretching; personal care; behaviour; seeing; hearing; continence; dexterity; intellectual functioning; consciousness; eating, drinking and digestion; and disfigurement. Questions were asked to derive the extent of disability in each of these domains and the three highest severity scores were weighted together to produce an overall disability score. Finally this weighted score, which ranged from 0.5 to 21.5, was assigned to a severity category ranging from 1 (least severe) to 10 (most severe). An example of someone in severity category 1 would be someone who had difficulty hearing someone talking in a normal voice in a quiet room. Someone in severity category 10 might not be able to walk at all, be unable to feed themselves or carry out other personal care activities without help, and be unable to carry out any activities involving holding, gripping and turning.

### Individual income

Net individual income refers to the gross weekly personal income of women and men less income tax and National Insurance contributions as reported in the Family Resources Survey. Gross income includes: earnings, income from self-employment, investments and occupational pensions/annuities, benefit income, and income from miscellaneous other sources. It excludes income which accrues at household level, such as council tax benefit. Income from couples' joint investment accounts is assumed to be received equally. Benefit income paid in respect of dependants such as Child Benefit is included in the individual income of the person nominated for the receipt of payments, except for married pensioner couples, where state retirement pension payments are separated and assigned to the man and woman according to their entitlements. Disposable individual income includes further deductions and additions which are potentially shared in different ways across the household (e.g. housing and maintenance), and after deduction of childcare and travel to work costs. Full details of the concepts and definitions used may be found in *Individual Income 1996/97 to 1998/99*, available from the Analytical Services Division, Department of Social Security.

### Equivalisation scales

The Department of Social Security (DSS), the Office for National Statistics (ONS), the Institute for Fiscal Studies (IFS) and the Institute for Social and Economic Research (ISER) all use McClements equivalence scales in their analysis of the income distribution, to take into account variations in the size and composition of households. This reflects the common sense notion that a household of five adults will need a higher income than will a single person living alone to enjoy a comparable standard of living. An overall equivalence value is calculated for each household by summing the appropriate scale values for each household member. Equivalised household income is then calculated by dividing household income by the household's equivalence value. The scales conventionally take a married couple as the reference point with an equivalence value of 1; equivalisation therefore tends to increase relatively the incomes of single person households (since their incomes are divided by a value of less than 1) and to reduce incomes of households with three or more persons. For further information see *Households Below Average Income*, Corporate Document Services, Department of Social Security.

The DSS and IFS use both before and after housing costs scales, although only before housing costs scales have been used in this chapter.

McClements equivalence scales:

| Household member | Before housing costs | After housing costs |
| --- | --- | --- |
| First adult (head) | 0.61 | 0.55 |
| Spouse of head | 0.39 | 0.45 |
| Other second adult | 0.46 | 0.45 |
| Third adult | 0.42 | 0.45 |
| Subsequent adults | 0.36 | 0.40 |
| Each dependent aged: | | |
| 0-1 | 0.09 | 0.07 |
| 2-4 | 0.18 | 0.18 |
| 5-7 | 0.21 | 0.21 |
| 8-10 | 0.23 | 0.23 |
| 11-12 | 0.25 | 0.26 |
| 13-15 | 0.27 | 0.28 |
| 16 or over | 0.36 | 0.38 |

### Redistribution of income (ROI)

Estimates of the incidence of taxes and benefits on household income, based on the Family Expenditure Survey (FES), are published by the ONS in *Economic Trends*. The article covering 1998-99 appeared in the April 2000 issue, and contains details of the definitions and methods used.

### Households Below Average Income (HBAI)

Information on the distribution of income based on the Family Resources Survey is provided in the DSS publication *Households Below Average Income: 1994/95 - 1998/99*. This publication provides estimates of patterns of personal disposable income in Great Britain, and of changes in income over time in the United Kingdom. It attempts to measure people's potential living standards as determined by disposable income. As the title would suggest, HBAI concentrates on the lower part of the income distribution, but provides comparisons with the upper part where appropriate.

Disposable household income includes all flows of income into the household, principally earnings, benefits, occupational and private pensions, investments. It is net of tax, National Insurance contributions, Council Tax, contributions to occupational pension schemes (including additional voluntary contributions), maintenance and child support payments, and parental contributions to students living away from home.

Two different measures of disposable income are used in HBAI: before and after housing costs are deducted. Housing costs consist of rent, water rates, community charges, mortgage interest payments, structural insurance, ground rent and service charges.

### Difference between Households Below Average Income and Redistribution of Income series

These are two separate and distinct income series produced by two different government departments. Each series has been developed to serve the specific needs of that department. The DSS series, HBAI, provides estimates of patterns of disposable income and of changes over time and shows disposable income before and after housing costs (where disposable income is as defined in the section on HBAI). The ONS series, ROI, shows how Government intervention through the tax and benefit system affects the income of households; it covers the whole income distribution and includes the effects of indirect taxes like VAT and duty on beer, as well as estimating the cash value of benefits in kind (e.g. from state spending on education and health care). The ROI results are designed to show the position in a particular year rather than trends in income levels over time, although trends in the distribution of income are given. An important difference between the two series is that HBAI counts individuals and ROI counts households. Also, whereas ROI provides estimates for the United Kingdom, from 1994/95 onwards HBAI provides estimates for Great Britain only.

### Net wealth of the household sector

Revised balance sheet estimates of the net wealth of the household (and non-profit institutions) sector were published in an article in *Economic Trends*, November 1999. These figures are based on the new international system of national accounting and incorporate data from new sources. Quarterly estimates of net financial wealth (excluding tangible and intangible assets) are published in Financial Statistics.

### Distribution of personal wealth

The estimates of the distribution of the marketable wealth of individuals relate to all adults in the United Kingdom. They are produced by combining Inland Revenue (IR) estimates of the distribution of wealth identified by the estate multiplier method with independent estimates of total personal wealth derived from the ONS national accounts balance sheets. Estimates for 1995 onwards have been compiled on the basis of the new System of National Accounts, but estimates for earlier years are on the old basis. The methods used were described in an article in *Economic Trends* (October 1990) entitled "Estimates of the Distribution of Personal Wealth". Net wealth of the personal sector differs from marketable wealth for the following reasons:

Difference in coverage: the ONS balance sheet of the personal sector includes the wealth of non-profit making bodies and unincorporated businesses, while the IR estimates exclude non-profit making bodies and treat the bank deposits and debts of unincorporated businesses differently from ONS;

Differences in timing: the ONS balance sheet gives values at the end of the year, whereas IR figures are adjusted to mid-year;

*Funded pensions*: are included in the ONS figures but not in the IR marketable wealth. Also the ONS balance sheet excludes consumer durables and includes non-marketable tenancy rights, whereas the IR figures include consumer durables and exclude non-marketable tenancy rights.

### Contributions to and receipts from the EC budget
The figures in Table 5.33 come from the European Court of Auditors (ECA) annual report concerning the financial year 1998 and have been converted to sterling at the following exchange rates:

1997 - £1 = 1.4510 ECU
1998 - £1 = 1.4896

Contribution figures are after account is taken of the United Kingdom's abatement and the bringing to account of surpluses and deficits in respect of member states' contributions in earlier years. The information in the ECA report does not attribute all Community expenditure to the member states. For example, not all administrative expenditure is attributed. The figures shown for the net position should not, therefore, be regarded as definitive for the member states.

### PART 6: EXPENDITURE

### Household expenditure
The national accounts definition of household expenditure, within household final consumption expenditure, consists of: personal expenditure on goods (durable and non-durable) and services, including the value of income in kind; imputed rent for owner-occupied dwellings; and the purchase of second-hand goods less the proceeds of sales of used goods. Excluded are: interest and other transfer payments; all business expenditure; and the purchase of land and buildings (and associated costs). This national accounts definition is also used for regional analysis of household income.

In principle, expenditure is measured at the time of acquisition rather than actual disbursement of cash. The categories of expenditure include that of non-resident as well as resident households and individuals in the United Kingdom.

The methods used for estimating expenditure at constant prices often depend on the methods used for the current price estimates. Where the current price estimate is in value terms only, it is deflated by an appropriate price index. The indices most widely used for this purpose are components of the retail prices index. The index does not, however, cover the whole range of household final consumer expenditure, and other indices have to be used or estimated where necessary. If no other appropriate price index is available the general consumer price index implied by the estimates of consumers' expenditure at current and constant prices on all other goods and services is used. Where the estimate at current prices is one of quantity multiplied by current average value, the estimate at constant prices is in most cases the same quantity multiplied by the average value in the base year. All these revaluations are carried out in as great detail as practicable.

For further details see the article entitled 'Consumers' expenditure' in *Economic Trends*, September 1983.

The Family Expenditure Survey definition of household expenditure represents current expenditure on goods and services. This excludes those recorded payments which are partly savings or investments (for example life assurance premiums). Similarly, income tax payments, national insurance contributions, mortgage capital repayments and other payments for major additions to dwellings are excluded. For purchases financed by hire purchase or loans, the amounts paid under the finance agreement are recorded as expenditure as they occur; the full cost of the item is not recorded at the time of the initial transaction. For further details see *Family Spending*.

### Retail prices index
The general index of retail prices (RPI) is the main domestic measure of inflation in the UK. It measures the average change from month to month in the prices of good and services purchased by most households in the United Kingdom. The spending pattern on which the index is based is revised each year, mainly using information from the Family Expenditure Survey. The expenditure of certain higher income households, and of pensioner households mainly dependent on state pensions, is excluded. These households are:

(a) the 4 per cent (approximately) where the total household recorded gross income exceeds a certain amount (£1,167 a week in 1997/98).

(b) 'pensioner' households consisting of retired people who derive at least three quarters of their income from state benefits.

Expenditure patterns of one-person and two-person pensioner households differ from those of the households upon which the general index is based. Separate indices have been compiled for such pensioner households since 1969, and quarterly averages are published in the ONS, *Consumer Price Indices (CPI) Business Monitor MM23*. They are chain indices constructed in the same way as the general index of retail prices. It should, however, be noted that the pensioner indices exclude housing costs.

A brief introduction to the RPI is given in the July 1999 issue of ONS, *CPI Business Monitor MM23*. Each month's edition of the *Business Monitor* contains further articles of interest, covering topics such as reweighting and indicator items.

### Harmonised index of consumer prices (Also published in *CPI Business Monitor MM23*)
The harmonised indices of consumer prices (HICPs) are calculated in each member state of the European Union for the purposes of European comparisons, as required by the Maastricht Treaty. From January 1999 it has been used by the European Central Bank as the measure for its definition of price stability across the Euro area. Further details are contained in an *ECB Press Notice* released on 13 October 1998: "*A stability oriented monetary policy strategy for the ESCB*".

The methodology of the HICP is similar to that of the retail prices index (RPI) but differs in the following ways:

(a) the geometric mean rather than the arithmetic mean is used to aggregate the prices at the most basic level.

(b) the coverage of the indices is based on the international classification system, COICOP (classification of individual consumption by purpose).

(c) a number of RPI series are excluded from the HICP; most particularly, housing costs (i.e. mortgage interest payments, council tax, house depreciation and buildings insurance)

(d) the HICP includes a series for air fares and boats which is not currently covered in the RPI.

(e) the index for new cars in RPI is imputed from movements in second hand car prices, whereas the HICP uses a quality adjusted index based on published prices of new cars.

(f) in the construction of the RPI weights, expenditure on insurance is assigned to the relevant insurance heading. For the HICP weights, the amount paid out in insurance claims is distributed amongst the COICOP headings according to the nature of the claims expenditure with the residual (i.e. the service charge) being allocated to the relevant insurance heading.

(g) the average household expenditure pattern on which the HICP is based is that of the all private households. In the RPI, the expenditure of highest income households, and of pensioner households mainly dependent on state benefits, are excluded.

With effect from the January 2000 index, the following changes were made to the HICP:

(a) coverage of goods and services was extended to include some health, education, insurance and social protection services which had been previously excluded.

(b) the population basis for the weights was broadened from private households to include expenditure by foreign visitors and residents of institutional households.

The March 2000 edition of *Economic Trends* contains an article describing these changes in more detail.

An article giving the background to the HICP and describing how it has been harmonised and how it compares with the RPI is available in the February 1998 edition of *Economic Trends*. Historical estimates of the HICP are given in an article in the November 1998 edition of *Economic Trends*.

### Consumer credit
The figures in Table 6.16 relating to bank loans cover banks and all other institutions authorised to take deposits under the *Banking Act 1987*.

Figures relating to other specialist lenders cover finance houses and credit companies excluding institutions authorised to take deposits under the *Banking Act 1987*.

### PART 7: HEALTH

### Expectation of life
The expectation of life, shown in Table 7.1, is the average total number of years which a person of that age could be expected to live, if the rates of mortality at each age were those experienced in that year. The mortality rates that underlie the expectation of life figures are based, up to 1999, on total deaths occurring in each year.

### Healthy life expectancy
Healthy life expectancy, defined as expected years of life in good or fairly good self-assessed general health, is one example of health expectancy. ONS calculates this measure using life tables from the Government Actuary's Department and morbidity data from the ONS General Household Survey, specifically responses to the question 'Over the last twelve months would you say your health has on the whole been good, fairly good, or not good?' 'Good' and 'Fairly good' responses are taken as a positive measure of

health. A second health expectancy, calculated using similar methodology, is expected years of life free from limiting long-standing illness.

### Standardised incidence rates
Directly standardised cancer incidence rates enable comparisons to be made over time, which are independent of changes in the age structure of the population. In each year, the crude incidence rates in each five-year age group are multiplied by the European standard population for that age group. These are then summed and divided by the total standard population to give an overall standardised rate.

### Standardised prevalence rates
Directly standardised prevalence rates enable comparisons to be made over time, between the sexes, between age groups and across area types, For each group under consideration, the age-specific rates are applied to the European standard population; the resulting 'expected cases' are then summed and divided by the total standard population to give an overall standardised rate.

### The ONS area classification
The ONS area classification is based on the analysis of a wide range of socio-economic and demographic variables from the 1991 Census which are used to group together areas with broadly similar characteristics. The group names generally reflect the socio-economic, and sometimes geographic, attributes of their members but they are not precise descriptions of all group members (*Wallace M. and Denham C. The ONS classification of local and health authorities of Great Britain*. London : HMSO 1996). In Table 7.6 the classification has been used to classify general practices by the 'area type' of the ward in which the practice is situated. In this table two area types, 'inner city estates' and 'deprived city areas', have been combined and jointly renamed as inner/deprived city; 'transient populations' do not feature as none of the included practices fall within such wards.

### Alcohol consumption
A unit of alcohol is 8 grams by weight or 10ml by volume of pure alcohol. This is the amount contained in half a pint of ordinary strength beer or lager, a single measure of pub spirits (1/6 gill or 25 ml), one glass of ordinary wine and a small pub measure of sherry or other fortified wine.

Sensible Drinking, the 1995 report of an inter-departmental review of the scientific and medical evidence of the effects of drinking alcohol, concluded that the daily benchmarks were more appropriate than previously recommended weekly levels since they could help individuals decide how much to drink on single occasions and to avoid episodes

of intoxication with their attendant health and social risks. The report concluded that regular consumption of between three and four units a day for men and two to three units for women does not carry a significant health risk. However, consistently drinking more than four units a day for men, or more than three for women, is not advised as a sensible drinking level because of the progressive health risk it carries. The government's advice on sensible drinking is now based on these daily benchmarks.

### Body mass index
The body mass index (BMI) shown in Table 7.13, is the most widely used index of obesity which standardises weight for height and is calculated as weight (kg)/height (m)2. Underweight is defined as a BMI of 20 or less, desirable over 20 to 25, overweight over 25 to 30 and obese over 30.

### Standardised death rates
To enable comparisons to be made over time which are independent of changes in the age structure of the population, directly standardised death rates have been calculated in Chart 7.19.

For each year, the age-specific death rates are multiplied by the European standard population for each age group. These are then summed and divided by the total standard population to give an overall standardised rate. Since the European population is the same for both males and females it is possible to directly compare male and female standardised death rates.

### International Classification of Diseases
The International Classification of Diseases (ICD) is a coding scheme for diseases and causes of death. England, Wales and Northern Ireland are currently using the Ninth Revision of the ICD (ICD9), and Scotland is using the Tenth Revision. The rest of the United Kingdom is due to start using the Tenth Revision in January 2001.

The causes of death included in Chart 7.19 correspond to the following ICD9 codes: circulatory diseases 390-459; cancer 140-208: respiratory diseases 460-519 and infectious diseases 001-139.

### Accidental deaths
The data in Table 7.21 exclude deaths where it was not known whether the cause was accidentally or purposely inflicted, misadventure during medical care, abnormal reactions and late complications.

### Immunisation
Data shown in Table 7.26 for 1991-92 onwards for England, Wales and Northern Ireland (1991-92 and subsequent years for NI) relate to children reaching their second birthday during the year and immunised by their second birthday. Data for 1981 in England, Wales and Northern Ireland relate to

children born two years earlier and immunised by the end of the second year. For Scotland, rates prior to 1995-96 have been calculated by dividing the cumulative number of immunisations for children born in year X and vaccinated by year X+2, by the number of live births (less neonatal deaths) during year X.

## PART 8: SOCIAL PROTECTION

### Benefit units

A benefit unit is a single or married couple living as married together with any dependent children. A pensioner benefit unit is where the head is over state pension age.

### Health and personal social services staff

Nursing, midwifery and health visitors comprises qualified and unqualified staff, and excludes nurse teachers, nurses in training and students on '1992' courses.

Other non-medical staff comprises Scientific & Professional and Technical staff.

General medical practitioners includes Unrestricted Principals, PMS contracted GPs, PMS salaried GPs, Restricted Principals, Assistants, GP Registrars and PMS others. It excludes GP Retainers.

General dental practitioners is a headcount of General Dental Service (GDS) at 30 September. It includes principals on a Health Authority / Family Health list, assistants and vocational dental practitioners.

Personal social services staff includes staff employed only at local authority social work departments (whole time equivalent). The figure for Scotland in 1999 is at 4 October.

### In-patient activity

In-patient data for England and later years for Northern Ireland are based on Finished Consultant Episodes (FCEs). Data for Wales and Scotland, and data for Northern Ireland except acute after 1986, are based on Deaths and Discharges and transfers between specialties (between hospitals in Northern Ireland). An FCE is a completed period of care of a patient using a bed, under one consultant, in a particular NHS Trust or directly managed unit. If a patient is transferred from one consultant to another within the same hospital, this counts as an FCE but not a hospital discharge. Conversely if a patient is transferred from one hospital to another provider, this counts as a hospital discharge and as a finished consultant episode.

### Recipients of benefits

The incapacity benefit and severe disablement figures are as at the end of February from 1996-97. Incapacity benefit was introduced in April 1995 to replace sickness and invalidity benefits.

Income-based Jobseeker's Allowance (JSA) replaced income support for the unemployed from October 1996. Income support includes some income-based JSA claimants.

The disability living allowance includes attendance allowance and, before 1992, mobility allowance.

The maternity allowance figures are February quarterly figures from 1996-97.

Family credit replaced the Family Income Supplement in April 1988. Family credit was replaced by the Working Families Tax Credit from October 1999.

Family Credit figures relate to February in each year given, except 1981-82 which is based on March data. The figures have been revised for 1996-97 and 1997-98. For 1996-97, figures are for March from a 4 per cent sample.

## PART 9: CRIME AND JUSTICE

### Types of offences in England and Wales

The figures are compiled from police returns to the Home Office or directly from court computer systems.

Recorded crime statistics broadly cover the more serious offences. Up to March 1998 most indictable and triable-either-way offences were included, as well as some summary ones; from April 1998, all indictable and triable-either-way offences were included, plus a few closely related summary ones. Recorded offences are the most readily available measures of the incidence of crime, but do not necessarily indicate the true level of crime. Many less serious offences are not reported to the police and cannot, therefore, be recorded while some offences are not recorded due to lack of evidence. Moreover, the propensity of the public to report offences to the police is influenced by a number of factors and may change over time.

In England and Wales, indictable offences cover those offences which must or may be tried by jury in the Crown Court and include the more serious offences. Summary offences are those for which a defendant would normally be tried at a magistrates' court and are generally less serious- the majority of motoring offences fall into this category. Triable either way offences are triable either on indictment or summarily.

### Types of offences in Northern Ireland

In recording crime, the Royal Ulster Constabulary broadly follow the Home Office rules for counting crime. As from 1st April 1998 notifiable offences are recorded on the same basis as those in England and Wales (i.e. under the revised Home Office rules – see above). Prior to the revision of the rules, criminal damage offences in Northern Ireland excluded those where the value of the property damaged was less than £200.

Notifiable offences: are broadly the more serious offences. They include most indictable offences and triable either way offences and certain summary offences (for example, unauthorised taking of a motor vehicle). Excludes criminal damage valued at less than £200. As from 1 April 1998, notifiable offences recorded in Northern Ireland are on the same basis as those in England and Wales.

Indictable only offences: are those for which an adult must be tried at the Crown Court, for example robbery, arson and rape. Figures for indictable offences given in this chapter include those for offences which are triable either way (see below).

Triable either way offences: are offences triable either on indictment or summarily. They may be tried in a magistrates' court unless either the defendant or the magistrate requests a Crown Court hearing. Most thefts, drug offences and less serious violence against the person offences fall into this category.

Summary offences: are those offences which are normally tried at a magistrates' court.

### Offences and crimes

There are a number of reasons why recorded crime statistics in England and Wales, Northern Ireland and Scotland cannot be directly compared:

Different legal systems: The legal system operating in Scotland differs from that in England and Wales and Northern Ireland. For example, in Scotland children aged under 16 are normally dealt with for offending by the Children's Hearings system rather than the courts.

Differences in classification: There are significant differences in the offences included within the recorded crime categories used in Scotland and the categories of notifiable offences used in England, Wales and Northern Ireland. Scottish figures of 'crime' have therefore been grouped in an attempt to approximate to the classification of notifiable offences in England, Wales and Northern Ireland.

Counting rules: In Scotland each individual offence occurring within an incident is recorded whereas in England, Wales and Northern Ireland only the main offence is counted.

Burglary: This term is not applicable to Scotland where the term used is 'housebreaking'.

Theft from vehicles: In Scotland data have only been separately identified from January 1992. The figures include theft by opening lockfast places from a motor vehicle and other theft from a motor vehicle.

### Offenders cautioned for burglary

In England and Wales offenders cautioned for going equipped for stealing, etc were counted against Burglary offences until 1986 and against Other offences from 1987. Historical data provided in Table 9.14 have been amended to take account of this change. Drug offences were included under Other offences for 1971.

### Sentences and orders

The following are the main sentences and orders which can be imposed upon those persons found guilty. Some types of sentence or order can only be given to offenders in England and Wales in certain age groups. Under the framework for sentencing contained in the Criminal Justice Acts 1991 and 1993, the sentence must reflect the seriousness of the offence. The following sentences are available for adults (a similar range of sentences is available to juveniles aged 10 to 17):

Absolute and conditional discharge: A court may make an order discharging a person absolutely or (except in Scotland) conditionally where it is inexpedient to inflict punishment and, before 1 October 1992, where a probation order was not appropriate. An order for conditional discharge runs for such period of not more than three years as the court specifies, the condition being that the offender does not commit another offence within the period so specified. In Scotland a court may also discharge a person with an admonition.

Attendance centre order: Available in England, Wales and Northern Ireland for offenders under the age of 21 and involves deprivation of free time.

Probation/supervision: An offender sentenced to a probation order is under the supervision of a probation officer (social worker in Scotland), whose duty it is (in England and Wales and Northern Ireland) to advise, assist and befriend him but the court has the power to include any other requirement it considers appropriate. A cardinal feature of the order is that it relies on the co-operation of the offender. Probation orders may be given for any period between six months and three years inclusive.

Community service: An offender who is convicted of an offence punishable with imprisonment may be sentenced to perform unpaid work for not more than 240 hours (300 hours in Scotland), and not less than 40 hours. Twenty hours minimum community service are given for persistent petty offending or fine default. In Scotland the Law Reform (Miscellaneous Provisions) (Scotland) Act 1990 requires that community service can only be ordered where the court would otherwise have imposed imprisonment or detention. Probation and community service may be combined in a single order in Scotland.

Combination order: The Criminal Justice Act 1991 introduced the combination order in England and Wales only, which combines elements of both probation supervision and community service. Meanwhile, Article 15 of the Criminal Justice (NI) Order 1996 introduced the combination order to Northern Ireland.

Imprisonment: is the custodial sentence for adult offenders. In the case of mentally disordered offenders, hospital orders, which may include a restriction order may be considered appropriate. Home Office or Scottish Executive consent is needed for release or transfer. A new disposal, the 'hospital direction', was introduced in 1997. The court, when imposing a period of imprisonment, can direct that the offender be sent directly to hospital. On recovering from the mental disorder, the offender is returned to prison to serve the balance of their sentence. The Criminal Justice Act 1991 abolished remission and substantially changed the parole scheme in England and Wales. Those serving sentences of under four years, imposed on or after 1 October 1992, are subject to Automatic Conditional Release and are released, subject to certain criteria, halfway through their sentence. Home Detention Curfews result in selected prisoners being released up to 2 months early with a tag that monitors their presence during curfew hours. Those serving sentences of four years or longer are considered for Discretionary Conditional Release after having served half their sentence, but are automatically released at the two-thirds point of sentence. The Crime (Sentences) Act 1997, implemented on 1 October 1997, included, for persons aged 18 or over, an automatic life sentence for a second serious violent or sexual offence unless there are exceptional circumstances. All offenders serving a sentence of 12 months or more are supervised in the community until the three quarter point of sentence. A life sentence prisoner may be released on licence subject to supervision and is always liable to recall. In Scotland the Prisoners and Criminal Proceedings (Scotland) Act 1993 changed the system of remission and parole for prisoners sentenced on or after 1 October 1993. Those serving sentences of less than four years are released unconditionally after having served half of their sentence, unless the court specifically imposes a Supervised Release Order which subjects them to social work supervision after release. Those serving sentences of four years or more are eligible for parole at half sentence. If parole is not granted then they will automatically be released on licence at two thirds of sentence subject to days added for breaches of prison rules. All such prisoners are liable to be 'recalled on conviction' or for breach of conditions of licence i.e. if between the date of release and the date on which the full sentence ends, a person commits another offence which is punishable by imprisonment or breaches his/her licence conditions, then the offender may be returned to prison for the remainder of that sentence whether or not a sentence of imprisonment is also imposed for the new offence.

Fully suspended sentences: may only be passed in exceptional circumstances. In England, Wales and Northern Ireland, sentences of imprisonment of two years or less may be fully suspended. A court should not pass a suspended sentence unless a sentence of imprisonment would be appropriate in the absence of a power to suspend. The result of suspending a sentence is that it will not take effect unless during the period specified the offender is convicted of another offence punishable with imprisonment. Suspended sentences are not available in Scotland.

Fines: The Criminal Justice Act 1993 introduced new arrangements on 20 September 1993 whereby courts are now required to fit an amount for the fine which reflects the seriousness of the offence, but which also takes account of an offender's means. This system replaced the more formal unit fines scheme included in the Criminal Justice Act 1991. The Act also introduced the power for courts to arrange deduction of fines from income benefit for those offenders receiving such benefits. The Law Reform (Miscellaneous Provision) (Scotland) Act 1990 as amended by the Criminal Procedure (Scotland) Act 1995 provides for the use of supervised attendance orders by selected courts in Scotland. The Criminal Procedure (Scotland) Act 1995 also makes it easier for courts to impose a supervised attendance order in the event of a default and enables the court to impose a supervised attendance order in the first instance for 16 and 17 year olds.

Custody Probation Order: an order unique to Northern Ireland reflecting the different regime there which applies in respect of remission and the general absence of release on licence. The custodial sentence is followed by a period of supervision for a period of between 12 months and three years.

### Young offender institutions
The Criminal Justice Act 1991 made a number of changes to the custodial sentencing arrangements for young offenders in England and Wales. A common minimum age of 15 for boys and girls was set for the imposition of a sentence of detention in a young offender institution thus removing boys aged 14 from the scope of this sentence.

### Civil courts
*England and Wales*: The main civil courts are the High Court and the county courts. Magistrates' courts also have some civil jurisdiction, mainly in family proceedings. Most appeals in civil cases go to the Court of Appeal (Civil Division) and may go from there to the House of Lords. Since July 1991, county courts have been able to deal with all contract and tort cases and actions for recovery of land, regardless of value. Cases are presided over by a judge who almost always sits without a jury. Jury trials are limited to specified cases, for example, actions for libel.

*Scotland*: The Court of Session is the supreme civil court. Any cause, apart from causes excluded by statute, may be initiated in, and any judgement of an inferior court may be appealed to, the Court of Session. The Sheriff Court is the principal local court of civil jurisdiction in Scotland. It also has jurisdiction in criminal proceedings. Apart from certain actions the civil jurisdiction of the Sheriff Court is generally similar to that of the Court of Session.

### Legal aid
Advice and assistance provided by a solicitor, short of actual representation in court or tribunal proceedings, may be obtained free by those whose capital and income are within certain financial limits. Assistance by way of representation covers the cost of a solicitor preparing a case and representing a client in court. It is available (either free or on payment of a contribution to those who are financially eligible) for some civil cases in the magistrates' court, for proceedings before Mental Health Review Tribunals', discretionary life prisoners before the parole board and disciplinary hearings before a prison governor, and for certain proceedings relating to the care of children and young people.

Legal aid in civil cases covers all work up to and including court proceedings and representing by a solicitor and a counsel if necessary. Legal aid in these cases is available for free or on a contributory basis to those whose capital and income are within certain financial limits. Applicants must show that they have reasonable grounds for asserting or disputing a claim. Certain types of action, including libel and slander, are excluded from this type of legal aid.

In the criminal courts in England and Wales a legal aid order may be made if this appears desirable in the interest of justice and the defendant's means are such that they requires financial help in meeting the costs of the proceedings in which they are involved. No limit of income or capital above which a person is ineligible for legal aid is specified, but the court must order a legally-aided person to contribute towards the cost of their case where their resources are such that they can afford to do so. Civil Legal Aid in Scotland operates on a similar basis to that operating prior to April 2000 in England and Wales. Advice and assistance has similar scope in Scotland but is available to those who are financially eligible either for free or on payment of a contribution. Assistance by way of representation (ABWOR) is granted mainly for summary criminal cases where a plea of guilty is made, though it also covers proceedings in mental health review cases, designated life prisoners before the parole board and disciplinary hearings before a prison governor, and other specified civil or criminal proceedings. Criminal Legal Aid, which is granted by the Scottish Legal Aid Board for summary cases and for all appeals, and by the courts for solemn cases, is not subject to a contribution.

### Drugs seizures
Seizures can involve more than one drug and so figures for individual drugs cannot be added together to produce totals. Seizures of unspecified quantities are not included.

## PART 10: HOUSING

### Dwelling stock
The definition of dwelling follows that adopted by the most recent Census. This definition has changed between censuses. In the 1991 Census, it has been defined as "structurally separate accommodation". It is meant to refer to a building, or part of a building which forms a separate, or reasonably separate and self-contained, set of premises designed to be occupied by a single household.

In all stock figures, permanent and non-permanent dwellings as well as vacant dwellings are included. For housebuilding statistics e.g. completions, only data on permanent dwellings are collected.

Estimates of the total dwelling stock, stock changes and the tenure distribution for each country are made by the Department of the Environment Transport and the Regions (DETR), the Scottish Executive, the National Assembly for Wales, and NI Department for Social Development. These are primarily based on census output data for the number of dwellings (or households converted to dwellings) from the

Censuses of Population for GB. Adjustments were carried out if there were specific reasons to do so. Census years' figures are based on outputs from the censuses. For in between census years, the total figures are obtained by projecting the base census year's figure forward yearly. The increment is based on the annual total number of completions plus the annual total net gain due to other housing flows statistics i.e. conversions, demolitions and change of use.

Estimates of dwelling stock by tenure category are primarily based on the census except in the situation where it is considered that for some specific tenure information, there are other more accurate sources. In this situation, it is assumed that the other data sources contain vacant dwellings also but it is not certain and it is not expected that these data are very precise. Thus the allocation of vacant dwellings to tenure categories may not be completely accurate. This means that the margin of error for tenure categories are wider than for estimates of total stock.

For the 1991 census, a comparison with other available sources indicated that for local authorities' stock, figures supplied by local authorities are more reliable. Similarly, it was found that Housing Corporation's own data is more accurate than those from the census for the Registered Social Landlord's (RSL's) stock. Hence only the rented privately or with a job or business tenure data directly from the census was used. The owner-occupied data was taken as the residual of the total from the census. For non census year, the same approach was adopted except for the privately rented or with a job or business for which Labour Force Survey results were considered to be appropriated for use.

For further information on the methodology used to calculate stock by tenure and tenure definitions, see Appendix B Notes and Definitions in DETR publication *Housing Statistics* annual volume.

### Dwellings completed
In principle, a dwelling is regarded as completed when it becomes ready for occupation whether it is in fact occupied or not. In practice, there are instances where the timing could be delayed and some completions are missed for example because no completion certificates were requested by the owner.

Tenure definition for housebuilding is only slightly different from that used for stock figures. For details see *Housing Statistics*.

### Homeless households
*England and Wales*: Households for whom local authorities accepted responsibility to secure accommodation under the *Housing Act 1985,* and subsequently the *Housing Act 1996*. Data for

Wales include some households given advice and assistance only. Figures for the period 1986-1996 are not strictly comparable with information provided for 1997 due to a change in legislation.

*Scotland*: Households assessed as being homeless or potentially homeless (likely to become homeless within 28 days) by local authorities.

*Northern Ireland*: Households for whom the Northern Ireland Housing Executive has accepted responsibility to secure permanent accommodation, not necessarily those for whom permanent accommodation has been found.

### Bedroom standard

The concept is used to estimate occupation density by allocating a standard number of bedrooms to each household in accordance with its age/sex/marital status composition and the relationship of the members to one another. A separate bedroom is allocated to each married or cohabiting couple, any other person aged 21 or over, each pair of children under 10. Any unpaired person aged 10-20 is paired if possible with a child under 10 of the same sex, or, if that is not possible, is given a separate bedroom, as is any unpaired child under 10. This standard is then compared with the actual number of bedrooms (including bedsitters) available for the sole use of the household, and deficiencies or excesses are tabulated. Bedrooms converted to other uses are not counted as available unless they have been denoted as bedrooms by the informants; bedrooms not actually in use are counted unless uninhabitable.

### The fitness standard

The new fitness standard in England and Wales was set out in section 604 of the *Local Government and Housing Act 1989* with guidance in DoE circulars 5/90 and 6/90. It came into operation from 1 April 1990. A property (including an HMO) is fit for human habitation unless it fails to meet any of the following requirements in the opinion of the local authority:

a)      It is structurally stable.
b)      It is free from serious disrepair
c)      It is free from dampness prejudicial to the health of any occupants.
d)      It has adequate provision for lighting, heating and ventilation.
e)      It has adequate supply of wholesome, piped water.
f)      It has satisfactory facilities for preparing and cooking food including a sink with supplies of hot and cold water.
g)      It has a suitably located WC.
h)      It has a bath or shower and basin, each with supplies of hot and cold water.
i)      It has an effective system for draining foul, waste and surface water.

There is also a separate fitness standard for HMOs, apart from the general standard described above, that compares the available facilities with the number of occupants, and that also ensures that there are adequate means of escape from fire and other fire precautions. When a property has been surveyed by the local authority and the condition assessed, the authority has then to decide on the most satisfactory course of action. If a property is identified as unfit, then the authority is obliged by statute to take action. This action can include serving a notice, making a closing order or a demolition order, or including the property in a clearance area. The authority can also consider if the property could be dealt with by including it in a group repair scheme. Lastly there is a direct link between the standard of fitness and eligibility for mandatory renovation grants. Thus applications for renovation grants must be approved where the work is to bring a property up to the fitness standard, and the applicant meets the various conditions and undergoes the test of resources.

### Property transactions

The figures are based on the number of particular delivered (PD) forms processed by the Stamp Office or District Land Registry. They relate to the transfer of sale of any freehold interest in land or property, or the grant or transfer or a lease of at least seven years, and therefore include some non-residential transactions. In practice there is an average lag of about one month between the transaction and the date on which the PD form is processed.

Over the period from 20 December 1991 to 19 August 1992, the stamp duty threshold was temporarily increased from £30,000 to £250,000.

### Sales and transfers of local authority dwellings

Right to buy was established by the Housing Act 1980 and was introduced across Great Britain in October 1980.

In England, Large Scale Voluntary Transfers (LSVTs) of stock have been principally to housing associations/registered social landlords; figures include transfers supported by Estate Renewal Challenge Funding (ERCF). The figures for 1993 includes 949 dwellings transferred under Tenants choice.

Scotland includes large scale voluntary transfers and trickle transfers to Housing Associations.

### PART 11: ENVIRONMENT

### Listed buildings

The Secretary of State for National Heritage is required to compile lists of buildings of special architectural or historic interest for guidance of local planning authorities in England. Buildings that qualify for listing are: all buildings built before 1700 which survive in anything like their original condition; most buildings built between 1700 and 1840 though selection is necessary; and between 1840 and 1914, only buildings showing definite quality and character. Selected buildings of high quality built between 1914 and 1939 are also considered, and particularly important post-war buildings more than 30 years old are also eligible for listing.

Buildings are classified in grades to show their relative importance.
Grade I: These are buildings of exceptional interest.
Grade II*: These are particularly important buildings of more than special interest.
Grade II: These are buildings of special interest, which warrant every effort being made to preserve them.
*Buildings at risk* are those historic buildings at risk through neglect and decay (rather than demolition) or vulnerable to becoming so.

### Rivers and canals

The chemical quality of rivers and canal waters in the United Kingdom are monitored in a series of separate national surveys in England and Wales, Scotland and Northern Ireland. In England and Wales the National Rivers Authority (now superseded by the Environment Agency) developed and introduced the General Quality Assessment (GQA) Scheme to provide a rigorous and objective method for assessing the basic chemical quality of rivers and canals based on three determinants: dissolved oxygen, biochemical oxygen demand (BOD) and ammoniacal nitrogen). The GQA grades river stretches into six categories (A-F) of chemical quality and these in turn have been grouped into two broader groups - good/fair (classes A, B C and D) and poor/bad classes E and F). In Northern Ireland, the grading is also based on the GQA scheme. In Scotland, water quality is based upon the Scottish River Classification Scheme of 20 June 1997. The chemical quality of rivers and canals is assessed using the following classes: excellent (A1), good (A2) fair (B), poor (C) and seriously polluted (D). Data exclude islands.

### European Blue Flag Campaign

The European Blue Flag is an annual award given to beaches and marinas across Europe which meet strict criteria for both water quality and environmental management. All beaches and marinas which fly the Blue Flag have been recommended by a national jury before being approved by an international panel made up from many of the participating counties. In the UK there are currently 535 beaches monitored as part of the Bathing Water Directive, of which 57 complied with the full range of Blue Flag Criteria. In addition, Blue Flag will fly at 29 UK marinas. Beaches and marinas include:

North West
(m) Maryport Marina

East Midlands
Sutton-on-Sea, Central

East of England
Sheringham
Cromer
Mundesley
Great Yarmouth, Central
Great Yarmouth, Gorleston
Lowestoft, South
(m) Lowestoft, Marina
Lowestoft, Victoria
Southwold
Felixstowe, South
(m)Woolverstone Marina

South East
Herne Bay, Central
Ramsgate, Main Sands
(m) Windsor Marina
(m) Bray Marina
(m) Penton Hook Marina
(m) Brighton Marina Mooring
West Wittering
(m) Northney Marina
West Beachlands, Central
West Beachlands, West
(m) Mercury Yacht Harbour
(m) Port Hamble Marina
(m) Shamrock Quay
(m) Hythe Marina Village
(m) Hamble Point Marina
(m) Ocean Village Marina

South West
Bournemouth, Durley
Bournemouth, Fisherman's Walk
Poole, Sandbanks
(m) Salterns Harbour
(m) Cobbs Quay
(m) Torquay Marina
Dawlish Warren
(m) Brixham Marina
Torbay, Breakwater, Shoalstone
Torbay, Meadfoot
Torbay, Oddicombe
Blackpool Sands
(m) Queen Anne's Battery Marina
Woolacombe

Wales
(m) Penarth Marina
Porthcawl, Rest Bay
Langland Bay
(m) Knab Rock
(m) Swansea Marina
Caswell Bay

Bracelet Bay
Port Eynon
Pembrey Country Park
Cefn Sidan
Amroth
Lydstep
Tenby, South
Tenby Castle
(m) Neyland Yacht Harbour
Newgale
St David's, Whitesands
Poppit Sands
Aberporth
Tresaith
New Quay, Traeth yr, Harbwr
Aberystwyth, North Traeth y Gogledd
Borth
Barmouth, Abermaw
(m) Pwllheli Yacht Haven
Pwllheli, Marian y De
(m) Port Dinorwic Marina
(m)Victoria Dock, State Quay
Newborough, Llanddwyn
Llanddona

Scotland
St Andrews, West Sands
Elie
Aberdour, Silver Sands

Northern Ireland
Benone Strand
Portrush, East Strand
Portrush, West Strand
Portstewert Strand
(m) Ballycastle Marina
Ballycastle
(m) Carrickfergus Marina
(m) Bangor Marina
Millisle Lagoon
Tyrella
Cranfield West

## Electricity produced by renewable sources

Hydro power figures in the renewable sources table exclude pumped storage stations. Capacities are as at the end of December, except for the capacities of installations of major power producing companies, which for 1995, are recorded as at the end-March of the following year. For both hydro power and onshore wind, actual generation figures are given where available, but otherwise are estimated using a typical load factor or the design load factor, where known. Figures for Municipal waste include combustion of refuse derived fuel pellets. The other category includes the use of farm waste digestion, sewage sludge digestion, waste tyre combustion, poultry litter, combustion and solar photovoltaics.

## PART 12: TRANSPORT

### Journey purpose

The purpose of a journey is normally taken to be the activity at the destination, unless that destination is 'home' in which case the purpose is defined by the origin of the journey. The classification of journeys to 'work' are also dependent on the origin of the journey. The following purposes are distinguished:

Commuting: journeys to a usual place of work from home, or from work to home.

Business: personal journeys in course of work, including a journey in the course of work back to work. This includes all work journeys by people with no usual place of work (e.g. site workers) and those who work at or from home.

Education: journeys to school or college, etc by full time students, students on day-release and part-time students following vocational courses.

Escort: used when the traveller has no purpose of his or her own, other than to escort or accompany another person; for example, taking a child to school. Escort commuting is escorting or accompanying someone from home to work or from work to home.

Shopping: all journeys to shops or from shops to home, even if there was no intention to buy.

Personal business: visits to services e.g. hairdressers, launderettes, dry-cleaners, betting shops, solicitors, banks, estate agents, libraries, churches; or for medical consultations or treatment, or for eating and drinking unless the main purpose was entertainment or social.

Social or entertainment: visits to meet friends, relatives, or acquaintances, both at someone's home or at a pub, restaurant, etc; all types of entertainment or sport, clubs, and voluntary work, non-vocational evening classes, political meetings, etc.

Holidays or day trips: journeys (within Great Britain) to or from any holiday (including stays of four nights or more with friends or relatives) or journeys for pleasure (not otherwise classified as social or entertainment) within a single day.

Just walk: walking pleasure trips along public highways including taking the dog for a walk and jogging.

### Car ownership

Car: the figures for household ownership include four wheeled and three wheeled cars, off-road vehicles, minibuses, motorcaravans, dormobiles, and light vans. Company cars normally available for household use are also included.

### Type of area

London borough - the 33 London boroughs;
Metropolitan built-up area - the built-up area within the administrative areas of the former metropolitan counties of Greater Manchester, Merseyside, the West Midlands, West Yorkshire, Tyne & Wear and Strathclyde;
Large urban - self-contained urban areas of more than 250,000 population in 1991;
Medium urban – self-contained urban areas of not more than 250,000 population in 1991, but more than 25,000;
Small urban – self-contained urban areas of not more than 25,000 population in 1991 but more than 3,000;
Rural - other areas are designated 'rural', including 'urban areas' under 3,000 population in 1991.

### Passenger death rates

Table 12.21 provides passenger death rates for passenger travel by air, road, rail and water. Wherever possible, travel by drivers and other crew in the course of their work has been excluded from the calculated rates for public transport modes. A casualty rate can be interpreted as the risk a traveller runs of being injured, per kilometre travelled. The coverage varies for each mode of travel and the definitions of deaths and accidents are different. Thus, care should be exercised in drawing comparisons between the rates for different modes.

The air travel data refer to passenger carrying services of United Kingdom airlines for fixed and rotary wing aircraft of over 2,300kg. The accidents therefore cover flights throughout the world, not just within the United Kingdom. The average number of fatal accidents is less than 1 per year, and may not necessarily occur within the United Kingdom.

The rail casualty data refer to passengers in train accidents and train movement accidents. They exclude non-movement accidents such as falling over packages on platforms, confirmed suicides and trespassers. The figures for air and water, similarly, exclude accidents on the land side of air terminals and seaports.

The data for travel by water cover both domestic and international passenger carrying services of United Kingdom registered vessels. Data are not available for non-fatal accidents to passengers prior to 1983. Casualties exclude deaths from disease and confirmed suicides. Injuries are those which incapacitate the person for more than 3 days.

The road data which refer to Great Britain, are for drivers/riders and passengers of vans, cars, two wheeled motor vehicles and pedal cycles. The data for buses and coaches refer to passengers only. They illustrate the risk to passengers of travel on the road system using both public and private transport. The casualty rates per billion kilometres for those on foot are based on estimates of distance walked obtained from National Travel Surveys. The article Comparative Accident Rates for Passengers by Modes of Transport, which provides additional information on the coverage and definitions used by the various modes was published in *Transport Statistics Great Britain 1994 edition*. These statistics of accidents and casualties are compiled from the reports submitted by the police to the Department of Environment, Transport and the Regions. More detailed information and analyses about road accidents and casualties is available in *Road Accidents Great Britain - the Casualty Report 1998*, published by the Stationery Office.

### PART 13: LIFESTYLES AND SOCIAL PARTICIPATION

### Socio-economic group

The basic occupational classification used is the Registrar General's socio-economic grouping in Standard Occupational Classification 1990, Volume 3 OPCS (HMSO, London 1991), pp13-14. Table 13.4 uses a collapsed version of this classification, which is as follows:

| Descriptive definition | SEG numbers |
|---|---|
| Professional | 3,4 |
| Employers and managers | 1,2,13 |
| Intermediate and junior non-manual | 5,6 |
| Skilled manual | 8,9,12,14 |
| Semi-skilled manual and personal services | 7,10,15 |
| Unskilled manual | 11 |

### Parliamentary elections

A general election must be held at least every five years or sooner, if the Prime Minister of the day so decides. The United Kingdom is currently divided into 659 constituencies, each of which returns one member to the House of Commons. To ensure equitable representation, four permanent Boundary Commissions (for England, Wales, Scotland, and Northern Ireland) make periodic reviews of constituencies and recommend any change in the number or redistribution of seats that may seem necessary in the light of population movements or for some other reason.

### Cultural events

Data from the Target Group Index 1987-1988 and 1991-1992, BMRB International, and the Target Group Index 1997-1998 Doublebase, BMRB International were used in Table 13.9.

# Articles published in previous editions

**No. 1 1970**
**Some general developments in social statistics** Professor C A Moser, CSO

**Public expenditure on the social services** Professor B Abel-Smith, London School of Economics and Political Science

**The growth of the population to the end of the century** Jean Thompson, OPCS

**A forecast of effective demand for housing in Great Britain in the 1970s** A E Holmans, MHLG

**No. 2 1971**
**Social services manpower** Dr S Rosenbaum, CSO

**Trends in certificated sickness absence** F E Whitehead, DHSS

**Some aspects of model building in the social and environmental fields** B Benjamin, CSC

**Social indicators - health** A J Culyer, R J Lavers and A Williams, University of York

**No. 3 1972**
**Social commentary: change in social conditions** CSO

**Statistics about immigrants: objectives, methods, sources and problems** Professor C A Moser, CSO

**Central manpower planning in Scottish secondary education** A W Brodie, SED

**Social malaise research: a study in Liverpool** M Flynn, P Flynn and N Mellor, Liverpool City Planning Department

**Crimes of violence against the person in England and Wales** S Klein, HO

**No. 4 1973**
**Social commentary: certain aspects of the life cycle** CSO

**The elderly** D C L Wroe, CSO

**Subjective social indicators** M Abrams, SSRC

**Mental illness and the psychiatric services** E R Bransby, DHSS

**Cultural accounting** A Peacock and C Godfrey, University of York

**Road accidents and casualties in Great Britain** J A Rushbrook, DOE

**No. 5 1974**
**Social commentary: men and women** CSO

**Social security: the European experiment** E James and A Laurent, EC Commission

**Time budgets** B M Hedges, SCPR

**Time budgets and models of urban activity patterns** N Bullock, P Dickens, M Shapcott and P Steadman, Cambridge University of Architecture

**Road traffic and the environment** F D Sando and V Batty, DOE

**No. 6 1975**
**Social commentary: social class** CSO

**Areas of urban deprivation in Great Britain: an analysis of 1971 Census data** S Holtermann, DOE

**Note: Subjective social indicators** Mark Abrams, SSRC

**No. 7 1976**
**Social commentary: social change in Britain 1970-1975** CSO

**Crime in England and Wales** Dr C Glennie, HO

**Crime in Scotland** Dr Bruce, SHHD

**Subjective measures of quality of life in Britain: 1971 to 1975** J Hall, SSRC

**No. 8 1977**
**Social commentary: fifteen to twenty-five: a decade of transition** CSO

**The characteristics of low income households** R Van Slooten and A G Coverdale, DHSS

**No. 9 1979**
**Housing tenure in England and Wales: the present situation and recent trends** A E Holmans, DOE

**Social forecasting in Lucas** B R Jones, Lucas Industries

**No. 10 1980**
**Social commentary: changes in living standards since the 1950s** CSO

**Inner cities in England** D Allnutt and A Gelardi, DOE

**Scotland's schools** D Wishart, SED
**No. 14 1984**
**Changes in the Life-styles of the Elderly 1959-1982** M Abrams

**No. 15 1985**
**British Social Attitudes** R Jowell and C Airey, SCPR

**No. 16 1986**
**Income after retirement** G C Fiegehen, DHSS

**No. 17 1987**
**Social Trends since World War II** Professor A H Halsey, University of Oxford

**Household Formation and Dissolution and Housing Tenure: a Longitudinal Perspective** A E Holmans and S Nandy, DOE; A C Brown, OPCS

**No. 18 1988**
**Major Epidemics of the 20th Century: from Coronary Thrombosis to AIDS** Sir Richard Doll, University of Oxford

**No. 19 1989**
**Recent Trends in Social Attitudes** L Brook, R Jowell and S Witherspoon, SCPR

**No. 20 1990**
**Social Trends, the next 20 years** T Griffin, CSO

**No. 21 1991**
**The 1991 Census of Great Britain: Plans for Content and Output** B Mahon and D Pearce, OPCS

**No. 22 1992**
**Crime statistics: their use and misuse** C Lewis, HO

**No. 24 1994**
**Characteristics of the bottom 20 per cent of the income distribution** N Adkin, DSS

**No. 26 1996**
**The OPCS Longitudinal Study** J Smith, OPCS

**British Household Panel Survey** J Gershuny, N Buck, O Coker, S Dex, J Ermish, S Jenkins and A McCulloch, ESRC Research Centre on Micro-social Change

**No. 27 1997**
**Projections: a look into the future** T Harris, ONS

**No. 28 1998**
**French and British Societies: a comparison** P Lee and P Midy, INSEE and A Smith and C Summerfield, ONS

**No. 29 1999**
**Drugs in the United Kingdom - a jigsaw with missing pieces** A Bradley and O Baker, Institute for the Study of Drug Dependence

**No. 30 2000**
**A Hundred Years of Social Change** A H Halsey, Emeritus Fellow, Nuffield College, Oxford

# Index

The references in this index refer to table and chart numbers, or entries in the Appendix.

# Index

Printed in the United Kingdom for The Stationery Office
TJ2691 C60 1/01 13110